Professional Enterprise .NET

Professional
Enterprise .NET

Professional
Enterprise .NET

Jon Arking
Scott Millett

WILEY

Wiley Publishing, Inc.

Professional Enterprise .NET

Published by
Wiley Publishing, Inc.
10475 Crosspoint Boulevard
Indianapolis, IN 46256
www.wiley.com

ISBN: 978-0-470-44761-1

Manufactured in the United States of America

10 9 8 7 6 5 4 3 2 1

For general information on our other products and services please contact our Customer Care Department within the United States at (877) 762-2974, outside the United States at (317) 572-3993 or fax (317) 572-4002.

Wiley also publishes its books in a variety of electronic formats. Some content that appears in print may not be available in electronic books.

Library of Congress Control Number: 2009933374

Dedicated to my wife Andrea, whose kindness, imagination, beauty, and patience make her the girl every man hopes to marry.

—Jon Arking

Dedicated to my beautiful Lynsey — thanks for the love, tea and the toast. And for Agatha and Columbo . . . probably the best rabbits in the world.

—Scott Millett

About the Author

Jon Arking is an enterprise software architect working in the greater Philadelphia region. He has been designing, developing, and managing multi-tiered systems for over 14 years, specializing in system migrations and the design of distributed architectures. Jon has experience programming in multiple languages and platforms, and has spent much of his career designing systems, managing teams, teaching classes, giving lectures and interviews, and publishing on a variety of technical topics. His company, Arking Technologies, specializes in designing enterprise systems for large companies in the Philadelphia area.

Scott Millett lives in Southsea, Portsmouth in the South of England where he is the senior developer for Wiggle.co.uk, an e-commerce company specializing in cycle and tri athlete sports based in the UK. He has been working with .NET since version 1.0 and has earned the Microsoft Certified Professional Web Developer certification. He is a regular contributor to the asp.net forums and when not writing about or working with .NET he can be found relaxing and enjoying the music at Glastonbury and all of the major music festivals in the UK during the summer. If you would like to talk to Scott about the book, anything .NET or the British music festival scene, then feel free to write to him at scott@elbandit.co.uk, or visit his blog at www.elbandit.co.uk/blog.

Credits

Acquisitions Editor
Paul Reese

Project Editor
Ed Connor

Technical Editor
Doug Parsons

Production Editor
Kathleen Wisor

Copy Editor
Foxxe Editorial Services

Editorial Director
Robyn B. Siesky

Editorial Manager
Mary Beth Wakefield

Production Manager
Tim Tate

Vice President and Executive Group Publisher
Richard Swadley

Vice President and Executive Publisher
Barry Pruett

Associate Publisher
Jim Minatel

Project Coordinator, Cover
Lynsey Stanford

Proofreader
Jen Larsen, Word One
Josh Chase, Word One

Indexer
Robert Swanson

Cover Image
© Digital Vision/Punchstock

Acknowledgments

I owe a lot of thanks to many people for helping to make this book a reality. Thanks to Ed Connor and Jim Minatel for their patience and understanding during a very busy time in my career. Huge thanks to my coauthor, Scott, for understanding my vision and helping to bring it to life. If you ever make it to Philly I'll have to show you how we roll on this side of the Pond! Thanks also to Vince, Sandra, John, and Ed at the Jug Handle Inn, who let a guy write a book at the bar on late Saturday nights. A special note of gratitude to my lovely mother, whose nagging and drama always kept me on course, and to my father who clearly helped shape me into the cantankerous, overbearing geek/meathead I am today. Most of all, thanks to my wife Andrea, and my children, Emma and Jake, who once again proved that their patience for me has no bounds!

—*Jon Arking*

First thanks to Jim Minatel at Wiley for giving me the opportunity of writing for Wrox and suggesting me to Jon. Thanks to Jon for the chance to get involved on such a great project and for all the help, support and guidance during the writing process. The next time you're in England I will take you on a good old fashioned pub crawl! Thank you to Doug Parsons, the technical editor, for all of his hard work and a big thanks to Ed Connor who had the unenviable task, as the book's Project Editor, to keep myself and Jon on track — thank you for all of your help. Finally special thanks to Lynsey, my beautiful wife to be for all the love and support you have given me before, during, and since writing this book and for reminding me what's important in life.

—*Scott Millett*

Contents

Contents

Contents

Contents

Introduction

Computer programming and developing business software are not the same thing. Though many think that writing code is the same no matter how you do it or who you do it for, nothing could be further from the truth. Sure, you've got to have coding skills in order to land some of those fancy, big-paying gigs, but that's just the beginning. Nowadays, creating software for businesses requires knowledge of many different languages and disciplines. It requires both low-level programming skills along with higher-level, comprehensive design experience. Most of all, it requires patience and tolerance of new ideas.

Of course, there are plenty of people out there who don't agree with us. Most of us know at least one or two programmers who do their best work locked away in a geek closet, insulated from the complexities of the business world. That's fine for some. After all, not everyone wants to build software that makes their whole company sing. Small application development will always have its rightful place in the community. Yet grow some of those applications into large, enterprise systems, and you're sure to run into trouble. More often than not, the small app development approach delivers wonderfully in the short term, then bites back hard as you expand its use and feature set. That's why when it comes to building company-wide enterprise systems, knowledge of enterprise design goes a long way.

The struggle for well-designed systems is far from new. Since the dawn of the computer age IT professionals have been debating how to strike a compromise between rapid application development and sound software design. It's a veritable tug-o-war between the best of design intentions and the very demanding hand that feeds you. Yet as businesses become more IT-savvy, they have begun investing in enterprise design with the hope that upfront costs will save money down the line. While the possibility of that is entirely real, developers need to know how to apply enterprise patterns correctly, in a manner best suited for their clients.

Microsoft developers are familiar with this argument. A platform almost exclusively dedicated to rapid application development, Microsoft applications have long been riddled with poor design, exchanging extensibility and flexibility for quick time-to-market. As enterprise methodologies become more widely embraced, a new generation of Microsoft developers find themselves faced with the daunting task of learning these new patterns and incorporating them into their existing skill sets and applications. This unfortunate gap between building well-designed applications and the high demand for rapid delivery has plagued the Microsoft community for years. With so many new enterprise patterns to learn, Microsoft programmers are in need of a practical resource to help guide them through each, and help them understand the best ways to update their own code and programming practices.

Enter *Professional Enterprise.Net* — the definitive guide for Microsoft programmers interested in learning the latest enterprise development methodologies. Our goal for this book is to educate developers on the different patterns and methodologies that can help to make their code cleaner, and more maintainable. It strives to provide a roadmap for mid-level and senior-level Microsoft programmers looking to migrate both their applications, as well as their own skill sets to newer, more flexible enterprise methodologies.

What This Book Covers

This book is meant to serve as an introduction to some of the more popular software development patterns and methodologies. It is intended for those with some background in Microsoft application development and is especially geared towards people with C# and ASP.NET development experience. This book does not intend to be a definitive all-in-one resource for all things enterprise. Enterprise design is an extremely broad subject, covering topics that warrant their own set of books and resources. Instead, this book provides a comprehensive look into a handful of widely embraced subjects. Readers looking for deep coverage of subjects such as Test Driven Development, middleware design patterns, or web MVC using ASP.NET would do better to find books dedicated to these topics exclusively. Beginning with a discussion on enterprise concepts and continuing through testable code methodologies and design patterns, you will first become familiar with some of the different ways to assemble your code in a loosely coupled, testable manner. Subsequent chapters delve into some of the tools that embrace these methodologies, such as Spring.Net, nHibernate, and ASP.NET MVC. The combination of these subjects will help to educate developers on the ways these different patterns work together, ultimately helping them to decide which pieces or portions are best suited for their business. Although this book does tell a story, it is also intended to be a useful reference for aspiring enterprise developers. Each chapter has been designed to stand on its own, without requiring the reader to first read all preceding chapters beforehand. With that in mind, here is a chapter-by-chapter synopsis:

Chapter 1: What Is Enterprise Design?

We begin by discussing some of the concepts at the core of enterprise development. These concepts have less to do with the physical act of coding and more to do with the spirit behind enterprise design and why we strive to embrace it. It begins with the concept of enterprise architecture, taking time to define what that means and to whom it applies. The reader then begins to explore the concept of enterprise development, focusing primarily on its core values, such as reliability, maintainability, and the separation of concerns. Then the chapter moves into some of the history of software design, walking the reader through the evolution of the core values. The chapter concludes with a discussion of some of the popular tools enterprise developers have come to embrace.

Chapter 2: The Enterprise Code

Chapter 2 introduces some of the new coding concepts germane to enterprise development. Concepts such as *modularity* and *loose coupling* are explained in detail, accompanied with some simple code samples to help demonstrate the concepts. Unit testing is a strong driving force in enterprise architecture, and it is carefully explained within the context of modularity and loose coupling. Inversion of Control is also introduced here, and it is explained how the creation of object instances can be made manageable within the rubric of a testable code base. The chapter concludes with a discussion of some of the tools available to help aid in enterprise coding, such as NUnit, Resharper, and Spring.Net.

Chapter 3: Emancipate Your Classes

Chapter 3 focuses on the concept of Dependency Inversion. This principle inverts the relationship between high level and low level modules, reducing their reliance on concrete implementations. The chapter ends with an application of the DI principle in the form of Dependency Injection, which is the process of injecting low-level objects into the higher-level objects.

Chapter 4: Test Driven Development

Chapter 4 introduces the Test Driven Development methodology, a development pattern that facilitates the design of loosely coupled, highly testable code. Using a comprehensive example, TDD is used to demonstrate how an application's design can be driven via unit tests. The chapter also covers the process of creating unit tests, discussing the compromise between a purist's approach to TDD and the practical application of the methodology.

The chapter concludes with a focus on unit testing modules with dependencies on expensive resources. The concept of mocking and stubbing is introduced, with an example using a popular mocking and stubbing framework.

Chapter 5: Make It Simple Again

Chapter 5 revisits the concepts introduced in Chapter 3, focusing on some of the tools and patterns that help to make enterprise development easier. After discussing the pros and cons of the Factory and Service Locator, you are introduced to the Inversion of Control principle, an abstract principle describing designs in which the flow of a system is inverted in comparison to procedural programming. The chapter ends with a simple build-your-own Inversion of Control container and a brief review of a popular open source product called Structure Map.

Chapter 6: Getting to the Middle of Things

Moving away from the core concepts and coding fundamentals germane to enterprise development, the reader now moves into the patterns portion of the book. Here, we discuss some of the popular design patterns and available frameworks for building a well-designed enterprise system. This first chapter tackles the concept of middleware. It begins with a look at the history of tiered design, starting from the legacy model of mainframe systems and moving through client-server architectures and web development. The chapter then explores some of the popular design patterns that are used in distributed systems today, such as services and message-oriented middleware.

Chapter 7: Writing Your Own Middleware

Chapter 7 focuses on the business logic contained with an application.

You will read about three popular middleware patterns: Transaction Script, Active Record, and the Domain Model pattern. You will then briefly explore Domain Driven Design, a design methodology currently gaining a notable degree of popularity. This emerging pattern focuses on the business logic of an application, strongly separating technical infrastructure concerns.

Chapter 7 ends with the building of a Domain Model for a fictitious Mortgage Loan Approval application, a project that will be reused in later chapters. Using some of the core principles of Domain Driven Design, you will walk through gathering requirements, talking to domain experts, and building a Domain Model using Test Driven Development principles.

Chapter 8: Mining Your Own Business

Chapter 8 addresses the concept of persistence. The chapter opens with a brief discussion on the responsibilities of the data access layer, and the traditional approach to hand-rolling with ADO.NET. The Object Relation Mapper is then introduced, followed by a discussion of the advantages and disadvantages of using a framework rather than doing it yourself.

You will then read about two methods of persistence management. The first is a data model approach using Microsoft's LinqToSQL. The second is a pattern that uses Microsoft's Entity Framework Object Relation Mappers with a pattern called the Data Access Object pattern.

Chapter 8 concludes with the provisioning of the Mortgage Loan Approval application created in Chapter 7 with a Repository layer built using nHibernate.

Chapter 9: Organizing Your Front End

Continuing with our exploration of system design, this next chapter explores the world of user interface development. Like Chapter 6, we begin with a discussion of the history of user interface design and programming. The reader is introduced to some of the influences of rapid application design and some platform tools that were available to support it. Moving through the period of drag-and-drop screen design and into web programming, we discuss some of the more popular emerging design patterns that eventually made their way into enterprise systems, such as the Model-View-Controller pattern.

Chapter 10: The Model-View-Presenter Pattern

Chapter 10 jumps squarely into user interface (UI) design with an in-depth review of the Model-View-Presenter pattern. Creating a testable user interface requires a loosely coupled pattern. However, applying such patterns to older user interface code can be difficult to do without breaking the application. The right pattern would enable unit testing on user interface code without being overly intrusive. Such is the goal of the Model-View-Presenter pattern. Arguably one of the most popular patterns used for enterprise user interface design, the Model-View-Presenter pattern helps to separate interface code from the visible artifacts themselves. Chapter 10 explains this pattern in detail, walking you through the individual components, explaining their interaction, and reviewing the various aspects of testability they provide. The chapter provides a detailed code sample of a simple mortgage calculator built using the Model-View-Presenter pattern, targeting both web and thick client platforms for demonstrative purposes.

Chapter 11: The Model-View-Controller Pattern

Following the themes outlined in Chapters 9 and 10, this chapter takes a deep dive into the Model-View-Controller pattern. A brief review of the history of this pattern is revisited, with an emphasis on the Ruby on Rails framework and the impact it has had. The reader is introduced to ASP.NET MVC, the web Model-View-Presenter pattern recently released by Microsoft for developing web applications on the Windows platform. This is followed with a detailed discussion of the core components and behaviors that the model exposes. We review the pros and cons of the web MVC model, with particular comparisons made with the Model-View-Presenter pattern introduced in Chapter 10. The chapter then moves into an aggressive code sample using the Mortgage Loan Model introduced in Chapters 7 and 8 and referenced again in Chapter 10.

Chapter 12: Putting It All Together

The book concludes with a comprehensive sweep of all concepts, methodologies, and design patterns discussed in all of the previous chapters. Taking a step back to the core values introduced in Chapter 1, a brief revisiting of each chapter is realized, summarizing the key points each chapter delivered and relating them to broader enterprise goals. We discuss how to apply the right pattern for the right type of system, picking only the frameworks and models suitable for a system's requirements. The chapter concludes with a brief walkthrough of a broad, multifaceted mortgage application that uses most of the themes and patterns explored in the book.

How This Book Is Structured

Professional Enterprise .NET is meant to be used as both a step-by-step guide as well as a continuous source of reference. The book is broken into distinct sections which can be read either as a whole, or piecemeal. The first portion of the book, Part I, addresses the philosophy behind enterprise development. Part II is a deeper discussion of coding patterns. It covers the concept of loose coupling, the best ways to decouple existing code, and the benefits of Test Driven Design. The third and final section, Part III, is a broad review of some of the more common design patterns used in enterprise systems. It reviews popular ways to structure your middleware, takes you through data minimizing and persistence techniques, and provides some background on enterprise UI design. Each chapter begins with an explanation of the subject matter, and most are complemented with a thorough code sample. Code samples can be reviewed on their own, or they can be assessed together for a more holistic system assessment.

Conventions

To help you get the most from the text and keep track of what's happening, we've used a number of conventions throughout the book.

> *Notes, tips, hints, tricks, and asides to the current discussion are offset and placed in italics like this.*

As for styles in the text:

❑   We *highlight* new terms and important words when we introduce them.

❑   We show keyboard strokes like this: Ctrl+A.

❑   We show file names, URLs, and code within the text like so: `persistence.properties`.

❑   We present code in two different ways:

```
We use a monofont type with no highlighting for most code examples.
We use gray highlighting to emphasize code that is of particular importance in
the present context.
```

Source Code

As you work through the examples in this book, you may choose either to type in all the code manually or to use the source code files that accompany the book. All of the source code used in this book is available for download at www.wrox.com. Once at the site, simply locate the book's title (either by using the Search box or by using one of the title lists) and click the Download Code link on the book's detail page to obtain all the source code for the book.

> *Because many books have similar titles, you may find it easiest to search by ISBN; this book's ISBN is 978-0-470-44761-1.*

Once you download the code, just decompress it with your favorite compression tool. Alternately, you can go to the main Wrox code download page at www.wrox.com/dynamic/books/download.aspx to see the code available for this book and all other Wrox books.

Errata

We make every effort to ensure that there are no errors in the text or in the code. However, no one is perfect, and mistakes do occur. If you find an error in one of our books, like a spelling mistake or faulty piece of code, we would be very grateful for your feedback. By sending in errata you may save another reader hours of frustration and at the same time you will be helping us provide even higher quality information.

To find the errata page for this book, go to www.wrox.com and locate the title using the Search box or one of the title lists. Then, on the book details page, click the Book Errata link. On this page you can view all errata that has been submitted for this book and posted by Wrox editors. A complete book list including links to each book's errata is also available at www.wrox.com/misc-pages/booklist .shtml.

If you don't spot "your" error on the Book Errata page, go to www.wrox.com/contact/techsupport .shtml and complete the form there to send us the error you have found. We'll check the information and, if appropriate, post a message to the book's errata page and fix the problem in subsequent editions of the book.

p2p.wrox.com

For author and peer discussion, join the P2P forums at p2p.wrox.com. The forums are a Web-based system for you to post messages relating to Wrox books and related technologies and interact with other readers and technology users. The forums offer a subscription feature to e-mail you topics of interest of your choosing when new posts are made to the forums. Wrox authors, editors, other industry experts, and your fellow readers are present on these forums.

At http://p2p.wrox.com you will find a number of different forums that will help you not only as you read this book, but also as you develop your own applications. To join the forums, just follow these steps:

1.   Go to `p2p.wrox.com` and click the Register link.

2.   Read the terms of use and click Agree.

3.   Complete the required information to join as well as any optional information you wish to provide and click Submit.

4.   You will receive an e-mail with information describing how to verify your account and complete the joining process.

   You can read messages in the forums without joining P2P, but in order to post your own messages, you must join.

Once you join, you can post new messages and respond to messages other users post. You can read messages at any time on the Web. If you would like to have new messages from a particular forum e-mailed to you, click the Subscribe to this Forum icon by the forum name in the forum listing.

For more information about how to use the Wrox P2P, be sure to read the P2P FAQs for answers to questions about how the forum software works as well as many common questions specific to P2P and Wrox books. To read the FAQs, click the FAQ link on any P2P page.

Setting Expectations

If you are a proficient, hard-blogging, forum-surfing open source guru, put this book down right now. This book is not a definitive resource for all things enterprise. It doesn't demand perfect Test First methodologies. It doesn't tout the Agile Manifesto at every turn, and it won't appeal to the enterprise perfectionists.

It is a book intended to introduce readers to the merits of good system design and how to apply it to large system projects. While we certainly don't want to incur the wrath of the enterprise/open source community, it is important to note that this book targets the *other side* of programming community. Our intention is to provide a simpler, less-rigid preface to modern software design principles. Although the book is tailored to Microsoft programmers, it is important to understand that the practices and methodologies discussed apply to all software development in any technical environment. Many of the tools and frameworks used have come from other development platforms, such as Java and Ruby on Rails. Some of these tools also come from Microsoft, but their mention in this piece has little to do with supporting the "Mother Ship" in Redmond and everything to do with good software design. The authors of this book are active supporters of the open source community. Both believe strongly that the best solution to a problem doesn't always come from the same company.

Over the next few months, you're bound to find lots of books on similar topics, many of which are dedicated to pitching a Microsoft solution. This book is about understanding the nature of good system design first and then choosing the path that best suits your needs. We'll be discussing some of the strong points of Microsoft technologies, as well as some of the notably weak ones. Understanding the pros and cons of the different tools that are available will help you make better decisions for your projects and ultimately lead to better system design.

Part I: Introduction to Practical Enterprise Development

What is Enterprise Design?

"Mr. Arking, your experience, certifications, and references are terrific, but unfortunately we can't hire you. Your resume just doesn't have enough enterprise experience . . . ."

That was the first time I had ever heard the word "enterprise." Wrapped subtly within a casserole of deprecating niceties and empty affirmations, assailing my staunch sense of geek-honor as I wrestled with the gravity of the moment. That was the first time I was ever turned away from a job in software development. Like most fallen nerds, I went through the normal stages of post-interview withdrawal. Similar to the departing of a close friend or relative, I felt denial, then outrage, then moved slowly into a state of grief. As the eccentric side of me skimmed through the torrent of emotions that accompany job overreaction, I began to evaluate what I did wrong. I have no enterprise experience? What does that mean? Didn't my interviewers read my resume? Weren't they impressed with my vast experience with different APIs? Didn't they appreciate my deep knowledge of different platforms and languages? I mean, look at all of the companies I worked for . . . all of the different applications I had built! Surely *some* of that demonstrated hands-on practice with enterprise!

After my failed interview I was determined to figure out what I had missed. I prided myself on being the consummate interviewee. I had all the right answers, knew all the best programming tricks. I had stacks of code samples and lots of great references to back up my work. I had to know where it all went wrong. My investigations inevitably led me back the job description which, among a great many requirements, listed the following work experience:

> *Ideal candidate will have extensive exposure to enterprise architecture, with a background in designing large systems for multifaceted, heterogeneous platform support.*

At first glance, this requirement didn't seem like much. Yet there must be something more to it than I was grasping. Multifaceted, heterogeneous platform support? What was that all about? I began to investigate what the employer meant by "enterprise patterns," expecting to find some subtlety of coding that I had likely touched on in one way or another. However, when I looked up enterprise architectures online, I was stunned to find a whole new level of design, one that had completely eluded me for over 8 years of computer programming. I took a good look at my resume and began to understand that I was a horrible fit for the position. I had built some great applications, but that's all they were: applications. Some of the things I had developed were very impressive, requiring a lot of knowledge in coding and multi-tiered design. Still, I had never actually developed an *enterprise system*. I had never designed an infrastructure or set of processes for other developers in other areas to support. I had never participated in an architectural process, never wrote tests before I wrote my code. I hadn't ever established patterns and practices to support a broad context of business needs. In fact, I had little or no experience in all of the key concepts behind all things enterprise.

I had no enterprise experience. Despite the fancy software that I had spent my career building, I hadn't even so much as dabbled in the enterprise fray. Like a great many before me, I had fallen prey to the enterprise assumption that haunts even the fanciest computer programmer. I presumed that if I've programmed enough powerful software, and learned everything there is to learn about platform libraries, APIs and SDKs, then I have earned the right to call myself an enterprise developer. Not only is this assumption wrong, it is a widely accepted assumption in Microsoft programming community. Unfortunately, I had to learn that the hard way.

And so it began, my long journey into the world of enterprise architecture and development. Wiping away all preconceived notions of what software development was supposed to be, I immersed myself into the very culture of enterprise architecture. I read books on different development processes. I purchased trade magazines and followed articles dedicated to large system development. I subscribed to countless blogs and forums published by some of the biggest players in the enterprise community. I went enterprise native, if you will. The result was a complete retooling of my skills, and a revision of my approach to software design.

In this first chapter, we will cover the following areas:

- ❑ Discuss enterprise architecture and what it means

- ❑ Discuss enterprise development and how it complements enterprise architecture

- ❑ Talk about tools, patterns, and features that enforce the key goals of an enterprise design for .NET

Enterprise design can be confusing. It requires knowledge of many different languages and disciplines. It requires both low-level programming skills and higher level, comprehensive design experience. Most of all, it requires patience and tolerance for new ideas. Enterprise design patterns and methodologies come in many different forms, each of which has slowly worked its way into the Microsoft development platform. A platform almost exclusively dedicated to rapid application development (RAD), Microsoft applications have long been riddled with poor design, exchanging extensibility and flexibility for quick time-to-market. As enterprise methodologies become more widely embraced by a new generation of Microsoft developers, many find themselves faced with the daunting task of learning these new patterns, and incorporating them into their existing skill sets and applications.

But what do we mean when we talk about enterprise architecture? What exactly is enterprise development? The term enterprise is used widely in today's technical vernacular. Most software programmers throw the term around far too casually, applying it to almost any type of application design or framework. Yet enterprise software is anything but application- or system-specific. To clarify the matter, it's best to begin with a common understanding of what enterprise means and how it changes the way you develop.

What Is Enterprise Architecture?

Enterprise architecture is typically used to describe an agency-wide or organization-wide framework for portraying and incorporating the business processes, information flows, systems, applications, data, and infrastructure to effectively and efficiently support the organization's needs. At the heart of this definition lies a very broad context aimed at including many different portions of an organization's participating branches, chief among them the business and information technology departments. We could wax intellectual all day long on the merits of these descriptions, but seeing as how this is a book for developers, let's cut to the chase. What does enterprise architecture mean from a developer's point of view? It means defining a process, framework, and set of patterns to design, develop, build, and maintain all of the software that an agency or company needs to operate. The operative phrase here is *all of the software*. It is a unified development platform for creating all elements of software at all levels of design. It includes reusable tools for building client applications, websites, databases, office applications, business automation tools, scripts, and just about anything else that a company may use to get things done. Enterprise architecture also endeavors to break down each of an application's layers into modular pieces for reusability. These reusable elements can then be used to feed or drive other applications with similar needs. Here's where the picture starts to get a bit fuzzy. Most developers take on projects with a finite set of business goals, goals that satisfy a specific need or company requirement. Within that scope, there is little consideration for modularity or reusability outside of the system that is being built. On the contrary, project goals rarely allot the time and resources needed to accommodate what is in essence the *possibility* of component reuse. Instead, typical projects focus development on the end goal only, marginalizing or downright ignoring the larger enterprise picture. Understanding enterprise development means first realizing that this kind of myopic, and often cavalier, development is ultimately counterproductive.

Enterprise architecture is also about defining a solid foundation of code and practices that eventually (and inevitably) facilitate interoperability in a heterogeneous software environment. This foundation provides both a toolset for creating software application, as well as a set of boundaries and rules within which those writings said applications need to work. The combination of both process and toolset is one of the key concepts to creating enterprise software. It expands on the otherwise traditional concepts of computer programming that concentrated on *what* one coded and mostly ignored *how* one coded. The incorporation of software development methodologies and lifecycle management becomes as important a part of building an application as the code itself.

Of course, chances are that if you're reading this book, you've already come to know some sort of development methodology. From the iterative and flexible like Agile and Extreme Programming, to the evolving and maturing like Six Sigma and the Capability Maturity Model, software development methodologies have worked their way into mainstream software development. Still, methodologies alone do not define an enterprise architecture. Plenty of shops that build applications apply these methodologies rigidly, and many of them do not have enterprise software. An organization that embraces enterprise architecture endeavors to combine a broad-context framework with a development approach, ultimately yielding code that conforms to a level of quality and design that suits the organization's core needs. Ideally, this approach can do wonders for a company, ensuring quality and uniformity throughout all tiers of design. Yet anyone who's participated or contributed to more than one enterprise shop would agree that the ideal is difficult to attain. Business needs and company politics often work counter to the spirit of enterprise planning. They force stringent timelines and tight project budgets, and don't easily allow for the sort of flexibility that a good enterprise architecture requires. The result is a hackneyed combination of some processes and standards that add little more than cumbersome meetings and a few tidy lifecycle diagrams that barely placate the folks in charge. Thus, a successful implementation of an enterprise system requires a comprehensive "buy-in" from both members of the business side and from the IT side.

What Is Enterprise Development?

Enterprise development commonly refers to the patterns and practices adopted by programmers endeavoring to implement enterprise architecture. It is the employment of certain approaches and methodologies that aim to achieve many of the root goals inherent to a successful enterprise system. What these goals are specifically changes from organization to organization; however, at the root, they address five key areas of system development:

1. Reliability

2. Flexibility

3. Separation of concerns

4. Reusability

5. Maintainability

These base tenets are embraced by all developers of enterprise systems, and they help to define the core of what most modern developers consider to be well-designed software. Enterprise development embraces these ideals, weaving them subtly into the tools and processes that drive software logic.

Reliability

Most would agree that designing systems that are reliable is a must. Yet coding for reliability is a departure from business as usual. This is especially true in the rapid application development community. Many enterprise enthusiasts exchange the term *reliability* for *testability*, since most modern enterprise coding patterns aim to facilitate unit testing. Writing code that can be well tested means changing the way that a system's functionality is modularized. It means flattening out otherwise bloated classes and removing dependencies, or rather, removing references to other code that prevent a class or module from being tested. Many of these design patterns are integral to a process known as Test Driven Development, or TDD. We will cover TDD in depth in Chapters 3 and 4.

Flexibility

Requirements can change. As a result, so must the software that supports them. If the code that you write prevents an application or system from being extensible or pliable, we would say it lacks flexibility. Many people mistake the need for flexibility for other popular engineering subjects, such as interoperability. However, enterprise flexibility addresses the ability of code to be broken down and shared by different systems applications. A program might be functional on different platforms, or contain logic for lots of different failure scenarios, but that wouldn't mean it was flexible. A flexible system allows for the changing of core features without violating unrelated services or attributes.

Separation of Concerns

Separation of concerns is simply the process of breaking a system or application down into distinct functional layers with limited overlapping of functionality. Like flexibility, separation of concerns addresses the ability to modularize code and make it more pliable, with the added benefit of logical division. Much of this division can be achieved through well-known object-oriented tenets, such as modularization and encapsulation. As we explore new patterns of development, separation of concerns becomes an all-important piece of the enterprise puzzle.

Reusability

Sharing features and services is tantamount to good enterprise design. As code is broken down and separated into logical pieces, these pieces should be designed to provide a distinct feature or satisfy a particular requirement of other systems that invoke it. The scope of a class's reusability depends on the context in which it is used; however, most agree that other modular pieces of code within a similar context should always be callable. In other words, classes at any one logical level should be reusable by other classes in the same logical level. Classes that provide data should be consumable by all other classes that demand data within scope. Classes that implement a user interface (UI) behavior should deliver the same behavior to all UI-implementing classes on the same UI tier. The notion of reusability is especially important when designing true enterprise architectures.

Maintainability

Maintainability refers to the capacity of a system to be altered or modified. Although most software engineers think they know what maintainability means, it actually has a distinct meaning in the world of software design. According to the international standard of software development defined in ISO 9126, the term maintainability actually means the ease with which a software product can be modified in order to support:

- ❑ Stability
- ❑ Analyzability
- ❑ Changeability
- ❑ Testability

Maintainable code should be the natural result of following these four tenets, provided that the designer has not introduced unnecessary levels of complexity. The inherent balance between complexity and maintainability will be explored further in Chapter 2.

For a great many software engineers this can be a dramatic shift in the way they program. It requires a rigid manner of programming, employing new concepts and demanding more upfront design than the typical developer usually executes. At close glance, one might think that simple, non-enterprise computer code that delivers a particular feature is identical in value to enterprise code that delivers precisely the same feature. Yet this shortsighted evaluation fails to address the greater needs of the system, namely core enterprise concepts. While the code may deliver similar results, the enterprise code takes strides to accommodate better design. So while the enterprise sample might look a bit more complex (only at first, mind you), the resulting class or module ultimately provides more reliability or is more maintainable.

Consider a simple example. Two developers are required to build a web page that displays dynamic feeds of financial data. These feeds can range from stock quotes to bond prices to billboard articles from popular financial journals. The non-enterprise developer might write an ASP.NET page with a set of data grids, each bound to different database calls and online web services. The bindings are created in the ASP.NET code-behind page directly, placing a good amount of data logic side by side with some of the user interface behaviors. The enterprise developer would take a slightly different tack. Using the Model-View-Presenter pattern widely embraced within the enterprise community, they define a class to garner and hold the data on its own. They then create another class to handle the user interface logic and events, defining both classes with an abstract interface that defines each of the classes' core methods. Finally, the developer writes a series of unit tests and mock classes to test the code and ensure that all portions function as intended. Figure 1-1 shows a diagrammatic depiction of the differences between the two patterns. The resulting software delivers precisely the same page and the same data, with much more orchestration and modularity. So the two efforts were a wash, right? Let's take this model a step further. The sample page hits its mark. Management is happy and they request that the page be published on the company website. The website requires a level of account authorization in order to query data from other data sources, but neither developer is aware of this. The non-enterprise developer deploys the web page directly and takes a quick look at it using a browser running on his/her desktop. They are logged in as an administrator, so the web page loads just fine. Unfortunately when others try to view the page they get a horrible system error that crashes the entire web session. On the other hand the enterprise developer took time to write a unit test that impersonates an anonymously authenticated user in the data access class. They run the test as a part of the build process and the problem becomes immediately apparent. The enterprise code is more reliable than the non-enterprise code. What's more, the composition of the web page code to support the unit tests allows for modularity and separation of concerns. So when management provides a new data service to use, the data layer can be altered with minimal impact on the user interface. The code is now more flexible, too. The added flexibility, along with the reliability and logical separation, makes the enterprise developer's web page far more maintainable than the non-enterprise developer's page.

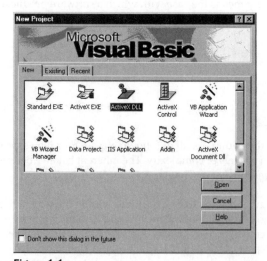

Figure 1-1

An enterprise architecture can be difficult to build in its entirety. Typically speaking, an individual software engineer has limited say over how a business expends its resources.

For most developers this is a game-changing approach to writing code. The vast majority of developers in the Microsoft world concentrate on developing software for a single system or application. This is completely understandable when you consider that an overwhelming number of career Microsoft developers began as business analysts or specialists who, thanks to the proliferation of rapid application development tools in the Microsoft software space, took on coding as a means of automation. Yet despite the upfront convenience of rapid application development, the cost in the long run can be, and usually is, very high. Enterprise development aims to reduce these long-term costs with prudent designs, approaches, and testability.

Where Is All of the Microsoft Enterprise?

Enterprise development is not new. In fact, many of the core values that drive enterprise architecture have been around for quite a few years. The problem is, if you're a Microsoft programmer, you probably haven't encountered any of them. Most enterprise patterns come from the great wide open world of common developer contribution known by most of us as *open source*. As a result, most enterprise systems have been built with platform-independent technologies such as Java or even C++. That's not to say that Microsoft technologies have never been used to build big systems for large organizations. Remember, enterprise architecture does not necessarily mean "made for big companies." We simply point out that the evolution of the patterns and methodologies driving the core values have depended on contributions from the developer community. Until recently Microsoft technologies were anything but open source. Since the open source community was the fecund environment from which modern enterprise concepts emerged, Microsoft software has played a relatively minor role in the evolution of enterprise architecture.

In the Microsoft world, a great deal of emphasis is placed on the ability to create applications quickly. Tools that provide quick automation and almost instant results can be found all over the Windows world. These tools generally fall within a category of software development known as rapid application development, or RAD. RAD-style programming isn't necessarily meant to deliver production-worthy code. Rather, its primary goal is to enable developers and analysts to emulate the core behaviors of a system quickly, intentionally ignoring patterns and process for a quick bang factor. Unfortunately, a good deal of RAD development is downright counter to the core values of enterprise development.

RAD culture has worked its way strongly into the large developer base of Microsoft programmers. At the heart of this pervasive movement lies the simple, easy-to-use language Visual Basic. First given the moniker "Project Thunder" and released as VB 1.0 in mid-1991, VB has since become the most popular programming language among Windows developers and one of the most widely used programming languages in the world. Its verbose, non-C-style syntax is easy for analysts and the less technically inclined to follow. The language itself has undergone a number of dramatic changes and enhancements over the years. However, until the language itself was retooled for the managed world and named VB.NET, its primary focus was to provide RAD tools for building powerful, production applications. At the height of its popularity, VB was most widely employed in one of two forms: Visual Basic 6.0, or Visual Basic for Applications (VBA). VB6 was its own development suite. It included tools for quickly creating object-structured applications using visual designers and wizard-like feature builders (Figure 1-1). VBA was, and still remains, the language of macros and automation within Microsoft Office applications. Between these two suites, new generations of coders were empowered. Forgoing a great deal of process and design, applications were churned out at alarming rates, with little planning and even less testing. Simple Word documents and Excel spreadsheets were fashioned with VB forms that provided a more flexible user experience than would otherwise have been achievable. Websites that once required complex Internet Server API (ISAPI) filters and direct Internet Information Server (IIS) extensions could now use VB6 ActiveX components, giving a website access to the entire Component Object Model (COM) library with very little development overhead. As usage increased, so did the power of VB. In time, Visual Basic eclipsed C++ as the Microsoft language of choice, yielding just about as much power as a complicated C module but without all of the messy planning beforehand.

Unfortunately, VB development led to some staggeringly bad applications. Once the emphasis was placed on delivery and away from design and process, a large number of companies found themselves stuck with unreliable, inflexible systems. They might have been delivered quickly, but the cost of maintenance over time became staggering. Note that we are not passing blanket judgment on the VB developer community. On the contrary, we too, found ourselves building systems in VB6 for quite a few years. We simply mean to demonstrate how this formidable trend in Microsoft development is one of the big reasons why enterprise design patterns still elude the common Microsoft programmer. The RAD culture that grew out of Visual Basic development polarized the pattern-minded from the results-oriented, ultimately blocking the mainstream Windows developers from participating in the enterprise effort.

The COM Factor

Of course, Visual Basic alone wasn't the only thing preventing enterprise patterns from making their way into Microsoft code. Some tend to think that Microsoft's previous software development platform had much to do with this as well. Before we had the neat and clean world of .NET, most C and C++ programmers were forced to use its predecessor, the Component Object Model, or COM. COM is a Windows-specific technology that allowed for components from different applications to communicate and interoperate with one another. Specifically, it is an interface standard that facilitates inter-process communication and object creation within any application, service, or system that supports the technology. COM patterns drive most objects that were used in Visual Basic programming, many of which are still in use on the Windows operating system. However, many developers felt that implementing COM introduced complexity that wasn't well suited to business applications. At the heart of every COM object lives a single common interface named `IUnknown`. This interface defines three key COM method definitions: `AddRef`, `Release`, and `QueryInterface`, each of which is used to manage objects in memory and communicate between objects.

As an object-oriented pattern, COM was well orchestrated and seemed to deliver on some of the goals that drive enterprise development. However, not everyone embraced COM programming. Implementing `IUnknown` generally meant that you had to write your program in a lower-level programming language such as C or C++. Since most Microsoft developers preferred to develop with RAD tools and languages, direct COM usage was hard to come by. Instead, COM-powered technologies such as Object Linking and Embedding (OLE) and ActiveX were provided to RAD programmers as a means to leverage COM objects without all of the hassle of the `IUnknown` plumbing. Unfortunately, COM-powered technologies were much heavier than straight COM. They introduced overhead and had a tendency to run more slowly than systems that implanted COM directly. Additionally, integration with other platforms became mostly impossible. COM objects became synonymous with Microsoft objects. As a pattern it didn't accommodate interoperability with non-Windows platforms. So, while COM was a fine pattern for designing enterprise architectures, it was only used as a means to define the Microsoft API itself. Precious few organizations employed the COM pattern directly within their own code.

The Shift to Java

Java, a (mostly) operating system-independent development platform, was released by Sun Microsystems in 1995 and gained popularity as a powerful alternative to otherwise limited Windows-based development. Long before .NET was released, Java developers enjoyed the use of well-designed APIs, automatic memory management, and just-in-time compilation. The Java community experienced a ground swell of low-level language programmers interested in porting their skills to more business-friendly development platforms. A large number of C and C++ developers were drawn to Java as a comfortable flavor of a C-style language that included some tenets of RAD without compromising some of the more academic portions of software engineering. As a platform, Java has also always been very community-oriented. It was released as free software under the GNU General Public Agreement and made freely available via downloading to programmers on different platforms. Other Java compilers have been released under the same set of public agreements, and although Sun never formalized Java with the ISO/IEC JTC1 standards body or the ECMA International, it quickly became the de facto standard for enterprise object-oriented systems. In late 2006, Sun released most of the Java SDK as free and open source software under the GNU General Public License.

As a result, the Java community was a fertile ground for the next generation of enterprise architecture. Large, multifaceted development patterns began to grow, weaving their way into medium-sized organizations at first and into vastly larger ones as time went on. The Java 2 Enterprise Edition (J2EE) provided distinct multi-tiered patterns, such as Servlets and Java Server Pages (JSP) for Web and *n*-tiered systems. Message Oriented Middleware (MOM) patterns began to form, evolving into Java Message Service (JMS) and facilitating asynchronous communication between disparate servers. Front-end orchestration patterns such as Struts paved the way for better decoupling of front-end interfaces from the code that handles data and application state. To this day, an overwhelmingly large percentage of the open source community is firmly rooted in Java and J2EE, contributing to public software projects and providing a loud voice in the enterprise community.

The .NET Revolution

In 2002, Microsoft officially released the .NET Framework version 1.0. .NET was a revolutionary departure from any development platform Microsoft had ever released. It came with a large set of pre-coded libraries that exposed or wrapped most of the core functionality within the Microsoft software development kit (SDK). It included a code management system known as the Common Language Runtime (CLR) that managed memory, loaded classes, and delivered just-in-time compilation to applications written in a .NET-enabled language. .NET languages run the gamut from script languages to older mainframe languages such as Cobol.net. However, the most popular are VB .NET, Microsoft's next generation of the popular Visual Basic language, and C#, a C-based language created by Microsoft specifically for building .NET applications. Unlike the COM and ActiveX of old, .NET was designed from the ground up to be a comprehensive development and runtime environment. Its mature combination of APIs, development tools, and runtime services makes it a far better candidate for building enterprise applications. .NET mirrors other managed software platforms in terms of tools and services provided, and it is still considered by most to be Microsoft's answer to the Java development platform. However, unlike Java, .NET didn't have the impetus of academic and enterprise developers driving it. On the contrary, at the time of .NET's release most Microsoft developers were RAD programmers or automation engineers. Thus, there wasn't a whole lot of enterprise development happening in the world of Windows.

In time, that began to change. As the .NET Framework became more mature (and as Microsoft was beefing up its server architecture a bit) more and more people began to recognize some of its enterprise advantages. .NET languages, particularly C#, were well suited for complex patterns. Language constructs such as delegates and events, properties, and indexers, made C# a suitable candidate for writing consumable, decoupled APIs. Microsoft has also taken a more accepting position to the world of open source. Upon initial release of the framework, Microsoft published the Common Language Infrastructure (CLI) and submitted it, along with specifications for the C# language and C++/CLI language, to both ECMA and ISO, making them accessible as open standards. Microsoft at first held tight to its patents on its core technologies such as its user interface API (Windows Forms) and their data access API (ADO.NET). However, in October of 2007, Microsoft announced that it would release much of the source code for the .NET base class libraries under the shared source Microsoft Reference License. This code was released in the next version of their popular interactive development environment, Visual Studio.NET 2008 edition. These steps helped to make .NET more attractive to a broader set of software engineers.

Over the last few years a number of .NET open source communities have emerged, driving new projects and embracing enterprise patterns as a means of more complicated system development. The Mono project (Figure 1-2), an initiative to create a suite of .NET tools and services targeting multiple operating systems, was established in July of 2001 and uses the public CLI specifications within its software. SourceForge.NET (see Figure 1-3), an open source community code repository, has a growing number of .NET projects.

Figure 1-2

Many of the popular Java open source projects, such as LogForJ and Hibernate, have .NET sister projects that started in SourceForge.NET.

Figure 1-3

SourceForge.net is a terrific resource for finding and exploring open source projects from all areas of the software development industry. It also includes community forums, information for system administrators, and a marketplace for buying and selling projects.

Perhaps most notable among the open source communities is Codeplex.com (Figure 1-4). Codeplex is Microsoft's open source project hosting site. Launched in June of 2006 and powered by Microsoft's Team Foundation Server, Codeplex had accumulated over 3500 public .NET projects by early 2008. It remains one of the primary avenues of code patterns used by Microsoft today.

Figure 1-4

Today, there are a number of tools and projects available for the .NET developer. Some these tools have grown out of existing enterprise projects for non-Windows platforms, while others have been created specifically for .NET development. Throughout this book, we will be exploring those tools and patterns, familiarizing you with the features they offer, as well as with the processes and frameworks in which they operate. Some patterns might seem confusing at first, adding layers of complexity to otherwise simple code samples. As you begin to get used to enterprise patterns within your code, the intrinsic value provided by enterprise design will become evident. As we cover more and more topics and your enterprise horizons broaden, this learning curve will become increasingly shallow until the patterns and processes become a part of your everyday development approach.

Summary

In this chapter, we began our journey into the professional enterprise development world by focusing on some of the key concepts and core values of enterprise development:

❑　We explored the nature of enterprise development, discussing how enterprise applications are fundamentally different from standalone applications.

❑　We defined enterprise architecture as a comprehensive set of tools, features, patterns, and processes that enable an organization to achieve its goals.

❑　We distinguished software development from the broader context of enterprise architecture, defining enterprise development as software programming that aims to achieve and support enterprise goals.

❑　We reviewed the core values of enterprise development, underscoring the five base tenets of well-designed code: reliability, flexibility, separation of concerns, reusability, and maintainability.

❑　We explored some of the background of Microsoft development.

❑　We reviewed the history of rapid application development within the Microsoft community, comparing it to the more rigid and well-defined Java development platform from which a great number of enterprise patterns emerged.

❑　Finally, we discussed Microsoft's.NET Framework, exploring some of its key benefits and explaining how and why .NET is well suited for the next generation of enterprise development.

In the next chapter we will begin to explore some of the code patterns and methodologies inherent to building enterprise systems. Using the information from this chapter as a theoretical foundation, we will focus on using programming patterns that help to increase code quality and flexibility.

2

The Enterprise Code

Before jumping head first into the land of Enterprise, you should take some time to understand how your code and development process will change. Making the shift to enterprise development requires more than just a cursory knowledge of academic patterns. Along with a new set of development tools and design patterns, enterprise development requires a change in methodologies. In this chapter we will:

❑ Explore new enterprise code patterns

❑ Discuss some of the changes you will make when writing new code

❑ Explore some of the tools you'll be using when writing enterprise code

❑ Review some of the facets of automation inherent to the enterprise environment

A New Way to Look At Code

Most people who begin learning enterprise development find that the best place to begin is the code. Readers should be familiar with a third generation object-oriented (OO) language to fully grasp some of the concepts discussed here. Considering that this book focuses exclusively on developing for the Microsoft platform, it is assumed that you have a moderate-to-advanced exposure to C#, Microsoft's preferred OO language for the ET.NET platform. If you are familiar with object-oriented programming but in need of a primer or refresher on C#, the tutorial found in Appendix A can serve as a good starting point. You'll want to be sure that you're acquainted with the language before digging deeper into the design patterns.

Over the course of the next few hundred pages, you'll become familiar with some pretty slick tools, some of which produce some pretty fancy behaviors. Yet these tools are each meant as a complement to a well-designed code base. Without good code design, these tools are rendered useless; many will fail to function at all. The reason for this failure is that a well-designed enterprise system should be constructed using code that adheres to one of the core values of enterprise design: separation of concerns. To achieve the correct degree of separation, developers should strive to write their code with a strong degree of modularity and loose coupling. At this point, readers should make sure that they have downloaded and installed the correct development tools to support the examples discussed in this book. The preferred development tool of choice for Microsoft developers is Visual Studio.NET 2008 Professional Edition. VS.NET Pro installs with all of the project templates needed for this book, including sample projects for ASP.NET, WPF (Windows Presentation Foundation), and WCF (Windows Communication Foundation) applications. Specifications and system requirements can be found at the following URL: `http://msdn.microsoft.com/en-us/visualc/aa700831.aspx`.

If you have VS.NET 2008 in an edition other than Professional, that may work too. Keep in mind, however, that this book does not focus on team collaboration, database programming, or testing exclusively. Therefore some of these suites might focus specifically on one area of development while excluding features for others. Editions such as Team Suite should work fine with this book's samples, but editions for database developers or testers might not.

The latest version of VS.NET installs with Service Pack 1 (SP1). SP1 contains newer features and templates required to follow the samples in later chapters, such as project templates for ASP.NET MVC, and plug-in tools for Microsoft Entity Framework. If you have VS.NET 2008 Pro but do not have the latest service pack, you can download it from the following address: `http://www.microsoft.com/downloads/details.aspx?FamilyId=FBEE1648-7106-44A7-9649-6D9F6D58056E&displaylang=en`.

If you do not have a version of Visual Studio.NET 2008 Professional Edition and prefer a more cost-effective solution, feel free to download the Visual Studio.NET Express editions. At the time of this writing, VS.NET Express editions have many of the same features and templates as the full editions, and they are 100% free to developers. However readers should keep in mind that some nuances between the editions may make the samples more difficult to reproduce. While there are a few different versions of the Express editions, you will only need to download two of them: Visual C#.NET 2008 Express edition, and Visual Web Developer 2008 Express edition. You can find the software specifications and system requirements at the following address: `http://www.microsoft.com/express/download/`.

Of course, if you are a diehard coding purist and despise using an interactive development environment (IDE) you can always download the .NET SDK by itself. The SDK comes with the same utilities and build tools used by the Visual Studio.NET IDE, but without the graphic user interface to launch them. All of the samples in this book assume that you are using a version of VS.NET. Still, if command line calls and batch files are more your style, you can download the .NET SDK at the following URL: `http://msdn.microsoft.com/en-us/windowsserver/bb986638.aspx`.

Some readers might want to explore other development suites as an alternative to VS.NET. Tools such as SharpDevelop are ideal for the open source community lover. However since this book is mostly intended for existing Microsoft developers, we assume readers have a certain degree of knowledge germane to the VS.NET environment, and tried to keep our samples simple by conforming to that knowledge base. Although none of our samples were created using SharpDevelop, interested readers can find out more about it at the following address: `http://www.icsharpcode.net/OpenSource/SD/`.

Modularity

The notion of code separation is one of the single most important facets of enterprise development. Traditional Microsoft developers have at their fingertips a wide array of powerful RAD tools that empower them to quickly automate macros and execute applications. Unfortunately, these tools don't enforce a strong degree of modularity. Although the code produces a desired result, the result is limited and not entirely reusable. Well-designed code must be broken down and divided into separate "vehicles of purpose." In the enterprise world, these are known as units of codes. Units of code are typically classes or types designed with a specific purpose in mind. The purpose should be well focused, striving to achieve the single desired goal for which the type was initially designed. As various units of code are developed, they can be designed to interact with one another in a manner that achieves a larger desired effect without violating the rules that drive their division.

We know this sounds pretty confusing at first, but take heart — most seasoned Microsoft developers still have a tough time thinking in terms of true separation. When it comes to developing business applications the vast majority of us are wired to think of the desired outcome and then work backward. Think about most of the business requirements for which you've developed code. A manager or project leader gives you the task of building a thing that does X. You then work backward from X, constructing the code line by line in your mind until you have a rough roadmap for a prototype. You then translate this roadmap into whatever code gets the desired outcome the quickest in order to produce the results for the tasking manager. Yet this process skips the critical step of assessing code design before you write the code. The result is a pile of spaghetti code that isn't reusable and, moreover, isn't testable. We'll be talking more about testing in the next section.

In cases such as these, it is critical for the developer to assess the design early, and understand the individual elements that will be needed to make the system function. Consider a requirement where you are tasked with creating a small client application that creates automated email newsletters advertising discounted auto parts. You're given a list of discounting rules based on the location where a user lives, and a small desktop database containing the list of automotive parts and their prices. Another database is given to you containing a list of user emails and the geographic location from which each user hails. Finally, you're provided with a brief list of preferred styles for HTML-compliant email clients. Generally speaking, an application like this is a no brainer. Most developers experienced with Microsoft Office automation or simple ET.NET forms programming could create a console application that gets the job done in a handful of function calls. Yet the resulting code is unorganized. It combines UI styles, database calls, and business rules into one convoluted stack of code.

Most developers have experimented with some modularity in the past. You might have moved recursive calls into a separate function, maybe created a class or two for accessing data, or perhaps you've dabbled with some object-oriented design patterns, like a Factory model or Decorator pattern. Wouldn't these deliver an acceptable amount of modularity? Not necessarily. Patterns such as these do provide a useful means of separation; however, when developing enterprise systems modularity isn't just about separation of your code for reusability. Enterprise development typically requires a strong degree of loose coupling.

Loosely Coupled Classes

Loose coupling is a pattern that embraces a high degree of entity separation. It describes a resilient relationship between two or more objects or systems where information can be exchanged or invoked with minimal dependency on one another. The term dependency can be used to describe a number of different aspects of reliance between two things, some of which may be more valid than others. In the case of enterprise development, a dependency is typically used to describe a runtime need for one class by another. The goal of loose coupling is to minimize these runtime links.

When it comes to enterprise development, loose coupling may be one of the strangest shifts you'll make when coding. Up until now you've likely been quite comfortable with a very traditional flavor of object-oriented programming. You define classes that perform various tasks, and provision them with attributes accordingly. The class might need some form of initialization so that you code a constructor that creates new objects, connects to different services, and populates properties accordingly. This approach is fine for small systems, but it's far from ideal for a large system that interacts with multiple services and consumers. The problem with this approach is that it prevents the creation of autonomous units. Recall that a unit of code is a class or entity designed to perform a single task. If a unit of code requires the consuming of services from other parts of the system, these services should be passed into the unit abstractly. It should never be the job of a unit to create the dependencies it needs.

Right about now you're likely sporting a tightly furrowed brow and a nasty, doubting scowl on your face. Object-oriented design has embraced the heavy constructor model for years. Some of the best books on C++ and C# list countless examples of classes that instantiate their own object instances. After all, isn't that a facet of well-encapsulated design? The answer of course is yes. All of the tenets of OO design still stand firm. Encapsulation and abstraction are still driving factors of your code design. Loose coupling does not aim to bend the time-honored rules of OO design; rather, it serves to embrace them at a new level. It combines OO methodologies and patterns with a much stronger degree of modularity. This approach not only yields much more reusability but also enables the designer to achieve perhaps the most important theme of enterprise programming: *testability*. We'll talk more on that in the next section. To better grasp this concept let's dig into a little bit of code. Think back to the list of discounted auto parts we discussed in the previous section. To simplify the example, we'll just assume that your job is to build a console application that uses a single database connection and a hard coded list of discounts based on geographic region in which a customer resides. We could take the quick-and-dirty approach and just throw all of the code together the non-enterprise way. By that we mean one big block of non-modularized code. The code block would likely be placed with a Console application's `Main` method. It would create all of the requisite ADOET.NET objects needed to extract data from a customer database and then loop through each data row. With each row iteration, the data would be pieced together starting with last name, first name, middle name, and then email address, ending finally with a price calculated on that row's value for the customer's region. The sample would look something like this:

```
class Program
    {
        const double basePrice = 35.00;
        static void Main(string[] args)
        {
            DataSet ds = new DataSet();
            OleDbCommand cmd = new OleDbCommand();
            string sql = "Select c.LastName, c.FirstName, c.MiddleName,
            c.CustomerRegion, c.EmailAddress
            from Customers c Inner Join Email e on c.ID =
            e.CustomerID Order By c.LastName ASC";
            string name = "";
            double price = 0.0;
            OleDbConnection conn = new OleDbConnection();
            OleDbDataAdapter adapter = new OleDbDataAdapter();

            cmd.Connection = conn;
            cmd.CommandType = CommandType.Text;
            cmd.CommandText = sql;
            adapter.SelectCommand = cmd;
```

```
try
{
    adapter.Fill(ds);
}
catch (Exception e)
{
    Console.WriteLine(String.Format("An error has occurred: {0}",
    e.Message));
}


foreach (DataRow dr in ds.Tables[0].Rows)
{
    name = String.Format("{0}, {1} {2}", dr["LastName"],
    dr["FirstName"], dr["MiddleName"]);

    switch (dr["CustomerRegion"].ToString())
    {
        case "1":
            price = (0.9 * basePrice);
            break;

        case "2":
            price = (0.85 * basePrice);
            break;

        case "3":
            price = (0.8 * basePrice);
            break;
    }
    Console.WriteLine(String.Format("Customer name: {0} Customer Email
    Address: {1} Customer's Price: {3}",
    name, dr["EmailAddress"]), price.ToString());

}
}
}
```

This code will work, but we would hardly call it good design. For starters, it severely breaks the rules of modularity. In a single method, there are at least three or four separate tasks being performed, including some tasks that contain distinct business rules. Each of these tasks should be separated out into a discreet unit of code, designed in a manner that best fits its needs. This sample also defies the basic tenets of loose coupling. The Program class and its Main method are tightly bound to instances of objects used to complete the mixed list of tasks. The Program class should have no reliance on any object other than those that directly relate to its scope of use. One might argue that all of these objects relate to its overall purpose, but as you'll see later in this chapter the true assessment of a loosely coupled class lies in the ability to write unit tests against it. In this example, we are unable to do so. A much better version of the same sample would probably break out the code into distinctly defined types, each adhering to the rules of modularity and loose coupling. The first class might be a simple data utility type. This object will perform simple data extraction and maybe return the data in a collection of ADOET.NET data rows.

```
class DataUtility
    {
        private string _connectionString;

        private DataSet _ds;
        private OleDbCommand _cmd;
        private OleDbConnection _conn;
        private OleDbDataAdapter _adapter;

        public DataUtility(string connectionString)
        {
            this._connectionString = connectionString;
        }

        public DataRowCollection GetData(string sql)
        {
            _ds = new DataSet();
            _conn = new OleDbConnection(_connectionString);
            _cmd = new OleDbCommand();
            _cmd.Connection = _conn;
            _cmd.CommandType = CommandType.Text;
            _cmd.CommandText = sql;
            _adapter = new OleDbDataAdapter(_cmd);

            try
            {
                _adapter.Fill(_ds);
            }
            catch (Exception e)
            {
                //handle exception and log the event
            }

            return _ds.Tables[0].Rows;
        }
    }
```

Notice that this class has been designed with one purpose in mind — to retrieve data. The only other objects that make up this class are used specifically for that purpose. We even left the catch block intentionally empty in the event that another class designed specifically for logging or error handling should be used. The only methods we defined are the constructor, which receives and holds a connection string and a method named GetData that receives the QLSql statement defining the query and returns a collection of rows reflecting the query's result.

> Other approaches to data utility classes like these might simplify the class even further, exposing only static methods and using of ADO.NET factories to further abstract the consumer.

The next class we need should perform rate calculations on a base price, varying the calculation based on different customer regions. A class like this requires a little more thought than the first one. Since these calculations represent a set of business rules, it's fair to say that different calculation classes might be needed in different contexts. Even more importantly, business rule classes might be used by other classes to do their jobs. So what we really want to do is define a set of rules that can represent all of these classes abstractly. We can use a C# interface for this:

```
public interface iCalcList
    {
        double this[int region]{get;}
        double GetPrice(int region);
        double BasePrice { get; set; }
    }
```

Now we have an abstract type that represents any list of calculations. Interfaces can be implemented by just about any C# class, allowing other developers to define their own versions of this business rule. Although the calculations might be defined differently for each implementation, every one of these classes should expose an indexer for quick reference of the calculation, a property named BasePrice, where an instance's original price can be set, and a method named GetPrice that returns a calculated value based on the region in which a customer lives. This abstract interface is an important element of design when it comes to building enterprise systems. They are a popular approach to type decoupling, which is needed when attempting to loosely couple classes that require interaction.

Now that you have a definition you can go ahead and create your Discount list:

```
class DiscountList : iCalcList
    {
        private Dictionary<int, double> _rates;
        private double _basePrice;

        public double BasePrice
        {
            get { return this._basePrice; }
            set { this._basePrice = value; }
        }

        public DiscountList()
        {
            _rates = new Dictionary<int, double>();
            _rates.Add(1, 0.9);
            _rates.Add(2, 0.85);
            _rates.Add(3, 0.8);
        }

        public double this [int region]
        {
            get{return _rates[region];}
        }

        public double GetPrice(int region)
        {
            return _rates[region] * BasePrice;
        }
    }
```

This class implements the same methods defined in the iCalcList interface. A generic Dictionary instance was also added to hold a very simple list of calculations, using the customer region numbers as keys for each entry. The indexer and GetPrice methods extract values from the Dictionary accordingly. What's important to note about this approach is that this class has been defined as two types: a parent type of iCalcList and a child type of DiscountList. Now any class that uses iCalcList can be handed an instance of DiscountList and invoke its members with (relative) impunity.

The next class we need should perform the formatting of the text from the data rows. As with the large code block sample, we'll need to loop through rows of data, extract the relevant column values, calculate each price by the customer region, and print it all out to a single line of text. Like DiscountList, this class represents a unit of business logic. So, we should take a minute to first define an interface that represents the abstract type and then implement our formatter.

```
public interface iTextFormatter
    {
        string GetFormattedText();
    }
```

Nice and simple, right? Now let's build the formatter itself. Most of that is straightforward, save for the calculation of the prices. If we define a class that formats text but then create another class that performs calculations we'll be violating the principals of loose coupling. Instead, we'll pass an instance of the calculation class into the constructor and hold it as a class field variable. Passing an object into another object's constructor limits the amount of coupling between the two and helps to remove the dependency of one class on another.

```
class DataToTextFormatter : iTextFormatter
    {
        private DataRowCollection _rows;
        private iCalcList _rateCalculator;

        public DataToTextFormatter(DataRowCollection rows, iCalcList rateCalculator)
        {
            _rows = rows;
            _rateCalculator = rateCalculator;
        }

        private string FormatLineEntry(DataRow dr)
        {
            string name = String.Format("{0}, {1} {2}", dr["LastName"],
            dr["FirstName"], dr["MiddleName"]);
            double price = _rateCalculator.GetPrice((int)(dr["CustomerRegion"]));
            string email = dr["EmailAddress"].ToString();
            return String.Format("Customer name: {0} Customer Email Address:
            {1} Customer's Price: {3}", name, email, price);
        }

        public string GetFormattedText()
        {
            StringBuilder sb = new StringBuilder();
            foreach (DataRow dr in _rows)
            {
                sb.Append(FormatLineEntry(dr));
            }
```

```
                    return sb.ToString();
            }
        }
```

Take a good look at the sample. You'll see that the constructor actually takes two parameters. One is a DataRowCollection object containing all of the data to be formatted, the other is an instance of iCalcList. Remember that DiscountList can be defined as two different types in this context. If our constructor is expecting an instance of iCalcList, it can easily accept an instance of its child type. Referencing the abstract type in the TextToDataFormatter class severs the ties between it and any concrete instance of a calculating class.

These classes effectively encapsulate all of the units you need to perform your tasks. You might want to invoke them directly in your console application's Main method, but we prefer to create one last class that performs that action for us. This class will have one method, GetList, and a constructor for initialization.

```
    class ListPresenter
    {
        private DataUtility _dUtil;
        private iCalcList _dList;
        private iTextFormatter _formatter;

        public ListPresenter(DataUtility dUtil, iCalcList dList, iTextFormatter
        formatter)
        {
            this._dUtil = dUtil;
            this._dList = dList;
            this._formatter = formatter;
        }

        public string GetList()
        {
            string sql = "Select c.LastName, c.FirstName, c.MiddleName,
            c.CustomerRegion, c.EmailAddress
            from Customers c Inner Join Email e on c.ID =
            e.CustomerID Order By c.LastName ASC";
            _dUtil = new DataUtility("");
            _dList = new DiscountList();
            _dList.BasePrice = 35.00;
            _formatter = new DataToTextFormatter(_dUtil.GetData(sql), _dList);
            return _formatter.GetFormattedText();
        }
    }
```

Unit Testing

Now that we've broken the code down into loosely coupled units, we can focus on one of the key concepts of enterprise development, unit testing. The term *unit testing* has come to mean many different things over the years. Conceptually, the definition remains the same. A unit test is construct or method for testing the smallest or most finite pieces of your source code. The application of unit tests has varied widely over time. This is especially true when one realizes that the use of unit tests depends entirely on the scope and design of one's code. There are plenty of systems that do not embrace enterprise programming tenets but that still use unit tests to verify physical layers, individual components, background processes, or other layers that can be divorced from the running system. The problem with this approach is the highly arbitrary nature of the unit. In these looser interpretations of unit tests, the scope of validation usually includes a number of different processes, preventing the ability to truly test at a level where useful action can be taken.

More recent uses of the term unit testing have come to focus on not only the high modular unit of testable code but also on the methodology of testing. In Test Driven Development, or TDD, the developer focuses on writing unit test *first*, prior to the code it is intended to validate. The programmer then writes the code to fit the test and refactors both in an iterative process. We'll be talking about Test Driven Development methodology in Chapter 4. Still, readers should take some time to familiarize themselves with a unit test early. In the enterprise world, unit tests are pieces of code that complement the modular pieces that make up a system. They almost always employ the use of a unit-testing framework, which is ostensibly another code library with methods that enable test automation. Herein lies one of the fundamental differences between older unit testing and Test Driven Development. The automation of tests is an integral part of the build process. As tests are written and new code checked into your code repository, tests are run against the new code and old code to ensure the durability of the new version of the system. This automation process ensures that developers are quickly alerted of any new code that breaks a previously valid system.

Let's take a look at a unit test for the small application we completed in the previous section. Developers would create tests like these in another project (or source code context) with a compilable version of the target source code. They would import the correct testing framework for building what is known as a test harness. The test harness contains both the individual tests to be executed, along with other pieces of code to create the various test conditions. We will discuss how to provision your test project in Chapter 4.

```
[TestFixture]
    class As_DataToTextFormatter
    {
        public void get_formatted_text_is_not_null()
        {
            iCalcList mock = new MockCalcList();
            DataSet sampleData = MockDataSets.MockSampleData();
            DataToTextFormatter d = new DataToTextFormatter(mock);

            Assert.IsNotNull(d.GetFormattedText(sampleData));
        }
    }
```

This code sample reflects a simple, but common, unit test. It checks that a valid instance of a DataToTextFormatter object returns a non-null object when provisioned correctly. The Assert object is a class found within the NUnit testing framework. With it, we pass in an instance of the DataToTextFormatter object, invoke the GetFormattedText method, and check to see if the value returned is not null. On the surface this test is deceptively simple. Yet readers should notice the use of the iCalcList instance labeled "mock," and the manner by which it is passed to the DataToTextFormatter instance. Since we defined iCalcList as a separate, loosely coupled object the DataToTextFormatter class has no direct dependency on it. If this class were defined within the DataToTextFormatter class we would have to use the same instance of the iCalcList each time we instantiated a DataToTextFormatter. Instead, we can easily create different instances of iCalcList, with completely different states and values, and pass them into the DataToTextFormatter class flexibly. This code pattern facilitates testability in all areas of your code base.

Inversion of Control Containers

As you begin to develop more and more decoupled code, you'll no doubt begin to feel some strain. Older object-oriented patterns allowed for the provisioning or initialization of complex objects within an object's constructor. This ensured that, when an object was created, all of its requisite dependencies were created and initialized as well, all from one line of consumer code. The result was simple to use and easy to proliferate. Now, when you strive to decouple your dependencies, you'll find yourself constantly creating and passing objects into other objects. That's fine the first time you define your object graph, but it gets very tedious over time. To resolve this tedium, enterprise developers employ the use of an Inversion of Control (IoC) container.

IoC containers, also known as Dependency Injection (DI) containers, help to maintain code modularity while automating a lot of the logic developers would otherwise need to write themselves. They can seem confusing at first as they seem to hide a lot of visible processing. However once you become accustomed to their patterns, they save a lot of time and frustration. The samples discussed in the next few paragraphs help to demonstrate some of these patterns. However bear in mind that they are necessarily simple examples, kept simple for demonstrative purposes. We will be diving much more deeply into Spring.NET and other IoC containers in Chapter 5.

Let's take a look at the two different approaches. Following is a code sample showing a series of classes that initialize their dependencies within their constructors:

```
class ComplexObject
    {
        private ObjA _classA;

        internal ObjA ClassA
        {
            get { return _classA; }
            set { _classA = value; }
        }
        private ObjB _classB;

        internal ObjB ClassB
        {
            get { return _classB; }
            set { _classB = value; }
        }
        private ObjC _classC;

        internal ObjC ClassC
        {
            get { return _classC; }
            set { _classC = value; }
        }


        public ComplexObject()
        {
            _classA = new ObjA();
            _classB = new ObjB();
```

```
            _classC = new ObjC();
        }
    }

    class ObjA
    {

    }

    class ObjB
    {

    }

    class ObjC
    {
        private ObjD _classD;

        internal ObjD ClassD
        {
            get { return _classD; }
            set { _classD = value; }
        }

        public ObjC()
        {
            _classD = new ObjD();
        }
    }

    class ObjD
    {
        private int _count;

        public int Count
        {
            get { return _count; }
            set { _count = value; }
        }

    }
```

Without defining any meaningful methods or member functions to these types, we can infer the basic relationships among them. The type named ComplexClass relies on instances of classes ObjA, ObjB, and ObjC, and ObjC relies on an instance of ObjD. ComplexClass creates instances of ObjA, ObjB, and ObjC in its constructor, and ObjC creates its dependant instance of ObjD within its constructor. This pattern abstracts any consuming code from the responsibility of object initialization. The resulting code might look something like this:

```
ComplexObject cObj = new ComplexObject();
cObj.ClassC.ClassD.Count = 5;
```

Nice and simple, no? One line of code invokes all of the work you need to create a live, initialized version of `ComplexObject`. Yet, as we've been discussing, this approach violates the rules of modularity and loose coupling, preventing us from being able to test each class separately. A cleaner version of the same code would look something like this:

```
class ComplexObject
    {
        private ObjA _A;

        internal ObjA A
        {
            get { return A; }
            set { _A = value; }
        }
        private ObjB _B;

        internal ObjB B
        {
            get { return _B; }
            set { _B = value; }
        }
        private ObjC _C;

        internal ObjC C
        {
            get { return _C; }
            set { _C = value; }
        }


        public ComplexObject(ObjA a, ObjB b, ObjC c)
        {
            _A = a;
            _B = b;
            _C = c;
        }
    }

    class ObjA
    {

    }

    class ObjB
    {

    }

    class ObjC
    {
        private ObjD _D;

        internal ObjD D
        {
            get { return _D; }
            set { _D = value; }
```

```
            }

        public ObjC(ObjD d)
        {
            _D = d;
        }
    }

    class ObjD
    {
        private int _count;

        public int Count
        {
            get { return _count; }
            set { _count = value; }
        }

    }
```

The differences here are subtle but important. The same dependencies exist, however the initializations have been removed. The objects now require Dependency Injection to receive the objects upon which they rely. Dependency Injection (or DI) is a term used to describe the process of passing dependant instances of objects into loosely coupled classes. It complements the abstract pattern embraced in loosely coupled modular design, typically referred to as Inversion of Control. While Inversion of Control (or IoC) renders classes far more flexible and testable, the process of DI can make the ComplexObject class very tedious to use. Now, every time you need an instance of ComplexObject you also need to explicitly create instances of ObjA, ObjB, and ObjC and pass them in. You also have the added inconvenience of creating objects out of order. Since ObjC depends on ObjD, you'll need to create ObjD first, pass that into ObjC's constructor, and then pass ObjC with the other objects into ComplexObject's constructor:

```
ObjA A = new ObjA();
ObjB B = new ObjB();

ObjD D = new ObjD();
ObjC C = new ObjC(D);

ComplexObject cObj = new ComplexObject(A, B, C);
```

As you can see, you need a lot more code in the consuming class just to create a single instance of ComplexObject. This is the unfortunate give and take of loosely coupled design. You get the flexibility of strongly typed independently testable units, but at a cost to the consumer. The compromise between loose coupling and development expedience can be achieved by using an Inversion of Control container. IoC containers (also referred to DI containers in varying contexts) provide a global set of definitions for developers to describe their objects at compile time. The container is aware of all objects in its definition file, along with an object's dependencies. Definition files are typically MLXML-based; however, some containers allow for programmatic configuration as well. When a consuming method or class needs to create a complex object, it need only request an instance of it from the IoC container, invoking a container Get method instead of the more typical new operator. The following is an example of an IoC container object definition for ComplexObject as defined in the popular Spring.NET IoC container:

```
<configuration>

  <configSections>
    <sectionGroup name="spring">
      <section name="context" type="Spring.Context.Support.ContextHandler, Spring.Core"/>
      <section name="objects" type="Spring.Context.Support.DefaultSectionHandler,
      Spring.Core" />
    </sectionGroup>
  </configSections>

  <spring>

    <context>
      <resource uri="config://spring/objects"/>
    </context>

    <objects xmlns="http://www.springframework.net">
      ...
    </objects>

  </spring>

</configuration>
```

The XML may seem a bit verbose to some, but it is considered a standard by many in the enterprise field. We'll be reviewing the programmatic approach to object definitions in Chapter 5.

Once the object is defined in the container, it can be instantiated by using the container reference:

```
IApplicationContext Context = ContextRegistry.GetContext();
ComplexObject cObj = (ComplexObject)Context.GetObject("etlPipelineEngine");
```

IApplicationContext is one of SpringET.NET's definitions of its consumable context. Once you have a handle to it, you can simply invoke an object by name using its various static Get methods. You can now create complex objects that are loosely coupled and fully testable without the overheard of manual Dependency Injection. IoC containers are good for a lot more than just simple object instantiation. They can help to speed the development of consuming code, create a tangible roadmap for your object model, even provide varying degrees of aspect-oriented programming. We will be covering the full use of IoC containers in Chapter 5.

Summary

In this chapter you took your first look at enterprise code patterns. Reflecting back to some of the core tenets reviewed in Chapter 1, we discussed some of the common code patterns seen in many enterprise systems and how they help to support these themes.

❑   We discussed the use of modularity in enterprise code. Using the rapid application development model as a basis for comparison, we reviewed the types of applications typically created for a

Windows system, and how they are fundamentally flawed. The term *unit of code* was introduced, helping to better to define the pattern of separation typically used in the enterprise community.

❑ We discussed the concept of loose coupling, and the role it plays in separation. Building on the example of a small database application that employs varying business rules, we broke down the application code into separate modular pieces. We then assembled the application following the rules of loose coupling and adhering to sounder, enterprise patterns.

❑ Building on the concepts of modularity and loose coupling, we then took a look at unit tests, and briefly discussed unit testing methodologies. Using a test built from the sample code in the proceeding section on loose coupling, we were able to see how the flexible relationship between the application's individual components allowed us to define tests easily, without having to initialize other unrelated sections of code.

❑ We concluded with a quick look at Inversion of Control containers. Since a well designed enterprise code base forces the consuming code to pass units of code into object constructors the resulting development effort can become tedious. An IoC container helps to minimize the instantiation process, automating the creation of related objects in a manner otherwise hidden from the developer.

Chapter 3 will further build on these concepts by taking a deeper dive into the process of loose coupling. We will review the different approaches developers can take when designing for the right degree of separation, and build a sample application that directly employs these concepts.

Part II: The New Code — Changing the Way You Build

3

Emancipate Your Classes

How many times have you been asked to modify a piece of existing code only to find that a small change has a rippling effect throughout the entire application, preventing it from compiling or worse still, introducing a bug that has a horrible knack of only surfacing just after you go live? What should have been a minor adjustment ends up becoming a massive task simply because your small change had an implicit effect on other portions of your code.

The problem is that software, for one reason or another, often requires changes. It's important for your code to be resilient, flexible, and adaptable, ultimately making your software more maintainable. Designing for maintainability is one of the most important goals when creating software. Maintenance is not just an important facet in making your job easier; it also makes the job of the next programmer easier when he or she takes over. By thinking about the future and how your code may evolve, you will be able to design applications in a way that makes them flexible and allows for easy modification as and when the business changes.

The biggest resisters to change are dependencies — classes that are dependent on other classes in your system. Dependencies can be found in all areas of code — high-level classes might be dependent on low-level classes, and vice-versa. If one portion of your code changes, other portions are required to change as well. In this chapter, you will learn what a dependency is, and how to invert it and make your code more manageable, testable, and flexible.

Evaluating Your Code for Dependencies

The real power in object oriented programming lies in the ability of objects to interact with each other thus coming together to form more complex modules or components and, by doing so, enabling the programmer to perform more complex processes. This translates into solving business problems via workflow. To understand this, however, one must first understand what a dependency is. As you might assume, a dependency is something that an object needs to function properly; in and of themselves dependencies are not a bad thing but it is the manner in which a dependency is bound to an object that can become problematic.

You read in the previous chapter that one of the easiest ways to identify dependencies in your code is to look for places where you are creating new instances of other classes. By creating an instance of a class within another, you are immediately creating a dependency and tightly coupling your code.

One of the best ways of learning is, of course, by example. So instead of another hello world code sample, you are going to get stuck into an exercise with a bit of meat on its bones, so you can take the concepts you learn and apply them to real world scenarios.

Imagine that you are working for a software company that has produced an e-commerce solution. The application currently only supports the PayPal merchant for taking order payments and making refunds. However, some customers using the software have shown an interest in using a different payment gateway, namely WorldPay. Your bosses have agreed to include this new payment merchant in the next release and have chosen to allow companies to specify a payment merchant via a configuration setting.

You have been given the task of modifying the code that deals with the return and refunding of orders to support the new payment merchant.

Figure 3-1 shows all the classes involved in the processing of customer returns.

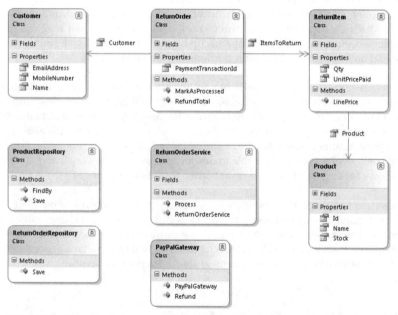

Figure 3-1

If you want to follow along in this exercise follow these simple steps:

1. Open up Visual Studio and create a new class library project named `ProEnt.Chap3.Returns`.

2. Delete the class named `Class1.cs` that Visual Studio automatically created and add three folders to the project named Model, Repositories and Services.

3. Add a new class to the Model folder named `Customer`, with the following definition. This class will represent the customer who is returning items.

```
namespace ProEnt.Chap3.Returns.Model
{
    public class Customer
    {
        private string _emailAddress;
        private string _name;
        private string _mobileNumber;

        public string EmailAddress
        {
            get { return _emailAddress; }
            set { _emailAddress = value; }
        }

        public string Name
        {
            get { return _name; }
            set { _name = value; }
        }

        public string MobileNumber
        {
            get { return _mobileNumber; }
            set { _emailAddress = value; }
        }
    }
}
```

4. Next add another new class to the Model folder named `Product`. This class will represent the product that a customer is returning and the code listing for the products is detailed below.

```
namespace ProEnt.Chap3.Returns.Model
{
    public class Product
    {
        private int _id;
        private int _stock;
        private string _name;

        public int Id
        {
            get { return _id; }
            set { _id = value; }
        }

        public int Stock
```

```
        {
            get { return _stock;}
            set { _stock = value;}
        }

        public string Name
        {
            get { return _name;}
            set { _name = value; }
        }
    }
}
```

5. The third class to add to the Models folder will represent the item that is being returned and will
    be named, rather imaginatively, ReturnItem; the listing for the class follows.

```
namespace ProEnt.Chap3.Returns.Model
{
    public class ReturnItem
    {
        private int _qty;
        private Product _product;
        private decimal _unitPricePaid;

        public int Qty
        {
            get { return _qty;}
            set { _qty = value; }
        }

        public Product Product
        {
            get { return _product;}
            set { _product = value;}
        }

        public decimal UnitPricePaid
        {
            get { return _unitPricePaid; }
            set { _unitPricePaid = value; }
        }

        public decimal LinePrice()
        {
            return UnitPricePaid * Qty;
        }
    }
}
```

6. Last, but by no means least, is the `ReturnOrder` class itself that will also be created within the Model folder. This class will represent the order that the customer is returning and this will hold a collection of items being returned. The `ReturnOrder` class also contains a property named `PaymentTransactionId`, which contains the unique payment transaction ID used to refund any monies back to the customer. The listing for the `ReturnOrder` class follows.

```
using System.Collections.Generic;
using System.Linq;

namespace ProfessionalEnterprise.Chap3.Rev_01.Model
{
    public class ReturnOrder
    {
        private Customer _customer;
        private IList<ReturnItem> _itemsToReturn;
        private string _paymentTransactionId;

        public string PaymentTransactionId
        {
            get { return _paymentTransactionId; }
            set { _paymentTransactionId = value;}
        }

        public Customer Customer
        {
            get { return _customer;}
            set { _customer = value; }
        }

        public IList<ReturnItem> ItemsToReturn
        {
            get { return _itemsToReturn; }
            set { _itemsToReturn = value; }
        }

        public void MarkAsProcessed()
        {
            // Changes the state of the order...
        }

        public decimal RefundTotal()
        {
            var query = from Item in ItemsToReturn
                        select Item;

            return query.Sum(a => a.LinePrice());
        }
    }
}
```

7. To enable the objects to be saved and retrieved from the data store you will be adding a Product and `ReturnOrder` repository. To keep the example simple these classes won't contain any code — just comments on their role within the application. In a real application this is where you would find all of your SQL code use to persist the business objects. Add a new class to the Repositories folder named `ProductRepository` with the following definition.

```
using ProEnt.Chap3.Returns.Model;

namespace ProEnt.Chap3.Returns.Repositories
{
    public class ProductRepository
    {
        public Product FindBy(long Id)
        {
            // Here you would find code to
            // retrieve a Product from the data store.
            return null;
        }

        public void Save(Product product)
        {
            // Here you would find code to persist
            // a Product to the data store.
        }
    }
}
```

8. Add a second class named `ReturnOrderRepository` to the Repositories folder, with the following listing.

```
using ProEnt.Chap3.Returns.Model;

namespace ProEnt.Chap3.Returns.Repositories
{
    public class ReturnOrderRepository
    {
        public void Save(ReturnOrder ReturnOrder)
        {
            // Here you would find code to persist
            // a ReturnOrder to the data store.
        }
    }
}
```

9. To enable PayPal refunds to be made you need a `PayPalPayment` gateway. Create a new class within the Services folder named `PayPalGateway` with the class definition below.

```
using System;

namespace ProEnt.Chap3.Returns.Services
{
    public class PayPalGateway
```

```
    {
        public PayPalGateway(string userName, string password)
        {
            // Here you would find code to login to the
            // PayPal payment merchant.
        }

        public Boolean Refund(decimal amount, string transactionId)
        {
            // Here you would find code to create a refund
            // transaction and send it to PayPal.
            return true;
        }
    }
}
```

10. Finally to complete the current implementation of the codebase you will need to add a class to the Services folder named `ReturnOrderService`. This class is responsible for the coordination of adjusting the stock of the returned items, refunding any monies back to the customer, and notifying the customer of the completion of the return order process. The definition for this class follows.

```
using System;
using System.Net.Mail;
using System.Text;
using ProEnt.Chap3.Returns.Repositories;
using ProEnt.Chap3.Returns.Model;

namespace ProEnt.Chap3.Returns.Services
{
    public class ReturnOrderService
    {
        private ProductRepository _productRepository;
        private ReturnOrderRepository _returnOrderRepository;
        private PayPalGateway _paypalGateway;
        // These settings would be stored in the AppSettings of the config file.
        // You can keep them as empty strings to keep this example code simple.
        private string _paypalUserName = string.Empty ;
        private string _paypalPassword =  string.Empty;
        private string _smtpHost = string.Empty;

        public ReturnOrderService()
        {
            _productRepository = new ProductRepository();
            _returnOrderRepository = new ReturnOrderRepository();
            _paypalGateway = new PayPalGateway(_paypalUserName, _paypalPassword);
        }

        public void Process(ReturnOrder ReturnOrder)
        {
            // 1) Update the stock.
            foreach (ReturnItem Item in ReturnOrder.ItemsToReturn)
```

```
        {
            // a) Find the product.
            Product product = _productRepository.FindBy(Item.Product.Id);
            // b) Increase the stock.
            product.Stock += Item.Qty;
            // c) Save the product.
            productRepository.Save(product);
        }

        // 2) Refund the payment back to the customer.
        _paypalGateway.Refund(ReturnOrder.RefundTotal(),
                              ReturnOrder.PaymentTransactionId);

        // 3) Mark the return order as processed.
        ReturnOrder.MarkAsProcessed();

        // 4) Save the updated return order.
        _returnOrderRepository.Save(ReturnOrder);

        // 5) Notify the customer on the processing of the return.
        String Recipient = ReturnOrder.Customer.EmailAddress;
        String From = "Returns@MyCompany.com";
        String Subject = "Your return order has been processed.";
        StringBuilder Message = new StringBuilder();

        Message.AppendLine
           (String.Format("Hello {0}", ReturnOrder.Customer.Name));
        Message.AppendLine
           ("You return order has been processed and you have been refunded.");

        Message.AppendLine("Items returned: ");
        foreach (ReturnItem ItemReturning in ReturnOrder.ItemsToReturn)
        {
            Message.AppendLine(String.Format("{0} of {1}",
                               ItemReturning.Qty, ItemReturning.Product.Name));
        }

        Message.AppendLine("Regards");
        Message.AppendLine("Returns Department");

        MailMessage msgMail = new MailMessage(From, Recipient,
                                              Subject, Message.ToString());

        SmtpClient smtp = new SmtpClient(_smtpHost);
        smtp.Send(msgMail);
    }
  }
}
```

The constructor method for the `ReturnOrderService` creates instances of three dependent classes.

- ❏   `ProductRepository`
- ❏   `ReturnOrderRepository`
- ❏   `PayPalGateway`

The `ProductRepository` and `ReturnOrderRepository` follow the Repository pattern; the Repository pattern acts like an in-memory collection. It is used to persist and retrieve the domain's business objects; in this instance, that means fulfilling the persistence and querying needs of the `ReturnOrder` and `Product` business objects; you will learn more about this pattern in Chapter 8. The `PayPalGateway` is a thin wrapper around the real PayPal web service and is used to communicate with the payment gateway.

The service class has a single method called `Process`. This method takes a `ReturnOrder` as an argument. The return order business object represents the real order that is being returned. It contains a collection of items with details on the products that are being returned and contains business logic to return the refund value of the order as well as a method to change its internal state.

The first step in the returns process is to enter the returned products back into stock. For each item being returned, the product is retrieved from the `ProductRepository`, its stock is adjusted to include the stock being returned, and then the changes to the Products stock value are persisted back into the datastore courtesy of the `ProductRepository save` method.

The second step in the process is issuing a refund to the customer for the returned items. As currently PayPal is the only supported payment merchant, a `PayPalGateway` object is created in the constructor of the `ReturnOrderService` with the required login details; in this example they are empty strings but typically these values would be pulled from some kind of configuration file or data store. To register a refund the `PayPalGateway`'s refund method is called with the total amount to refund along with the transaction ID used to pay for the orignal order.

Step three simply involves the order changing its internal state to mark it as being processed. Step four saves the changes to the state of the `ReturnOrder` via the `ReturnOrderRepository`'s `save` method.

The final step in the process notifies the customer that the returned order has been processed. This is acheived by building a message from the collection of return items, then creating an instance of a `MailMessage` object with the customer's email address and the returns department email address, via a configuration file setting. Finally, you send the email, using a new instance of the SMTP class, again with details stored in the configuratation file.

Now that you understand the inner workings of the `ReturnOrderService` class you decide to add the code to support the `WorldPay` payment merchant. You figure the easiest way to do this is just add a new payment gateway, the `WorldPayGateway`, to abstract away the details of refunding to a World Pay account in the same manner as the `PayPalGateway`. Then to enable the `ReturnOrderService` class to use it you add a logic check to see which payment merchant the system has been set up to work with.

If you are working your way through this exercise simply follow these steps. You will need to create a new class named `WorldPayGateway` in the Services folder, with the following code definition.

```
namespace ProEnt.Chap3.Returns.Services
{
    public class WorldPayGateway
    {
        public WorldPayGateway(string MerchantAccount,
                               string userName,
                               string password)
        {
            // Here you would find code to login to the
            // WorldPay payment merchant.
        }

        public Boolean Refund(decimal Amount, string TransactionId)
        {
            // Here you would find code to create a refund
            // transaction and send it to the WorldPay payment merchant.
            return true;
        }
    }
}
```

Now you can amend the `ReturnOrderService` as displayed below.

```
using System;
using System.Net.Mail;
using System.Text;
using ProEnt.Chap3.Returns.Repositories;
using ProEnt.Chap3.Returns.Model;

namespace ProEnt.Chap3.Returns.Services
{
    public class ReturnOrderService
    {
        private ProductRepository _productRepository;
        private ReturnOrderRepository _returnOrderRepository;
        private PayPalGateway _paypalGateway;
        private WorldPayGateway _worldPayGateway;
        // These settings would be stored in the AppSettings of the config file.
        private string _paypalUserName = string.Empty ;
        private string _paypalPassword =  string.Empty;
        private string _worldpayUserName = string.Empty;
        private string _worldpayPassword = string.Empty;
        private string _worldpayMerchantId = string.Empty;
        private string _paymentGatewayType = string.Empty;
        private string _smtpHost = string.Empty;

        public ReturnOrderService()
```

```
        {
            _productRepository = new ProductRepository();
            _returnOrderRepository = new ReturnOrderRepository();
            if (_paymentGatewayType == "PayPal")
                _paypalGateway = new PayPalGateway(_paypalUserName,
                                                  _paypalPassword);
            else
            {
                _worldPayGateway = new WorldPayGateway
                        (worldpayMerchantId, _worldpayUserName, _worldpayPassword);
            }
        }

        public void Process(ReturnOrder ReturnOrder)
        {
            // 1) Update the stock.
            foreach (ReturnItem Item in ReturnOrder.ItemsToReturn)
            {
                // a) Find the product.
                Product product = _productRepository.FindBy(Item.Product.Id);
                // b) Increase the stock.
                product.Stock += Item.Qty;
                // c) Save the product.
                _productRepository.Save(product);
            }

            // 2) Refund the payment back to the customer.
            if (_paymentGatewayType == "PayPal")
                _paypalGateway.Refund(ReturnOrder.RefundTotal(),
                             ReturnOrder.PaymentTransactionId);
            else
                _worldPayGateway.Refund(ReturnOrder.RefundTotal(),
                                ReturnOrder.PaymentTransactionId);


            // 3) Mark the return order as processed.
            ReturnOrder.MarkAsProcessed();

            // 4) Save the updated return order
            _returnOrderRepository.Save(ReturnOrder);

            // 5) Notify the customer on the processing of the return.
            String Recipient = ReturnOrder.Customer.EmailAddress;
            String From = "Returns@MyCompany.com";
            String Subject = "Your return order has been processed.";
            StringBuilder Message = new StringBuilder();

            Message.AppendLine
                (String.Format("Hello {0}", ReturnOrder.Customer.Name));
```

```
    Message.AppendLine
      ("You return order has been processed and you have been refunded.");

    Message.AppendLine("Items returned: ");
    foreach (ReturnItem ItemReturning in ReturnOrder.ItemsToReturn)
    {
        Message.AppendLine(String.Format("{0} of {1}",
                ItemReturning.Qty, ItemReturning.Product.Name));
    }

    Message.AppendLine("Regards");
    Message.AppendLine("Returns Department");

    MailMessage msgMail = new MailMessage(From, Recipient, Subject,
                                          Message.ToString());

    SmtpClient smtp = new SmtpClient(_smtpHost);
    smtp.Send(msgMail);
        }
    }
}
```

Because you are pressed for time, you have added the WorldPay payment option using the same style of procedural coding as the previous developer; this seemed like the easiest and quickest solution. You took the option of retrieving the payment merchant setting via the configuration setting as was done with the email settings and PayPal credentials. Needless to say, when you test the code, it works. It is built, packaged, and put into production, and you receive plenty of pats on the back from your bosses — a job well done . . . or was it?

After a review of the `ReturnOrderService` class, you can see that it's tightly coupled to the following dependent classes:

❏ `ProductRepository`

❏ `ReturnOrderRepository`

❏ `PayPalGateway`

❏ `WorldPayGateway`

❏ Notifying via the `System.Net.Mail` classes

You should also note that the service class requires deep knowledge of how to correctly instantiate a valid instance of each dependency; for example, the class needs to know what are valid values for the `WorldPayGateway` constructor arguments, and where to find them.

The design of the `ReturnOrderService` class is poor — however you need to quantify this statement. It's important to understand what makes a poor design and why loose coupling is important. By understanding these concepts you can begin to understand why patterns, principles and practices have evolved to guide developers to build software in a maintainable and flexible manner. You can measure the effectiveness of the code against the following tenets of enterprise development as you read about back in Chapter 1.

Rigidity

How rigid is the code in the above listing? In order for you to change any aspect of the low level concerns, such as how the `PayPalGateway` is constructed, you will need to modify the high-level class, in this case the `ReturnOrderService` class, this demonstrates that the class is inflexible and thus rigid to change.

Flexibility

Flexibility measures how susceptible your code is to change. If you look at the `ReturnOrderService` class, as it stands, it could break or give unexpected results, if there are any changes to the classes it depends on. For example, a change in the way the PayPal API works or a change in the way that the application settings are stored would cause the return process code to break. Put another way, a change to a dependent lower module will have an effect on the high-level module.

Separation of Concerns

Are the concerns of the `ReturnOrderService` separated? You can see that they are not because the `ReturnOrderService` should be concerned only with coordinating the workflow of processing a return order and not be bogged down with the low-level details such as formatting and sending emails.

Reusability

Could you use parts of the code in the process method in other classes? Wouldn't it be great if you could reuse the email logic? Or perhaps leverage the code that deals with stock adjustments in another part of your application? Reusability measures how mobile your code is and to what degree it can be reused elsewhere in your software.

Maintainabilty

How easy is it to understand what is going on in the `ReturnOrderService` class. Perhaps it's helped by the many lines of comments scattered throughout the listing? Methods should be short and precise; they should be named in a manner that immediately describes what role they perform. Other developers should be able to understand a methods purpose and logic after a quick look and without having to spend time dissecting the code. It is clear that the current implementation of the `ReturnOrderService` class is very unreadable and requires more than a few minutes to fully understand the process of returning an order, which after modification and added features will only become worse. With the tightly coupled dependencies the lack of clear code will prove very hard for yourself and others to maintain the code base as features are added.

In the procedural style of programming used within the `ReturnOrderService`, the high-level module, `ReturnOrderService`, is dependent upon the low-level modules. When they change, it has to change. This is what is making the code fragile and likely to cause problems in the future. You can also see that, by no means, does the `ReturnOderService` class adhere to the Single Responsibility Principle. It simply has too many reasons to change, is concerned with too many low-level issues, and is responsible for a lot more than just the workflow of returning an order. It's not just the addition of a new payment merchant that has demonstrated the fragility of the class; any number of these features could have been implemented, causing problems:

❑ PayPalGateway wrappers implementation could alter which would require a change to the `ReturnOrderService` which is dependent upon it.

❑ The process of returning stock could require that all stock adjustments be logged into an aduit table.

❑ Changes to configuration settings that hold information on the payment gateway credentials would involve the service class being updated to reflect these changes.

You can see how changes to lower level details can result in the need to update the high level ReturnOrderService class. This is obviously a bad situation as the service class should really only change if the workflow relating to the processing of a return order changes.

Okay, okay, I can hear you saying, yeah, but what if those things never happen? Remember the YAGNI principle — you ain't gonna need it; the principle is about resisting the temptation to write code that is not necessary at the moment, but might be in the future. However the job and purpose of the `ReturnOrderService` is to coordinate the process of returning an order, but in its present form, it is getting involved in too much of the low-level details and becoming responsible for the payment merchant APIs and email classes. You can see that, as time goes on, more and more features will be added to the process method, design rot will set in, and it will become ever more difficult to maintain the class.

Another issue with the code block is one of testing. You read in the previous chapter that the goal of unit testing is to isolate each part of the program and verify that each individual part is behaving as expected. A unit test provides a strict, written contract that the module of code under test must satisfy.

How would you test the logic of the `ReturnOrderService` class in isolation? Testing the class in isolation is made all the more difficult because the `ReturnOrderService` is instantiating its dependencies within its own constructor. This makes it impossible to pass in a fake or mock object as an alternate to the real dependency. Therefore, the only real tests you can perform are integration testing, which is certainly not ideal. You will learn a lot more about unit testing and mocking dependencies in the next chapter.

As stated before the `ReturnOrderService` should only be concerned with the coordination and workflow of the process of returning an order and not get bogged down in the implementation details of how monies get refunded and how customers are notified when the process is complete. Furthermore it should be easy from another developer's point of view to scan the process method and be able to understand the workflow relating to the process of returning an order. To achieve this you need to separate the concerns of the lower level modules from the high level ones and modularize the code. And that's exactly what you are going to look at doing in the next section.

Separation of Concerns and Identifying Modularity

Now that you have identified what's wrong with the code, it's time to refactor it and address those issues raised in the previous section. To start off, you need to separate each of the concerns that are taking place in the `ReturnOrderService` class. You read about separation of concerns in Chapter 2 but let's recap exactly what the principle is all about.

The Separation of Concerns (SoC) Principle is the process of dissecting a piece of software and splitting it down into discrete features that encapsulate distinct behavior and data that can be used by other classes. Generally, a concern represents a feature or behavior of a class. You can achieve SoC by modularizing your code and encapsulating distinct and specific data and behavior. Modules are self-contained units of code, which, if designed correctly, can improve your code and the way you manage it. Benefits of writing modular code units include:

- ❏ It is easier to manage small self-contained classes.

- ❏ It's easier to allow teams of developers to work together when a problem is separated into small modules.

- ❏ Code reuse significantly increases when concerns are split into modules with distinct responsibility.

- ❏ It is easier to identify where bugs are occurring when issues arise in your code, if you use small modules rather than monolithic methods with hundreds of lines.

- ❏ It's easier to test small class modules in isolation.

Very closely associated with the SoC is another principle that you read about in Chapter 2, namely the Single Responsibility Principle (SRP). SRP states that every object should have a single responsibility and only have one reason to change. If you take a look at the `ReturnOrderService`, it is clear that it is taking a fair bit of responsibility that should really be dealt with by a separate module. The `ReturnOrderService` is currently concerned with and responsible for determining which payment gateway to use to refund a payment to a customer and taking responsibility on how the stock is updated. The real and only responsibility of the `ReturnOrderService` class should be to coordinate the process and workflow of returning orders, and it should not get bogged down in the details of each of the lower-level modules. It is clear that the `ReturnOrderService` class is breaking the Single Responsibility Principle, as it has a host of reasons to change. By focusing your efforts to ensure that the `ReturnOrderService` adheres to the SRP, you will make the class more robust and easier to maintain, and to achieve this you will refactor the code.

Refactoring is the process of modifying how a piece of code works without changing its external behavior or existing functionality. You typically refactor code to improve the readability or architecture, increase performance/extensibility, and/or simplify maintenance.

The refactoring that will take place in this class will include:

- ❏ **Extract Method:** You will use this to move code that can be logically grouped together into a method. The name of the method should fully explain its purpose.

- ❏ **Extract Class:** This technique can be employed when you have one class performing a role that would be better handled by two. A new class can be created, and the logic from the old class can be moved into the new class, which should be named suitably.

- ❏ **Extract SuperClass:** This is used to provide a base class that can be inherited from when you have two or more classes with similar features.

Visual Studio provides you with some handy tools when it comes to refactoring. If you right-click on a code page and select Refactor, you will open up the Refactor context menu, as can be seen in Figure 3-2.

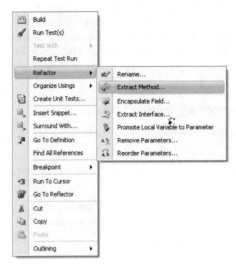

Figure 3-2

The first piece of code you can take a look at is the logic for entering the stock back into the inventory. This is an ideal candidate to be modularized, as you can encapsulate the process of adjusting stock and keep this concern separate from the return order workflow.

Highlight the code within the `ReturnOrderService` process method that deals with updating stock (highlighted below), right click and select Refactor ⇨ Extract Method. The dialog box as shown in Figure 3-3 will be shown; name the new method `ReturnStockFor` and click OK.

```
public void Process(ReturnOrder ReturnOrder)
    {
        // 1) Update the stock.
        foreach (ReturnItem Item in ReturnOrder.ItemsToReturn)
    {
            // a) Find the product.
            Product product = _productRepository.FindBy(Item.Product.Id);
            // b) Increase the stock.
            product.Stock += Item.Qty;
            // c) Save the product.
            _productRepository.Save(product);
    }
```

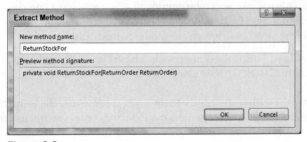

Figure 3-3

```
public class ReturnOrderService
    {
        ...


        public void Process(ReturnOrder ReturnOrder)
        {
            ReturnStockFor(ReturnOrder);

            // 2) Refund the payment back to the customer.
            if (_paymentGatewayType == "PayPal")
               _paypalGateway.Refund(ReturnOrder.RefundTotal(),
                               ReturnOrder.PaymentTransactionId);
            else
               _worldPayGateway.Refund(ReturnOrder.RefundTotal(),
                                 ReturnOrder.PaymentTransactionId);


            // 3) Mark the return order as processed.
            ReturnOrder.MarkAsProcessed();

            // 4) Save the updated return order.
            _returnOrderRepository.Save(ReturnOrder);

            // 5) Notify the customer on the processing of the return.
            String Recipient = ReturnOrder.Customer.EmailAddress;
            String From = "Returns@MyCompany.com";
            String Subject = "Your return order has been processed.";
            StringBuilder Message = new StringBuilder();

            Message.AppendLine(
               String.Format("Hello {0}", ReturnOrder.Customer.Name));
            Message.AppendLine
               ("You return order has been processed and you have been refunded.");

            Message.AppendLine("Items returned: ");
            foreach (ReturnItem ItemReturning in ReturnOrder.ItemsToReturn)
            {
                Message.AppendLine(String.Format("{0} of {1}",
                              ItemReturning.Qty, ItemReturning.Product.Name));
            }

            Message.AppendLine("Regards");
            Message.AppendLine("Returns Department");

            MailMessage msgMail = new MailMessage(From, Recipient, Subject,
                                          Message.ToString());

            SmtpClient smtp = new SmtpClient(_smtpHost);
            smtp.Send(msgMail);
        }
```

```
        private void ReturnStockFor(ReturnOrder ReturnOrder)
        {
            // 1) Update the stock.
            foreach (ReturnItem Item in ReturnOrder.ItemsToReturn)
            {
                // a) Find the product.
                Product product = _productRepository.FindBy(Item.Product.Id);
                // b) Increase the stock.
                product.Stock += Item.Qty;
                // c) Save the product.
                _productRepository.Save(product);
            }
        }
    }
```

Unfortunately, the `ReturnOrderService` still has the responsibility of knowing all about how to adjust returned stock; you have simply moved the logic into a separate method. What you really need to do is move it into its own code module. To do this you can perform an extract class refactoring. It makes sense to call this new class `ProductService`, as this class will provide a service on the product inventory to adjust stock.

Create a new class within the Services folder named `ProductService`, with the following code listing.

```
using ProEnt.Chap3.Returns.Repositories;
using ProEnt.Chap3.Returns.Model;

namespace ProEnt.Chap3.Returns.Services
{
    public class ProductService
    {
        private ProductRepository _productRepository;

        public ProductService()
        {
            _productRepository = new ProductRepository();
        }
    }
}
```

Now move the newly created `ReturnStockFor` method from the `ReturnOrderService` class into the `ProductService` class and change the accesor of the method from private to public. The `ProductService` class will now look like the following.

```
using ProEnt.Chap3.Returns.Repositories;
using ProEnt.Chap3.Returns.Model;

namespace ProEnt.Chap3.Returns.Services
{
    public class ProductService
```

```
{
    private ProductRepository _productRepository;

    public ProductService()
    {
        _productRepository = new ProductRepository();
    }

    public void ReturnStockFor(ReturnOrder ReturnOrder)
    {
        // 1) Update the stock.
        foreach (ReturnItem Item in ReturnOrder.ItemsToReturn)
        {
            // a) Find the product.
            Product product = _productRepository.FindBy(Item.Product.Id);
            // b) Increase the stock.
            product.Stock += Item.Qty;
            // c) Save the product.
            _productRepository.Save(product);
        }
    }
}
}
```

You can now go back to the ReturnOrderService and remove all references to the
ProductRepository class and the ReturnStockFor method and instead replace it with a call to the
new ProductService class as can be seen in the updated code below.

```
public class ReturnOrderService
{
    private ProductService _productService;

    ...

    public ReturnOrderService()
    {
        _productService = new ProductService();
        ...
    }

    public void Process(ReturnOrder ReturnOrder)
    {
        _productService.ReturnStockFor(ReturnOrder);

        ...
    }
}
```

Did you notice how fluent the method name and parameter arguments were when you performed the refactors; you can almost read them as a sentence:

"Return the stock for the given return order."

```
_productService.ReturnStockFor(ReturnOrder))
```

It's a great idea to ensure that your method and parameter names give a real insight into what the method is really all about. A reader can then get a good understanding of your code without having to dig down into the lower levels.

The next piece of code to tackle is the email logic. First; you can extract the section of code that creates the body of the message into a new method, called `BuildReturnMessageFrom`, in the same manner as you did for the last extract method refactor by highlighting the code shown below, right clicking and selecting Refactor ⇨ Extract Method.

```
public class ReturnOrderService
    {
        ...

        public void Process(ReturnOrder ReturnOrder)
        {
            _...

            // 5) Notify the customer on the processing of the return.
            String Recipient = ReturnOrder.Customer.EmailAddress;
            String From = "Returns@MyCompany.com";
            String Subject = "Your return order has been processed.";
            StringBuilder Message = new StringBuilder();

            Message.AppendLine(
                String.Format("Hello {0}", ReturnOrder.Customer.Name));
            Message.AppendLine
                ("You return order has been processed and you have been refunded.");

            Message.AppendLine("Items returned: ");
            foreach (ReturnItem ItemReturning in ReturnOrder.ItemsToReturn)
            {
                Message.AppendLine(String.Format("{0} of {1}",
                            ItemReturning.Qty, ItemReturning.Product.Name));
            }

            Message.AppendLine("Regards");
            Message.AppendLine("Returns Department");

            MailMessage msgMail = new MailMessage(From, Recipient, Subject,
                                            Message.ToString());

            SmtpClient smtp = new SmtpClient(_smtpHost);
            smtp.Send(msgMail);
        }
    }
```

Next extract the method that sends the email into a new method, entitled
SendReturnOrderNotificationFor, again by highlighting the code shown below,
right clicking and selecting Refactor ⇨ Extract Method.

```
public class ReturnOrderService
{
    ...

    public void Process(ReturnOrder ReturnOrder)
    {
        ...

        // 5) Notify the customer on the processing of the return.
        String Recipient = ReturnOrder.Customer.EmailAddress;
        String From = "Returns@MyCompany.com";
        String Subject = "Your return order has been processed.";
        StringBuilder Message = BuildReturnMessageFrom(ReturnOrder);

        MailMessage msgMail = new MailMessage(From, Recipient, Subject,
                                              Message.ToString());

        SmtpClient smtp = new SmtpClient(_smtpHost);
        smtp.Send(msgMail);
    }

    private static StringBuilder BuildReturnMessageFrom
                                        (ReturnOrder ReturnOrder)
    {
        StringBuilder Message = new StringBuilder();

        Message.AppendLine(
            String.Format("Hello {0}", ReturnOrder.Customer.Name));
        Message.AppendLine
            ("Your return order has been processed and you have been refunded.");

        Message.AppendLine("Items returned: ");
        foreach (ReturnItem ItemReturning in ReturnOrder.ItemsToReturn)
        {
            Message.AppendLine(String.Format("{0} of {1}",
                    ItemReturning.Qty, ItemReturning.Product.Name));
        }

        Message.AppendLine("Regards");
        Message.AppendLine("Returns Department");
        return Message;
    }
}
```

After these refactorings your `ReturnOrderService` class will look like this:

```
public class ReturnOrderService
{
    ...

    public void Process(ReturnOrder ReturnOrder)
    {
        _productService.ReturnStockFor(ReturnOrder);

        // 2) Refund the payment back to the customer.
        if (_paymentGatewayType == "PayPal")
           _paypalGateway.Refund(ReturnOrder.RefundTotal(),
                            ReturnOrder.PaymentTransactionId);
        else
           _worldPayGateway.Refund(ReturnOrder.RefundTotal(),
                                ReturnOrder.PaymentTransactionId);


        // 3) Mark the return order as processed.
        ReturnOrder.MarkAsProcessed();

        // 4) Save the updated return order.
        _returnOrderRepository.Save(ReturnOrder);

        SendReturnOrderNotificationFor(ReturnOrder);
    }

    private void SendReturnOrderNotificationFor(ReturnOrder ReturnOrder)
    {
        // 5) Notify the customer on the processing of the return.
        String Recipient = ReturnOrder.Customer.EmailAddress;
        String From = "Returns@MyCompany.com";
        String Subject = "Your return order has been processed.";
        StringBuilder Message = BuildReturnMessageFrom(ReturnOrder);

        MailMessage msgMail = new MailMessage(From, Recipient, Subject,
                                        Message.ToString());

        SmtpClient smtp = new SmtpClient(_smtpHost);
        smtp.Send(msgMail);
    }

    private static StringBuilder BuildReturnMessageFrom
                                        (ReturnOrder ReturnOrder)
    {
        StringBuilder Message = new StringBuilder();

        Message.AppendLine(
          String.Format("Hello {0}", ReturnOrder.Customer.Name));
        Message.AppendLine
          ("Your return order has been processed and you have been refunded.");

        Message.AppendLine("Items returned: ");
        foreach (ReturnItem ItemReturning in ReturnOrder.ItemsToReturn)
```

```
        {
            Message.AppendLine(String.Format("{0} of {1}",
                    ItemReturning.Qty, ItemReturning.Product.Name));
        }

        Message.AppendLine("Regards");
        Message.AppendLine("Returns Department");
        return Message;
    }
}
```

Again, by giving the new methods intention-revealing names, you are making it easier for yourself in the future to quickly understand the purpose and role of the method call when you need to revisit the code for updates and maintenance.

Now that the two email methods have been extracted, you can create a new class to separate the act of notification from the workflow of returning an order.

Create a new service class within the Services folder named EmailNotificationService and move the two email methods from the ReturnOrderService class into it, so that the class is the same as the definition below.

```
using System;
using System.Net.Mail;
using System.Text;
using ProEnt.Chap3.Returns.Model;

namespace ProEnt.Chap3.Returns.Services
{
    public class EmailNotificationService
    {
        // This settings would be stored in the AppSettings of the config file.
        private string _smtpHost = string.Empty;

        public void SendReturnOrderNotificationFor(ReturnOrder ReturnOrder)
        {
            // 5) Notify the customer on the processing of the return.
            String Recipient = ReturnOrder.Customer.EmailAddress;
            String From = "Returns@MyCompany.com";
            String Subject = "Your return order has been processed.";
            StringBuilder Message = BuildReturnMessageFrom(ReturnOrder);

            MailMessage msgMail = new MailMessage(From, Recipient, Subject,
                                        Message.ToString());

            SmtpClient smtp = new SmtpClient(_smtpHost);
            smtp.Send(msgMail);
        }

        private StringBuilder BuildReturnMessageFrom(ReturnOrder ReturnOrder)
```

```
        {
            StringBuilder Message = new StringBuilder();

            Message.AppendLine(
              String.Format("Hello {0}", ReturnOrder.Customer.Name));
            Message.AppendLine
              ("Your return order has been processed and you have been refunded.");

            Message.AppendLine("Items returned: ");
            foreach (ReturnItem ItemReturning in ReturnOrder.ItemsToReturn)
            {
                Message.AppendLine(String.Format("{0} of {1}",
                        ItemReturning.Qty, ItemReturning.Product.Name));
            }

            Message.AppendLine("Regards");
            Message.AppendLine("Returns Department");
            return Message;
        }
    }
}
```

You can now update the `ReturnOrderService` class by removing the email methods and making a reference to the new `EmailNotificationService` class. The `ReturnOrderService` class will now resemble the following code listing.

```
using ProEnt.Chap3.Returns.Repositories;
using ProEnt.Chap3.Returns.Model;

namespace ProEnt.Chap3.Returns.Services
{
    public class ReturnOrderService
    {
        private EmailNotificationService _notificationService;
        private ProductService _productService;
        private ReturnOrderRepository _returnOrderRepository;
        private PayPalGateway _paypalGateway;
        private WorldPayGateway _worldPayGateway;
        // These settings would be stored in the AppSettings of the config file.
        private string _paypalUserName = string.Empty ;
        private string _paypalPassword =  string.Empty;
        private string _worldpayUserName = string.Empty;
        private string _worldpayPassword = string.Empty;
        private string _worldpayMerchantId = string.Empty;
        private string _paymentGatewayType = string.Empty;

        public ReturnOrderService()
        {
            _notificationService = new EmailNotificationService();
            _productService = new ProductService();
```

```
        _returnOrderRepository = new ReturnOrderRepository();
        if (_paymentGatewayType == "PayPal")
            _paypalGateway = new PayPalGateway(_paypalUserName,
                                               _paypalPassword);
        else
        {
            _worldPayGateway = new WorldPayGateway(_worldpayMerchantId,
                                                   _worldpayUserName,
                                                   _worldpayPassword);
        }
    }

    public void Process(ReturnOrder ReturnOrder)
    {
        _productService.ReturnStockFor(ReturnOrder);

        // 2) Refund the payment back to the customer.
        if (_paymentGatewayType == "PayPal")
            _paypalGateway.Refund(ReturnOrder.RefundTotal(),
                            ReturnOrder.PaymentTransactionId);
        else
            _worldPayGateway.Refund(ReturnOrder.RefundTotal(),
                                ReturnOrder.PaymentTransactionId);


        // 3) Mark the return order as processed.
        ReturnOrder.MarkAsProcessed();

        // 4) Save the updated return order.
        _returnOrderRepository.Save(ReturnOrder);

        _notificationService.SendReturnOrderNotificationFor(ReturnOrder);
    }


    }
    }
```

For your last refactor you need to extract the logic that handles the payment methods. You could simply perform the Extract Method refactoring, as you did for the email and stock adjusting code, but you can do better than that. If you look at the refund method for both of the payment gateways you can see that they are identical; and both require the `TransactionId` and the `Amount` to process a refund. You can extract a superclass for both of the payment gateways to inherit from; this will give you a consistent API to program against and enable the method call to be oblivious to which payment merchant it is using.

The first step is to construct an abstract base class that the PayPal and WorldPay Gateway classes can inherit from, which contains a common refund method that can be used by the `ReturnOrderService` class. Unfortunately there isn't a wizard within the refactor menu to perform this particular refactor so we will just have to do it by hand.

Add a new class to the Services folder named `PaymentGateway` with the following definition:

```
using System;

namespace ProEnt.Chap3.Returns.Services
{
    public abstract class PaymentGateway
    {
        public abstract Boolean Refund(decimal amount, string transactionId);
    }
}
```

With the base class in place all you need to do is simply amend the `PayPalGateway` and `WorldPayGateway` class so that they inherit from it, as can be seen in the code below.

```
public class PayPalGateway : PaymentGateway
{
    public PayPalGateway(string userName, string password)
    {
        // Here you would find code to login to the
        // PayPal payment merchant.
    }

    public override Boolean Refund(decimal amount, string transactionId)
    {
        // Here you would find code to create a refund
        // transaction and send it to PayPal.
        return true;
    }
}

public class WorldPayGateway : PaymentGateway
{
    public WorldPayGateway(string MerchantAccount,
                           string userName,
                           string password)
    {
        // Here you would find code to login to the
        // WorldPay payment merchant.
    }

    public override Boolean Refund(decimal amount, string transactionId)
    {
        // Here you would find code to create a refund
        // transaction and send it to the WorldPay payment merchant.
        return true;
    }
}
```

The `ReturnOrderService` can now use the new `PaymentGateway` abstract base class in the `Process` method to perform the refund and leave the problem of determining which payment service implementation to use in the constructor method, as can be seen in the following amended `ReturnOrderService` class.

```csharp
public class ReturnOrderService
{
    private EmailNotificationService _notificationService;
    private ProductService _productService;
    private ReturnOrderRepository _returnOrderRepository;
    private PaymentGateway _paymentGateway;
    // These settings would be stored in the AppSettings of the config file.
    private string _paypalUserName = string.Empty ;
    private string _paypalPassword =  string.Empty;
    private string _worldpayUserName = string.Empty;
    private string _worldpayPassword = string.Empty;
    private string _worldpayMerchantId = string.Empty;
    private string _paymentGatewayType = string.Empty;

    public ReturnOrderService()
    {
        _notificationService = new EmailNotificationService();
        _productService = new ProductService();
        _returnOrderRepository = new ReturnOrderRepository();
        if (_paymentGatewayType == "PayPal")
            _paymentGateway = new PayPalGateway(_paypalUserName,
                                               _paypalPassword);
        else
        {
            _paymentGateway = new WorldPayGateway(
                                              worldpayMerchantId,
                                              _worldpayUserName,
                                              _worldpayPassword);
        }
    }

    public void Process(ReturnOrder ReturnOrder)
    {
        _productService.ReturnStockFor(ReturnOrder);

        // 2) Refund the payment back to the customer.
        _paymentGateway.Refund(ReturnOrder.RefundTotal(),
                          ReturnOrder.PaymentTransactionId);

        // 3) Mark the return order as processed.
        ReturnOrder.MarkAsProcessed();

        // 4) Save the updated return order.
        _returnOrderRepository.Save(ReturnOrder);

        _notificationService.SendReturnOrderNotificationFor(ReturnOrder);
    }
}
```

You may have noticed that the logic to construct the PayPal or WorldPay gateway is still present in the constructor of the `ReturnOrderService` class, and the class is still responsible for knowing how to create the correct payment gateway. In fact, the `ReturnOrderService` is still responsible for the construction of *all* of its dependencies so you still have a long way to go to separate your high-level and low-level modules. A little patience please—this exercise is all about emancipating your classes. The next section will deal with the responsibility for getting the dependencies into your `ReturnOrderService` class without it having to worry about them.

As a side note, you may have also noticed that a lot of the comments in the `Process` method have now been removed. This is simply because the method names are now so descriptive that there is no longer a need for them. You can now go back and remove the remaining comments from the process method. After doing this the process method will now look like the code snippet below:

```
public void Process(ReturnOrder ReturnOrder)
{
    _productService.ReturnStockFor(ReturnOrder);

    _paymentGateway.Refund(ReturnOrder.RefundTotal(),
                            ReturnOrder.PaymentTransactionId);

    ReturnOrder.MarkAsProcessed();

    _returnOrderRepository.Save(ReturnOrder);

    _notificationService.SendReturnOrderNotificationFor(ReturnOrder);
}
```

The `Process` method is now entirely clutter-free of comments and lower-level details, and crystal clear on the role that it performs and what its responsibilities are. It is now very easy to see with just a glance the entire workflow relating to the processing of a return order.

Code Comments

Don't rely on comments in your code to help the reader understand the role of your method or class. Remember that the reader could be you looking back at some code you wrote months earlier. Your method names should be written with a clear indication of what they do. Nobody likes to update documentation, and code comments are the same, so it is better to have a fluent method name and be able to read from left to right than to rely on comments that will surely never be updated.

In this section, you looked at how to identify the parts of the code that you could separate and then refactored them using well-known techniques. The upshot of this was that it made the code more maintainable and testable. You also looked at isolating your code so that you had a separation of concerns: one class, one job, and one reason to change it. In the next section, you will look at how to decouple the dependencies entirely from your `ReturnOrderService` class so that it does not require the knowledge to create lower-level details itself.

The Dependency Inversion Principle

In the last section, you modularized the code, applied the Single Responsibility Principle and the Separation of Concerns Principle to the `ReturnOrderService` class example. But, as was pointed out, nothing was done with regard to the concrete dependencies that the `ReturnOrderService` class still held on the lower-level modules. You still have the dependencies that you had before refactoring and the problem of the high-level module, the `ReturnOrderService`, being dependent on the lower-level modules of the `EmailNotificationService`, `PaymentGateway`, `ProductService`, and the `ReturnOrderRepository`. You need a way to remove the concrete dependencies so that changes to the lower-level modules will not have an affect on the `ReturnOrderService` class.

As you have already learnt the `ReturnOrderService` should only deal with the real business logic and workflow and not be responsible for the construction of lower-level details. At the moment the lower-level modules are still imposing themselves on the `ReturnOrderService` and causing it to change whenever they do, hardly an ideal scenario. This situation should be reversed, which some have termed the "Hollywood Principle": "Don't call us, we'll call you." This is all about having the lower-level modules referenced as abstractions rather than concrete implementations.

The Dependency Inversion Principle (DIP) is all about isolating your classes from the concrete implementations and having them depend on abstract classes or interfaces. You can see in the `ReturnOrderService` that the high-level `Process` method is dependent on the lower-level modules for refunding payment, notifying customers via email, and adjusting the stock, and if you wanted to change one of these services or add a new payment gateway you would need to alter the `ReturnOrderService` class. Applying the DIP can help to resolve such an issue.

Robert C. Martin defines the DIP like this:

1. High-level modules should not depend on low-level modules. Both should depend on abstractions.

2. Abstractions should not depend upon details. Details should depend upon abstractions.

When you buy into the two principles of DIP and apply it in your code, you will find that your modules become less fragile and rigid. By using it, you will find that changes to a lower-level module will no longer have an unwanted impact on the high-level modules that you saw in the preceding code listing.

The first step in applying the DIP is to extract the interfaces for each of the low-level dependencies. You can start by extracting the interface for the `ProductService`. Open the `ProductService` class and right-click to display the context sensitive menu and select Refactor ⇨ Extract Interface as can be seen in Figure 3-4. From the popup dialog box as shown in Figure 3-5 click Select All and click OK.

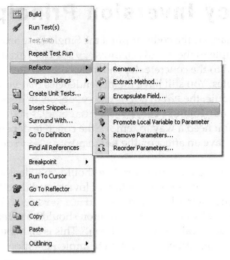

Figure 3-4

Figure 3-5

Visual Studio will build the Interface and automatically have the ProductService class implement it as can been in the code listing below.

```
using ProEnt.Chap3.Returns.Model;

namespace ProEnt.Chap3.Returns.Services
{
    interface IProductService
    {
        void ReturnStockFor(ReturnOrder ReturnOrder);
    }
}

public class ProductService : IProductService
{
        ...
}
```

Now that you have an interface for the `ProductService` you can use this in your
`ReturnOrderService` class.

```
public class ReturnOrderService
    {
        private EmailNotificationService _notificationService;
        private IProductService _productService;
        private ReturnOrderRepository _returnOrderRepository;
        private PaymentGateway _paymentGateway;
        // These settings would be stored in the AppSettings of the config file.
        private string _paypalUserName = string.Empty ;
        private string _paypalPassword =  string.Empty;
        private string _worldpayUserName = string.Empty;
        private string _worldpayPassword = string.Empty;
        private string _worldpayMerchantId = string.Empty;
        private string _paymentGatewayType = string.Empty;

        ...
    }
```

Perform the same Extract Interface refactor on the following classes and replace the concrete variable
declaration to a declaration using the interface.

❑   EmailNotificationService

    Name the Interface INotificationService.

❑   ReturnOrderRepository

    Name the Interface IReturnOrderRepository.

❑   ProductRepository

    Name the Interface IProductRepository.

❑   PaymentGateway

    Name the Interface IPaymentGateway.

After you have done this your `ReturnOrderService` class will now look like the following.

```
public class ReturnOrderService
    {
        private INotificationService _notificationService;
        private IProductService _productService;
        private IReturnOrderRepository _returnOrderRepository;
        private IPaymentGateway _paymentGateway;
        // These settings would be stored in the AppSettings of the config file.
        private string _paypalUserName = string.Empty ;
        private string _paypalPassword =  string.Empty;
        private string _worldpayUserName = string.Empty;
        private string _worldpayPassword = string.Empty;
        private string _worldpayMerchantId = string.Empty;
        private string _paymentGatewayType = string.Empty;

        ...
    }
```

Now that you have the interfaces in place you have inverted all the dependences that the `ReturnOrderService` held on each of the lower level details. The service now depends on abstractions in the form of interfaces rather than direct concrete implementations; Figure 3-6 shows this concept.

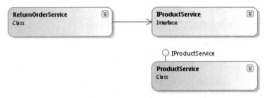

Figure 3-6

You have done a great job of inverting the dependencies and thus have made the `ReturnOrderService` less susceptible to changes in the lower-level modules. However one problem still remains, even though the `ReturnOrderService` class is now only dependent on abstractions its still tightly coupled to a specific implementaion of each interface and in the case of the payment gateways it still needs to know how to create specific implementations. You will learn how to resolve this issues in the next section.

Turning Classes Inside Out Using Dependency Injection

The `ReturnOrderService` class is still tied to a single implementation of each interface and is still responsible for creating those dependencies; for example, if you want to use a different type of `INotificationService` you will have to modify the `ReturnOrderService` class and maybe pick up some more configuration settings. This is obviously not a great place to be, however fear not as there is a pattern called Dependency Injection that can help you out. The Dependency Injection (DI) pattern refers to the act of supplying an external dependency to high-level module. It is a type of Inversion of Control whereby the process of obtaining a lower-level module is the concern being inverted. Inversion of Control, which is often used interchangeably with Dependency Injection, is a high-level abstract principle that deals with inverting the flow or process of system in contrast to the procedural style of workflow; you will learn more about this in Chapter 5.

There are three flavors in which you can perform Dependency Injection to obtain a reference to an external module.

- ❑ **Constructor injection:** which you applied in the last refactoring session, is the process of supplying dependencies through the class constructor.

- ❑ **Setter injection:** is the process of injecting dependent modules via a setter property on the dependent module.

- ❑ **Method injection:** requires the dependency to implement an interface that the high-level module will reference and inject at runtime.

Let's apply the Constructor Injection flavor of DI to the `ReturnOrderService` so that an instance of the `INotificationService` is injected into the service class rather than being created in the constructor. Amend the `ReturnOrderService` class as shown in the code listing below.

```
public class ReturnOrderService
{
    private INotificationService _notificationService;
    private IProductService _productService;
    private IReturnOrderRepository _returnOrderRepository;
    private IPaymentGateway _paymentGateway;
    // These settings would be stored in the AppSettings of the config file.
    private string _paypalUserName = string.Empty ;
    private string _paypalPassword =  string.Empty;
    private string _worldpayUserName = string.Empty;
    private string _worldpayPassword = string.Empty;
    private string _worldpayMerchantId = string.Empty;
    private string _paymentGatewayType = string.Empty;

    public ReturnOrderService(INotificationService notificationService)
    {
        _notificationService = notificationService;
        _productService = new ProductService();
        _returnOrderRepository = new ReturnOrderRepository();
        if (_paymentGatewayType == "PayPal")
            _paymentGateway = new PayPalGateway(_paypalUserName,
                                               _paypalPassword);
        else
        {
            _paymentGateway = new WorldPayGateway
                (_worldpayMerchantId,
                 _worldpayUserName,
                 _worldpayPassword);
        }
    }

    public void Process(ReturnOrder ReturnOrder)
    {
        _productService.ReturnStockFor(ReturnOrder);

        _paymentGateway.Refund(ReturnOrder.RefundTotal(),
                               ReturnOrder.PaymentTransactionId);

        ReturnOrder.MarkAsProcessed();

        _returnOrderRepository.Save(ReturnOrder);

        _notificationService.SendReturnOrderNotificationFor(ReturnOrder);
    }
}
```

As you can see the responsibility of creating a valid instance of the `NotificationService` has now been removed from the `ReturnOrderService` class, and more importantly the service class is not tied to just one implementation of `INotificationService`; any implementation of the

`INotificationService` can be used with the `ReturnOrderService`, such as a Fake implementation for use in testing or perhaps an SMS service to send a message to the customer's mobile phone, as can be seen in Figure 3-7.

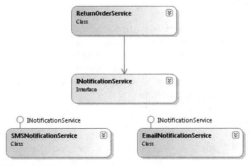

Figure 3-7

By placing the dependency on the `INotifcationService` as a parameter of the `ReturnOrderService`'s constructor, the client code using it will immediately be aware that it needs to supply a valid instance of an `INotificationService`, and without a valid instance the `ReturnOrderService` will not be able to instantiate.

Setter injection involves the use of properties on the high-level modules to inject the dependencies of the low-level modules. The benefits of this include allowing you to swap dependencies at will. It may not be as intention-revealing as the constructor approach, but it does offer more flexibility. For a rather convoluted example, you could add a property to `ReturnOrderService` to inject the `INotificationService` instance via a setter property as opposed to the constructor. If you didn't want to send a customer a notification of the returned order, you could opt to not inject it or perhaps use a stub implementation. The code listing below shows how this can be achieved.

```
public class ReturnOrderService
{
    private INotificationService _notificationService;
    private IProductService _productService;
    private IReturnOrderRepository _returnOrderRepository;
    private IPaymentGateway _paymentGateway;
    // These settings would be stored in the AppSettings of the config file.
    private string _paypalUserName = string.Empty ;
    private string _paypalPassword =  string.Empty;
    private string _worldpayUserName = string.Empty;
    private string _worldpayPassword = string.Empty;
    private string _worldpayMerchantId = string.Empty;
    private string _paymentGatewayType = string.Empty;

    public ReturnOrderService()
    {
        _productService = new ProductService();
        _returnOrderRepository = new ReturnOrderRepository();
        if (_paymentGatewayType == "PayPal")
            _paymentGateway = new PayPalGateway(_paypalUserName,
                                                _paypalPassword);
        else
```

```
        {
            _paymentGateway = new WorldPayGateway
                    (_worldpayMerchantId,
                    _worldpayUserName,
                    _worldpayPassword);
        }
    }

    public void Process(ReturnOrder ReturnOrder)
    {
        _productService.ReturnStockFor(ReturnOrder);

        _paymentGateway.Refund(ReturnOrder.RefundTotal(),
                            ReturnOrder.PaymentTransactionId);

        ReturnOrder.MarkAsProcessed();

        _returnOrderRepository.Save(ReturnOrder);

        if (_notificationService != null)
            _notificationService.SendReturnOrderNotificationFor(ReturnOrder);
    }

    public INotificationService NotificationService
    {
        get { return _notificationService ; }
        set { _notificationService = value ; }
    }
}
```

As noted the only drawback with the setter injection is that you need to make a check to ensure that the dependency has been set before using it. This is because the client using the ReturnOrderService doesn't have to set it as with the Constructor Injection method.

The setter injection method may not be as clear as a constructor injection, but if you have a mass of other dependencies being injected at constructor time, it may make sense to move the optional ones to a setter-based approach to make the classes' construction easier to understand.

A great use of the Method Injection is for when you need to have some logic that is not applicable to place in a property. Imagine you need to add logging support to the ReturnOrderService and all of the lower-level dependencies. You could add a single method to the ReturnOrderService class that would then update all of the dependencies with the logger. An example of this can be seen in the code snippet below.

```
public class ReturnOrderService
    {
        ...

        public ReturnOrderService(INotificationService notificationService
```

```
    {
        _...
    }

    public void Process(ReturnOrder ReturnOrder)
    {
        _...
    }

    public void SetLogger(ILogger logger)
    {
        _notificationService.SetLogger(logger);
        _paymentGateway.SetLogger(logger);
        _productService.SetLogger(logger)
        _returnOrderRepository.SetLogger(logger);
    }
}
```

The choice of when to opt for one implementation over another is completely up to you. Although many believe that the constructor injection is more intention-revealing, it may not be appropriate in every case, especially if you have many dependencies or optional ones.

As you want to ensure that all dependencies are injected into the ReturnOrderService class when it's created, you can opt for the Constructor Injection flavor of DI. Start with the ProductService class and amend its constructor as below.

```
public class ProductService : IProductService
{
    private IProductRepository _productRepository;

    public ProductService(IProductRepository productRepository)
    {
        _productRepository = productRepository;
    }

    public void ReturnStockFor(ReturnOrder ReturnOrder)
    {
        // 1) Update the stock.
        foreach (ReturnItem Item in ReturnOrder.ItemsToReturn)
        {
            // a) Find the product.
            Product product = _productRepository.FindBy(Item.Product.Id);
            // b) Increase the stock.
            product.Stock += Item.Qty;
            // c) Save the product.
            _productRepository.Save(product);
        }
    }
}
```

Next amend the Constructor of the `ReturnOrderService` class so that all dependencies are injected at construction time. Your code should match the listing below.

```
public class ReturnOrderService
    {
        private INotificationService _notificationService;
        private IProductService _productService;
        private IReturnOrderRepository _returnOrderRepository;
        private IPaymentGateway _paymentGateway;

        public ReturnOrderService(INotificationService notificationService,
                                  IProductService productService,
                                  IReturnOrderRepository returnOrderRepository,
                                  IPaymentGateway paymentGateway )
        {
            _notificationService = notificationService;
            _productService = productService;
            _returnOrderRepository = returnOrderRepository;
            _paymentGateway = paymentGateway;
        }

        public void Process(ReturnOrder ReturnOrder)
        {
            _productService.ReturnStockFor(ReturnOrder);

            _paymentGateway.Refund(ReturnOrder.RefundTotal(),
                                   ReturnOrder.PaymentTransactionId);

            ReturnOrder.MarkAsProcessed();

            _returnOrderRepository.Save(ReturnOrder);

            _notificationService.SendReturnOrderNotificationFor(ReturnOrder);
        }
    }
```

As you can see all references to variables that hold configuration settings have been removed, the `ReturnOrderService` class no longer needs to know which payment gateway implementation to instantiate and it no longer needs to know how to instantiate it.

In this section, you came to grips with how you can get references to those pesky low-level dependencies into your high-level modules with the three forms of Dependency Injection. You also learned that Dependency Injection is an implementation of the high-level Dependency Inversion Principle and itself is a form of Inversion Control. These were all very high-level abstract principles. But with the code example you have been dealing with since the beginning of this chapter, you should have understood how these principles can be practical and how they can guide you to improve your code's flexibility and understanding.

The `ReturnOrderService` class is no longer fragile, as then only changes that will require modification will be changes to the workflow of returning an order. The class is also very easily unit tested, and each of the dependencies can be tested in isolation.

You can now compare the new code to the metrics evaluated against the original code remove a few pages back.

Rigidity

The dependencies the `ReturnOrderService` class are now very easy to change without fear of impacting on the `ReturnOrderService` class itself. Because the dependencies implement the contract of an interface their internal working can change as long as the contract is met. Now all of the dependencies can be substituted for alternatives, new payment gateways and notification services notification services can be used with no impact to the `ReturnOrderService` class.

Flexibility

There is now no danger of the `ReturnOrderService` class breaking due to changes in lower-level details; this is due to the `ReturnOrderService` depending on interfaces instead of concrete types.

Separation of Concerns

The concerns of each process involved in the returning of a return order are now in separate classes referenced by interfaces. The `ReturnOrderService` class is now only responsible for the coordination of the workflow and does not handle any low-level details; this is all delegated to the low-level modules.

Reusability

The `ReturnOrderService` can now be reused with any number of new implementations of the low-level modules without any changes to it.

Maintainability

As you read earlier it's now crystal clear as to the responsibilities of the `ReturnOrderService` class. You were able to remove all the '"helpful" comments, as well as naming the services and method calls in an intention-revealing manner, enabling other developers, and yourself, to quickly scan the body of the high-level process method and be able to understand from a high level what is happening. This level of opacity in conjunction with the separation of concerns will make maintenance easy for yourself and other developers to come.

Figure 3-8 shows the complete set of classes you have created to refactor and loosely couple the original code.

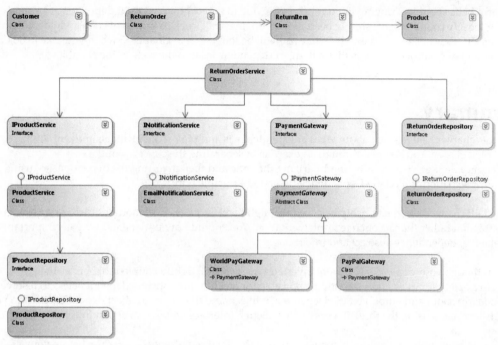

Figure 3-8

Don't be put off by that fact that you have created lots of extra classes to get the job done. It's better to have lots of small concise classes that do one job than a monolithic class trying to do everything — remember the Single Responsibility Principle: every object should have a single responsibility and one reason to change.

Before we wrap up this chapter let's see how you might use the `ReturnOrderService` class from the client point of view. Examine the code snippet below.

```
ReturnOrderService returnOrderService;
INotificationService notificationService =
                    new EmailNotificationService();
IProductRepository productRepository = new ProductRepository();
IProductService productService = new ProductService(productRepository);
IPaymentGateway paymentGateway =
                    new PayPalGateway("USERNAME", "PASSWORD");
IReturnOrderRepository returnOrderRepository =
                    new ReturnOrderRepository();

returnOrderService = new ReturnOrderService(
                        notificationService,
                        productService,
                        returnOrderRepository,
                        paymentGateway);
```

Alarm bells should be ringing in your head now due to the fact that the tight dependencies you spent so long loosely coupling have simply been moved up, they call stack to the client code and you are no better off. Fear not as this is exactly what you will be looking at in Chapter 5 when you take a look at Inversion of Control containers that will inject dependencies into the code at the client level.

Summary

In this chapter, you learned about what a dependency is and the problems that come with tightly coupled classes. You stepped through an exercise of separating the concerns of the ReturnOrderService class by modularizing the code and then inverting the dependencies, using an enterprise pattern called the Dependency Inversion Principle (DIP).

The DIP changed the relationship between the high-level and low-level modules by basing it on an abstraction rather than a concrete implementation. You should now understand why it's important to make that dependency abstract and invert it.

Even though your dependencies were inverted you were still tightly coupled to them as the ReturnOrderService class was still responsible for creating the concrete dependencies. To resolve this you learnt about and employed the Dependency Injection (DI) pattern to inject dependencies into your high-level class using the three flavors of DI — Setter, Interface and Construction Injection.

You saw how, in the procedurally focused style of the ReturnOrderService class before your refactorings, the high-level module controlled the creating of the lower-level modules. When you applied the Dependency Injection (DI) and extracted the interfaces, the control was inverted. Following this design will enable you to build enterprise applications involving complex logic and processes in a more testable and maintainable manner.

To recap, you should now be familiar with and understand these principles:

- ❑ Separation of Concerns (SoC)
- ❑ Single Responsibility Principle (SRP)
- ❑ Dependency Inversion Principle (DIP)
- ❑ Dependency Injection (DI) and the three forms of it
- ❑ The benefits of programming to interfaces and not implementations

One thing that this chapter should have prepared you for is change. If you are writing good software, people are going to use it, and if people are using it, you can bet they will want tweaks and features added. If you can easily add features, modify processes, and extend your applications, you will be in a great position to offer real value to your business. By putting in just a small amount of extra effort and adhering to these very simple principles — DIP, DI, SRP, and SoC — you will make your code maintainable and extensible.

The next chapter will show you how, by applying the Dependency Injection Pattern, you can increase the testability of your classes. You will learn about substituting fakes for real implementations and leverage mocking frameworks to dynamically build pretend implementations with known results to ensure that you are testing the smallest piece of functionality in isolation. The chapter will also introduce you to the methodology of Test Driven Design and how it relates to unit testing as well as covering a few of the major unit-testing frameworks available to the .NET developer.

4

Test Driven Development

Wouldn't it be great if you had full confidence in the code you had written, you knew it worked, and you had only written the bare minimum of code to the meet the requirements? Test Driven Development (TDD) is all about addressing the needs of software development — writing something that works, something that meets a set of requirements, and something that is easy to maintain.

Despite the name, it may surprise you to learn that Test Driven Development is as much about the design of your software as it is about ensuring that your code is behaving and functioning in the way it was required to. The concept behind Test Driven Development is a simple one: write a test before you write any production code, watch the test fail, write just enough code to get the test to pass, then clean the code up and repeat. This has come to be known as the Red, Green, Refactor mantra (see Figure 4-1).

When you start with Test Driven Development, you write a test that fails; the test will fail because you haven't written the functionality in the production code. Most unit testing frameworks will display a red marker next to the test, indicating a failure, and this is where the "Red" comes from. After you have a failing test, you write the minimum amount of code to get it to pass and rerun the test. In most of the testing frameworks, a green marker will be displayed, indicating that the test is now satisfied; this is where the "Green" comes from. Last, you clean up the code, or refactor it if you can. Refactoring enables you to clean up, remove duplication from, and simplify your code for maintenance purposes, and because you have the tests as a safety net, you can refactor and get immediate feedback to ensure that you have only altered the internal and not external behavior of your modules.

Test Driven Development forces you to work in very short cycles and only on the requirements specifically needed for your program. You write short tests and the minimum amount of code in order for them to pass, refactor, and repeat. The idea of working in small steps is key and will enable you to define small, concise, loosely coupled code modules. You know when you're done when all the tests pass, and you have a full suite of tests that verify your software does what it's supposed to do.

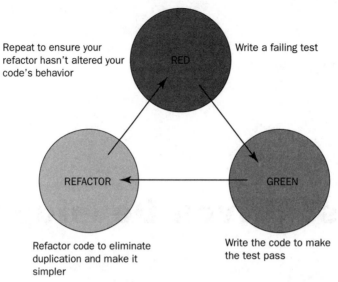

Repeat to ensure your
refactor hasn't altered your
code's behavior

RED

Write a failing test

REFACTOR

GREEN

Refactor code to eliminate
duplication and make it
simpler

Write the code to make
the test pass

Figure 4-1

By now you are either thinking that Test Driven Development is a brilliant idea or you're scratching your head still trying to figure out just how writing tests for nonexistent code is ever going to help drive the design of your software and increase the speed at which it's delivered. You could read more on the benefits that Test Driven Development can bring you, but your time may be served better by running through a small example of Test Driven Development. This practice should help you get a good understanding of the process before you read about the other benefits it can offer you.

Tic Tac Toe and Test Driven Development: An Example

You are going to write a program which will allow you to play the game of Tic Tac Toe, also known as Noughts and Crosses. Through this simple example, you will learn exactly what Test Driven Development is and how it can drive your application design. Before you start writing the program, it may be a good idea to remind yourself of the rules of the game, especially if you have never played or heard of it.

Tic Tac Toe is a simple game played by two people; the first player is represented by an X and the second by an O. The goal of Tic Tac Toe is to be the first player to get three in a row on a 3 × 3 grid. Player X always goes first, then players take turns in placing Xs and Os on the board until either one player has three in a row, horizontally, vertically, or diagonally or all nine squares are filled. The first player with three Xs or three Os in a row wins. If all nine squares are filled and neither player has three in a row, the game is a draw.

Before practicing Test-Driven Development, it's always a good idea to start with a list of requirements or user stories for the application you are about to build.

Tic Tac Toe Requirements

❏ A game should be played on a grid of 3 × 3 squares.

❏ The game is played by two players, one with an X marker and one with an O marker.

❏ Each player takes turns placing a marker onto an empty square.

❏ A game is won when either player gets three of their markers in a line. A line can be across any row, down any column, or diagonal from left to right, or right to left.

❏ A game is a draw when all the squares are filled and there is no winner.

The problem with a list of requirements, from a TDD point of view, is that they don't make for good unit tests. Unit tests need to be far more specific than the generic-sounding requirements; each test needs to express the expected behavior and outcome for a specific example with known inputs. Here is a list of tests based on the preceding requirements. This initial set of tests will grow as you start to build your program, as you will undoubtedly think of more tests as you progress and you can add them to this list.

Initial Tests

❏ Player X is the first player to place a marker.

❏ A player cannot place a marker on a full square.

❏ After Player X places an X marker the square is unavailable.

❏ Player O will be next to take a turn after Player X has placed a marker.

❏ A player cannot place a marker in a zone that does not exist.

❏ An exception will be thrown if a player attempts to place a marker in an occupied square.

❏ If Player X gets three Xs in a row, then the game is won by Player X.

❏ If Player X gets three Xs in a column, then the game is won by Player X.

❏ If Player X Gets three Xs in a diagonal line the game is won by Player X.

❏ When all squares are full and there is no winner, the game is a draw.

Before you write your first test, you need to set up your project. In this exercise, you will use the NUnit testing framework.

1. Start by downloading the latest version of the NUnit framework from `http://www.nunit.org`. NUnit 2.4.8 is the current production release at the time of writing.

2. Once you have downloaded the framework, run the msi installer. After NUnit has been installed, you will find a new folder in your program files.

Now that you have the NUnit framework installed, you can begin.

1. Open Visual Studio and create a new blank solution called ProEnt.Chap4, as shown in Figure 4-2 in the location C:\Projects.

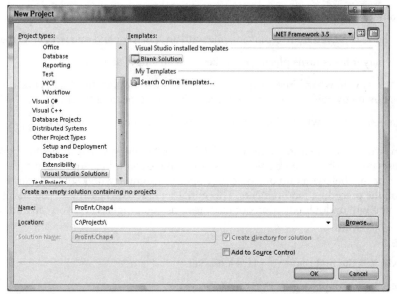

Figure 4-2

2. Add a Class Library project to the solution by following these steps:

    1. From the File menu, select Add ➪ New Project.

    2. Select a C# Class Library.

    3. Name the Class Library ProEnt.Chap4.TicTacToe.Model.

3. Add a second Class Library project to the solution in the same manner, but this time name it ProEnt.Chap4.TicTacToe.ModelTests.

4. After you have created all of the projects, navigate to the folder structure by right clicking on the solution name and selecting Open Folder In Windows Explorer. Add a new folder called lib, and copy the NUnit.Framework.dll from the NUnit directory on your machine (by default this can be found at %systemdrive%\%programfiles directory%\NUnity 2.4.8\bin) into the newly created lib folder.

5. Now add a new solution folder to the solution, called Lib. To do this, right-click on the solution root, then select Add ➪ Add New Solution Folder.

6. Add the NUnit.Framework.dll to your solution by right-clicking on the lib solution folder and selecting Add ➪ Add Existing Item, then navigating to the NUnit.Framework.dll in the lib folder at the root of your application.

Add a reference to the NUnit.Framework.dll from the ProEnt.Chap4.TicTacToe.ModelTests project by right-clicking on the ProEnt.Chap4.TicTacToe.ModelTests project name and selecting Add Reference. From the dialog window that appears select the Browse tab and navigate to the Lib folder and select the NUnit.Framework.dll, and click Add Reference.

7. Lastly add a reference to the `ProEnt.Chap4.TicTacToe.Model` project by right clicking on the `ProEnt.Chap4.TicTacToe.ModelTests` name and selecting Add Reference. This time select the Project tab from the dialog window that appears and select the `ProEnt.Chap4.TicTacToe.Model` project.

Your solution should now resemble Figure 4-3.

Figure 4-3

Before you get started on the Tic Tac Toe game, it's worth getting up to speed on how to use NUnit.

Create a class within the `ProEnt.Chap4.TicTacToe.ModelTests` project, named `SimpleTest`, and add the following code definition:

```
using System;
using NUnit.Framework;

    namespace ProEnt.Chap4.TicTacToe.ModelTests
    {
        [TestFixture()]
        public class SimpleTest
        {
            [Test()]
            public void My_First_NUnit_Test()
            {
                int expectedResult = 3;

                Assert.AreEqual(expectedResult, 1 + 1);
            }
        }
    }
```

The `[TestFixture]` attribute on the `SimpleTest` class tells NUnit that this class that will contain unit tests. The test methods themselves are always public methods that have no return value, expect no parameters and are decorated with the `[Test]` attribute.

The call to the static method `Assert` class has a collection of methods that are used to verify that the expected state is correct, in a number of different ways. The `AreEqual` method compares the expected result to the actual value.

Build the project and navigate to the NUnit folder in the program files via your start menu and click on the NUnit application. Click File ⇨ Open Project, navigate to your `ProEnt.Chap4.TicTacToe` `.ModelTests` project debug folder, and open the `ProEnt.Chap4.TicTacToe.ModelTests.dll` file. When the `ProEnt.Chap4.TicTacToe.ModelTests.dll` is loaded, you will see a test tree structure in the left panel (see Figure 4-4).

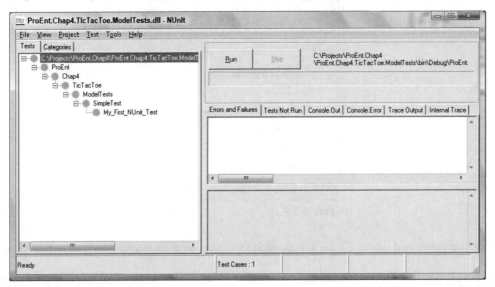

Figure 4-4

Click Run (see Figure 4-5).

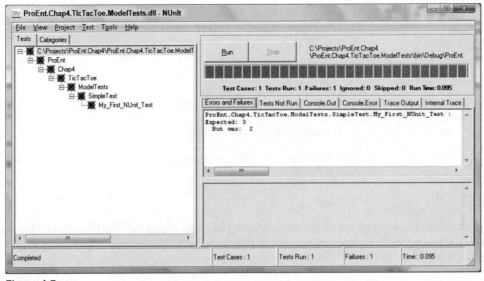

Figure 4-5

Your test will fail because you were expecting the result to be 3, but 2 was produced. Go back to **Visual Studio** and amend the code to:

```
using System;
using NUnit.Framework;

namespace ProEnt.Chap4.TicTacToe.ModelTests
{
    [TestFixture()]
    public class SimpleTest
    {
        [Test()]
        public void My_First_NUnit_Test()
        {
            int expectedResult = 3;

            Assert.AreEqual(expectedResult, 2 + 1);
        }
    }
}
```

Rebuild the project and rerun the test (see Figure 4-6).

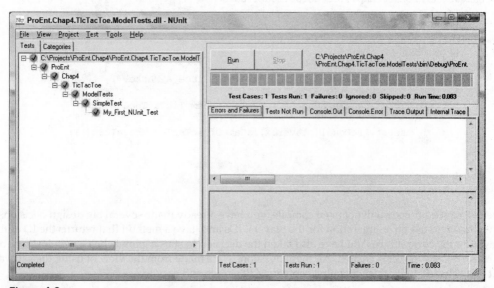

Figure 4-6

Your test will now pass and you will see a nice green glow, and that's all there is to it. Later in the chapter, you will learn about other testing frameworks that are available and programs that integrate with NUnit into Visual Studio itself.

Now that you have had a quick introduction on how to use the NUnit framework, you can start to create the Tic Tac Toe game using a Test Driven Development methodology. The first test on your list is "Player X is the first player to place a marker," so why not use this as the title for your test? It's a good idea to name your tests in a verbose manner so that it's very obvious what they are testing, especially as the number of your tests grows. A good pattern to follow when structuring the name of your tests is to first state what you are testing and then state what it should be doing, that is, "Player X is the first player to place a marker."

When you write a test, you have the ability from the outset to make the API for the program simple and fluent. Imagine that you are the user of the finished piece of software. How would you like to program against it? You are in a position to create the perfect interface for your software, so remember to keep things simple and logical when you're creating your tests, and this will help to drive your development toward a very usable piece of software. To begin your Test Driven Design experience start by creating a class that will hold all of your tests to verify the rules of the Tic Tac Toe game. Create a new class in the ProEnt.Chap4.TicTacToe.ModelTests project named TicTacToeGameTests. As discussed above create your first test entitled "Player_X_Is_The_First_To_Place_A_Marker," and copy the following code definition.

```
using System;
using NUnit.Framework;
using ProEnt.Chap4.TicTacToe.Model;

namespace ProEnt.Chap4.TicTacToe.ModelTests
{
    [TestFixture]
    public class TicTacToeGameTests
    {
        [Test]
        public void Player_X_Is_The_First_To_Place_A_Marker()
        {
            TicTacToeGame aGameOfTicTacToe = new TicTacToeGame();

            Assert.AreEqual(player.x, aGameOfTicTacToe.WhoseTurn());
        }

    }
}
```

Even though your code will not even compile, you have already made several big design decisions. You have chosen to use an enumeration for the players' IDs and have a method that returns the ID of the player for the current turn. You have also taken the decision to start a game when a new instance of the TicTacToeGame object is created. All these decisions were made from the view of using the software as if it were already built; this will help keep your API simple and easy to use.

Of course, the test you just typed in won't compile, so you will need to write the minimum amount of code to get it to compile and fail. It's vitally important to start with a failing test because you want to write the test before the code functionality is implemented. To get the test to compile, you can create the skeleton of the TicTacToeGame class as well as the player enumeration with a Player X defined. So create a new enumeration named Player and a new class named TicTacToeGame with the following code definitions.

```
namespace ProEnt.Chap4.TicTacToe.Model
{
    public class TicTacToeGame
    {
        public TicTacToeGame()
        {
        }

        public player WhoseTurn()
        {
            return player.o;
        }
    }
}

namespace ProEnt.Chap4.TicTacToe.Model
{
    public enum player
    {
        x = 1,
        o = 2
    }
}
```

Remember, you want the test to fail before you can start coding to make it pass, so even though every bone in your body is telling you to change the return value of WhoseTurn() method to Player.x, don't do it! Compile the project and run the test and you will receive a failing result (see failing test as shown in Figure 4-7). Great! This is what you want; you can now start to add the code to get the test to pass.

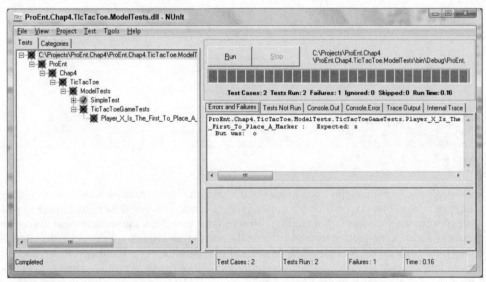

Figure 4-7

Update the `WhoseTurn()` method to return `player.x`. Rebuild the test project and re-run the test within the NUnit test program and you will see that it now passes, as shown in Figure 4-8.

```
namespace ProfessionalEnterprise.Chap4.Model
{
    public class TicTacToeGame
    {
        public TicTacToeGame()
        {
        }

        public player WhoseTurn()
        {
            return player.x;
        }
    }
}
```

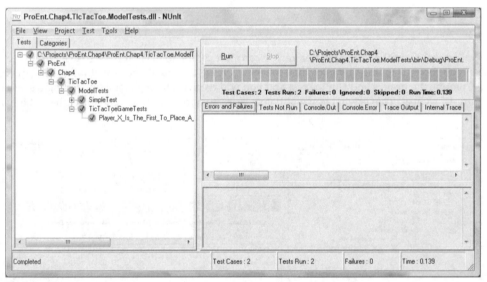

Figure 4-8

You are probably screaming at this book by this point, thinking that cannot be correct, as surely the result of `WhoseTurn()` won't be Player X for the duration of the game, and you'd be right. However you shouldn't concern yourself with what might happen or what you think the software will need to do it. You should be focusing on getting the code to pass the test in the simplest way possible and moving on to the next test. If you do think of new tests as you are programming, add them to your list and carry on. Don't try to implement a feature if the test does not require it — remember you are meant to be taking small steps. As you progress through this example, you will start to see some sense in what this simple example is demonstrating, so bare with it. As you have written the simplest piece of code, there isn't anything to refactor, so you can go on to the next test.

Taking a look at the list of tests you initially wrote, you can see that the next test is "A player cannot place a marker on a full square." Thinking about this, it may be a good idea to test if the first player can place their marker anywhere. So add the test "The first player can place their marker anywhere," and you can come back to the other test.

```
[Test]
public void The_First_Player_Can_Place_Marker_Anywhere()
{
        TicTacToeGame aGameOfTicTacToe = new TicTacToeGame();

        Assert.IsTrue(aGameOfTicTacToe.CanPlaceMarkerAt(0, 0));
        Assert.IsTrue(aGameOfTicTacToe.CanPlaceMarkerAt(0, 1));
        Assert.IsTrue(aGameOfTicTacToe.CanPlaceMarkerAt(0, 2));
        Assert.IsTrue(aGameOfTicTacToe.CanPlaceMarkerAt(1, 0));
        Assert.IsTrue(aGameOfTicTacToe.CanPlaceMarkerAt(1, 1));
        Assert.IsTrue(aGameOfTicTacToe.CanPlaceMarkerAt(1, 2));
        Assert.IsTrue(aGameOfTicTacToe.CanPlaceMarkerAt(2, 0));
        Assert.IsTrue(aGameOfTicTacToe.CanPlaceMarkerAt(2, 1));
        Assert.IsTrue(aGameOfTicTacToe.CanPlaceMarkerAt(2, 2));
}
```

Hmmm — is there anything smelly about the code you have written and the design decision you have made? You are assuming that the board from the game has a zero base index; is that a good idea? Also is the first integer the row or column? If you were using the code, you would only learn this by trial and error, so why not write what you mean? Okay, you can refactor the test to something very easy to understand and that cannot be misunderstood.

```
[Test]
public void The_First_Player_Can_Place_Marker_Anywhere()
{
        TicTacToeGame aGameOfTicTacToe = new TicTacToeGame();

        Assert.IsTrue(aGameOfTicTacToe.CanPlaceMarkerAt(Row.One,
                                                 Column.One));
        Assert.IsTrue(aGameOfTicTacToe.CanPlaceMarkerAt(Row.One,
                                                 Column.Two));
        Assert.IsTrue(aGameOfTicTacToe.CanPlaceMarkerAt(Row.One,
                                                 Column.Three));
        Assert.IsTrue(aGameOfTicTacToe.CanPlaceMarkerAt(Row.Two,
                                                 Column.One));
        Assert.IsTrue(aGameOfTicTacToe.CanPlaceMarkerAt(Row.Two,
                                                 Column.Two));
        Assert.IsTrue(aGameOfTicTacToe.CanPlaceMarkerAt(Row.Two,
                                                 Column.Three));
        Assert.IsTrue(aGameOfTicTacToe.CanPlaceMarkerAt(Row.Three,
                                                 Column.One));
        Assert.IsTrue(aGameOfTicTacToe.CanPlaceMarkerAt(Row.Three,
                                                 Column.Two));
        Assert.IsTrue(aGameOfTicTacToe.CanPlaceMarkerAt(Row.Three,
                                                 Column.Three));
}
```

That's more readable isn't it? It is a very simple refactor but one that clearly demonstrates which parameter is which and doesn't leave the user to guess if you are using a zero-based index or not.

Once again the test won't compile, so the first thing to do is sort that out: by first creating two new enumeration classes, one named `Column` and the other named `Row`; copy the following code listing into the new enumerations respectively.

```
namespace ProfessionalEnterprise.Chap4.Model
{
    public enum Column
    {
        One = 0,
        Two = 1,
        Three = 2
    }
}
namespace ProfessionalEnterprise.Chap4.Model
{
    public enum Row
    {
        One = 0,
        Two = 1,
        Three = 2
    }
}
```

With the two new enumerations in place, you can create the method to get the test to compile by updating the existing `TicTacToeGame` class with the following modified code.

```
namespace ProfessionalEnterprise.Chap4.Model
{
    public class TicTacToeGame
    {
        public TicTacToeGame()
        {
        }

        public player WhoseTurn()
        {
            return player.x;
        }

        public bool CanPlaceMarkerAt(Row row, Column column)
        {
            return false;
        }
    }
}
```

Again, remember that you are trying to get the test to compile and not to pass, so hard-coding a false return in the new `CanPlaceMarkerAt` method is exactly what you want to do, even though it's probably making your head spin. The test, after a quick rebuild of the model project, can now compile and when run will return a failing result; this is exactly what you wanted. Now you can write the simplest amount of code to get the test to pass.

The simplest way you can see to pass the test is surely to change the hard-coded false return value to a hard-coded true. Yes? Well why not do that then?

```
namespace ProfessionalEnterprise.Chap4.Model
{
    public class TicTacToeGame
    {
        public TicTacToeGame()
        {
        }

        public player WhoseTurn()
        {
            return player.x;
        }

        public bool CanPlaceMarkerAt(Row row, Column column)
        {
            return true;
        }
    }
}
```

Rerun the test, and this time it passes. By now, you are probably thinking that this is a waste of time and you can't see the benefit in TDD. But what this simple exercise is teaching you is that you must write extra tests to ensure that the behavior of the software is correct. Up to now, you have written the code to pass the first two tests. As you carry on, you will add more tests to ensure that the code you wrote to pass the initial tests is correct. This is known as testing triangulation. *Triangulation* is the process of creating a number of different tests to ensure that you are testing a function from a number of viewpoints. So in other words, you will write other tests that will confirm that the WhoseTurn and CanPlaceMarkerAt methods are doing what they are supposed to.

Now on to the next test, which is "After a player places a marker the square is unavailable."

```
[Test]
public void After_A_Player_Places_A_Marker_The_Square_Is_Unavailable()
{
        Row rowToPlace = Row.One;
        Column columnToPlace = Column.One;
        TicTacToeGame aGameOfTicTacToe = new TicTacToeGame();

        aGameOfTicTacToe.PlaceMarkerAt(rowToPlace, columnToPlace);

        Assert.IsFalse(aGameOfTicTacToe.CanPlaceMarkerAt(rowToPlace,
                                                    columnToPlace));

}
```

Because the PlaceMarkerAt method has not been written, as with the previous tests, you must first create it to get the test to compile:. Amend the TicTacToeGame class to include the new PlaceMarkerAt method referenced in the Test project, as shown in the following code listing, then rebuild the Model project.

```
namespace ProfessionalEnterprise.Chap4.Model
{
    public class TicTacToeGame
    {
        public TicTacToeGame()
        {
        }

        public player WhoseTurn()
        {
            return player.x;
        }

        public bool CanPlaceMarkerAt(Row row, Column column)
        {
            return false;
        }

        public void PlaceMarkerAt(Row row, Column column)
        {

        }
    }
}
```

You can probably guess that, when you compile and run the test, it fails. Now you can start to create the code to get the test to pass. As the test case uses two methods of the TicTacToeGame to verify the expected behavior, you will need to amend both of them as shown in the following listing. However as you already have another test that verifies the CanPlaceMarkerAt method in the context of a brand new game, you can't simply hard code a false as the return value for the method; you need a way to hold the state of each square on the board. To achieve this you can create a multidimensional array to represent the 3 × 3 grid. What you have done here is to triangulate your tests so that you're not relying only on one test to verify behavior; you will more read about this a little later.

But now, without further ado, amend the TicTacToeGame class so that it resembles the following code definition.

```
namespace ProfessionalEnterprise.Chap4.Model
{
    public class TicTacToeGame
    {
        private int[,] Board = new int[3, 3];

        public TicTacToeGame()
        {
        }

        public player WhoseTurn()
        {
            return player.x;
        }

        public bool CanPlaceMarkerAt(Row row, Column column)
```

```
        {
            return this.Board[(int)row, (int)column] == 0;
        }

        public void PlaceMarkerAt(Row row, Column column)
        {
            this.Board[(int)row, (int)column] = (int)WhoseTurn();
        }
    }
}
```

Even though you have only added three lines of code, compared to what you have been writing, that was a big step. The first thing you have done is create a multidimensional array with a 3 × 3 array of integers to hold the markers. You have then changed the CanPlaceMarkerAt method to check if the integer at the given position is equal to 0, that is, does that square have a marker? Last, you filled the integer at the given position in the PlaceMarkerAt method with the value of the WhoseTurn method. You can now compile and run all three tests to ensure that you haven't broken an earlier test with the code update. It's important to run all of the tests, as the changes and refactors could have an effect on an earlier test. You can run all of your tests, and they will pass, which is good — you get immediate feedback that your refactor hasn't broken the code logic.

Having had a look at the code, you can probably see that even though the CanPlaceMarkerAt method returns false when a square is occupied, there is nothing to stop a player placing a marker on it. You could just add the code to ensure that this doesn't happen, but it's better to write a test first and test for this behavior — remember, you only want to write code that makes a test pass.

So, why don't you write this test now? As there is a method to check if a player can place a marker at a given position, it seems logical that, if a user were to ignore this, the program should throw an exception. So add a test to the TicTacToeGameTests class that checks for this to see if an exception should be thrown as defined in the following listing.

```
[Test]
[ExpectedException(typeof(System.ApplicationException),
"Square Row:One, Column:One already occupied by x" )]
public void
    Exception_Will_Be_Thrown_If_Player_Tries_To_Place_Marker_In_A_Taken_Square()
{
        Row rowToPlace = Row.One;
        Column columnToPlace = Column.One;
        TicTacToeGame aGameOfTicTacToe = new TicTacToeGame();

        aGameOfTicTacToe.PlaceMarkerAt(rowToPlace, columnToPlace);
        aGameOfTicTacToe.PlaceMarkerAt(rowToPlace, columnToPlace);
}
```

This test is slightly different from the ones you have written previously, as it is decorated by a second attribute and contains no assert statement. The ExpectedException attribute just above the method definition tells NUnit to pass the test if an exception of the same type and with the same message is thrown.

When you run the test, it will of course fail. You can now add some code to check if the square that the player is trying to mark is in fact vacant, and if it's not, throw an appropriate exception. Amend the `PlaceMarkerAt` method with the following code.

```
namespace ProfessionalEnterprise.Chap4.Model
{
    public class TicTacToeGame
    {
        private int[,] Board = new int[3, 3];

        public TicTacToeGame()
        {
        }

        public player WhoseTurn()
        {
            return player.x;
        }

        public bool CanPlaceMarkerAt(Row row, Column column)
        {
            return this.Board[(int)row, (int)column] == 0;
        }

        public void PlaceMarkerAt(Row row, Column column)
        {
            if (CanPlaceMarkerAt(row, column))
            {
                this.Board[(int)row, (int)column] = (int)WhoseTurn();
            }
            else
            {
                throw new ApplicationException(
                string.Format("Square Row:{0}, Column:{1} already occupied by {2}",
                row.ToString(), column.ToString(),
                (player)Enum.ToObject(typeof(player),
                        this.Board[(int)row, (int)column])));
            }
        }
    }
}
```

Now if you were sticking to the rules of Test Driven Development to the letter, you would have written the simplest piece of code to get the test to pass, which would resulted in code that looks like this:

```
namespace ProfessionalEnterprise.Chap4.Model
{
    public class TicTacToeGame
    {
        ...
```

```
public void PlaceMarkerAt(Row row, Column column)
{
    if (CanPlaceMarkerAt(row, column))
    {
        this.Board[(int)row, (int)column] = (int)WhoseTurn();
    }
    else
    {
        throw new ApplicationException(
            "Square Row:One, Column:One already occupied by x")
    }
}
```

However, you know that the exception will need to dynamically inject the row and column numbers into the error message, so you can make a small compromise on the purist approach to Test Driven Development and take a more pragmatic point of view. Nonetheless you should still take small steps to ensure that you are not running before you can walk and you are not trying to do too much in one test. Remember, you are only trying to get the test to pass and not write the entire program; or put another way, know the ground rules first and know what you are doing; then you can cut a few corners to pick up the speed.

Hopefully, you can see the value in that small deviation from the rules of Test Driven Development. You didn't do the simplest thing to get the test to pass, but then again you didn't overcomplicate the design. You made a judgment call, knowing that the combination of row and column will change and that you would add that functionality instead of writing a test later that would prove that your original test didn't work. This is just a small compromise between the purist academic approach to Test Driven Development and the approach that uses a little common sense. As you gain more experience with Test Driven Development, you will become confident and identify what parts of your system don't require testing or where you can bend the rules a little. You will read more about that in the section that follows this exercise. Now that you understand what you just did, you can continue with creating the rest of the Tic Tac Toe game functionality.

If you look back at your list of tests, the next one is "Player O will be next to take a turn after Player X has placed a marker." This is the test that will expose the WhoseTurn method as a method that doesn't actually do what it is supposed to. This helps to triangulate the tests to ensure that you have tested what you think you are testing. Add a new test to your growing suite of tests within the TicTacToeGameTests as defined below.

```
[Test]
public void Player_O_Will_Be_Next_To_Take_A_Turn_After_Player_X_Has_Placed_A_
Marker()
{
        Row rowToPlace = Row.One;
        Column columnToPlace = Column.One;
        TicTacToeGame aGameOfTicTacToe = new TicTacToeGame();

        Assert.AreEqual(player.x, aGameOfTicTacToe.WhoseTurn());
        aGameOfTicTacToe.PlaceMarkerAt(rowToPlace, columnToPlace);
        Assert.AreEqual(player.o, aGameOfTicTacToe.WhoseTurn());
}
```

You can now run the test, and it will fail; this, if you remember, is because the return value of the WhoseTurn() method is hard-coded to always return player.x, which is exactly what you wanted at the time to pass the earlier tests. You can now refactor the code to ensure that the current player alternates after each marker is placed. To do this, simply add a variable to hold the current player and set it to Player X in the constructor, then change it after a marker is placed in a square. The code you need to amend to hold the current player correctly is highlighted in the code listing below.

```
namespace ProfessionalEnterprise.Chap4.Model
{
    public class TicTacToeGame
    {
        private int[,] Board = new int[3, 3];
        private player currentplayer;

        public TicTacToeGame()
        {
            currentplayer = player.x;
        }

        public player WhoseTurn()
        {
            return currentplayer;

        }

        public bool CanPlaceMarkerAt(Row row, Column column)
        {
            return this.Board[(int)row, (int)column] == 0;
        }

        public void PlaceMarkerAt(Row row, Column column)
        {
            if (CanPlaceMarkerAt(row, column))
            {
                this.Board[(int) row, (int) column] = (int) WhoseTurn();

                if (this.currentplayer == player.x)
                {
                    this.currentplayer = player.o;
                }
                else
                {
                    this.currentplayer = player.x;
                }
            }
            else
            {

                throw new ApplicationException(
                    string.Format(
                    "Square Row:{0}, Column:{1} already occupied by {2}",
                    row.ToString(), column.ToString(),
```

```
                    (player)Enum.ToObject(typeof(player),
                        this.Board[(int)row, (int)column])));
                }
            }
        }
    }
```

You can now run all of the tests, and they will all pass. The `PlaceMarkerAt` method is starting to get a little too big. You can perform an extract method refactoring to separate the changing of the current player from the placing of the marker, to make the code easier to read. Select the code that checks and changes the current player, right-click, and select refactor ⇨ Extract Method. In the pop-up window, enter the method name called `ChangeCurrentPlayer`.

```
namespace ProfessionalEnterprise.Chap4.Model
{
    public class TicTacToeGame
    {
        ...

        public void PlaceMarkerAt(Row row, Column column)
        {
            if (CanPlaceMarkerAt(row, column))
            {
                this.Board[(int) row, (int) column] = (int) WhoseTurn();

                ChangeCurrentPlayer();
            }
            else
            {
                throw new ApplicationException(
                    string.Format(
                    "Square Row:{0}, Column:{1} already occupied by {2}",
                    row.ToString(), column.ToString(),
                    (player)Enum.ToObject(typeof(player),
                        this.Board[(int)row, (int)column])));
            }
        }

        private void ChangeCurrentPlayer()
        {
            if (this.currentplayer == player.x)
            {
                this.currentplayer = player.o;
            }
            else
            {
                this.currentplayer = player.x;
            }
        }
    }
}
```

You can now rerun all of the tests to ensure that nothing has broken with this refactor. On to the next test, which if you check your list, is "A player cannot place a marker in a zone that does not exist." When you write the code that follows to test for this behavior, you will notice that it will not compile.

```
[Test]
public void A_Player_Cannot_Place_A_Marker_In_A_Zone_That_Does_Not_Exist()
{
        TicTacToeGame aGameOfTicTacToe = new TicTacToeGame();
        Assert.IsFalse(aGameOfTicTacToe.CanPlaceMarkerAt(33 , 11));
}
```

The reason why the code does not compile is due to the fact that you decided to use an enumeration for the row and column values, something that you couldn't have known about when you were creating your initial list of tests. Due to your design decision you have verified that users can only input valid values for the row and column positions, so you can dispense with this test by commenting it out and moving onto the next on your list.

```
//[Test]
//public void A_Player_Cannot_Place_A_Marker_In_A_Zone_That_Does_Not_Exist()
//{
//        TicTacToeGame aGameOfTicTacToe = new TicTacToeGame();
//        Assert.IsFalse(aGameOfTicTacToe.CanPlaceMarkerAt(33 , 11));
//}
```

The next test on your list determines if there is a winner or not: "If Player X gets three Xs in a row then the game is won by Player X."

```
[Test]
public void If_Player_X_Gets_Three_Xs_In_A_Row_Then_The_Game_Is_Won_By_Player_X()
{
        Row PlayerX_RowMove123 = Row.One;
        Column PlayerX_ColumnMove1 = Column.One;
        Column PlayerX_ColumnMove2 = Column.Two;
        Column PlayerX_ColumnMove3 = Column.Three;

        Row PlayerO_RowMove12 = Row.Two;
        Column PlayerO_ColumnMove1 = Column.One;
        Column PlayerO_ColumnMove2 = Column.Two;

        TicTacToeGame aGameOfTicTacToe = new TicTacToeGame();

        // Player X Move 1
        // X| |
        //  | |
        //  | |
        aGameOfTicTacToe.PlaceMarkerAt(PlayerX_RowMove123,
                                 PlayerX_ColumnMove1);
        // Player O Move 1
        // X| |
        // O| |
        //  | |
        aGameOfTicTacToe.PlaceMarkerAt(PlayerO_RowMove12,
                                 PlayerO_ColumnMove1);
```

```
// Player X Move 2
// X|X|
// O| |
//  | |
aGameOfTicTacToe.PlaceMarkerAt(PlayerX_RowMove123,
                              PlayerX_ColumnMove2);
// Player O Move 2
// X|X|
// O|O|
//  | |
aGameOfTicTacToe.PlaceMarkerAt(PlayerO_RowMove12,
                              PlayerO_ColumnMove2);

// Player X Move 3
// X|X|X
// O|O|
//  | |
aGameOfTicTacToe.PlaceMarkerAt(PlayerX_RowMove123,
                              PlayerX_ColumnMove3);

Assert.AreEqual(GameStatus.PlayerXWins, aGameOfTicTacToe.Status());
}
```

To get the test to even compile, you will need to add an enumeration class for the status as well as a method to return the current status of a game. The game of Tic Tac Toe can only ever be in one of five states:

1. Game won by Player X

2. Game won by Player O

3. Game is a draw

4. Waiting for Player X to place marker

5. Waiting for Player O to place marker

Create a new enumeration class in the Model project named GameStatus with the enumerations defined below.

```
namespace ProfessionalEnterprise.Chap4.Model
{
    public enum GameStatus
    {
        PlayerXWins = 1,
        PlayerOWins = 2,
        GameDrawn = 3,
        AwaitingPlayerXToPlaceMarker = 4,
        AwaitingPlayerOToPlaceMarker = 5
    }
}
```

You can now create a method to return the current state of the game and to allow the test to compile as shown below.

```
namespace ProfessionalEnterprise.Chap4.Model
{
    public class TicTacToeGame
    {
        ...

        public GameStatus Status()
        {
            return GameStatus.GameDrawn;
        }
    }
}
```

Okay, now you have a compiling test that fails. Again, if you were to continue to strictly follow the Test Driven Development rules, you would write the simplest piece of code to get the test to pass, namely by amending the Status method as shown in the following listing.

```
namespace ProfessionalEnterprise.Chap4.Model
{
    public class TicTacToeGame
    {
        ...

        public GameStatus Status()
        {
            return GameStatus.PlayerXWin;
        }
    }
}
```

However, you may find it better to keep to the spirit of Test Driven Development by implementing the rules but not adhering to them as if they were a law. So, perhaps a better use of your time is to write the code that checks each row to see if the game has a winner.

```
namespace ProfessionalEnterprise.Chap4.Model
{
    public class TicTacToeGame
    {
        ...

        public GameStatus Status()
        {
            GameStatus GameStatus = Model.GameStatus.GameDrawn;

            for (int Row = 0; Row <= 2; Row++)
            {
                if ((this.Board[Row, (int)Column.One] == (int)player.x &&
                    this.Board[Row, (int)Column.Two] == (int)player.x &&
                    this.Board[Row, (int)Column.Three] == (int)player.x))
                {
                    GameStatus = GameStatus.PlayerXWins;
                }
```

```
                 if ((this.Board[Row, (int)Column.One] == (int)player.o &&
                      this.Board[Row, (int)Column.Two] == (int)player.o &&
                      this.Board[Row, (int)Column.Three] == (int)player.o))
                 {
                     GameStatus = GameStatus.PlayerOWins;
                 }
            }

            return GameStatus;
        }
    }
}
```

That passes the test, but it's pretty ugly and you know that there are going to be other results that need to be checked for, so it's a good candidate for refactoring. You can use the Extract Method refactor to clean up the Status method.

```
namespace ProfessionalEnterprise.Chap4.Model
{
    public class TicTacToeGame
    {
        ...

        public GameStatus Status()
        {
            GameStatus GameStatus = Model.GameStatus.GameDrawn;

            if (isAWinner(player.o))
            {
                GameStatus = Model.GameStatus.PlayerOWins;
            }
            else if (isAWinner(player.x))
            {
                GameStatus = Model.GameStatus.PlayerXWins;
            }

            return GameStatus;
        }

        private bool isAWinner(player Player)
        {
            bool winner = false;

            for (int Row = 0; Row <= 2; Row++)
            {
                if ((this.Board[Row, (int)Column.One] == (int)Player &&
                     this.Board[Row, (int)Column.Two] == (int)Player &&
                     this.Board[Row, (int)Column.Three] == (int)Player))
                {
                    winner = true;
```

```
                }
            }

            return winner;
        }
    }
}
```

You can run all the tests to ensure that it passes. One test that springs to mind when writing the code for that last test is that the game status should be awaiting either Player X or Player O if the game is not won or drawn. Currently, the status will return with Game Drawn if there is no winner.

To verify this expected behavior you write the test before rushing off to try and implement the code. Create a method that will verify this status with the following definition.

```
[Test]
public void
The_Game_Status_Should_Be_Awaiting_Either_Player_X_Or_O_If_The_Game_Is_Not_Won_
Or_Drawn()
{
        Row PlayerXrowToPlace = Row.One;
        Column PlayerXcolumnToPlace = Column.One;

        TicTacToeGame aGameOfTicTacToe = new TicTacToeGame();

        Assert.AreEqual(GameStatus.AwaitingPlayerXToPlaceMarker,
                    aGameOfTicTacToe.Status());

        aGameOfTicTacToe.PlaceMarkerAt(PlayerXrowToPlace, PlayerXcolumnToPlace);

        Assert.AreEqual(GameStatus.AwaitingPlayerOToPlaceMarker,
                    aGameOfTicTacToe.Status());
}
```

To get this test to pass, it's a simple case of adding code to check if either player has won; if not then find out whose turn it is; this can be seen in the following amendment to the Status method.

```
namespace ProfessionalEnterprise.Chap4.Model
{
    public class TicTacToeGame
    {
        ...

        public GameStatus Status()
        {
            GameStatus GameStatus = Model.GameStatus.GameDrawn;

            if (IsAWinner(player.o))
                GameStatus = Model.GameStatus.PlayerOWins;
            else if (IsAWinner(player.x))
                GameStatus = Model.GameStatus.PlayerXWins;
```

```
            else if (WhoseTurn() == player.x)
                GameStatus = Model.GameStatus.AwaitingPlayerXToPlaceMarker;
            else
                GameStatus = Model.GameStatus.AwaitingPlayerOToPlaceMarker;

            return GameStatus;
        }


        ...

    }

}
```

Rebuild the Model and Test projects and run the suite of tests to verify that the status is correct during a game and while there is no winner or that the game is drawn before moving on.

The next test on your list is "If Player X gets three Xs in a column then the game is won by Player X." This test is similar to the last one, but this time you are checking for a winning line on a row. The code for this test is defined below.

```
[Test]
public void
If_Player_X_Gets_Three_Xs_In_A_Column_Then_The_Game_Is_Won_By_Player_X()
{
        Row PlayerX_RowMove1 = Row.One;
        Row PlayerX_RowMove2 = Row.Two;
        Row PlayerX_RowMove3 = Row.Three;
        Column PlayerX_ColumnMove123 = Column.One;

        Row PlayerO_RowMove12 = Row.One;
        Column PlayerO_ColumnMove1 = Column.Two;
        Column PlayerO_ColumnMove2 = Column.Three;

        TicTacToeGame aGameOfTicTacToe = new TicTacToeGame();

        // Player X Move 1
        // X| |
        //  | |
        //  | |
        aGameOfTicTacToe.PlaceMarkerAt(PlayerX_RowMove1,
                                PlayerX_ColumnMove123);
        // Player O Move 1
        // X|O|
        //  | |
        //  | |
        aGameOfTicTacToe.PlaceMarkerAt(PlayerO_RowMove12,
                                PlayerO_ColumnMove1);

        // Player X Move 2
        // X|O|
        // X| |
        //  | |
        aGameOfTicTacToe.PlaceMarkerAt(PlayerX_RowMove2,
                                PlayerX_ColumnMove123);
```

```
                    // Player O Move 2
                    // X|O|O
                    // X| |
                    // | |
                    aGameOfTicTacToe.PlaceMarkerAt(PlayerO_RowMove12,
                                            PlayerO_ColumnMove2);

                    // Player X Move 3
                    // X|O|O
                    // X| |
                    // X| |
                    aGameOfTicTacToe.PlaceMarkerAt(PlayerX_RowMove3,
                                            PlayerX_ColumnMove123);

                    Assert.AreEqual(GameStatus.PlayerXWins, aGameOfTicTacToe.Status());
        }
```

When you run the test, it fails. This happens because you have only implemented the code to check for a winning line on the horizontal rows. You need to write the code that will check for combinations of three Xs in a row. Amend the `IsAWinner` method within the `TicTacToeGame` class to include a check for a winning row of Xs or Os.

```
namespace ProfessionalEnterprise.Chap4.Model
{
    public class TicTacToeGame
    {
        ...

        private bool IsAWinner(player Player)
        {
            bool winner = false;

            for (int Row = 0; Row <= 2; Row++)
            {
                if ((this.Board[Row, (int)Column.One] == (int)Player &&
                    this.Board[Row, (int)Column.Two] == (int)Player &&
                    this.Board[Row, (int)Column.Three] == (int)Player))
                {
                    winner = true;
                }
            }

            for (int Column = 0; Column <= 2; Column++)
            {
                if ((this.Board[(int)Row.One, Column] == (int)Player &&
                    this.Board[(int)Row.Two, Column] == (int)Player &&
                    this.Board[(int)Row.Three, Column] == (int)Player))
                {
                    winner = true;
                }
            }
```

```
                    return winner;
            }
        }
    }
```

You can now rerun all of the tests, after rebuilding the Model and then the Test project, and they will all pass. The IsAWinner method is starting to get big. It may be a good idea to refactor it. The next test is to check for a diagonal line of Xs, so why not get that test out of the way and then refactor the complete IsAWinner method?

```
[Test]
public void
If_Player_X_Gets_Three_Xs_In_A_Diagonal_Line_The_Game_Is_Won_By_Player_X()
{
            Row PlayerX_RowMove1 = Row.One;
            Row PlayerX_RowMove2 = Row.Two;
            Row PlayerX_RowMove3 = Row.Three;
            Column PlayerX_ColumnMove1 = Column.One;
            Column PlayerX_ColumnMove2 = Column.Two;
            Column PlayerX_ColumnMove3 = Column.Three;

            Row PlayerO_RowMove12 = Row.One;
            Column PlayerO_ColumnMove1 = Column.Two;
            Column PlayerO_ColumnMove2 = Column.Three;

            TicTacToeGame aGameOfTicTacToe = new TicTacToeGame();

            // Player X Move 1
            // X| |
            // | |
            // | |
            aGameOfTicTacToe.PlaceMarkerAt(PlayerX_RowMove1, PlayerX_ColumnMove1);
            // Player O Move 1
            // X|O|
            // | |
            // | |
            aGameOfTicTacToe.PlaceMarkerAt(PlayerO_RowMove12, PlayerO_ColumnMove1);

            // Player X Move 2
            // X|O|
            // |X|
            // | |
            aGameOfTicTacToe.PlaceMarkerAt(PlayerX_RowMove2, PlayerX_ColumnMove2);
            // Player O Move 2
            // X|O|O
            // |X|
            // | |
            aGameOfTicTacToe.PlaceMarkerAt(PlayerO_RowMove12, PlayerO_ColumnMove2);

            // Player X Move 3
            // X|O|O
            // |X|
            // | |X
```

```
        aGameOfTicTacToe.PlaceMarkerAt(PlayerX_RowMove3, PlayerX_ColumnMove3);

        Assert.AreEqual(GameStatus.PlayerXWins, aGameOfTicTacToe.Status());
    }
```

It won't surprise you to learn that when you run the test it fails. You now need to add the code that will check for a winning line on either of the diagonals. This code will be added to the IsAWinner method. For the sake of space, we have not included a test to check for a winner from the top right to the bottom left, but you should be able to work it out for yourself, and, if not it is included in the code download. The same is true of checking for a win with Os.

```
namespace ProfessionalEnterprise.Chap4.Model
{
    public class TicTacToeGame
    {

        ...

        private bool IsAWinner(player Player)
        {
            bool winner = false;

            for (int Row = 0; Row <= 2; Row++)
            {
                if ((this.Board[Row, (int)Column.One] == (int)Player &&
                    this.Board[Row, (int)Column.Two] == (int)Player &&
                    this.Board[Row, (int)Column.Three] == (int)Player))
                {
                    winner = true;
                }
            }

            for (int Column = 0; Column <= 2; Column++)
            {
                if ((this.Board[(int)Row.One, Column] == (int)Player &&
                    this.Board[(int)Row.Two, Column] == (int)Player &&
                    this.Board[(int)Row.Three, Column] == (int)Player))
                {
                    winner = true;
                }
            }

            if ((this.Board[(int)Row.One, (int)Model.Column.One] == (int)Player &&
                this.Board[(int)Row.Two, (int)Model.Column.Two] == (int)Player &&
                this.Board[(int)Row.Three, (int)Model.Column.Three] == (int)Player
                ))
            {
                winner = true;
            }

            if ((
                this.Board[(int)Row.One, (int)Model.Column.Three] == (int)Player &&
                this.Board[(int)Row.Two, (int)Model.Column.Two] == (int)Player &&
                this.Board[(int)Row.Three, (int)Model.Column.One] == (int)Player))
```

```
            {
                winner = true;
            }

            return winner;
        }
    }
}
```

Now that you have satisfied all of the winning conditions, you can refactor the IsAWinner method. You can split the three methods of determining if you have a winner into methods themselves by using the Extract Method refactor. This, again, serves to make the code more readable and understandable.

```
namespace ProfessionalEnterprise.Chap4.Model
{
    public class TicTacToeGame
    {
        ...

        private bool IsAWinner(player Player)
        {
            bool winner = false;

            if (IsThreeInARowWinner(Player) |
                IsThreeInAColumnWinner(Player) |
                IsThreeInADiagonalWinner(Player) )
            {
                winner = true;
            }

            return winner;
        }

        private bool IsThreeInADiagonalWinner(player Player)
        {
            bool winner = false;
            if ((
                this.Board[(int)Row.One, (int)Model.Column.One] == (int)Player &&
                this.Board[(int)Row.Two, (int)Model.Column.Two] == (int)Player &&
                this.Board[(int)Row.Three, (int)Model.Column.Three] == (int)Player
              ))
            {
                winner = true;
            }

            if ((
                this.Board[(int)Row.One, (int)Model.Column.Three] == (int)Player &&
                this.Board[(int)Row.Two, (int)Model.Column.Two] == (int)Player &&
                this.Board[(int)Row.Three, (int)Model.Column.One] == (int)Player
              ))
```

```
            {
                winner = true;
            }
            return winner;
        }

        private bool IsThreeInAColumnWinner(player Player)
        {
            bool winner = false;
            for (int Column = 0; Column <= 2; Column++)
            {
                if ((this.Board[(int)Row.One, Column] == (int)Player &&
                     this.Board[(int)Row.Two, Column] == (int)Player &&
                     this.Board[(int)Row.Three, Column] == (int)Player))
                {
                    winner = true;
                }
            }
            return winner;
        }

        private bool IsThreeInARowWinner(player Player)
        {
            bool winner = false;
            for (int Row = 0; Row <= 2; Row++)
            {
                if ((this.Board[Row, (int)Column.One] == (int)Player &&
                     this.Board[Row, (int)Column.Two] == (int)Player &&
                     this.Board[Row, (int)Column.Three] == (int)Player))
                {
                    winner = true;
                }
            }
            return winner;
        }
    }
}
```

The final tests on your list and the final state of a game is "When all squares are full and there is no winner the game is a draw."

```
[Test]
public void When_All_Squares_Are_Full_And_There_Is_No_Winner_The_Game_Is_A_Draw()
{
        TicTacToeGame aGameOfTicTacToe = new TicTacToeGame();
        Row currentRow;

        for (int R = 0; R <= 2; R++)
        {
            currentRow = (Row)Enum.ToObject(typeof(Row), R);

            aGameOfTicTacToe.PlaceMarkerAt(currentRow, Column.One );
```

```
            aGameOfTicTacToe.PlaceMarkerAt(currentRow, Column.Three);
            aGameOfTicTacToe.PlaceMarkerAt(currentRow, Column.Two );
        }
        // Game Board After All Moves
        // X|X|O
        // O|O|X
        // X|X|O

        Assert.AreEqual(GameStatus.GameDrawn, aGameOfTicTacToe.Status());
    }
```

A game is a draw when all of the squares are covered and there is no winner. You can add code to check for all of the squares being covered after you have checked for a winner.

```
namespace ProfessionalEnterprise.Chap4.Model
{
    public class TicTacToeGame
    {
        ...

        public GameStatus Status()
        {
            GameStatus GameStatus = Model.GameStatus. Draw;

            if (isAWinner(player.o))
                GameStatus = Model.GameStatus.PlayerOWins;
            else if (isAWinner(player.x))
                GameStatus = Model.GameStatus.PlayerXWins;
            else if (GameIsDrawn())
                GameStatus = Model.GameStatus. Draw;
            else if (WhoseTurn() == player.x)
                GameStatus = Model.GameStatus.AwaitingPlayerXToPlaceMarker;
            else
                GameStatus = Model.GameStatus.AwaitingPlayerOToPlaceMarker;

            return GameStatus;
        }

        private bool GameIsADraw()
        {
            bool allSquaresUsed = true;

            for (int Row = 0; Row <= 2; Row++)
            {
                for (int Column = 0; Column <= 2; Column++)
                {
                    if (this.Board[Row, Column] == 0)
                    {
                        allSquaresUsed = false;
                    }
                }
            }
```

```
          return allSquaresUsed;
      }


  ...

  }
}
```

One test that you didn't have down on your initial list is one that addresses what happens after a game is won. It makes sense to not allow the game to continue, so you must test for this edge case. Add a test entitled "A player can make no more moves after a game is won." It's not just production code that you can t refactor. Because you need to have a game in a won state, you can reuse the code from an earlier test by using the Extract Method refactor.

```
using Microsoft.VisualStudio.TestTools.UnitTesting;
using ProfessionalEnterprise.Chap4.Model;

namespace ProfessionalEnterprise.Chap4.MSTests
{
    [TestFicture]
    public class TicTacToeGameTests
    {

        ...

        [Test]
        public void
        If_Player_X_Gets_Three_Xs_In_A_Row_Then_The_Game_Is_Won_By_Player_X()
        {
            TicTacToeGame aGameOfTicTacToe = GetThreeXsInARowWinningGame();

            Assert.AreEqual(GameStatus.PlayerXWins, aGameOfTicTacToe.Status());
        }

        private TicTacToeGame GetThreeXsInARowWinningGame()
        {
            Row PlayerX_RowMove1 = Row.One;
            Row PlayerX_RowMove2 = Row.Two;
            Row PlayerX_RowMove3 = Row.Three;
            Column PlayerX_ColumnMove123 = Column.One;

            Row PlayerO_RowMove12 = Row.One;
            Column PlayerO_ColumnMove1 = Column.Two;
            Column PlayerO_ColumnMove2 = Column.Three;

            TicTacToeGame aGameOfTicTacToe = new TicTacToeGame();

            // Player X Move 1
            // X| |
            //  | |
            //  | |
```

```
            aGameOfTicTacToe.PlaceMarkerAt(PlayerX_RowMove1,
                                           PlayerX_ColumnMove123);
        // Player O Move 1
        // X|O|
        // | |
        // | |
        aGameOfTicTacToe.PlaceMarkerAt(PlayerO_RowMove12,
                                       PlayerO_ColumnMove1);

        // Player X Move 2
        // X|O|
        // X| |
        // | |
        aGameOfTicTacToe.PlaceMarkerAt(PlayerX_RowMove2,
                                       PlayerX_ColumnMove123);
        // Player O Move 2
        // X|O|O
        // X| |
        // | |
        aGameOfTicTacToe.PlaceMarkerAt(PlayerO_RowMove12,
                                       PlayerO_ColumnMove2);

        // Player X Move 3
        // X|O|O
        // X| |
        // X| |
        aGameOfTicTacToe.PlaceMarkerAt(PlayerX_RowMove3,
                                       PlayerX_ColumnMove123);
        return aGameOfTicTacToe;
    }
```

```
    ...

    [Test]
    public void A_Player_Can_Make_No_More_Moves_After_A_Game_Is_Won()
    {
        TicTacToeGame aGameOfTicTacToe = GetThreeXsInARowWinningGame();

        Assert.AreEqual(GameStatus.PlayerXWins, aGameOfTicTacToe.Status());

        // Should not be able to place a marker in an empty
        // square after the game has ended.
        Assert.IsFalse(aGameOfTicTacToe.CanPlaceMarkerAt(Row.Three,
                                                         Column.Three ));

    }
  }
}
```

The test fails because you have no method in place to test if the game is over. To get the test to pass, you simply have to check the status of the game to ensure that it has not been won or tied or a draw. The easiest way to do this is to check if the game is awaiting a player's move.

```
namespace ProfessionalEnterprise.Chap4.Model
{
    public class TicTacToeGame
    {
        ...

        public bool CanPlaceMarkerAt(Row row, Column column)
        {
            if (Status() == GameStatus.AwaitingPlayerOToPlaceMarker |
                Status() == GameStatus.AwaitingPlayerXToPlaceMarker )
            {
                return this.Board[(int)row, (int)column] == 0;
            }
            return false;
        }

        ...
    }
}
```

All of the tests on your initial list have passed, so you can be confident that the software has satisfied all of the initial requirements, plus you now have the benefit of fast feedback if you ever need to change or refactor the code. The tests also read as a rulebook for the game of Tic Tac Toe, so future developers will be able to understand the business rules of your small game application.

Here is the full code listing for the Tic Tac Toe game.

```
namespace ProfessionalEnterprise.Chap4.Model
{
    public class TicTacToeGame
    {
        private int[,] Board = new int[3, 3];
        private player currentplayer;

        public TicTacToeGame()
        {
            currentplayer = player.x;
        }

        public player WhoseTurn()
        {
            return currentplayer;
        }

        public bool CanPlaceMarkerAt(Row row, Column column)
        {
            if (Status() == GameStatus.AwaitingPlayerOToPlaceMarker |
                Status() == GameStatus.AwaitingPlayerXToPlaceMarker )
```

```
    {
        return this.Board[(int)row, (int)column] == 0;
    }
    return false;
}

public void PlaceMarkerAt(Row row, Column column)
{
    if (CanPlaceMarkerAt(row, column))
    {
        this.Board[(int) row, (int) column] = (int) WhoseTurn();

        ChangeCurrentPlayer();
    }
    else
    {
        throw new ApplicationException(
        string.Format("Square Row:{0}, Column:{1} already occupied by {2}",
        row.ToString(), column.ToString(),
        (player)Enum.ToObject(typeof(player),
                this.Board[(int)row, (int)column])));

    }
}

private void ChangeCurrentPlayer()
{
    if (this.currentplayer == player.x)
    {
        this.currentplayer = player.o;
    }
    else
    {
        this.currentplayer = player.x;
    }
}

public GameStatus Status()
{
    GameStatus GameStatus = Model.GameStatus.Draw;

    if (IsAWinner(player.o))
        GameStatus = Model.GameStatus.PlayerOWins;
    else if (IsAWinner(player.x))
        GameStatus = Model.GameStatus.PlayerXWins;
    else if (GameIsADraw())
        GameStatus = Model.GameStatus.Draw;
    else if (WhoseTurn() == player.x)
        GameStatus = Model.GameStatus.AwaitingPlayerXToPlaceMarker;
    else
        GameStatus = Model.GameStatus.AwaitingPlayerOToPlaceMarker;

    return GameStatus;
}
```

```
private bool GameIsADraw()
{
    bool allSquaresUsed = true;

    for (int Row = 0; Row <= 2; Row++)
    {
        for (int Column = 0; Column <= 2; Column++)
        {
            if (this.Board[Row, Column] == 0)
            {
                allSquaresUsed = false;
            }
        }
    }

    return allSquaresUsed;
}

private bool IsAWinner(player Player)
{
    bool winner = false;

    if (IsThreeInARowWinner(Player) |
        IsThreeInAColumnWinner(Player) |
        IsThreeInADiagonalWinner(Player) )
    {
        winner = true;
    }

    return winner;
}

private bool IsThreeInADiagonalWinner(player Player)
{
    bool winner = false;
    if ((
        this.Board[(int)Row.One, (int)Model.Column.One] == (int)Player &&
        this.Board[(int)Row.Two, (int)Model.Column.Two] == (int)Player &&
        this.Board[(int)Row.Three, (int)Model.Column.Three] == (int)Player
        ))
    {
        winner = true;
    }

    if ((
        this.Board[(int)Row.One, (int)Model.Column.Three] == (int)Player &&
        this.Board[(int)Row.Two, (int)Model.Column.Two] == (int)Player &&
        this.Board[(int)Row.Three, (int)Model.Column.One] == (int)Player
        ))
    {
        winner = true;
    }
    return winner;
}
```

```
private bool IsThreeInAColumnWinner(player Player)
{
    bool winner = false;
    for (int Column = 0; Column <= 2; Column++)
    {
        if ((this.Board[(int)Row.One, Column] == (int)Player &&
             this.Board[(int)Row.Two, Column] == (int)Player &&
             this.Board[(int)Row.Three, Column] == (int)Player))
        {
            winner = true;
        }
    }
    return winner;
}

private bool IsThreeInARowWinner(player Player)
{
    bool winner = false;
    for (int Row = 0; Row <= 2; Row++)
    {
        if ((this.Board[Row, (int)Column.One] == (int)Player &&
             this.Board[Row, (int)Column.Two] == (int)Player &&
             this.Board[Row, (int)Column.Three] == (int)Player))
        {
            winner = true;
        }
    }
    return winner;
}
    }
}
```

In this exercise, you really got to grips with what Test Driven Development is all about. You created no upfront design, but you still managed to create the entire game with the minimum amount of code, and you only wrote what you needed to get you test cases to pass. Better still, you knew when you were done because all of the tests passed and you could think of no functionality needed to write a test for. Think about what the code would have looked like if you had created a design for the program first. You might have created a board object and maybe a player object and created elaborate class diagrams without knowing what exactly their roles would be. You would then have started to meet the requirements of the program and may or may not have added some unit tests to verify the behavior at the end.

By letting your tests drive your design, you were able to satisfy the requirements in the simplest manner possible. The best thing is that if you do feel that one or two of the methods are doing more than they ought to or if you believe that the checking for a winning line should be performed by another class, you can easily refactor the design, and your suite of tests will immediately tell you if your refactor has broken the external behavior of the TicTacToeGame class.

Testing Frameworks

You used the NUnit framework for the Test Driven Development exercise, but NUnit is not the only testing framework, and running the standalone NUnit application is not the only way to run your tests.

NUnit

You have been using the NUnit framework during the exercise to create the Tic Tac Toe game. NUnit is an open source product ported from the popular JUnit and one of the most popular unit testing frameworks in .NET land.

For more information on NUnit, visit `http://www.NUnit.org`.

MS Test

Microsoft's integrated unit testing framework tool can do much the same as NUnit, albeit with a very slight syntax difference, but has the bonus of being integrated into Visual Studio.

MS Test is included with the Professional and above editions of Visual Studio 2008.

MbUnit

MbUnit is another open source unit testing framework. It has a vast feature array and can easily be extended. Once you have pushed NUnit and MStest to their limits, maybe MbUnit can offer you the flexibility that you need.

For more information on MbUnit visit `http://www.mbunit.com`.

TestDriven.Net

Although not a testing framework itself, TestDriven.Net is an add-in for Visual Studio that will integrate your open source testing framework of choice into Visual Studio. It integrates with NUnit, MbUnit, and MS Test as well as a whole host of other open source testing frameworks to improve your testing experience.

The personal version is free of charge, and more information can be found by visiting `http://www.testdriven.net`.

Identifying Testable Elements

Now that you understand the process and methodology behind Test Driven Development, the next question you will be asking yourself is what should I be testing? One hundred percent code coverage does not mean that you have a perfect set of unit tests — think quantity rather than quality. There is always going to have to be a compromise between following the rules of a development methodology and using it in a pragmatic manner for business needs. This section will detail what you should and shouldn't be looking at testing.

Don't Test Trivial Code

As you read earlier in the introduction, Test Driven Development is as much about driving the design of your code as it is about creating the unit tests that will verify the behavior of your code modules. Your tests should initially come from a high level of abstraction. Think about your high-level needs rather than the low-level details. These initial high-level tests will sometimes spawn smaller lower-level objects, but it's not always advantageous to unit test them. Take the example of a test that you write to verify that a service returns all available currencies for an e-commerce store, would you want to test the getters and setters of a simple currency object that is used as a data transfer object with no behavior?

There is no value in testing simple objects with no behavior that just have getters and setters. The testing of these objects does not add any value to the suite of unit tests and at its worst clutters the suite of tests, obscuring the more valuable unit tests. There needs to be a compromise between following the Test Driven Development process to the letter and making a good judgment call on identifying the real parts of your system that need to be isolated and unit tested.

In effect, unit tests should be targeting what's likely to go wrong and what's likely to change in the future. If you created tests for every single scenario, you would end up with hundreds of thousands of tests that really don't give you an awful amount of value.

Testing Third-Party Modules

Another series of unit tests to avoid are any that test the .NET Framework itself or third-party APIs. If you don't trust the third-party tool that you are referencing in your module, then maybe that's a sign that you shouldn't be using it. Again, you need to use your judgment. If the reference assembly is key to the functionality of the system and is business-critical, you may just want to make sure that it's doing what its supposed to do, or in other words, if you are ever in doubt, you can always write that unit test.

Testing at the Right Level of Abstraction

The purpose of your unit tests is to reduce the overall risk of the logic in your application failing, so it's important to ensure that your tests are specifically aimed at the high-level abstractions of your software's modules. Blindly testing the low-level details of your code can be tiresome and mundane, and after a time this could lead you to skipping the testing altogether. It's not always in the best interests of the business to have every little piece of code verified by a unit test; developers need use their best judgment and experience to decide if code logic is best proven to work with the use of a unit test or just by running their eyes over it.

Testing Boundary Conditions

The purist would tell you that, if you want to thoroughly test your code, you should test all of the boundary conditions. Testing boundary conditions is all about using various extremes of values in your test. If a method that accepts a date in the future was passed a date in the past or today's date, how would it handle it? Again, just because you can test boundary conditions, should you? Like many answers to software development problems, it depends. It depends on what might happen if something went wrong. If it's business-critical, then test a host of different boundary conditions. If it's not business-critical and the worst that can happen is an `InvalidArgumentException` is thrown, it may not be the end of the world; the judgment will lie with the developer.

Knowing what to test and what not to test is all about using your common sense. This will get better with experience; weigh up what having a unit test for every single piece of code will get you and if 100% code coverage really is as good as a metric as it sounds. As you become more and more experienced with Test Driven Development, you will be able to take small shortcuts to get the job done quicker, as there will always need to be a tradeoff between following a methodology to the letter and living in the real world. As mentioned, you will arrive at this compromise over time when you are comfortable of what you and the rest of your team can achieve. In the end, if all else fails and you're still in doubt, write a test first, as you can always remove it later.

Now that you have an idea what to test you should ensure that the tests you write and include in your suite of tests are effective and helpful.

Writing Unit Tests That Work and Help

What makes a good unit test? Here is a list of metrics to determine if you have an effective unit test, which is going to work and give you real value when refactoring:.

- ❏ Tests should run fast.
- ❏ Tests should run automatic.
- ❏ Tests should be atomic.
- ❏ Tests should be repeatable.
- ❏ Tests should be explicit and readable.
- ❏ Tests should be independent.
- ❏ Tests should be easy to set up.
- ❏ Tests should cover all angles by triangulation.

Tests Should Run Fast

Put simply, if your tests take an age to run, they're not going to be run very often, by you or anyone else, which makes them of very little use. You are going to be spending an awful lot of time running your tests, so you need to ensure that they run fast. This will assist you in working in quick cycles and will enable you to check that you haven't introduced bugs when adding your feature or refactoring code. One way to ensure that your tests run smoothly and speedily is to remove the dependencies on outside systems, by using mock or stub objects. If your unit tests hit a database or call out to a web service, they are going to run slower than tests run in memory. By faking the interface of the dependency, you can isolate the code you are testing and ensure that your tests always run with consistent results. You will learn more about mocks and stub objects later in this chapter. When it comes to writing integration tests that may involve connecting to a database, try to keep them in separate assembly so that your unit tests can still run fast.

Many software houses run the full suite of unit tests prior to checking in source code to the source control repository, so it's vital that these tests run fast, as slow check-ins will lead to developers becoming reluctant to check their code in at the end of the day.

Tests Should Run Automatically

Your tests should run automatically at the touch of a button for you and the rest of the developers on your team, giving you immediate feedback on your code modifications. If your tests aren't easy to run and require configuration, then developers will be less likely to want to run them. In short, when developers check out the latest version from your source control repository, they should be able to run the tests without the need of any configuration setup procedure.

Tests that are automatic and easy to run will help developers when the time comes to update code. If the tests are failing because of a configuration problem, developers will lose confidence in the tests and the tests will become worthless. So, ensure that all your tests are good to go.

Tests Should Be Atomic

Your tests should be fine-grained and aimed at the smallest piece of logic in a module. When a test fails it should be very easy to identify the point at which your code is failing. If you need to F5 (run the debugger) your way through your code, this should be a sign that maybe your tests aren't fine-grained enough and are testing too much. If your code under test has external dependencies, use mock and stub objects to ensure that it is isolated from those dependencies. By using mock objects with known behavior, you can eliminate the risk of the dependencies causing a test to fail and make certain that it's the code under test failing.

Your test should really only validate one piece of logic and have only one reason to fail. It's a good idea to have a single assert statement for each unit test, or ensure that if there is more than one assert, they are all confirming the same piece of logic.

Tests Should Be Repeatable

No matter how many times you run your tests, they should always give the same result. You shouldn't rely on uncontrollable variables like the time, date, or state of a database. Instead, use parameters that will always be consistent and will allow your tests to be run at any time and any number of times.

Your tests should ensure that any dependent resources are in a known state before running, and they should be returned to that state after the test is complete. You can use the setup and teardown events to set up before and clean up after any test. This will give you a clean slate when running your tests.

Tests Must Be Explicit and Readable

A suite of tests can act as a living form of documentation on what your system can and can't do, so it's a good idea to give tests meaningful and verbose names to help other developers to immediately understand what they are verifying.

As well as being named in an intention-revealing manner the tests themselves should be clear and simple to understand. Your tests are a demonstration as to how the program's interface should be used, so it's important that they are presented in a readable manner.

If you treat your tests with as much professionalism as your production code, remove duplicated tests, delete old tests, and keep tests clean and easy to read, they will become much more useful and valuable to you.

Tests Should Be Independent

Your tests should be isolated from each other and not dependent on any other tests. Assume that tests will be run in no specific order so that you are not relying on earlier tests to set up the state of an object for an upcoming test.

The success or failure of one test should not have an impact on another test. Tests that alter the state of an object or external resource or create/remove files/records should clean up after themselves by restoring the state after the test has run through use of a teardown method.

Tests Should Be Easy to Setup

If you are spending too much time setting up tests and not enough time on writing your production code, then something is amiss. Your tests should be straightforward and easy to set up. If you're spending your time writing masses of setup code, then try to break up what you are testing into meaningful sections or create setup routines that can be shared by other tests cases that require the same object in the same state.

Test Coverage and Testing Angles/Triangulation

Just because one test passes, this doesn't mean that your logic has been verified as working. As you saw in the Tic Tac Toe exercise earlier in this chapter, you write the minimum amount of code to get a test to pass. Sometimes, however, you knew that the code would not work under different test case scenarios. You need to test your code with some extreme boundary parameters as well as the usual arguments that will be passed to your code 99% of the time.

In summary, treat your unit tests with as much professionalism as you do your production code, and your unit tests will look after you. They will provide you with a safety net, which will alert you when you are deep into a project. When tests become obsolete, delete them from your test suite to keep your tests uncluttered with irrelevant code. Name your tests in as an intention-revealing verbose manner as possible. Remember, this isn't your production code, and your tests are there to remind you what your program can and can't do, so the better named the tests are, the more value they will be to you and other developers. Last, ensure that your tests are easy to set up and easy to run. Difficult or slow-running tests are going to put you and other developers off running them. This will lead to bugs being introduced and poor-quality code. Again, as with anything in life, you will need to make a judgment call. If your test is taking you an age to set up, and you are spending more time on it than on the production code, maybe your time would be better spent on manually testing the functionality or breaking your code down into smaller units.

Up to now, you have learned what Test Driven Development is, how to apply those concepts, what to test for, and how to make those tests effective. Now it's time to turn to the tangible benefits of following Test Driven Development and what you get in return for the upfront investment.

Automating — the Real Benefit

One of the first benefits of Test Driven Development that springs to mind is the fact that, after you have completed your program, you will be left with a suite of tests for each piece of logic in your code base. This battery of tests will act an insurance policy, giving you fast feedback on any later changes to the code and ensuring that you are alerted immediately if a change has introduced a bug into an existing module. What you have achieved by following a Test Driven Development methodology is a reduction in risk to your software. At the touch of a button, you can verify that your software is behaving in the manner that it is required to, and more importantly, other developers can run these tests and eliminate the need to debug their way through reams of code after each modification.

A big practical advantage of automating your unit tests is the reduction in the requirements for manual testing. Automating the majority of your testing efforts will remove the need for human intervention. It's easy for a testing framework to fire off 1000 tests than it is for a developer to have to mercilessly debug and manually test each and every code scenario. No two developers are alike. Some are better at testing than others, so to remove this reliance on the developer to test every piece of logic after every code change, and moving it to your testing framework, should give you far more confidence that bugs will be picked up. In addition, it gives you the added advantage of freeing up time to work on the next feature of the software.

By definition, by following a Test Driven Development methodology, you will be producing testable code. Testable code will be loosely coupled and modular in design. Having small units of functionality isolated in single responsibility classes will decrease maintenance and extensibility requirements, allowing your code to be more flexible when the business needs change. Later in the chapter you will learn how mock and stub objects help you to keep code modules loosely coupled by allowing you to switch a real version of a code dependency for a fake or mock version. This is all achieved because you, as a developer, will have total confidence when it comes to refactoring your code and making design decisions. Your tests will give you immediate feedback on whether or not your code is working. Later in this chapter you will learn how you can simplify the design of your code by refactoring toward design patterns.

As you read in the introduction to this chapter, Test Driven Development is not just about ensuring that you are certain your code works and satisfies the requirements but is also just as important in the design and architecture of your software. Test Driven Development compels you to ensure that you have a full understanding of the problem you are trying to solve by making you test for the desired result before writing any production code. Not only does this ensure that you are clear on the requirements of the software, but it also puts you in the position of someone coding against the finished API. By designing code test first, you will need to imagine how the interface will work. You will be writing tests from the point of view of a consumer of your module. You will be focused first instance on the interface of the code, then with the functionality. This requires you to think about the interaction between the client (tests) and the API before getting the functionality to work, which will force you write a simple and fluent API that will be easy to use and intention-revealing for other developers.

Your completed suite of tests acts as a list of what the software can and can't do; the tests act as a suite of sample code, showing how to interact with the API. They form a living breathing documentation that will evolve and stay up to date as your code base grows and develops. This is why it's important to name your tests in a verbose manner and keep your tests themselves clear and simple. By reading the tests that you built for the Tic Tac Toe example at the beginning of this chapter, you will be able to learn everything you needed to know about the game and its rules.

As was pointed out in the earlier section identifying what to test, your initial tests will focus on high-level abstractions rather than the low-level details of your modules. This will allow developers to focus on the real business value of a module, then after this is verified, triangulation can be used to test the boundary cases such as error handling and validation. This can help to get key pieces of functionality up and running and really drive your production efforts.

Because code is only ever going to be written to pass failing tests, you are immediately subscribing to the YAGNI ("You Aren't Gonna Need It") design pattern. By only ever writing code that the program needs and doing so in response to a failing test, you will have a series of tests that cover all code paths. This, coupled with writing only the minimum amount of code, will help to reduce the needless complexities sometimes introduced to projects through over-engineering. Only ever writing code that is needed will improve your productivity and your teams.

A good suite of unit tests will also remove the reliance on a single programmer; this is often called the "'truck factor". The truck factor is the number of people on your team who have to be hit with a truck before the project is in serious trouble. By creating a suite of tests, new developers will have an easier integration time and will be able to come to grips with the existing code base quicker, as the tests will provide a guidance that will alert the developer if any existing behavior has been broken. The suite of tests will also be of great value to new developers, as they are a demonstration of how the production code should be used. This ties in with the organic documentation nature of Test Driven Development.

To summarize, Test Driven Development has a lot of practical benefits that can immediately provide a big help for your software development efforts. By automating your tests and creating them before you create your production code, you are taking the stress out of your development. You will be confident that your code works and that you have only written the code to get the job done and nothing more. Other developers that work on the code base will be confident that the changes they make or extra functionality that they add will not have broken the behavior of the existing code because the test will give them feedback instantly and act as an early warning alert. By taking small steps and working in quick cycles, you can build your software in a disciplined manner that will produce high quality code that's loosely coupled, extensible, and maintainable.

Last, if you are going to take anything away from the benefits of Test Driven Development, then trust in your code should be the most important. Code covered by a suite of tests that can give you quick feedback on fixes and add functionality will be invaluable to you and your team. If you can trust your code, then you will be more confident during production releases and when it comes time to modify or add functionality.

Through the first part of this chapter, you have read about the importance of keeping your code clean as well as working. This cleaning process, as you have read, is known as refactoring and is as important a topic as writing the tests themselves.

Refactoring

We briefly touched on refactoring in the previous chapter and as the third step of the Test Driven Development mantra — Red, Green, Refactor. Refactoring is all about improving the design of existing code. After you got the code working and the green light in the Tic Tac Toe game, you were then in a position to refactor the code into a cleaner and more maintainable state without changing its external behavior. Simple, but not simplistic, code is always going to be less expensive to change.

So why should you worry about refactoring your code? Shouldn't the saying "if it ain't broke, don't fix it" be the view to take? Refactoring your code does not fix bugs and it does not add any functionality, so what's the value of it, you may ask? The real value of refactoring your code is to improve its understandability, making it easier for other developers and yourself to maintain it. A great quote from Martin Fowler really sums up what refactoring is all about: "Any fool can write code that a computer can understand. Good programmers write code that humans understand." (Fowler, *Refactoring*, 1999 Addison-Wesley Object Technology Series.)

If you don't refactor your code regularly, it will soon become a problem when it comes to adding or modifying functionality. Without refactoring your code to a cleaner state, you could end up with a tangled spaghetti-like structure, impossible to work with and very hard to maintain. As you refactor, you will begin to understand your code better; you will then be able to refactor it to a better architecture and a simpler design. You will also be able to refactor towards known design patterns to make your code more accessible to other developers.

Refactoring isn't exclusive to the realm of Test Driven Development, but what Test Driven Development gives you is the confidence to refactor knowing that you will get instant feedback on your code changes so that you know your internal changes don't affect the external behavior of your modules.

One of the most important points to remember when refactoring is to refactor in small steps and run your tests after each refactor. As with Test Driven Development, by working in small cycles you are lowering the risk of introducing bugs and making it easier on yourself to spot issues that break existing tests. Refactoring goes hand in hand with Test Driven Development. Your tests enable you to refactor confidently, and your code refactoring helps to improve the cleanliness and simplicity of your code, which in turn makes it easy to test.

Refactoring Tools

As with testing frameworks, there are a number of tools available to help you with refactoring.

ReSharper

ReSharper is a Visual Studio add-in that, as well as a host of other enhancements, adds powerful refactoring abilities to your development efforts. It also integrates with NUnit to provide a one-click integrated unit testing framework to boot.

For more information visit `http://www.jetbrains.com/resharper`.

Refactor Pro

Refactor Pro has pretty much all the functionality of ReSharper minus the integrated testing user interface. Choosing one over another is purely a matter of personal taste, as they are both great products.

For more information visit `http://www.devexpress.com/Products/Visual_Studio_Add-in/Refactoring/`.

Dealing with Dependencies in Test Driven Development — Mocking, Stubs, and Fakes

One of the key attributes when writing tests is being able to test functionality in isolation. However, as you saw in Chapter 3 with the `ReturnOrderService`, the strength of programming comes when objects collaborate to solve complex problems. In the `ReturnOrderService`, the `Process` method delegated the work of refunding the customer to the `IPaymentGateway` implementation; it also delegated the work of notifying the customer of the refund to the `INotificationService`. When trying to unit test a small piece of logic that depends on other modules, the process often turns into a full integration test involving many different modules. Things are even worse when we are writing tests against objects that don't exist and their dependencies may not exist as well.

If you are writing tests on objects that have dependencies, then you can create stub (sometimes called fake) objects to act as stand-ins for the real object. The role of the Stub object is to provide simulated responses to give data to the object under test. Stub objects typically do not directly cause the unit test to fail. They are used simply to provide the object under test with the data it needs to complete its work.

Stubs enable you to easily replace expensive dependencies such as a service that calls to a database or a web service with a dummy object that will stand in for the real implementation and make the same noises, which will enable your test to run consistently and fast every time you run it.

To demonstrate stubs and mocking, you will use a simple holiday request booking system. Figure 4-9 shows the classes involved in this system.

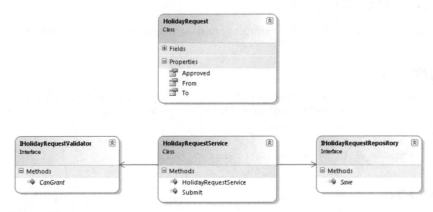

Figure 4-9

Before you start to write some tests you will need to create the classes in Figure 4-9.

1. Open up Visual Studio and create a new solution named `ProEnt.Chap4.Mocking`.

2. Add a new class library project to the solution by right clicking on the solution named and selecting Add ⇨ New Project; name the `Project ProEnt.Chap4.Mocking.Model`.

3. Add a second class library to the solution in the same way but call this one `ProEnt.Chap4.Mocking.Model.Tests`.

4. After you have created all of the projects, navigate to the folder structure by right-clicking on the solution name and selecting Open Folder in Windows Explorer. Add a new folder called lib, and copy the Nunit.Framework.dll from the NUnit directory on your machine (by default this can be found at `%systemdrive%\%programfiles directory%\NUnity 2.4.8\bin`) into the newly created lib folder.

5. Now add a new solution folder to the solution, called lib. To do this, right-click on the solution root, then select Add ⇨ Add New Solution Folder.

6. Add the NUnit.Framework.dll to your solution by right-clicking on the lib solution folder and selecting Add ⇨ Add Existing Item, then navigating to the NUnit.Framework.dll in the lib folder at the root of your application.

7. Add a reference to the NUnit.Framework.dll from the `ProEnt.Chap4.Mocking.Model/Tests` project by right clicking on the project name and selecting Add Reference. From the dialog window that appears select the Browse tab and navigate to the Lib folder and select the NUnit. Framework.dll.

8. From the `ProEnt.Chap4.Mocking.Model.Tests` project add a project reference to the `ProEnt.Chap4.Mocking.Model` project.

9. From within the `Project ProEnt.Chap4.Mocking.Model` add a new class named `HolidayRequest` with the listing below. This class will represent the `HolidayRequest` itself.

```
namespace ProEnt.Chap4.Mocking.Model
{
    public class HolidayRequest
    {
        private DateTime _from;
        private DateTime _to;
        private string _employeeId;
        private bool _approved;

        public DateTime From
        {
            get { return _from; }
            set { _from = value; }
        }

        public DateTime To
        {
            get { return _to; }
            set { _to = value; }
        }

        public bool Approved
        {
            get { return _approved; }
            set { _approved = value; }
        }

    }
}
```

10. Add a new interface to the project `ProEnt.Chap4.Mocking.Model` named `IHolidayRequestValidator` with the following definition.

```
namespace ProEnt.Chap4.Mocking.Model
{
    public interface IHolidayRequestValidator
    {
        bool CanGrant(HolidayRequest holidayRequest);
    }
}
```

The `IHolidayRequestValidator` interface defines the contract that a class must implement to be used as a holiday request validator; in basic terms the holiday request validator determines if an employee can have the specified holiday request.

11. Add a second interface to the `ProEnt.Chap4.Mocking.Model` named `IHolidayRequestRepository`.

```
namespace ProEnt.Chap4.Mocking.Model
{
    public interface IHolidayRequestRepository
    {
        void Save(HolidayRequest holidayRequest);
    }
}
```

The `IHolidayRequestRepository` simply defines a contract that has a single method which enables the `HolidayRequestService` to save a `HolidayRequest`.

12. Finally add a new class named `HolidayRequestService` to the project with the following code listing.

```
namespace ProEnt.Chap4.Mocking.Model
{
    public class HolidayRequestService
    {
        private IHolidayRequestValidator _holidayRequestValidator;
        private IHolidayRequestRepository _holidayRequestRepository;

        public HolidayRequestService(
            IHolidayRequestValidator holidayRequestValidator,
            IHolidayRequestRepository holidayRequestRepository)
        {
            _holidayRequestValidator = holidayRequestValidator;
            _holidayRequestRepository = holidayRequestRepository;
        }

        public void Submit(HolidayRequest holidayRequest)
        {
            if (_holidayRequestValidator.CanGrant(holidayRequest))
```

```
                    {
                        holidayRequest.Approved = true;
                        _holidayRequestRepository.Save(holidayRequest);
                    }
                }
            }
        }
    }
```

The `HolidayRequestService` simply coordinates the process of approving and saving a `HolidayRequest` to the datastore, which involves using instances of the `IHolidayRequestValidator` and the `IHolidayRequestRepository`.

If you were to write a test that confirms that a `HolidayRequest` that passes the validation check is approved, you would need to supply implementations for all of the dependencies. In this case that is an implementation for the `IHolidayRequestValidator` and the `IHolidayRequestRepository`. You don't really want to be supplying a real implementation of either of these dependencies as testing will be slow because a real implementation may connect to an slow resource like a database or a web service, so instead you can create stub versions of these implementations.

If you did not create a stub version and a test failed, you would not be able to be certain the test failed with the object under test, so you would have to step through the debugger to find the root cause. With stubs, however, you are hard-coding the behavior, so you know exactly how it will react, and you can be confident that you are only testing the object that you think you are testing.

Add a new folder to the `ProEnt.Chap4.Mocking.Model.Tests` project named Stubs and within this folder add a new class named `AlwaysValidHolidayRequestValidator` with the following definition.

```
using ProEnt.Chap4.Mocking.Model;

namespace ProEnt.Chap4.Mocking.Model.Tests.Stubs
{
    public class AlwaysValidHolidayRequestValidator : IHolidayRequestValidator
    {
        public bool CanGrant(HolidayRequest holidayRequest)
        {
            return true;
        }
    }
}
```

Add a second class to the same folder named `StubHolidayRequestRepository` with the code listing below.

```
using ProEnt.Chap4.Mocking.Model;

namespace ProEnt.Chap4.Mocking.Model.Tests.Stubs
{
    public class StubHolidayRequestRepository : IHolidayRequestRepository
    {
        public void Save(HolidayRequest holidayRequest)
        {
            // Do nothing.
        }
    }
}
```

These classes will be used in place of real implementations so that you can isolate and test only the parts of the HolidayRequestService that you want to test. You have hard-coded the CanGrant method of the AlwaysValidHolidayRequestValidator class to always return true; this will enable you to test that the HolidayRequestService correctly approves a HolidayRequest that is granted by the HolidayRequestValidator.

Add a new class to the ProEnt.Chap4.Mocking.Model.Tests Project named HolidayRequestServiceHandRolledTests with the code listing below.

```
using NUnit.Framework;
using ProEnt.Chap4.Mocking.Model;
using ProEnt.Chap4.Mocking.Model.Tests.Stubs;
using ProEnt.Chap4.Mocking.Model.Tests.Mocks;

namespace ProEnt.Chap4.Mocking.Model.Tests
{
    [TestFixture()]
    public class HolidayRequestServiceHandRolledTests
    {
        [Test()]
        public void
The_HolidayRequestService_Will_Approve_A_Holiday_Request_That_Is_Granted_By_The_
Validator()
        {
            HolidayRequest holidayRequest = new HolidayRequest();
            AlwaysValidHolidayRequestValidator alwaysValidHolidayRequestValidator =
                            new AlwaysValidHolidayRequestValidator();
            StubHolidayRequestRepository holidayRequestRepository =
                            new StubHolidayRequestRepository();
            // Class under test
            HolidayRequestService holidayRequestService =
                            new HolidayRequestService(
                                alwaysValidHolidayRequestValidator,
                                holidayRequestRepository);

            holidayRequest.Approved = false;
            holidayRequestService.Submit(holidayRequest);

            Assert.AreEqual(true, holidayRequest.Approved);

        }
    }
}
```

The test uses both of the stub implementations of the depenedencies to check if a HolidayRequest is approved by the service if it passes validaition. If you used a real implementaion of the IHolidayRequestValidator and the test failed how could you be sure that it was because of the service method when it could be equally the fault of the IHolidayRequestValidator implementation?

Run the test to verify that it passes.

What you have done is to hard-code the behavior of the stub implementations. This enables you to know exactly how it will behave without having to rely on external dependencies. The stubs in this case were simple objects with only one of the classes needing a return value; in real world scenarios you could be dealing with modules with complex dependencies such as web services or databases. The example only had two simple dependencies, so it was relatively inexpensive to manually code the stub classes by hand. If you are in the position of having a complex stub or a large number of stubs to create, you could employ a mocking framework to auto-create your stubs. A mocking framework makes it very easy to automatically create stub objects to use in place of real dependencies by creating them dynamically at runtime.

For this example, you will use a mocking framework called Rhino Mocks to generate the stubs, using reflection. Other mocking frameworks are discussed at the end of this section.

To download Rhino Mocks, navigate to `http://ayende.com/projects/rhino-mocks/downloads` `.aspx`. The version at the date of writing was Rhino Mocks 3.5, for .NET 3.5. Unlike NUnit, Rhino Mocks does not have an installer. You simply download the compressed file, unzip it, and add a reference to the Rhino.Mocks.dll assembly to your test class project. To keep things organized, copy the Rhino.Mocks.dll and place it in the lib folder in the root of the project and then add it to the lib solution file within Visual Studio.

Now add a new class to the test project named `HolidayRequestServiceRhinoMockTests` with the following definition.

```
using NUnit.Framework;
using Rhino.Mocks;

namespace ProEnt.Chap4.Mocking.Model.Tests
{
    [TestFixture()]
    public class HolidayRequestServiceRhinoMockTests
    {
        [Test()]
        public void
The_HolidayRequestService_Will_Approve_A_Holiday_Request_That_Is_Granted_By_The_
Validator()
        {
            HolidayRequest holidayRequest = new HolidayRequest();
            MockRepository mocks = new MockRepository();
            var alwaysValidHolidayRequestValidator =
                    mocks.Stub<IHolidayRequestValidator>();
            var holidayRequestRepository = mocks.Stub<IHolidayRequestRepository>();

            using ((mocks.Record()))
            {
                // Configure Results for the Stub
                SetupResult.For(
                    alwaysValidHolidayRequestValidator.CanGrant(holidayRequest))
                    .Return(true);
            }
```

```
        using ((mocks.Playback()))
        {
            // Class under test
            HolidayRequestService holidayRequestService =
                new HolidayRequestService(alwaysValidHolidayRequestValidator,
                                          holidayRequestRepository);

            holidayRequest.Approved = false;
            holidayRequestService.Submit(holidayRequest);

            Assert.AreEqual(true, holidayRequest.Approved);
        }

    }

}
```

Take a look at what's going on in this test; the first step is to create an instance of the RhinoMocks `MockRepository`. This can then be used to generate a stub object based on the `IHolidayRequestValidator` interface and the `IHolidayRequestRepository`. The method `mocks .Stub<IHolidayRequestValidator>()` creates an instance of the class, using reflection. The class can now be used as a normal instance of an `IHolidayRequestValidator`. The next step is to set up the response to the `CanGrant` method. You wrap the `SetUpResult.For` method within a using statement that calls the `mocks.Record()` method. The role of the `Record` method is to set up how the stub class will respond when its methods are called. Different responses can be set up for different parameters or a response can be set up for any set of parameters passed. Finally, you can code the actual result by using the static `SetupResult` class, which is used to set the return value for the `alwaysValidHolidayRequestValidator.CanGrant()` method. When the `CanGrant()` method is called with the matching `HolidayRequest` argument, the class will return true. You can now run the test to verify that it passes.

You can see that; by using a mocking framework you eliminate the need to manually create the stub objects yourself. Sometimes, however, you need to test the interaction between the object under test and the dependency; for example, to see if the correct information is being sent to a logging mechanism that was injected into the module under test. These types of tests are known as integration tests and verify the interaction between modules of code.

You will now write a test to ensure that the `HolidayRequest` is sent to the repository for saving if it is approved. Firstly you are going to hand roll a test. Add a folder to the test project named Mocks and within this folder add a new class named `MockHolidayRequestRepository` with the following definition.

```
using ProEnt.Chap4.Mocking.Model;

namespace ProEnt.Chap4.Mocking.Model.Tests.Mocks
{
    public class MockHolidayRequestRepository : IHolidayRequestRepository
    {
        private HolidayRequest _holidayRequestSaved;

        public HolidayRequest HolidayRequestSaved
```

```
        {
            get { return _holidayRequestSaved; }
            set { _holidayRequestSaved = value; }
        }

        public void Save(HolidayRequest holidayRequest)
        {
            HolidayRequestSaved = holidayRequest;
        }
    }
}
```

This class is slightly different from the hand rolled stub equivalent as it exposes a new property that will return the HolidayRequest that has been passed to the Save method.

Add a new test to the HolidayRequestServiceHandRolledTests file as shown in the listing below.

```
using NUnit.Framework;
using ProEnt.Chap4.Mocking.Model;
using ProEnt.Chap4.Mocking.Model.Tests.Stubs;
using ProEnt.Chap4.Mocking.Model.Tests.Mocks;

namespace ProEnt.Chap4.Mocking.Model.Tests
{
    [TestFixture()]
    public class HolidayRequestServiceHandRolledTests
    {
        [Test()]
        public void
The_HolidayRequestService_Will_Approve_A_Holiday_Request_That_Is_Granted_By_The_
Validator()
        {
            ...
        }

        [Test()]
        public void
A_Holiday_Request_That_Is_Approved_By_The_Request_Service_Is_Save_By_The_
Repository()
        {

            HolidayRequest holidayRequest = new HolidayRequest();
            AlwaysValidHolidayRequestValidator alwaysValidHolidayRequestValidator =
                    new AlwaysValidHolidayRequestValidator();
            MockHolidayRequestRepository holidayRequestRepository =
                    new MockHolidayRequestRepository();
            // Class under test
            HolidayRequestService holidayRequestService =
                new HolidayRequestService(alwaysValidHolidayRequestValidator,
                                    holidayRequestRepository);

            holidayRequestService.Submit(holidayRequest);
```

```
            Assert.AreEqual(holidayRequest,
                holidayRequestRepository.HolidayRequestSaved);
        }
    }
}
```

This test is verifying that the `HolidayRequestService` is saving a `HolidayRequest` via an instance of the `IHolidayRequestRepository` if the `HolidayRequest` passes the approval stage. An assert is used to check the value of the `HolidayRequestSave` on the special Mock object against the `HolidayRequest` you passed into the service. Again this is a rather trival example but if you are working with complex dependencies that have many interactions with your classes you could spend all day creating your own mock classes; luckily Rhino Mocks' (the hint is in the name) provides a framework for enabling you to create mocks easily.

To demonstrate Rhino Mocks' mocking capabilities you will add a new test to the `HolidayRequestServiceRhinoMockTests` class as displayed in the code listing below.

```
using NUnit.Framework;
using Rhino.Mocks;

namespace ProEnt.Chap4.Mocking.Model.Tests
{
    [TestFixture()]
    public class HolidayRequestServiceRhinoMockTests
    {
        [Test()]
        public void
The_HolidayRequestService_Will_Approve_A_Holiday_Request_That_Is_Granted_By_The_
Validator()
        {
            ...
        }

        [Test()]
        public void
A_Holiday_Request_That_Is_Approved_By_The_Request_Service_Is_Save_By_The_
Repository()
        {
            HolidayRequest holidayRequest = new HolidayRequest();
            MockRepository mocks = new MockRepository();
            var alwaysValidHolidayRequestValidator =
                mocks.Stub<IHolidayRequestValidator>();
            var holidayRequestRepository =
                mocks.CreateMock<IHolidayRequestRepository>();

            using ((mocks.Record()))
            {
                // Configure Results for the Stub
                SetupResult.For(
                    alwaysValidHolidayRequestValidator.CanGrant(holidayRequest)).
                    Return(true);

                // Set Up Expectations
```

```
                    holidayRequestRepository.Save(holidayRequest);
                    LastCall.Repeat.Once();
                }
            using ((mocks.Playback()))
            {
                    // Class under test
                    HolidayRequestService holidayRequestService =
                        new HolidayRequestService(alwaysValidHolidayRequestValidator,
                                                  holidayRequestRepository);

                    holidayRequestService.Submit(holidayRequest);
                }
            }
        }
    }
```

The first thing you will notice in this test is that there is no Assert call, so where is the verification call for this test you might ask? Because you cannot directly call an asset Rhino Mocks instead verifies that all expected behavior, as set up in the line below, occurs in the playback statement. If it does not then Rhino Mocks will cause the test to fail.

```
                    holidayRequestRepository.Save(holidayRequest);
                    LastCall.Repeat.Once();
```

If you don't want to use Rhino Mocks or any other mocking framework, you could hand roll your own mock objects that register if a certain method or series of methods were called, but as mocking frameworks exist, it seems a waste not to take advantage of them to cut down on your development time.

In this short section, you learned about integration testing and how to verify that objects are behaving and interacting as you expect them to. You first looked at replacing dependences for the objects under test with stub objects, first by hand rolling them yourself and then later with a mocking framework. Second, you looked at how to verify interactive behavior by using mock objects. You recorded the mock dependencies and set up some expectations. You then ran the tests, and the mocking framework verified if those expectations were met, making the test pass or fail.

It's important to note the subtle difference between the stub and mock objects. Put simply, stubs cannot fail a test. They are simply there to replace an external dependency so that the object under test can run and be tested. Mocks, on the other hand, can fail a test and are used to verify that the interaction between two objects took place as you expected.

Mocking Frameworks

There's more than one way to mock a dependency and there are a host of mocking frameworks available to you. Here are some of the major players.

Rhino Mocks

This was the mocking framework you used in the demonstration code in the previous section. Rhino Mocks is to mocking what NUnit is to unit testing; it's a popular and open source framework with a host of features.

For more information on Rhino Mocks, visit `http://ayende.com/projects/rhino-mocks.aspx`.

Moq

Moq is one the newer mocking frameworks. Like Rhino Mocks, it's also open source. Moq uses some of the latest enhancements included with .NET 3.5 such as lambdas, Linq, and extension methods. If you are comfortable with the newer aspects of the C# language and the latest .NET features, it's a good choice for a mocking framework.

For more information on Moq, visit `http://code.google.com/p/moq/`.

NMock

NMock is another open source mocking framework, which was originally ported from the Java JMock mocking framework. With its latest release, it's looking to give Rhino Mocks a run for its money with a very fluent interface that may be on the verbose side of things but is very easy to use.

For more information on NMock, visit `http://www.NMock.org`.

Summary

Concepts learnt in this chapter:

- ❏ Test Driven Development
- ❏ Metrics of Good Unit Tests
- ❏ Refactoring
- ❏ Testing with Dependencies using Mocking and Stubs

You started off this chapter by looking at the concepts behind Test Driven Development and how these concepts can help to address the challenges of developing and delivering high-quality software that you can be confident in. You then applied those concepts to a build a Tic Tac Toe game. You initially created a list of general requirements, then turned them into explicit tests. You tackled one test at a time and built the program in small increments, adding functionality with a failing test, making the test pass, and then refactoring it to a simpler; cleaner solution. This process is known as "Red, Green, Refactor," with the red and green coming from the colors displayed on the many testing frameworks graphical user interfaces. In the end, you had written the minimum amount of code needed to meet the design requirements, and you had a simple program with a full suite of tests that will enable you and other developers to modify and add functionality with confidence.

Having understood the key concepts of Test Driven Development, you then learned how to take a more pragmatic view of Test Driven Development and how to separate the key elements of your system that require testing from the trivial errors that do not. It's all about keeping to the spirit of Test Driven Development, in combining a purist academic approach with common sense, treating the methodology as a set of guidelines rather than iron-clad rules governing how you must develop. All of this judgment calling will, of course, improve with experience and depends on how you and your team choose to adopt a new developing methodology.

In the next section of the chapter, you learned what metrics you could measure your tests against to ensure that they were valuable and effective in meeting your development needs. Tests are susceptible to design rot and code smells as much as your production code, so they need to be looked after if they are going to be effective. Simple, clean, and understandable tests that are easy to setup and fast to run will give you and your team reliable and trustworthy benchmarks to run your production code against.

The most tangible benefit that Test Driven Development and automated unit testing frameworks give you is confidence in your code. By removing the risk from your code and not relying on a developer to manually test a lot of the logic, you will be able to reliably refactor and modify it, knowing that you have a safety net of tests ready to alert you if you have inadvertently introduced a bug into the code base.

Refactoring is the technique of altering the internal state of a program to make it cleaner and clearer, while keeping the external behavior the same. During the Tic Tac Toe exercise you were constantly refactoring to ensure you had a clean and maintainable code base.

Last, you learned about the role mocks and stubs play in isolating integration code when it comes to unit testing. The knowledge you gained from the previous chapter was used to ensure that all dependencies required by a module were injected into it and were referenced by a shared interface. By using this interface, you were able to mock and stub those dependencies and isolate the code under test.

In the next chapter, you will learn how to instantiate all of the dependences that are required for your module to perform. Up to now you have only seen the classes that require external dependencies, and you have seen code that consumes these modules. It's all well and good to loosely couple code by injecting dependencies into modules, but somewhere up the line something needs to create the dependencies and that means something will be tightly coupled to those creations. This is where an Inversion of Control Container helps out, and you will learn more about that next.

5

Make It Simple Again —
Inversion of Control

In Chapter 3, you read about the principles of Dependency Inversion and Dependency Injection, and learned how objects collaborating together in modules can be built in a loosely coupled fashion by inverting the relationship of a dependent to its dependencies. However after moving the responsibility of creating the dependencies out of the service modules, you have been left with the problem of where and when the concrete implementations are created.

Creating Dependencies

To demonstrate the problems of constructing objects with dependencies, let's consider a simple example of a service that requires two low-level detail objects.

The `TouristInformationService` is a service that pinpoints places of interest on a map. The service requires a map and a dictionary of places of interest. The service has a single method, `FindInterestingPlacesNear`, which takes a location object and returns a map filled with places of interest. The service has been designed in a loosely coupled fashion, via a Test Driven Design methodology and you have been very strict about not to tying yourself down to any concrete implementation. Figure 5-1 shows the class diagram of the `TouristInformationService`.

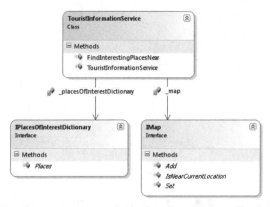

Figure 5-1

You will be using this sample code to demonstrate the concepts of Inversion of Control, so let's first build the sample.

1. Create a new blank solution named `ProEnt.Chap5`.

2. Add three class library projects to the solution by following these steps:

   ❏ From the File menu, select Add ⇨ New Project.

   ❏ Select C# Class Library.

   Name the class libraries `ProEnt.Chap5.Infrastructure`, `ProEnt.Chap5.Model`, and `ProEnt.Chap5.Tests`.

3. Navigate to the folder structure by right-clicking on the solution name and selecting Open Folder In Windows Explorer. Add a new folder called `Lib`, and copy the `Nunit.Framework.dll` from `C:\Program Files\NUnit 2.4.8\bin` into the newly created `Lib` folder. Refer to Chapter 3 for where to download the NUnit framework from.

4. Now add a new solution folder to the solution, called `Lib`. To do this, right-click on the solution root, then select Add ⇨ Add New Solution Folder.

5. Add the `NUnit.Framework.dll` to your solution by right-clicking on the `Lib` solution folder and selecting Add ⇨ Add Existing Item, then navigating to the `NUnit.Framework.dll` in the `Lib` folder at the root of your application.

6. Create two folders in the `ProEnt.Chap5.Model` project named `Maps` and `PlacesOfInterest`.

7. Add a reference to the `NUnit.Framework.dll` from the `ProEnt.Chap5.Tests` project by right-clicking on the `ProEnt.Chap5.Tests` project name and selecting Add Reference. From the dialog window that appears, select the Browse tab and navigate to the `Lib` folder and select the `NUnit.Framework.dll`.

8. Finally, add a project reference to `ProEnt.Chap5.Infrastructure`, `ProEnt.Chap5.Model` from the `ProEnt.Chap5.Tests` project by right-clicking on the `ProEnt.Chap5.Tests` name and selecting Add Reference. This time select the Project tab from the dialog window that appears, and select both the `ProEnt.Chap5.Infrastructure` and `ProEnt.Chap5.Model` projects.

Your solution should now look like Figure 5-2.

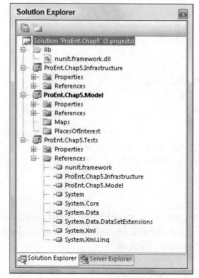

Figure 5-2

With your solution set up, you can build the demonstration application. Start by adding a new class in the root of the `ProEnt.Chap5.Model` project, named `Location`; this is a blank class used to represent the current location of a user.

```
namespace ProEnt.Chap5.Model
{
    public class Location
    {
    }
}
```

Next add a new class to the `PlacesOfInterest` folder, named `PlaceOfInterest`, which is again a dumb class that is used to represent a place of interest that can be added to a map:

```
namespace ProEnt.Chap5.Model.PlacesOfInterest
{
    public class PlaceOfInterest
    {
    }
}
```

Add an interface called `IPlacesOfInterestDictionary` to the `PlacesOfInterest` folder with the following definition:

```
namespace ProEnt.Chap5.Model.PlacesOfInterest
{
    public interface IPlacesOfInterestDictionary
```

```
    {
        IList<PlaceOfInterest> Places();
    }
}
```

Add a second interface to the Maps folder named IMap with the following definition using `ProEnt.Chap5.Model.PlacesOfInterest;`

```
namespace ProEnt.Chap5.Model.Maps
{
    public interface IMap
    {
        void Set(Location currentLocation);
        void Add(PlaceOfInterest placeOfInterest);
        bool CurrentLocationIsNear(PlaceOfInterest placeOfInterest);
    }
}
```

Now that you have two interfaces, you can create a couple of concrete types that can be used in the upcoming `TouristInformationService`. Create a new class in the Maps folder, named SatelliteMap, with the following code listing:

```
using ProEnt.Chap5.Model.PlacesOfInterest;

namespace ProEnt.Chap5.Model.Maps
{
    public class SatelliteMap : IMap
    {
        public void Set(Location currentLocation)
        {  }

        public void Add(PlaceOfInterest placeOfInterest)
        {  }

        public bool CurrentLocationIsNear(PlaceOfInterest placeOfInterest)
        {
            return true;
        }
    }
}
```

Don't worry that SatelliteMap doesn't do anything; in reality this would be a complex class probably with many dependencies of its own. In this context, we are using it as a dependency for the TouristInformationService.

Create another new class, named EnglishPlacesOfInterestDictionary, but this time in the PlacesOfInterest folder:

```
namespace ProEnt.Chap5.Model.PlacesOfInterest
{
    public class EnglishPlacesOfInterestDictionary : IPlacesOfInterestDictionary
    {
        public IList<PlaceOfInterest> Places()
```

```
        {
            return new List<PlaceOfInterest>();
        }
    }
}
```

Again, this class would hook up to a database or a web service to obtain a list of `PlaceOfInterest` objects; here, you are simply returning an empty list.

Finally, you can add a class named `TouristInformationService` to the root of the `ProEnt.Chap5` `.Model` project and enter the following code:

```
using ProEnt.Chap5.Model.Maps;
using ProEnt.Chap5.Model.PlacesOfInterest;

namespace ProEnt.Chap5.Model
{
    public class TouristInformationService
    {
        private IMap _map;
        private IPlacesOfInterestDictionary _placesOfInterestDictionary;

        public TouristInformationService(IMap map,
                    IPlacesOfInterestDictionary placesOfInterestDictionary)
        {
            _map = map;
            _placesOfInterestDictionary = placesOfInterestDictionary;
        }

        public IMap FindInterestingPlacesNear(Location currentLocation)
        {
            _map.Set(currentLocation);

            foreach (PlaceOfInterest place in _placesOfInterestDictionary.Places())
            {
                if (_map.CurrentLocationIsNear(place))
                {
                    _map.Add(place);
                }
            }

            return _map;
        }
    }
}
```

The `TouristInformationService` uses the constructor flavor of dependency injection to inject the `IMap` and `IPlacesOfInterestDictionary` into the service. The single method takes a `Location` as an argument and sets the current location on the map, then for each of the `PlacesOfInterest` a call is made to determine if the `PlaceOfInterest` is near to the current location. If it is, it is then added to the map and, finally, the map is returned.

After adding all of the preceding classes, you will have a solution that resembles Figure 5-3.

Figure 5-3

You've now got your loosely coupled, dependency-injected service — you have done a great job to ensure that you can easily maintain and extend the service and provide different implementations for the dependencies. However, you now find yourself in a bit of dilemma, as you need to start using this wonderful service that you have made, but "newing" up instances of it and its dependencies will leave you tightly coupled to those implementations, making it hard to maintain your code when requirements change or new options for an IMap or IPlacesOfInterestDictionary are built. Hmmm, what's a developer to do?

Before you learn about the frameworks that have been designed to solve such a problem, it's first important to fully understand the problem and see why other options just aren't up to scratch.

To use the TouristInformationService in your client code, you need to create a valid IMap and IPlacesOfInterestDictionary instance to inject into it. Let's first look at the most simplest way you can create a valid TouristInformationService with the required combination of dependencies.

Create a new class in the ProEnt.Chap5.Tests project, named ManualWireUpTest, with the following code definition, then build your solution and run the test to ensure that it passes. Again, if you are unsure of how to set up NUnit, please refer to the previous chapter.

```
using ProEnt.Chap5.Model;
using ProEnt.Chap5.Model.Maps;
using ProEnt.Chap5.Model.PlacesOfInterest;
```

```
using NUnit.Framework;

namespace ProEnt.Chap5.Tests
{
    [TestFixture]
    public class ManualWireUpTest
    {
        [Test]
        public void Can_Manually_Create_A_Valid_TouristInformationService()
        {
            TouristInformationService touristInformationService;
            IMap map = new SatelliteMap();
            IPlacesOfInterestDictionary placesOfInterestDictionary =
                                new EnglishPlacesOfInterestDictionary();

            touristInformationService =
                new TouristInformationService(map, placesOfInterestDictionary);

            Assert.IsInstanceOfType(
                typeof(TouristInformationService), touristInformationService);
        }
    }
}
```

You have no doubt seen thousands of lines of code like this before. A service is needed in the client, so the client just creates it and creates its dependencies. The problem with this is that all the hard work you have done in keeping the service module loosely coupled, testable, and easily maintainable has been undone in four lines of code. By having the client code do all the dirty work of creating the concrete implementations, you have simply moved the problem of tying yourself to an implementation up the code chain. You now have all of the same problems that were identified in Chapter 3:

❑   If the implementations of `SatelliteMap` or `EnglishPlacesOfInterestDictionary` change, your code will break.

❑   If you need to swap the `SatelliteMap` and `EnglishPlacesOfInterestDictionary` for different implementations, you are going to have to modify all instances in your client code where you create a `TouristInformationService`.

In a nutshell, your client code has to know far too much about the construction of not only `TouristInformationService` but of both its dependencies, and this will make your code brittle and highly likely to break if a change to any one of those three classes is needed.

Let's have a looked at a graphical representation of what is going on here, in Figure 5-4.

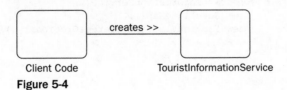

Figure 5-4

You can see in the diagram that the client code is responsible for creating `TouristInformationService` and the dependencies it requires. This results in the client code becoming tightly coupled to the `TouristInformationService` implementation. One way to remove the responsibility for creating the service from your client code is by employing the Gang of Four Factory design pattern.

Factory Pattern

The Factory pattern is a creation design pattern, whose sole purpose is to deal with the problem of creating objects, while hiding any complexities such as creating and wiring up dependant objects — sounds like exactly what we are after! The `Factory` class is a standalone class, typically with static methods that provide ready-made valid instances — this is sounding better and better. Figure 5-5 shows a graphical representation of the way the client code interacts with the `Factory` class to obtain the `TouristInformationService`.

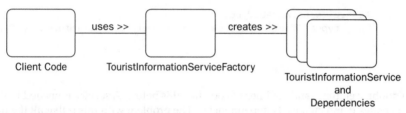

Figure 5-5

Now that you know what the Factory pattern is and how it can help, let's see how you can use it to solve the problem of creating a `TouristInformationService` without jeopardizing your commitment to keeping your modules loosely coupled.

Create a new class in the root of the `ProEnt.Chap5.Model` project, named `TouristInformationServiceFactory`, with the following code:

```
using ProEnt.Chap5.Model.Maps;
using ProEnt.Chap5.Model.PlacesOfInterest;

namespace ProEnt.Chap5.Model
{
    public static class TouristInformationServiceFactory
    {
        public static TouristInformationService
                        GetTouristServiceSatelliteMapEnglish()
        {
            return new TouristInformationService(
                new SatelliteMap(),
                new EnglishPlacesOfInterestDictionary());
        }
    }
}
```

The `TouristInformationServiceFactory` has one static method, called `GetTouristServiceSatelliteMapEnglish`. The method will create a `TouristInformationService` and create and build the required dependences, all unknown to the client code.

It is now very simple for the client code to obtain an instance of `TouristInformationService`. To demonstrate this, create a new class in the `ProEnt.Chap5.Tests` project, named `FactoryPatternTests`, with the following code definition, then build and run the test to ensure that the `Factory` is creating a valid instance of `TouristInformationService`.

```
using ProEnt.Chap5.Model;
using NUnit.Framework;

namespace ProEnt.Chap5.Tests
{
    [TestFixture]
    public class FactoryPatternTests
    {
        [Test]
         public void
              Prequalification_Factory_Should_Create_A_Valid_
TouristInformationService()
        {
            TouristInformationService touristInformationService;
            touristInformationService =
              TouristInformationServiceFactory
            .GetTouristServiceSatelliteMapEnglish();

            Assert.IsInstanceOfType(typeof(TouristInformationService),
                              touristInformationService);
        }
    }
}
```

By using a Factory class the client code no longer requires the knowledge of how to create a valid `TouristInformationService`. Also, the code to create a `TouristInformationService` is now centralized and all client code can use the factory, thus making it trivial to update if the `TouristInformationService` is ever modified. Utilizing the `Factory` class has completely abstracted away the responsibility of creating the `TouristInformationService` and, thus, decoupled the client code from the service implementation.

At this stage, you may be thinking that a `Factory` class is the solution to the problem of where and how a service is created. However, things are not always as they seem. The problem with the Factory pattern becomes apparent as you start to add more variants to the dependants when creating a `TouristInformationService`.

Create a new class in the `ProEnt.Chap5.Model` project `PlacesOfInterest` folder, named `GermanPlacesOfInterestDictionary`, that implements the `IPlacesOfInterestDictionary` interface:

```
namespace ProEnt.Chap5.Model.PlacesOfInterest
{
    public class GermanPlacesOfInterestDictionary : IPlacesOfInterestDictionary
    {
        public IList<PlaceOfInterest> Places()
        {
            return new List<PlaceOfInterest>();
        }
    }
}
```

You now need to update the `TouristInformationServiceFactory` class to include a new method that takes into account the new implementation of an `IMap`:

```
using ProEnt.Chap5.Model.Maps;
using ProEnt.Chap5.Model.PlacesOfInterest;

namespace ProEnt.Chap5.Model
{
    public static class TouristInformationServiceFactory
    {
        public static TouristInformationService
                    GetTouristServiceSatelliteMapEnglish()
        {
            return new TouristInformationService(
                    new SatelliteMap(),
                    new EnglishPlacesOfInterestDictionary());
        }

        public static TouristInformationService
                    GetTouristServiceSatelliteMapGerman()
        {
            return new TouristInformationService(
                    new SatelliteMap(),
                    new GermanPlacesOfInterestDictionary());
        }
    }
}
```

Again, if you were to add a couple of different `IMap` classes, such as a `RoadMap` and a `NonGraphicalMap`, to the `Maps` folder in the `ProEnt.Chap5.Model` project, the factory would need another four methods:

```
    public static class TouristInformationServiceFactory
    {
        public static
                TouristInformationService GetTouristServiceSatelliteMapEnglish()
        {
            return new TouristInformationService(new SatelliteMap();
```

```
                                   new EnglishPlacesOfInterestDictionary());
    }

        public static TouristInformationService
                GetTouristServiceSatelliteMapGerman()
        {
            return new TouristInformationService(new SatelliteMap(),
                    new GermanPlacesOfInterestDictionary());
        }

        public static TouristInformationService GetTouristServiceRoadMapEnglish()
        {
            return new TouristInformationService(new RoadMap(),
                    new EnglishPlacesOfInterestDictionary());
        }

        public static TouristInformationService GetTouristServiceRoadMapGerman()
        {
            return new TouristInformationService(new RoadMap(),
                    new GermanPlacesOfInterestDictionary());
        }

        public static TouristInformationService
                GetTouristServiceNonGraphicalMapEnglish()
        {
            return new TouristInformationService(new NonGraphicalMap(),
                    new EnglishPlacesOfInterestDictionary());
        }

        public static TouristInformationService
                GetTouristServiceNonGraphicalMapGerman()
        {
            return new TouristInformationService(new NonGraphicalMap(),
                    new GermanPlacesOfInterestDictionary());
        }
    }
```

Clearly, the more dependencies you have, the more methods you will end up with, as you will require a Factory method for each `TouristInformationService` variation, which is not ideal. That's not the only problem with the `Factory` pattern, as it suffers from the same issues as constructing the service by hand. If you take a closer look at the figure depicting the relationship between the client code and the Factory class, you will see that the client code is still tightly coupled to a specific implementation of the `TouristInformationService` even though the complexities of creating the dependency objects have been removed.

You need something a lot more flexible and generic. You need something that will locate the `TouristInformationService` on behalf of the client code. Enter the Service Locator pattern.

Service Locator

The role of the Service Locator is to act as a central service repository with a simple interface that knows how to get hold of any service required by the application. A Service Locator provides methods to register services and usually takes a literal name value of a service or an object type to resolve them.

Think of a Service Locator as a kind of beefed up factory. Instead of having a mass of different factory methods for variants of your service, you have a single `Resolve` method that will allow you to obtain any service for a given key.

Like the Factory pattern the Service Locator pattern hides the complexities of wiring up a service with its required dependant objects, except that the service locator can be reused in many applications and is a lot more abstract than the Factory design pattern.

Take a look at a graphical representation of the Service Locator pattern in Figure 5-6 before we check out some code.

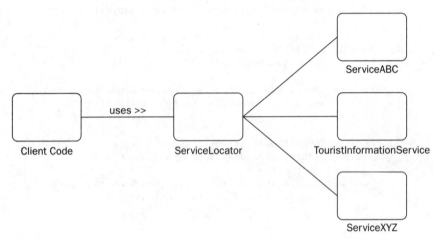

Figure 5-6

On first glance, the Service Locator pattern seems very similar to the Factory pattern, but if you take a look at code, you can see that the client is passing a key to the Service Locator, which then looks up and returns the required service fully constructed with all dependencies supplied. with all the necessary dependencies. There's no need to add this code to any of your classes, but the code snippet below shows a client using the Service Locator to obtain an instance of the `TouristInformationService` class in English using a `SatelliteMap`.

```
TouristInformationService touristInformationService;
TouristInformationService =
    serviceLocator.Locate<TouristInformationService>(
                          "TouristServiceSatelliteMapEnglish");
```

For completeness, you can add a very simple example of a Service Locator to the `ProEnt.Chap5`
`.Infrastructure` project with the following definition:

```
namespace ProEnt.Chap5.Infrastructure
{
    /// <summary>
    /// Basic implementation of a service locator
    /// </summary>
    public class ServiceLocator
    {
        private IDictionary<string, Object> registeredTypes =
                                    new Dictionary<string, Object>();

        public void Register<T>(string ServiceName, T obj)
        {
            registeredTypes.Add(ServiceName, obj);
        }

        public T Locate<T>(string ServiceName)
        {
            return (T)registeredTypes[ServiceName];
        }

    }
}
```

This can then be used in a test, which verifies its behavior. Create a new class in the `ProEnt.Chap5.Tests`
project, named `ServiceLocatorPatternTest`, then build your solution and verify that the test passes.

```
using ProEnt.Chap5.Model;
using ProEnt.Chap5.Model.Maps;
using ProEnt.Chap5.Model.PlacesOfInterest;
using ProEnt.Chap5.Infrastructure;
using NUnit.Framework;

namespace ProEnt.Chap5.Tests
{
    [TestFixture]
    public class ServiceLocatorPatternTest
    {
        [Test]
        public void
Prequalification_Service_Locator_Should_Create_A_Valid_TouristInformationService()
        {
            ServiceLocator serviceLocator = new ServiceLocator();

            serviceLocator.Register("TouristServiceSatelliteMapEnglish",
                            new TouristInformationService(
                            new SatelliteMap(),
                            new EnglishPlacesOfInterestDictionary()));

            TouristInformationService touristInformationService;
            touristInformationService =
```

```
serviceLocator.Locate<TouristInformationService>(
                        "TouristServiceSatelliteMapEnglish");

        Assert.IsInstanceOfType(typeof(TouristInformationService),
                                    touristInformationService);
        }
    }
}
```

Typically, the code to register the service would reside in a startup class, ideally in the `global.asax` file of a web application or the main module of a Windows Forms application.

The Service Locator is a far easier model to work with and does not need lots of explicitly named methods to provide implementations of the `TouristInformationService`.

As great as the Service Locator is, it still has issues similar to those of the Factory pattern. The client code is just supplying a string describing which implementation of a `TouristInformationService` is required instead of calling a method on a `Factory` class, so it's just as tightly coupled to a specific implementation as before. That said, the Service Locator does go some way toward providing a workable solution. The problem, however, still exists, as the client code is still responsible in the end for obtaining the service. Let's turn this problem inside out, or invert it, if you will.

Inversion of Control and IoC Containers

All the options you have looked you have looked at so far have one thing in common and that is the fact that the client code is responsible for obtaining or fetching a service and all its dependencies. The Factory and Service Locator patterns remove the need to know how to construct the service but still place the burden on the client code to specify which service implementation is required. What an IoC (Inversion of Control) Container does is to completely invert this relationship by injecting the service into the client, thus pushing rather than pulling, if you will. The term *Inversion of Control* describes the act of the client relinquishing control to the IoC Container, that is the Inversion of Control from client to container. There is another name for this pattern, which is a lot more descriptive, and is known as the Hollywood principle: "Don't call us, we'll call you." Essentially, Inversion of Control is all about taking the traditional flow of control — the client code creating the service, and inverting it — using the IoC Container to inject the service into the client code.

By using an IoC Container, the client code can simply depend on an interface or abstract class and not have a care in the world as to what is providing it with the concrete implementation at runtime. Let's have a look at how the graphical representation of the IoC Container, shown in Figure 5-7, differs from those of the Factory and Service Locator patterns.

TouristInformationService

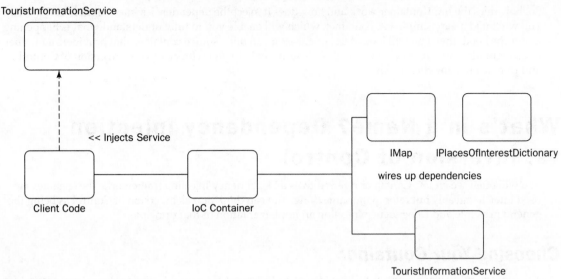

<< Injects Service

Client Code

IoC Container

IMap   IPlacesOfInterestDictionary

wires up dependencies

TouristInformationService

Figure 5-7

As you can see in the diagram, the client code has no influence on the type of
TouristInformationService that is constructed. The IoC container takes the burden from the client
code and performs this task of construction and injecting the dependencies. The IoC Container has
completely inverted the relationship between the client code and the TouristInformationService.

Let's take a look at how the client code would use an IoC Container to obtain a
TouristInformationService. There's no need to add this code to any of your classes.

```
TouristInformationService touristInformationService =
        (TouristInformationService) simpleIoCContainer.
                        GetInstance<TouristInformationService>();
```

What's happening here is the client code is asking the container to provide an instance of the
TouristInformationService, similar to the way in which the Service Locator worked, but the crucial
difference in this example is that the client code is not telling the container how it wants the
TouristInformationService constructed. It is the job of the container to inject the correct
dependencies into the TouristInformationService and return it to the client code.
All of this results in the client code no longer being tied to a specific implementation of
the TouristInformationService. It simply instructs the container to inject the
TouristInformationService along with its dependencies into the code at runtime. All the knowledge
of how to create a TouristInformationService is now handled by the container and knowing which
exact implementation will be used is no longer of any concern of the client code. This subtle difference
means that the client code is completely decoupled from any concrete implementation in regard to how
the TouristInformationService is constructed, resulting in a very loosely coupled design that is very
easy to test.

So, how does the IoC Container work and how does it inject the dependencies into the client code? Next, you will build a very simple IoC container, which will enable you to fully understand what is happening under the hood, then you will look at StructureMap, an open source container that providers a number of configuration options and some powerful features to help you with all of your Inversion of Control and Dependency Injection needs.

What's in a Name? Dependency Injection vs. Inversion of Control

You will often see an IoC Container referred to as a Dependency Injection framework. These names are used interchangeably but refer to the same thing. You can think of it as Inversion of Control as being the general principle and Dependency Injection an implementation of that principle.

Choosing Your Container

The concept of Inversion Control and the idea of an Inversion of Control Container have been around for a while. Many frameworks have been built, but to understand the concepts fully you will start by building your own IoC Container, before looking at some enterprise level IoC Container frameworks that you can use in your applications.

Build Your Own Lightweight IoC Container

In its most basic sense an IoC Container is simply a dictionary of types and implementations. Typically, as with the Service Locator during application startup, you would register all of the services in your IoC Container, then throughout your application you can obtain them from the container.

As an IoC Container is not strictly part of the domain of the mortgage application; it makes sense to keep it separate, so create a new class in ProEnt.Chap5.Infrastructure, named SimpleIoCContainer, with the following class definition:

```
namespace ProEnt.Chap5.Infrastructure
{
    public class SimpleIoCContainer
    {
        private IDictionary<Type, Object> objectsRegistered =
                                    new Dictionary<Type, Object>();

        public void Add<T>(T Instance)
        {
            objectsRegistered.Add(typeof(T), Instance);
        }

        public T GetInstance<T>()
        {
            return (T)objectsRegistered[typeof(T)];
        }
    }
}
```

The `SimpleIoCContainer` has only two methods, one to add a new instance and a second to retrieve it. Internally, the class is storing each service using a dictionary with the type of object and the key, and the object itself as the value. The next thing to do is to see if the simple IoC Container works.

Add a new class to the `ProEnt.Chap5.Tests` project, named `SimpleIoCContainerTests`, with the following definition:

```
using ProEnt.Chap5.Model;
using ProEnt.Chap5.Model.Maps;
using ProEnt.Chap5.Model.PlacesOfInterest;
using ProEnt.Chap5.Infrastructure;
using NUnit.Framework;

namespace ProEnt.Chap5.Tests
{
    [TestFixture]
    public class SimpleIoCContainerTests
    {
        [Test]
        public void SimpleIoCContainer_Can_Create_An_Instance_Of_SatelliteMap()
        {
            // Register Type in IoC Container
            SimpleIoCContainer simpleIoCContainer;
            simpleIoCContainer = new SimpleIoCContainer();
            simpleIoCContainer.Add<IMap>(new SatelliteMap());

            // Let the container inject the map into the client code
            IMap map = (IMap)simpleIoCContainer.GetInstance<IMap>();

            // Verify that it's the type of Map you were expecting
            Assert.IsNotNull(map);
            Assert.IsInstanceOfType(typeof(SatelliteMap), map);
        }
    }
}
```

The `SimpleIoCContainer_Can_Create_An_Instance_Of_SatelliteMap()` method creates an instance of `SimpleIoCContainer` and adds an instance of the `SatelliteMap` specified with the `IMap` type. As mentioned before, this code would typically be placed in some kind of bootstrapper code that ran when your application started. After the `SatelliteMap` is added, you check to see if it can be retrieved. Note that you are not specifying the concrete type of `IMap`. You are using the interface only and letting the container work out which concrete type to return. You can write a similar method for the `EnglishPlacesOfInterestDictionary`:

```
using NUnit.Framework;
using ProEnt.Chap5.Model;
using ProEnt.Chap5.Model.Maps;
using ProEnt.Chap5.Infrastructure;
using ProEnt.Chap5.Model.PlacesOfInterest;

namespace ProEnt.Chap5.Tests
```

```
{
    [TestFixture]
    public class SimpleIoCContainerTests
    {
        SimpleIoCContainer simpleIoCContainer;

        [SetUp]
        public void SetUp()
        {
            // Register Types in IoC Container
            simpleIoCContainer = new SimpleIoCContainer();

            simpleIoCContainer.Add<IMap>(new SatelliteMap());
            simpleIoCContainer.Add<IPlacesOfInterestDictionary>(
                            new EnglishPlacesOfInterestDictionary());
        }

        [Test]
        public void SimpleIoCContainer_Can_Create_An_Instance_Of_SatelliteMap()
        {
            IMap map = (IMap)simpleIoCContainer.GetInstance<IMap>();

            Assert.IsNotNull(map);
            Assert.IsInstanceOfType(typeof(SatelliteMap), map);
        }

        [Test]
        public void
SimpleIoCContainer_Can_Create_An_Instance_Of_EnglishPlacesOfInterestDictionary()
        {
            IPlacesOfInterestDictionary placeOfInterest =
                    (IPlacesOfInterestDictionary)simpleIoCContainer.
                    GetInstance<IPlacesOfInterestDictionary>();

            Assert.IsNotNull(placeOfInterest);
            Assert.IsInstanceOfType(typeof(EnglishPlacesOfInterestDictionary),
                            placeOfInterest);
        }
    }
}
```

As the `SimpleIoCContainer_Can_Create_An_Instance_Of_EnglishPlacesOfInterestDictionary()` method is very similar to the `SimpleIoCContainer_Can_Create_An_Instance_Of_SatelliteMap()` method, you can extract the method of registering the concrete types into the NUnit setup method, which will be run before every test is run. You can run the tests and everything should pass. The last test you need to perform is the test to ensure that you can get an instance of the `TouristInformationService`. Amend the code in the `SimpleIoCContainerTests` class to the following:

```
namespace ProEnt.Chap5.Tests
{
    [TestFixture]
    public class SimpleIoCContainerTests
```

```
    {
        SimpleIoCContainer simpleIoCContainer;

        [SetUp]
        public void SetUp()
        {
            // Register Types in IoC Container
            simpleIoCContainer = new SimpleIoCContainer();

            simpleIoCContainer.Add<IMap>(new SatelliteMap());
            simpleIoCContainer.Add<IPlacesOfInterestDictionary>(
                                new EnglishPlacesOfInterestDictionary());
            simpleIoCContainer.Add<TouristInformationService>
                (new TouristInformationService(
                            new SatelliteMap(),
                            new EnglishPlacesOfInterestDictionary()));
        }

        [Test]
        ...

        [Test]
        public void
        SimpleIoCContainer_Can_Create_An_Intance_Of_A_
TouristInformationService()
        {
            TouristInformationService touristInformationService =
                    (TouristInformationService)
                    simpleIoCContainer.GetInstance<TouristInformationService>();

            Assert.IsNotNull(touristInformationService);
            Assert.IsInstanceOfType(typeof(TouristInformationService),
                                        touristInformationService);
        }
    }
}
```

As in the other two tests, you are again registering the concrete type, in this instance, the TouristInformationService in the setup method, and then testing that is can be successfully retrieved in the test. The annoying thing is that you have already registered both of the dependencies required to create a valid TouristInformationService already, so shouldn't the container be clever enough to inspect the type you are trying to obtain an instance for and inject the dependences for you? This process is known as auto-wiring and can be added to your simple IoC Container with a bit more code; the problem is that spending all of your development time on infrastructure concerns does not get your application built any quicker.

Don't worry, though, you don't need to spend your valuable time writing your own IoC Container; some other clever fellows have done all the hard work for you. There are a host of options when it comes to choosing an IoC Container, but you will look in detail at an open source product called StructureMap before having a quick read on the other options out there for all your IoC needs.

StructureMap

From the definition on the StructureMap home page, `http://structuremap.sourceforge.net/`:

> StructureMap is a Dependency Injection / Inversion of Control tool for .Net [sic] that can be used to improve the architectural qualities of an object oriented system by reducing the mechanical costs of good design techniques. StructureMap can enable looser coupling between classes and their dependencies, improve the testability of a class structure, and provide generic flexibility mechanisms. Used judiciously, StructureMap can greatly enhance the opportunities for code reuse by minimizing direct coupling between classes and configuration mechanisms.

To get started with StructureMap, the first thing you will need to do is download the framework and add it to your solution.

1. Navigate to `http://sourceforge.net/projects/structuremap` and download the latest version of StructureMap. Once the compressed file has downloaded, unzip it, extract all files, then copy the `StructureMap.dll` to the `Lib` folder in the root of the `ProEnt.Chap5` solution by navigating to it via Windows Explorer.

2. From within the `ProEnt.Chap5` solution, right-click on the `Lib` solution folder and select Add Existing and add the `StructureMap.dll`.

3. Finally, add a reference to `StructureMap.dll` to the `ProEnt.Chap5.Tests` project. Your solution should now resemble Figure 5-8.

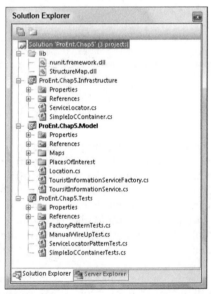

Figure 5-8

Wire Up Using the Fluent Interface

There are a number of ways you can configure and use StructureMap, the first of which is the fluent interface. Add a new class to the ProEnt.Chap5.Tests project, named StructureMap_FluentTests. For the StructureMap container, you are going to write the same tests you wrote for the IoC Container you created. With that in mind, enter the following for the class definition:

```
using ProEnt.Chap5.Model;
using ProEnt.Chap5.Model.Maps;
using ProEnt.Chap5.Model.PlacesOfInterest;
using NUnit.Framework;
using StructureMap;
using StructureMap.Configuration.DSL;

namespace ProEnt.Chap5.Tests
{
    [TestFixture]
    public class StructureMap_FluentTests
    {
        [SetUp]
        public void SetUp()
        {
// TODO: Register the types...

        }

        [Test]
        public void StructureMap_Can_Create_A_Valid_SatelliteMap()
        {
// TODO...
        }

        [Test]
        public void
          StructureMap_Can_Create_An_Instance_Of_EnglishPlacesOfInterestDictionary()
        {
// TODO...
        }

        [Test]
        public void StructureMap_Can_Create_A_Valid_TouristInformationService()
        {
// TODO...
        }
    }
}
```

The first thing you need to do is register all of the concrete types, just as you did for the simple IoC Container you wrote earlier. StructureMap has a special class called Registry. You can inherit from this class and use it to initialize all of your chosen concrete types. Create a new class within the test class, named TouristInformationRegistry.

```
namespace ProEnt.Chap5.Tests
{
    [TestFixture]
    public class StructureMap_FluentTests
    {
        ...
    }

    public class TouristInformationRegistry : Registry
    {
        public TouristInformationRegistry()
        {
            ForRequestedType<IMap>().TheDefaultIsConcreteType<SatelliteMap>();

            ForRequestedType<IPlacesOfInterestDictionary>()
                .TheDefaultIsConcreteType<EnglishPlacesOfInterestDictionary>();
        }
    }
}
```

The `TouristInformationRegistry` class is simply setting up the concrete implementations to return when a specific type if asked for. This is very similar to the way your `SimpleIoCContainer` worked. Before you write a test for this, you need to ensure that StructureMap uses this registry when you tell it to `Initialize`. This is achieved by amending the `SetUp` method with the following code:

```
[SetUp]
    public void SetUp()
    {
        // Initialize the registry
        ObjectFactory.Initialize(x =>
        {
            x.AddRegistry<TouristInformationRegistry>();

        });
    }
```

You can now add the code for the `StructureMap_Should_Create_A_Valid_SatelliteMap()` and `StructureMap_Can_Create_An_Instance_Of_EnglishPlacesOfInterestDictionary()` methods to test the StructureMap framework:

```
[Test]
    public void StructureMap_Can_Create_A_Valid_SatelliteMap()
    {
        IMap map = (IMap)ObjectFactory.GetInstance<IMap>();

        Assert.IsNotNull(map);
        Assert.IsInstanceOfType(typeof(SatelliteMap), map);
    }

    [Test]
    public void
        StructureMap_Can_Create_An_Instance_Of_EnglishPlacesOfInterestDictionary()
```

```
{
        IPlacesOfInterestDictionary placesOfInterestDictionary =
                (IPlacesOfInterestDictionary)ObjectFactory
                        .GetInstance<IPlacesOfInterestDictionary>();

        Assert.IsNotNull(placesOfInterestDictionary);
        Assert.IsInstanceOfType(typeof(EnglishPlacesOfInterestDictionary),
                        placesOfInterestDictionary);
}
```

If you run the tests, you will find that they pass and StructureMap does what it's supposed to do. Now on to the next test which, if you remember from your `SimpleIoCContainer`, was to create the `TouristInformationService`. Now because StructureMap is a little more advanced than our simple effort it has the ability to auto-wire-up the dependencies for the `TouristInformationService` based on the types that have already been registered. To prove that this is what happens, add this code for the final test:

```
[Test]
public void StructureMap_Can_Create_A_Valid_TouristInformationService()
{
        TouristInformationService touristInformationService =
                (TouristInformationService)ObjectFactory
                        .GetInstance(typeof(TouristInformationService));

        Assert.IsNotNull(touristInformationService);
        Assert.IsInstanceOfType(typeof(TouristInformationService),
                        touristInformationService);
}
```

When you compile and run the test, it passes even though you didn't even explicitly register the `TouristInformationService`. This happens because StructureMap auto-wires the dependencies based on what it already has in its container. Having StructureMap, or any other IoC container, auto-wire your dependencies is where you get the maxim benefit from using a container.

Wire Up Using Attributes — the Plugin Family

A second way to configure your objects to be used by StructureMap is to decorate them with attributes and have StructureMap scan your assembly to add it to its container.

Create a new class in the `ProEnt.Chap5.Tests` project, named `StructureMap_AttributeTests`. This will contain the same tests as the previous class.

```
using ProEnt.Chap5.Model;
using ProEnt.Chap5.Model.Maps;
using ProEnt.Chap5.Model.PlacesOfInterest;
using NUnit.Framework;
using StructureMap;
using StructureMap.Configuration.DSL;

namespace ProEnt.Chap5.Tests
```

```
    {
        [TestFixture]
        public class StructureMap_AttributeTests
        {
            [SetUp]
            public void SetUp()
            {
                // TODO....
            }


            [Test]
            public void StructureMap_Can_Create_A_Valid_SatelliteMap()
            {
                IMap map = (IMap)ObjectFactory.GetInstance<IMap>();

                Assert.IsNotNull(map);
                Assert.IsInstanceOfType(typeof(SatelliteMap), map);
            }

            [Test]
            public void
               StructureMap_Can_Create_An_Instance_Of_EnglishPlacesOfInterestDictionary()
            {
                IPlacesOfInterestDictionary placesOfInterestDictionary =
                    (IPlacesOfInterestDictionary)ObjectFactory
                        .GetInstance<IPlacesOfInterestDictionary>();

                Assert.IsNotNull(placesOfInterestDictionary);
                Assert.IsInstanceOfType(typeof(EnglishPlacesOfInterestDictionary),
                                        placesOfInterestDictionary);
            }

            [Test]
            public void StructureMap_Can_Create_A_Valid_TouristInformationService()
            {
                TouristInformationService touristInformationService =
                        (TouristInformationService)ObjectFactory
                            .GetInstance(typeof(TouristInformationService));

                Assert.IsNotNull(touristInformationService);
                Assert.IsInstanceOfType(typeof(TouristInformationService),
                                        touristInformationService);
            }
        }
    }
```

Before you can test, you need to decorate each of the dependencies with attributes that will allow StructureMap to identify which implementation you wish to use.

1. Open the `ProEnt.Chap5.Model` project, and add a reference to `StructureMap.dll`.

2. Open the `IMap` interface, and add a `using` statement to import the Structure Map namespace and decorate the class in the following manner:

```
using ProEnt.Chap5.Model.PlacesOfInterest;
using StructureMap;

namespace ProEnt.Chap5.Model.Maps
{
    [PluginFamily("Default")]
    public interface IMap
    {
        void Set(Location currentLocation);
        void Add(PlaceOfInterest placeOfInterest);
        bool CurrentLocationIsNear(PlaceOfInterest placeOfInterest);
    }
}
```

3. Open the `SatelliteMap` class, add the using StructureMap statement, and decorate the class with the `Pluggable` attribute.

```
using ProEnt.Chap5.Model.PlacesOfInterest;
using StructureMap;

namespace ProEnt.Chap5.Model.Maps
{
    [Pluggable("Default")]
    public class SatelliteMap : IMap
    {
        public void Set(Location currentLocation)
        {  }

        public void Add(PlaceOfInterest placeOfInterest)
        {  }

        public bool CurrentLocationIsNear(PlaceOfInterest placeOfInterest)
        {
            return true;
        }
    }
}
```

4. Open the `IPlacesOfInterestDictionary`, add the using statement to pull in the StructureMap namespace, and decorate the interface with the `PluginFamily` attribute.

```
using System.Collections.Generic;
using StructureMap;

namespace ProEnt.Chap5.Model.PlacesOfInterest
```

```
    {
        [PluginFamily("Default")]
        public interface IPlacesOfInterestDictionary
        {
            IList<PlaceOfInterest> Places();
        }
    }
```

5. Open the `EnglishPlacesOfInterestDictionary`, and add the `Pluggable` attribute to the class, along with the `using StructureMap` statement:

```
using System.Collections.Generic;
using StructureMap;

namespace ProEnt.Chap5.Model.PlacesOfInterest
{
        [Pluggable("Default")]
        public class EnglishPlacesOfInterestDictionary : IPlacesOfInterestDictionary
        {
            public IList<PlaceOfInterest> Places()
            {
                return new List<PlaceOfInterest>();
            }
        }
}
```

What you have done is mark both of the dependency interfaces (`IMap` and `IPlacesOfInterestDictionary`) with a `PluginFamily` attribute. This lets StructureMap know that it needs to register these types in a similar way to the way you manually registered the types using the fluent method. The `Pluggable` attribute registers concrete implementations with StructureMap which it will use when resolving services that require these dependencies.

Before you can start to test the container using the attribute configuration, you need to first instruct StructureMap to scan the assembly so that it can register the types before using them.

Add a new class within the `StructureMap_AttributeTests` class of the `ProEnt.Chap5.Tests` project named `TouristInformationScanningRegistry`:

```
namespace ProEnt.Chap5.Tests
{
    [TestFixture]
    public class StructureMap_AttributeTests
    {
        ...
    }

    public class TouristInformationScanningRegistry : Registry
    {
        public TouristInformationScanningRegistry()
        {
            Scan(x =>
```

```
        {
            x.Assembly("ProEnt.Chap5.Model");
        });

    }

}
}
```

This class, like the `Registry` in the fluent interface example, inherits from the StructureMap `Registry` class, but this time instead of manually registering types, you are instructing the container to scan the assembly to look for the classes decorated with the attributes and build the registered types from that. Just as before, you are required to initialize the container with the registry, so add the following code to the `SetUp` method:

```
[SetUp]
public void SetUp()
{
    ObjectFactory.Initialize(x =>
    {
        x.AddRegistry<TouristInformationScanningRegistry>();

    });
}
```

You can now run the tests, and StuctureMap will resolve the types to make the tests pass.

Wire Up Using Configuration Meta Data

The final way to configure StructureMap is by using a configuration file. In this example, you will use the default `StructureMap.Config` file, but if you wanted to, you could always stick the configuration into a the application or web configuration file.

We are going to demonstrate using StructureMap with a configuration file in the same way that we tested the previous two methods — by writing tests to confirm our expectations. So, the first thing to do is a add a new class to the `ProEnt.Chap5.Tests` project, named `StructureMap_ConfigurationFileTests`, with the following class: definition.

```
using ProEnt.Chap5.Model;
using ProEnt.Chap5.Model.Maps;
using ProEnt.Chap5.Model.PlacesOfInterest;
using NUnit.Framework;
using StructureMap;

namespace ProEnt.Chap5.Tests
{
    [TestFixture]
    public class StructureMap_ConfigurationFileTests
```

```
    {
        [SetUp]
        public void SetUp()
        {
            ObjectFactory.Initialize(x =>
            {
                x.PullConfigurationFromAppConfig = true;

            });
        }

        [Test]
        public void StructureMap_Can_Create_A_Valid_SatelliteMap()
        {
            IMap map = (IMap)ObjectFactory.GetInstance<IMap>();

            Assert.IsNotNull(map);
            Assert.IsInstanceOfType(typeof(SatelliteMap), map);
        }

        [Test]
        public void
         StructureMap_Can_Create_An_Instance_Of_EnglishPlacesOfInterestDictionary()
        {
            IPlacesOfInterestDictionary placeOfInterest =
                    (IPlacesOfInterestDictionary)ObjectFactory
                            .GetInstance<IPlacesOfInterestDictionary>();

            Assert.IsNotNull(placeOfInterest);
            Assert.IsInstanceOfType(typeof(EnglishPlacesOfInterestDictionary),
                            placeOfInterest);
        }

        [Test]
        public void StructureMap_Can_Create_A_Valid_TouristInformationService()
        {
            TouristInformationService touristInformationService =
                    (TouristInformationService)ObjectFactory
                            .GetInstance(typeof(TouristInformationService));

            Assert.IsNotNull(touristInformationService);
            Assert.IsInstanceOfType(typeof(TouristInformationService),
                            touristInformationService);
        }
    }
}
```

This class is very similar to the other two test classes with one difference, and it's in the setup method. Instead of having a registration class that is responsible for wiring up your dependencies, you are instead instructing StructureMap to look in a configuration file. So with that in mind, you had better create one. Add an `App.Config` file to the `ProEnt.Chap5.Tests` project with the following meta data:

```xml
<?xml version="1.0" encoding="utf-8" ?>
<configuration>
  <configSections><section name="StructureMap"
   type="StructureMap.Configuration.StructureMapConfigurationSection,StructureMap"/>
  </configSections>

    <StructureMap>


    </StructureMap>
</configuration>
```

Declaring the `StructureMap` section within the `configSections` will allow ASP.NET to handle StructureMap settings within the configuration file. To get the tests to pass, you must define which concrete types you want StuctureMap to inject into your `TouristInformationService`.

Add the following meta data between the `StructureMap` tags:

```xml
<StructureMap>

        <Assembly Name="ProEnt.Chap5.Model" />
        <Assembly Name="ProEnt.Chap5.Tests" />

        <PluginFamily Assembly="ProEnt.Chap5.Model"
                      Type="ProEnt.Chap5.Model.Maps.IMap" DefaultKey="Default">
            <Plugin Assembly="ProEnt.Chap5.Model"
                    Type="ProEnt.Chap5.Model.Maps.SatelliteMap"
                    ConcreteKey="Default"/>
        </PluginFamily>

        <PluginFamily Assembly="ProEnt.Chap5.Model"
            Type="ProEnt.Chap5.Model.PlacesOfInterest.IPlacesOfInterestDictionary"
            DefaultKey="Default">
        <Plugin
            Assembly="ProEnt.Chap5.Model"
            Type="ProEnt.Chap5.Model.PlacesOfInterest.EnglishPlacesOfInterestDictionary"
            ConcreteKey="Default"/>
        </PluginFamily>
</StructureMap>
```

What you are doing here is very similar to the pattern you followed when you added attributes to the interfaces and concrete implementations. As with the attribute option, the `PluginFamily` section defines which type StructureMap will be registered in the container. The `Plugin` section defines the concrete implementation that is required and is equivalent to the `Pluggable` attribute.

When you rebuild the `ProEntt.Chap5.Tests` project and run the tests, you will find that all of the tests that verify the configuration file settings pass.

To XML or Not to XML, That Is the Question

So with three ways to wire up your services in StructureMap, which is best? As with most things in software development, it depends. If you read the notes on the StructureMap site, the preferred method of configuration is using the fluent interface method of creating a Registry to initialize the container. However if you don't want your configuration data to be embedded in code, you can always opt for an XML configuration file. The attributes are deprecated and largely unnecessary now but still supported for backward compatibility. You can even use the three methods together, but you may not want to decorate all of your domain model with infrastructure attributes if you are trying to keep a clean line of separation.

Other IoC Frameworks

There are a number of IoC Containers available to the .NET developer. Here is a brief list of some of the most popular:

Windsor Container

The Castle Project is open source framework providing a set of tools for .NET development. Windsor Container is part of the Castle Project and is an IoC Container similar to StructureMap.

To find out more information, navigate to `www.castleproject.org/container/index.html`.

MS Unity

The Microsoft Patterns and Practices team is up to version 4.0 of the Enterprise Library, which is a framework comprising a collection of software application blocks all following best practice guidelines. It was created to provide a common toolset for developers working on enterprise development solutions. One of these application blocks is Unity, Microsoft's IoC Container, which, just like Castle Windsor and StuctureMap, can be configured from a variety of different sources.

To find out more navigate to `www.codeplex.com/entlib`.

Spring.Net

Spring.Net's IoC Container, Spring.Core is a port from the Java Spring application framework. It's part of a larger framework covering many topics similar to those of Microsoft's Enterprise Library framework. The only key difference with Spring.Net is that the set up only supports XML configuration, but don't let that put you off. The IoC Container is part of a large set of libraries.

Find out more at `www.springframework.net/`. Whichever IoC Container you choose to use, they all do the same job. Sure there are a few minor differences with initializing your container and retrieving objects, but these are largely syntactical, so the flavor of the IoC you opt for is purely personal.

Summary

In this chapter, you dealt with the issues that arise when client code or any other part of your system needs to use a service that has dependencies on other objects. The service module itself was designed in a loosely coupled fashion, ensuring that anything it needed was injected into it, avoiding tightly coupled code and the knowledge needed to construct dependencies. This means something else has to know how to create these dependencies and be responsible for constructing them and injecting them into the service.

You first looked at a very common way that client code obtains an instance of a service, namely constructing it and wiring up all the dependencies. This, of course, undoes all of the good work you did to ensure your code was loosely coupled. In identifying these issues with manual construction, you investigated two other methods used to create objects in a manner that hides all of the complexities involved in the creation of the services.

The methods you looked at to resolve the issue of tightly coupled code in the client were:

❑   Factory Method

❑   Service Locator

❑   Inversion of Control Container

The first method saw you employing the Factory design pattern. This pattern completely removes the responsibility from the client code and provides very simple methods to obtain a complex service. However, introducing the Factory pattern simply changed the type of object that the client code was coupled to. Now the client code had to know which method of the factory class it needed to call. So, in fact, the client was still responsible and very much tied to a concrete implementation.

After the shortcomings of the Factory pattern were exposed, you looked at another very popular pattern for creating services, namely the Service Locator pattern. The Service Locator pattern was a lot more flexible than the Factory pattern, allowing the client code to pass a literal string, which the locator would use to look up and return a service. This pattern appeared to be exactly what you were after, but on closer inspection it suffered from the same problems as the Factory pattern. The client code still had the responsibility for knowing what implementation of service it required, so the Service Locator was not much of an improvement on the factory pattern.

To resolve the issue of the client code being tightly coupled to a certain implementation, you inverted the relationship, and instead of the client code asking for the service, the service was injected into the client. This Inversion of Control was provided by an Inversion of Control Container. By using the IoC Container the knowledge of how to create the `TouristInformationService` was removed from the client code completely. This pattern also goes under another name — the Hollywood principle: "Don't call us, we'll call you." This refers to the fact the client code doesn't ask for a service; it's explicitly injected into it. Inversion of Control and the IoC Container solved the problem of ensuring your code is not tightly coupled when it comes time to actually instantiating and using services in the client.

In the next chapter, you will start to look at the how you can organize your front-end user interfaces and how this fits in with what you have learned so far about keeping your code modules loosely coupled and highly maintainable.

Part III: Enterprise Design Patterns

6

Getting to the Middle
of Things

We began our journey discussing the tenets and core values behind enterprise architecture. We then spent ample time exploring the base coding patterns and methodologies that help to achieve these goals, including loose coupling, Test Driven Development, Dependency Injection, and Inversion of Control. It's now time to focus back on the practical. In this third section of the book, we are going to spend some time exploring some of the popular design patterns commonly found in different enterprise systems. In this chapter, we will:

❑ Discuss the different conceptual tiers of design and their relevant roles in enterprise architecture

❑ Explore the history of middleware and how it has evolved in the enterprise world

❑ Review some of the popular design patterns implemented for enterprise middleware

❑ Explore a code sample using Windows Communication Foundation services.

On Middleware

The term *middleware* means different things to different people. For some, middleware is the code that powers an application. It can contain the logic for driving screen behaviors, database queries, simple validation, and message exchange. For others, it is the code that runs a website, including the HTML-generating pages and the web server that hosts the site. Some even think that middleware includes business logic within a relational database, such as stored procedures, functions, and triggers that join data and deliver to other consumers of the data. In fact at the time of this writing the Wikipedia definition for Middleware is notably simple:

Middleware is computer software that connects software components or applications.

In truth, middleware can be considered all of these things depending on your point of view. Older perceptions of middleware imply the creating application servers to handle web hosting and business logic. Other, newer, definitions apply an enterprise theme, relegating middleware to complex service-oriented tiers for system-to-system interoperability. The history of middleware development is somewhat muddled. As technology has changed over time, so too has our definition of middleware and the purpose it serves.

The Wild West

In the early days of computer programming, software architecture was simple. Most systems were written for mainframe environments, with a single, monolithic tier that processed incoming data, executed business rules, and served out user interfaces via terminal inputs. Enterprise concepts such as separation of concerns had little bearing as the internal application logic was naturally mixed together with the rest of the system code. Even the data was housed within the same codebase. This was fine for early programs, but as companies grew their systems to support a widening range of business needs, this inherent mixing of code became difficult to maintain. Often companies would separate applications into different mainframe systems, communicating electronically between mainframe computers for the purposes of simple synchronization.

This approach was a mixed bag for businesses. It allowed for a separation of logic and data; however, the sharing and synchronizing of data between the systems became as difficult to maintain as the nonseparated approach. A lack of communication standards also complicated matters. Systems attempting to exchange data with mainframes in other departments or even in other companies had to figure out each system's default byte format to be able to parse information effectively. The result of these hackneyed designs was sort of Wild West of software development, with each company adopting an every-man-for-himself attitude in order to get the job done quickly.

The need to completely separate data from the many different systems that consumed it became quickly apparent to all businesses. The mainframe world allowed for a very tight coupling of data with the core application code, more often than not mixing logic between these two conceptual layers. As other systems needed to consume the same data, the limitations of the architecture impeded development progress. Data was often modified and transformed by code that could only be executed within a working mainframe session, requiring a user to physically interact with the data in order to change it to its correct state. Much of this changed when the software industry began to migrate toward tiered architectures.

Tiered Designs

The first pervasive move toward tiered architecture was the client-server pattern. Client-server architecture began almost exclusively with an isolation of the database in its own shared layer. Some of this was realized during the mainframe era, resulting in the beginning versions of database systems. Some products were released for data-specific mainframe programming, such as PIC and Adabas; however, their uses were limited, as they supported limited querying on a flat data model. Various technological developments quickly put this model to rest. The rise of the relational database management system changed the way software developers thought of their data, and the way their data is stored and shared. Relational data models were better suited for sharing data as they allowed for data normalization.

> *Normalization is a systematic way of ensuring that a database structure is suitable for general-purpose querying and free of certain undesirable characteristics that could lead to a loss of data integrity.*

Likewise, relational database management systems came with tools and features that easily enabled developers to administer their data in a manner that was completely divorced from other applications. The database server quickly became the de facto server in the client-server model.

The evolution of the client also changed the way developers designed their systems. In a mainframe model, all application logic lived in a single physical and conceptual layer. User displays were delivered in thin terminals, which were little more than computer screens and keyboards hooked directly into the mainframe itself. Some terminals contained supporting code or stub applications to complement the mainframe programs with which they interacted; however these systems still relied on the mainframe logic for most of the interface behaviors. The user interface behavior was contained within the same system that handled the business logic and data code. The proliferation of the Windows platform throughout the business world had a major effect on this design. The PC became the ruling class of the software world, delivering a fully functional computer system to the desks of millions workers. System development moved away from the monolithic, centralized mainframe pattern and toward a distributed architecture. Applications became standalone executables that installed on individual PCs, connecting to a single centralized data tier across an internal network. The natural separation of business code from the data code was quickly realized, enabling systems to grow organically, and without the technical impedances inherent to monolithic mainframe architectures.

Of course, the client-server model had its disadvantages as well. As many readers may remember, distributed application code was difficult to maintain. As new versions of the system were released, developers and system administrators struggled to dispense with patches and updates to dozens, if not hundreds of clients at a time. Versions easily fell out of sync, leaving users confused and frustrated as applications on different PCs often behaved differently. Business code was difficult to lock down. As most companies couldn't predict the rate at which changes were required, patches and updates would double on each other. This made the process cumbersome to manage, and managers were frustrated with a seemingly inflexible system.

To alleviate issues pertaining to distribution many designers attempted to centralize logic within the database. Most client-server models during this period provided for a central database repository as a means to ensure that all applications were working with the most up-to-date information. As relational database management systems grew in functionality, they provided more objects and mechanisms to manipulate the data. Although these objects may not have been originally intended for complex logic, business rules inevitably made their way into them. Objects such as database functions and stored procedures became flush with rules for calculations, validation, even authorization. As a result, client applications began to grow thinner as they became increasingly dependent upon these centralized devices. Of course, with centralization came the unavoidable issues relating to the mixing of code. Similar to the mainframe problem, databases bogged down with business logic grew overly complex. Data that was once designed with reuse in mind became tightly coupled with the business logic. As the tight coupling increased, more and more processing was required by the database system to serve the consuming applications it supported. This awkward balance of shifting purpose and oscillating logic continued throughout most of the early to mid-1990s.

The Internet Age

The mid- to late 1990s marked the dramatic transition to Internet-powered software systems. Though the history of the Internet itself dates back to the late 1970s, it was the advent and growth of the World Wide Web that truly catalyzed the explosion of wide-networked communicative applications. Initially there were many different protocols by which information was exchanged, and myriad online services to support them. Yet the eventual shift towards hypertext and HTTP led to the remarkable proliferation of browser-based applications and corporate web sites. With that shift came the inevitable move toward *n*-tiered architectures.

N-tiered architectures build on the traditional client-server designs most companies had used previously. Taking advantage of the natural centralization provided by the web model, web architectures typically employed three physical layers: the presentation layer, the application server, and the database server. At first, the presentation layer was notably thin. It consisted of hypertext markup written in the form of HTML and rendered directly with a web browser. Browsers were equipped at this point to handle little more than static displays, such as tables, text, and images. In time, however, web browsers expanded their features to accommodate client scripting. Scripting allowed relatively simple logic to run in the browser, for purposes such as data entry validation and user interface behaviors. The combination of static HTML and scripting enabled developers to run almost all user interface logic within the browser code, facilitating a strong degree of separation from business logic.

The database server experienced the least amount of change. Most companies had enjoyed the centralization of their data within a single physical tier and had little reason to change that model when web applications became the design standard. Databases lived behind the veil of the application server and, therefore, well behind the Internet boundary. The presence of a presentation layer and an application server did allow for the removal of logic from the relational database management software itself, as new tiers were now available to house these awkwardly placed pieces of code. Databases were now free to focus on what they did best — maintain and serve data.

Perhaps the biggest change for system designers was the application server. Application servers were required to host the code that served the web pages that composed the presentation layer, as well as the code that responded to user input from said pages. The server typically consisted of a web server system, such as Apache, or Internet Information Services, which can be configured to accept requests and post responses to and from a number of installed web applications. The web applications themselves housed the business code that lived in between the data and the presentation layer. This code marks the first industry-wide shift toward standardized business rule separation and can be thought of as the first form of true middleware found pervasively in the corporate software world.

Web applications changed a great deal in form and design. For the first few years of the web, dating roughly from 1995 to 1999, most complex web systems were designed using a model known as Common Gateway Interface, or CGI. CGI was a standard protocol for interfacing external application software with a web server. A CGI system could work in tandem with an existing web server, but could also stand on its own as the server itself, accepting requests from client browsers and sending responses back to them. The internals of a CGI system were somewhat disjointed. Command-line utilities contained the logic pertinent to a request and were invoked through the CGI at runtime. This was generally considered a low-tech approach, as business rules were spread across a wide range of executable files. As each request came in, a new process was required to execute the intended command-line utility, using a lot of processing power per each user request. Since compiled executables were difficult to maintain, many early web developers depended on script files to run the server code. Script files written in languages such as Perl and UNIX shell scripts were powerful and easy to modify, but they required compilation at runtime. This amounted to more processing power being needed per request, making the user experience slower. The vast majority of CGI implementations provided for a single cgi-bin directory to house all of the application scripts and utilities. CGI was a popular model because of its standardization during the early web years.

The advent of application server software helped to simplify and unify the web application tier. Like CGI implementations, these systems were installed to receive browser requests and respond accordingly. However, in contrast to CGI, these models allowed for a more flexible web application model. Rather than forcing designers to create scripts in a single directory, these systems could be configured to work with various compiled frameworks better suited to coordinate business logic. The Apache web server defined and supported configurable modules ("mods") that extend the system's core functionality. These can range from server-side programming language support to different schemes of authentication. Other systems such as Microsoft's Internet Information Server, or IIS, can be configured to work with various web extensions, such as the native Internet Server Application Programming Interface (ISAPI). These sorts of models were well suited for business logic as they provided a framework that empowered developers to use a wide range of features within the operating system in a manner that was mostly divorced from the web communication pattern. Although these systems never enjoyed the standardization afforded to the CGI model, they were widely embraced and remain popular tools for website support currently.

The application server itself wasn't the proverbial agent of good software design, but rather an important stepping stone on the path to the middleware age. Application servers provided the flexibility to enhance and expand the frameworks that support the business code. These newer development frameworks proliferated at a surprising rate, and led to the development of advanced business applications. On the Windows platform, Microsoft created the Active Server Page model, or ASP, for developing intricate web applications using the programming model with which most Windows developers were already familiar. Exposing no more than five core objects for web-specific logic, ASP exposed simple hooks for invoking Component Object Model (COM) objects and ActiveX classes. Both COM and ActiveX were established programming frameworks that accommodated different popular Microsoft programming languages, such as Visual Basic, C, and C++, and integrated well with other deeper Windows frameworks, such as the Active Template Library (ATL) and Microsoft Foundation Classes (MFC) Likewise, on non-Windows platforms, frameworks such as the Java 2 Enterprise Edition provided classes such as Servlets and Java Server Pages, or JSP, that acted as a natural, logical separation of web-specific code while also enabling developers to leverage the entirety of the Java programming framework. Popular scripting models such as PHP1 have also grown to accommodate complex business logic. PHP is a scripting language originally intended for producing dynamic web pages and has since evolved into a command-line interface and a tool for non-web programming. Using both dynamic web pages and standalone scripts configured with Apache modules, PHP platforms provide low-cost solutions for web development. As these frameworks grew in popularity, so did the strongly tiered designs they supported.

The Enterprise Middleware Age

Since the growth of the web distributed models have become the de facto standard of the corporate software industry. *N*-tiered models allowed for the simple decoupling of layers both physically and conceptually. This is so because of the frameworks available that support their individual technical purposes, as well as because of the lower cost of hardware needed to house these systems. The web model took a firm architectural hold in the early 2000s. Even systems requiring or preferring the use of thick client installations shifted toward an application server to handle business rules external to the database. Yet as these distributed models grew, another technical dilemma surfaced: interoperability.

The world was smaller now, and systems were being developed with communications in mind. Systems were expected to transmit data between servers and PCs to perform even the simplest of business tasks. Businesses increased the number of applications they built to support business needs, which now needed to communicate with each other to share logic and services. Even the exchange of data had now complicated a bit as each application required a number of dedicated data servers for redundancy and high availability. Which server was the right one to use? How would a process running on server X know how to access logic from a class on server Y? The answer was the creation of enterprise middleware.

Enterprise middleware can be considered any model that handles the communication of computers between platforms and systems. The job of middleware software is to abstract the consuming systems so that they don't have to understand the technical particulars of the system they are calling. A Java-based system making a call into a service on a Windows server would do so through the use of a middleware server, which handles the translation between platforms in a manner that isolated one from the other. However, disparate operating systems weren't the only impediment that made interoperability so difficult. Varying architectures had a similar need for middleware. A system that used a web model for housing application logic would often need to invoke the services of a client application on a limited number of distributed machines. Likewise, client applications often had the need to call into an application server as a web request, even though no implicit web communication model was built into the software. The complexities of interoperability increased dramatically as systems began to depend on isolated servers for broad, comprehensive tasks, such as authentication and authorization. Authentication servers built on the Lightweight Directory Access Protocol, or LDAP model, became the standard for network security calls. As more systems began to rely on services from other systems, they also required iterative calls into LDAP servers. Taking this model a step further, increased data needs also lead to increased interoperability demands. Consuming applications in need of data from multiple systems began connecting to different relational database management systems at runtime. Each database had its own security roles and levels of authorization, requiring even more calls into security LDAP servers. Now, even a simple task might require communication between three, four, or even five different systems, each one using its own architecture and technical platforms.

Enterprise middleware evolved with the industry's communication needs. Early middleware models were somewhat rudimentary. Organizations in need of complex interoperability often attempted to design their own middleware, complete with a set of messages and protocols that were entirely of their own devising. Simple text-based patterns such as string delimiters were used in flat file exchanges to transmit data from one machine to another. The limitations of this approach were almost immediately apparent. As organizations attempted to share system services with other organizations, a considerable amount of work was required to translate the nonstandard message patterns. Even when the translation was in place, maintaining and updating these patterns was a cumbersome task.

The task of translation was moderately simplified with the emergence of Extensible Markup Language, or XML, as the primary means of message exchange. XML provided a language pattern for conveying message-based concepts common to all systems. XML's rich format allowed for the defining of data structure, especially pertaining to parent-child relationships inherent to data hierarchies. XML also provided a means for the defining of basic data types, such as integers, strings, and double-precision floats. XML documents such as the Document Type Definition (DTD) and XML Schema (XSD) quickly became the industry standard for defining types and applying simple validation to the fields each type supported. All of these patterns eased the pain of defining the system-to-system messages, but designers still needed to come up with their own message structures to match the requisite invocation signatures of the target services. There was no standard methodology for these messages, and there were no mechanisms in place to provide a well-known model to act as a roadmap for new consumers.

The emergence of web services helped to lower the interoperability curve. Web services were one of the first widely embraced machine-to-machine interactions over a network using non-platform-specific conveyances. They provide an open means of invoking methods on another system, most commonly known as a remote procedure call, or RPC. RPC models have been around for quite some time, with support from varying invocation frameworks such as XML-RPC, the Common Object Request Broker Architecture (CORBA), the Distributed Component Object Model (DCOM) and the Java platform's Remote Method Invocation (RMI) framework. RPC models can be either synchronous or asynchronous. However, the former has proven to be a more commonly embraced model than the latter. Web services provide a framework for synchronous remote procedure calls over a network and are a useful layer within an enterprise middleware system.

The architecture of a web service can be fairly complex; a full description of web service architecture lies outside of the scope of this book. However, some of the core principles behind them are important keys to understanding enterprise middleware as it has evolved. A true web service exposes a public endpoint often referred to as a web method. A web method uses basic HTTP communication standards for sending text-based data across a network in a format known as Simple Object Access Protocol, or SOAP. SOAP messages are written using XM, and expose two key elements: the envelope and the message body. The envelope contains critical metadata about the message being passed, while the body contained the data to be delivered to the service. Web services were also required to publish a service descriptor file, using a pattern known as Web Services Description Language, or WSDL. A WSDL file was served out with the public method, providing up-to-date information and instructions for calling the web method. To discover web services, various service broker models began to pop up, delivering a sort of online yellow pages for available web services. Overall, however, the SOAP model has remained consistent enough to provide organizations with a stable model for requesting and responding to networked service calls.

Web services helped the software industry realize a level of predictability otherwise unseen in the enterprise community. Since the web service model was both transparent and pervasive, tools began to surface to eliminate the need for developers to understand the service architecture itself. Since the XML was standardized, each development platform could implement features and utilities to automatically create the XML messages and corresponding files on the fly, without forcing the programmer to write a lot of markup to expose their methods.

Web services on the Windows platform have evolved along with some of the latest web services trends. With the initial release of ASP.NET in the .NET 1.0 Framework (2002) Microsoft provided a mechanism for defining and consuming web services on top of the ASP.NET model with relative ease. Readers with experience using ASP.NET are likely familiar with .asmx files. The .NET SDK came complete with a set of command-line utilities for interrogating online web services using the web standard published by the W3C. These utilities could be used to define web methods in an ASP.NET project, and expose them as public web services in a file known as an .asmx file. These files translated the web method requests and responses into SOAP-based messages and exposed a WSDL file for other downstream consumers. These same utilities could also be used by calling .NET clients to read the published WSDL file and generate a local proxy class through which web methods could be invoked. The generated proxy classes would translate incoming and outgoing messages to and from XML SOAP, eliminating the need for the consuming developer to write any XML messages.

ASP.NET web services were popular for small application data exchange but fell short of delivering an enterprise model for system-to-system interoperability. The tools provided were Microsoft-specific. While they worked well for communicating between Windows applications, there were various technical nuances that made communicating with a non-Windows platform difficult to accomplish. The SOAP messages used were not entirely standardized, leaving developers at a loss when choosing the right SOAP version for their calls. Moreover, the communication model was irregular. The .asmx web service model was built directly on top of the ASP.NET framework, coupling the web service model with the ASP.NET event lifecycle. This added runtime overhead and made maintenance efforts harder. Since then, Microsoft has released the Windows Communication Foundation, or WCF framework. WCF is a framework and API dedicated to all manner of machine-to-machine communication. Like Java and other popular development platforms, WCF aims to unify the communication stack for all Microsoft systems. This new communication model is far better suited for growing systems with changing communication needs and is ideal for building true enterprise middleware.

A WCF Web Service

WCF web services are still simple to build. They can be created and consumed using many of the same command line and IDE-integrated tools used for building similar ASP.NET web services. The difference with WCF utilities is that the services are always created with the same base components. WCF is an expansive subject with a lot of interesting features. A full study of it falls outside of the scope of this chapter. Still, it's important for readers to familiarize themselves with at least a handful of core WCF components. Readers interested in familiarizing themselves with WCF should start with this tutorial on the MSDN website: http://msdn.microsoft.com/en-us/library/ms734712.aspx.

All WCF applications define a *service contract*. A service contract defines the functionality offered by an available service to external callers, and describes to potential users how to communicate with the service. Service contracts are defined using WCF descriptors in a C# interface file. The Interface declaration is decorated with the WCF attribute [ServiceContract], indicating that the interface contains definitions that will be exposed in a WCF service. The Interface also contains descriptors for identifying which methods will be available for invocation by the contract. Each of these methods is decorated with the WCF attribute [OperationService], indicating that the method and its provided signature will be publicly, available for invocation through the service. A concrete class implementing the interface is then created, satisfying the terms of the service contract in the same manner the compiler forces it to satisfy all other interface methods. Other WCF attributes, such as [DataContract] and [DataMember] can be defined with the service contracts to convey a form of binding translation for complex types as well. Both the service contract operational contracts, as well as its concrete implementation, can reference these complex types directly, allowing the WCF engine to translate the type's internals to consuming entities.

WCF samples are extra components needed to host the concrete service and expose it through a well-known URI. However since we are focusing on web services in this section, we don't need to go there. Instead, let's jump right in with what we know so far and create a simple, synchronous WCF web service.

Open up Visual Studio .NET 2008 and create a new project in your C:\Projects directory. In the New Project dialog window, select WCF Service Application and name it ProEnt.Chap6.SimpleWebService, as shown in Figure 6-1.

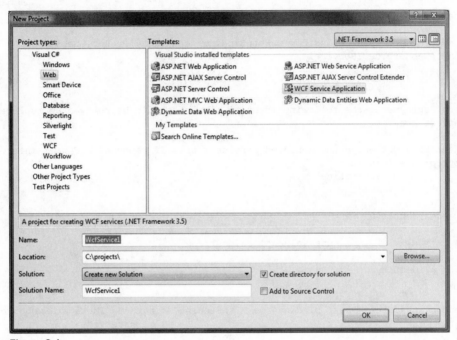

Figure 6-1

The project template provides a lot of the basic components needed for any WCF service, including the web services you are going to build. A look at the Solution Explorer window will reveal three essential files needed to write and expose a service so that it is available across the network. The first of these files is IService1.cs. In here, you'll find a stubbed-out sample of a service contract, along with a few operational contracts and a data contract. The service and operational contracts have automatically been added to a C# interface named IService1, which can be used to implement WCF-provided services to downstream consumers. The next file is the Service1.cs class. This is the concrete implementation of the IService1 interface and, therefore, the main class for implementing your WCF service functionality. The last file is the web.config file used to configure the service behavior with the WCF engine. web.config files can get very busy in the WCF world. They are more complicated than the comparatively simple web.config files used in ASP.NET applications, and readers should take the time to understand the different elements when administering their services. The project template has preconfigured this project for web service functionality. If you crack open the `web.config` and look toward the bottom of the screen, you'll find the following snippet:

```
<system.serviceModel>
                                        <services>
                                                <service name="ProEnt.Chap6.
SimpleWebService.Service1" behaviorConfiguration="ProEnt.Chap6.SimpleWebService.
Service1Behavior">
                                                                <!-- Service
Endpoints -->

<endpoint address="" binding="wsHttpBinding" contract="ProEnt.Chap6.
SimpleWebService.IService1">

    <!--

Upon deployment, the following identity element should be removed or replaced to
reflect the

identity under which the deployed service runs.  If removed, WCF will infer an
appropriate identity
            automatically.
        -->

    <identity>

                    <dns value="localhost"/>

    </identity>
                                                                </endpoint>

<endpoint address="mex" binding="mexHttpBinding" contract="IMetadataExchange"/>
                                        </service>
                        </services>
                        <behaviors>
                                        <serviceBehaviors>

<behavior name="ProEnt.Chap6.SimpleWebService.Service1Behavior">


<!-- To avoid disclosing metadata information, set the value below to false and
remove the metadata endpoint above before deployment -->

    <serviceMetadata httpGetEnabled="true"/>

    <!-- To receive exception details in faults for debugging purposes, set the
value below to true.  Set to false before deployment to avoid disclosing exception
information -->
```

```
                <serviceDebug includeExceptionDetailInFaults="false"/>

    </behavior>

                                                        </serviceBehaviors>
                                            </behaviors>
                        </system.serviceModel>
```

Here is where you'll find the declaration of the service itself by type, `ProEnt.Chap6.SimpleWebService.Service1`, along with the definition of a WCF endpoint with `wsHttpBinding` declared and a contract that matches the fully qualified name of your WCF service contract (`IService1`). Since we are just walking through a simple WCF web service example, let's keep the names and types the same. Until you fully grasp all of the dependent elements that require configuration, changes to your type names will likely result in a broken sample.

Let's quickly add a WCF service call by adding to the definitions files. In the `IService1.cs` file add a method named `GetFriendlyTime` directly beneath the `GetData` method. You file should look like this now:

```
using System;
using System.Collections.Generic;
using System.Linq;
using System.Runtime.Serialization;
using System.ServiceModel;
using System.Text;

namespace ProEnt.Chap6.SimpleWebService
{
    // NOTE: If you change the interface name "IService1" here, you must also update
the reference to "IService1" in Web.config.
    [ServiceContract]
    public interface IService1
    {

        [OperationContract]
        string GetData(int value);

        [OperationContract]
        string GetFriendlyTime(string name);

        [OperationContract]
        CompositeType GetDataUsingDataContract(CompositeType composite);


        // TODO: Add your service operations here
    }


    // Use a data contract as illustrated in the sample below to add composite types
to service operations.
    [DataContract]
    public class CompositeType
    {
```

```
            bool boolValue = true;
            string stringValue = "Hello ";

            [DataMember]
            public bool BoolValue
            {
                get { return boolValue; }
                set { boolValue = value; }
            }

            [DataMember]
            public string StringValue
            {
                get { return stringValue; }
                set { stringValue = value; }
            }
        }
    },
```

You will also need to add this method to the concrete implementation class, satisfying the `IService1`
interface, as well as the WCF service contract. Replace the `Service1.svc` file code with the
following code:

```
using System;
using System.Collections.Generic;
using System.Linq;
using System.Runtime.Serialization;
using System.ServiceModel;
using System.Text;

namespace ProEnt.Chap6.SimpleWebService
{
    // NOTE: If you change the class name "Service1" here, you must also update the
//reference to "Service1" in Web.config and in the associated .svc file.
    public class Service1 : IService1
    {
        public string GetData(int value)
        {
            return string.Format("You entered: {0}", value);
        }

        public string GetFriendlyTime(string name)
        {
            return String.Format("Hello {0}, the current time is now: {1}", name,
            DateTime.Now.ToString("HH:mm"));
        }


        public CompositeType GetDataUsingDataContract(CompositeType composite)
        {
            if (composite.BoolValue)
```

```
            {
                composite.StringValue += "Suffix";
            }
            return composite;
        }
    }
}
```

The `GetFriendlyTime` function is simple. It just takes the name passed into the method, and concatenates it into a friendly return message with a formatted instance of the current time. That's it! If the names of the types remain the same, the internals of the WCF engine will provide all of the particulars needed to consume these methods.

We now need to quickly build a small consuming service. Open up a separate instance of Visual Studio. NET 2008 and create a new project. This time in the New Project dialog window, select Windows from the left-hand pane and then select WPF Application from the right-hand pane. Place it into the `C:/Projects` directory and name it `ProEnt.Chap6.SimpleClient`.

The first thing this project needs is a quick-and-dirty entry form. You need a field for adding your name, a button for invoking the WCF service, and a label for displaying the results. Find the file named `Window1.Xaml` and open it. Make sure that you are opening the XAML viewer and not the C# code. Replace the XAML with the following code:

```
<Window x:Class="SimpleClient.Window1"
    xmlns="http://schemas.microsoft.com/winfx/2006/xaml/presentation"
    xmlns:x="http://schemas.microsoft.com/winfx/2006/xaml"
    Title="Window1" Height="230" Width="450">
    <Grid HorizontalAlignment="Center" Width="397" Height="190">
        <Grid.ColumnDefinitions>
            <ColumnDefinition/>
        </Grid.ColumnDefinitions>
        <Grid.RowDefinitions>
            <RowDefinition/>
            <RowDefinition/>
            <RowDefinition/>
            <RowDefinition/>
            <RowDefinition/>
            <RowDefinition/>

        </Grid.RowDefinitions>
        <TextBox x:Name="nameField" Grid.Row="0" Grid.RowSpan="2" Margin=
        "20,0,12,0" />

        <Button x:Name="callWebMethod" Grid.Row="2" HorizontalAlignment="Center"
         Content="Call Web Method" Click="callWebMethod_Click" />

        <Label x:Name="results" Grid.Row="4" HorizontalAlignment="Center" Content=""
        Foreground="Red"/>
    </Grid>
</Window>
```

Now, you need to make a service reference to your WCF web service and invoke it when you add your name to the text field. In the Solution Explorer, right-click on References and select Add Service Reference. You should see a dialog window appear for adding the service reference and configuring it with your project (see Figure 6-2).

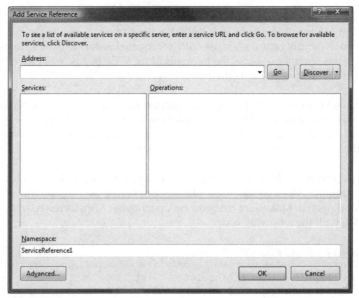

Figure 6-2

Don't enter anything yet. Since you used all of the default settings in your WCF service project, you won't be sure what the service URI will be. This is due to the fact that Visual Studio .NET uses a random port number generator when running a web project. Run the WCF web service project from the Visual Studio .NET IDE, and you should see a directory listing in your web browser, as shown in Figure 6-3.

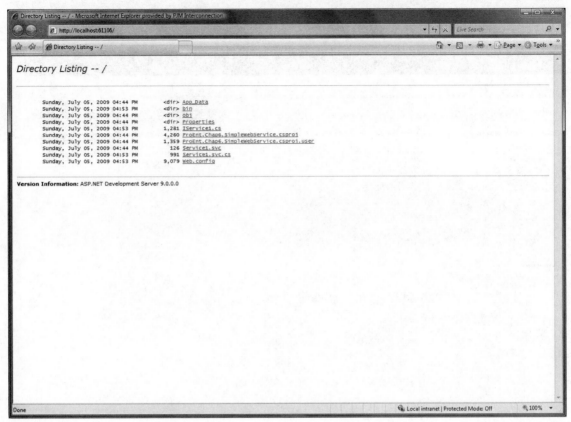

Directory Listing -- /

http://localhost:61106/

Directory Listing -- /

Sunday, July 05, 2009 04:44 PM	<dir>	App_Data
Sunday, July 05, 2009 04:53 PM	<dir>	bin
Sunday, July 05, 2009 04:44 PM	<dir>	obj
Sunday, July 05, 2009 04:44 PM	<dir>	Properties
Sunday, July 05, 2009 04:53 PM	1,281	IService1.cs
Sunday, July 05, 2009 04:44 PM	4,260	ProEnt.Chap6.SimpleWebService.csproj
Sunday, July 05, 2009 04:44 PM	1,359	ProEnt.Chap6.SimpleWebService.csproj.user
Sunday, July 05, 2009 04:44 PM	126	Service1.svc
Sunday, July 05, 2009 04:53 PM	991	Service1.svc.cs
Sunday, July 05, 2009 04:53 PM	9,079	Web.config

Version Information: ASP.NET Development Server 9.0.0.0

Figure 6-3

Click on the link labeled `Service1.svc`, and a system-generated test page for the service should appear, just like the one showing in Figure 6-4.

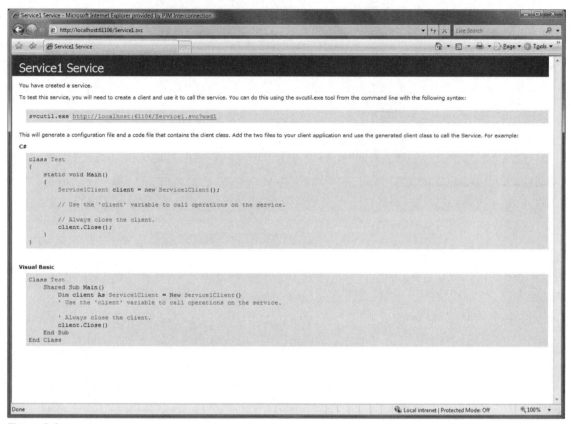

Figure 6-4

This page contains helpful information for building your consumer code. Notice at the top of the page are the following lines:

> To test this service, you will need to create a client and use it to call the service. You can do this using the svcutil.exe tool from the command line with the following syntax:

```
svcutil.exe http://localhost:[asp.net port number]/Service1.svc?wsdl
```

The svcutil.exe utility referenced here is a useful tool in the .NET SDK. You can use it to create proxy classes for different consumers and it can be leveraged in batch files for updating project builds and deployments. In this case, the utility has a graphic user interface built into the IDE you saw in Figure 6-2. Copy the URI, starting from the http. Now go back to the web reference dialog still showing in your client project, and paste that into the top text field. Click the Go button, and the service information should be found. The window should now appear as it does in Figure 6-5.

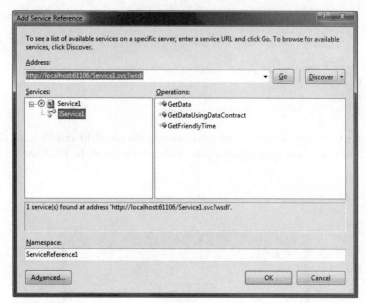

Figure 6-5

You should see the name of the three methods defined in the service contract, including the one that you added. Replace the Namespace field with `SimpleWebReference` and click OK.

We now have a valid web reference to use in our project. Be sure that you keep the WCF service project running to ensure that the port number doesn't change. Find the code-behind file for the XAML page by right-clicking in the `Window1.Xaml` node in the Solution Explorer and selecting View Code. Replace the contents of this page with the following:

```
using System;
using System.Windows;
using System.Windows.Controls;


namespace SimpleClient
{
    /// <summary>
    /// Interaction logic for Window1.xaml
    /// </summary>
    public partial class Window1 : Window
    {
        public Window1()
        {
            InitializeComponent();
        }

        private void callWebMethod_Click(object sender, RoutedEventArgs e)
        {
```

```
        SimpleWebReference.IService1 serv = new SimpleWebReference.
        Service1Client();
        string retval = serv.GetFriendlyTime(this.nameField.Text.ToString());

        this.results.Content = retval;
    }
  }
}
```

Now compile and run the application. Enter your name in the text field and click the Call Web Method button. You should see a red label display with the output of the WCF service call as shown in Figure 6-6.

Figure 6-6

This simple example demonstrates the essentials of service-base communication, and represents the latest platform available for building RPC-based middleware for the Windows platform using WCF.

The Messaging Model

This sample demonstrated how to build synchronous, remote procedure call middleware using the latest Microsoft communication framework. Other design patterns available don't rely on web service calls, but rather the notion of asynchronous messaging. There are a handful of message-based patterns, many with dedicated protocols to support them. Chief among these patterns is Message-Oriented Middleware, or MOM. MOM is a design pattern focused on the sending and receiving of discreet messages between systems in an effort to facilitate interoperability, portability, and system flexibility. Unlike the request/ response model of the web services pattern, MOM blurs the line between client and server, treating all participating systems as peers in a distributed, oftentimes heterogeneous environment. MOM systems are typically more complex than those dedicated to synchronous messaging models. Dedicated servers are configured for the generation, passing, and consuming of messages over broad network topography. As messages are moved from server to server, they may change state, undergo transformation, get split amid other consumers, or get removed from the system altogether. The key facet of this model is that each member in the MOM infrastructure operates independently from other members in the system, allowing the messages to be modified or adjusted with minimal dependencies.

In the Java community the Java Messaging Service is an API dedicated to the development and support of message-based systems. It provides a set of structured, unified interfaces for message creation, message passing, durability, broadcasting, and publication-subscription patterns. There are other MOM-supporting platforms available, but JMS is the most pervasive of these APIs. Unfortunately, Message-Oriented Middleware has a somewhat confusing history in the Windows community. Although the Microsoft pundits beat their chest and declare that there are plenty of options for .NET developers interested in MOM, most of us in the trenches know better. A solid MOM platform requires a unified technology to support its many different flavors. The Distributed Component Object Model (DCOM) was a step in the right direction for Microsoft, but it lacked teeth. DCOM was fine for remote invocation but less than ideal for asynchronous messaging, especially for ActiveX programmers working in higher-level languages like Visual Basic (VB). The WCF platform has some features that support asynchronous messaging; however these come in the form of simple signatures and hooks for building your own messaging model. Microsoft does provide a technology for creating and storing durable messages called Microsoft Message Queuing (MSMQ), but the supporting API is fairly anemic, and falls a bit flat compared to the power of the Java Messaging Service. And of course, we would be remiss not to mention Microsoft's enterprise middleware server product, BizTalk. BizTalk can be configured to drive a message-based system, but be forewarned: BizTalk lives in its own corner of the Microsoft development community. Understanding how to leverage its services has become an entire career for some. Unlike an API like JMS that builds on the skills of common developers, BizTalk is more of a departure from other types of Microsoft programming. It is more of a product than an API, or a set of design patterns. There are plenty of organizations that can benefit from BizTalk; however a deeper discussion of it lies beyond the scope of this book.

A Brief Note on SOA

As the technology that supports each of these communication patterns has evolved, their presence in the software community has grown. Nowadays it is not uncommon for even small and mid-sized organizations to embrace service-based and message-based mechanisms to drive their software. These patterns lessen an organization's need to focus on technical issues, such as system interoperability, and instead to focus on building the best solution to fit their needs. Arising from this trend comes the concept of Service Oriented Architecture, or SOA. SOA is both an architectural pattern, as well as a business and development process. It focuses on the creation and maintenance of discreet pieces of logic known as services. Each service is defined as a loosely coupled function, made available over a network to other consuming systems. The core principles of a service-oriented system demand the use of a federation of interoperable functions that can be invoked independently of one another. These services or functions should be platform independent, relying on common formats and protocols for invocation. Conceptually it is a much broader pattern than the ones we have discussed so far, incorporating aspects of different communication patterns into a single, ubiquitous set of programmatic interfaces. SOA infrastructures often support different avenues of communication. Message queuing, publication-subscription, and request/response are communication patterns that can live side-by-side with each other in an SOA-based environment.

SOA implementations come in many forms. As an emerging trend in the enterprise community there is considerable debate and confusion about what a "true SOA" system should look like, and how it should function. A deeper discussion of an SOA system would include service coupling, orchestration, granularity, as well as a review of infrastructure patterns such as cloud computing services. Aside from noting the basic rules of a service-oriented system, we prefer to avoid a deep dive into the topic. The processes that drive SOA development lie outside of the scope of this book. However the models, principles, and patterns covered are all integral pieces of a well-designed SOA system. We will discuss service-based patterns in more depth in Chapter 7.

No matter what sort of communication pattern you choose, there are varied levels of complexity each may incur. Most advanced service-based systems rely on asynchronous models such as message passing and publication-subscription patterns. Moreover, uncomplicated code samples such as this one rely on very simple signatures, exchanging strings, integers and other primitives to accomplish a task. Complex models tend to pass full messages, oftentimes containing live objects with state to be handled by n number of downstream systems. These models use similar plumbing to the same we just built, with some changes to the protocol and contracts to accommodate for lower-level communications. Yet models like these blur the lines between tiers. They require the client consumer to know something about the server. For example, a system passing a customer record from one server to another might choose to package up the domain object "Customer" and send it across the wire. The client receives the object and its data, but also all of the methods and properties the object implements. Most would agree that violates separation of concerns, not to mention security. In cases such as these a Data Transfer Object, or DTO should be used. DTOs have all of the data needed by the client, but with absolutely no behavior built in. Rather, they are simple data containers, created solely for the use of exchanging information. We will see an example of how simple DTOs are used when we get to Chapter 12.

Summary

In this chapter, we began to discuss the architectures that rely on enterprise development concepts. Moving away from the focus on coding practices we had in previous chapters, this chapter shifts focus to the broader design patterns used to construct enterprise systems.

❑ We discussed the concept of middleware and its many different definitions. We explored the history behind distributed software design, following the emergence of middleware as a housing for business rules and a means of intersystem communication.

❑ As we traced the emergence of the web model, we began to explore the idea of enterprise middleware as both a physical and conceptual tier dedicated to interoperability. The impediments to machine-to-machine communication were reviewed, as well as some of the emerging technologies that helped to facilitate the exchanging of messages.

❑ Web services were then reviewed, followed by a quick, hands-on sample of a WCF web service using the WCF Visual Studio .NET project template.

❑ We concluded with a brief discussion of other enterprise middleware patterns such as SOA and MOM, and how the right system should be embraced for the right enterprise architecture.

Chapter 7 digs deeper into some of these patterns, focusing on the business logic portion of your middleware.

7

Writing Your Own Middleware

Up to now you have concentrated your efforts on learning the patterns and principles to keep your code modular and loosely coupled. These are valuable techniques that will allow you to build applications that will be maintainable and flexible to meet you business needs. However, these principles and practices are merely a side show, a collection of tools in your coding toolbox, if you will, that enable you to carry out your work. The main purpose of your application and the sole purpose of our existence as developers is to solve business problems. It's odd then that a large proportion of development time is spent writing plumbing code instead of business logic; this chapter is all about refocusing your efforts and readdressing the balance by providing you with some practical patterns that will enable you to map your business goals effectively. Before you read about the many patterns at your disposable to organize your business logic it's important that we define what exactly the role of the business logic layer is and how it fits in with the rest of your applications layers.

Business Logic Layer

The business logic layer is an abstract layer that contains all the rules, workflow and validation that define and deal with the business complexities that your software has been designed to meet. Typically, the business logic layer will fit between your user interface, service, or presentation layer and your data access layer, as shown in Figure 7-1. By separating the business logic from other layers in your applications you are separating your concerns and keeping your code loosely coupled and allowing for different implementations to be used with the business logic layer; for example, changing the UI from a web application to a WPF application.

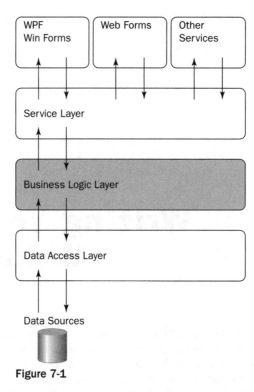

Figure 7-1

Depending on the complexities of the business model that your application has been designed for, the structure of your business logic layer may differ considerably. For instance a complex banking application will have a rich Domain Model that represents the real banking domain with hundreds of small business entities representing loans, customers, and accounts. For a simpler application, such as a blogging engine, you may have a number of fairly simple business objects that map very closely to your underlying Data Model with little or no business logic, simply acting as a method to add and retrieve data. In the next section, you will look at the various patterns at your disposal to structure your business logic layer.

Patterns for Your Business

❑   There are a number of design patterns that you can follow that will help you to organize your business logic. In this section, you will be introduced to three of the main patterns found in the business logic layer: the Transaction Script, Active Record, and the Domain Model pattern.

Transaction Script

Transaction Script is a very simple business design pattern, which follows a procedural style of development rather than an object-oriented approach. Simply create a single procedure for each of your business transactions with each procedure containing all of the business logic that is required to complete the business transaction from the workflow, business rules, and validation checks to persistence in the database.

Let's take a look at how you could leverage the Transaction Script pattern in an application that deals with the workflow of processing an order in an e-commerce store.

```
public class OrderManager
{
    public void PlaceOrder(OrderDTO order)
    {
        // Validate order based on business rules
        // Check for stock availablity on items ordered
        // Add the order to the database
        // Set the order id on the OrderDTO object
    }

    public bool CancelOrder(Guid orderId)
    {
        // Retrieve order from database
        // Determine if the order can be canceled
        // if order can be canceled, set as canceled
        // return true/false if order was canceled
    }

    public bool AddItemToOrder(Guid orderId, OrderItemDTO ItemToAdd)
    {
        // Retrieve order from database
        // Determine if the item can be added to the order
        // Add a new item row in the database
        // return true/false if item was added to the order
    }

    public bool ProcessOrder(Guid orderId)
    {
        // Check to ensure this order can be processed.
        // Validate order based on business rules
        // Update the stock levels of products ordered
        // return true/false if order was processed
    }
}
```

All of the transactions that relate to an order are grouped together under the order manager class. Each method maps to a business use case or transaction involved in the processing of an order. If you take a look at the first method PlaceOrder it takes an OrderDTO, which is a very simple data transfer object used to pass data around an application and avoid the need to have long lists of parameters on the methods. The PlaceOrder method then checks if the order is in a valid state according to any business rules governing the creation of orders and then checks for the availability of stock for the products ordered. Finally, the order data is persisted to the database and a new order number is generated and returned, indicating a successfully placed order. The other methods in the manager class all follow a similar approach, with the full spectrum of details relating to a transaction being handled by the single method.

One of the strengths of the Transaction Script pattern is that it is very simple to understand and clear to see what is going on without any prior knowledge of the pattern. If a new business case needs to be handled, it is straightforward enough to add a new method to handle it, which will contain all of the related business logic.

The problems with the Transaction Script pattern are revealed when an application grows and the business complexities increase. It is very easy to see many management or application classes with hundreds of fine-grained transaction methods that map directly to a business use cases. Submethods can be used to avoid repetitive code such as the validation and business rules, but duplication in the workflow cannot be avoided, and the code base can quickly become unwieldy and unmanageable as the application grows.

If you have a simple application with minimal business logic, which doesn't warrant a fully object-oriented approach, the Transaction Script pattern can be a good fit. However, if your application will grow, you may need to rethink your business logic structure and look to a more scalable pattern like the Active Record pattern.

Active Record Pattern

The Active Record pattern is very popular pattern and is especially effective when your underlying database model matches your business model. Typically, a business object will exist for each table in your database. The business object represents a single row in that table and contains both data and behavior as well as a means to persist itself and methods to add new instances and find collections of objects. Figure 7-2 shows how an order and order items objects relate to their orders and order items tables.

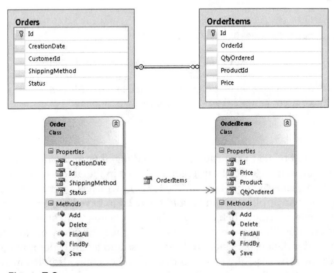

Figure 7-2

In the Active Record pattern, each business object is responsible for its own persistence and related business logic. The following code shows an Active Record implementation of the `Order` business object from the Transaction Script example.

```
public class Order
{
    private Guid _id;
    private DateTime _creationDate;
    private int _shippingMethod;
    private int _status;
    private List<OrderItems> _orderItems;

    public Guid Id
    {
        get { return _id;}
        set { _id = value; }
    }

    ...

    public List<OrderItems> OrderItems
    {
        get { return _orderItems; }
        set { _orderItems = value; }
    }

    // Business Logic
    public void Place()
    {
        // Validate order based on business rules to ensure it is in
        // a good state to add to the database
        // Check for stock availablity on items ordered
        this.Add();
    }

    public void Cancel()
    {
        // Check to ensure this order can be canceled.
        this.Status = Status.Cancelled();
        this.Save();
    }

    public void ProcessOrder()
    {
        // Check to ensure this order can be processed.
        // Validate order based on business rules
        // Udpate the stock levels of products ordered
    }

    // Data Access Methods
    public void Save()
    {
        // Code to persist changes to the database
    }
```

```
        public void Add()
        {
            // Code to Add this object to the database
        }

        public void Delete()
        {
            // Code to remove this object from the database
        }

        public static List<Order> FindAll()
        {
            // Code to retrieve all Orders from the database
        }

        public static Order FindBy(Guid id)
        {
            // Code to retrive a specific Order from the database
        }
    }
```

As you can see, the `Order` object contains behavior as well as data in the form of the three business methods `Place`, `Cancel`, and `Process`. These three methods in turn utilize the data access methods on the order object to persist changes.

The Active Record pattern is great for very simple applications where there is a one-to-one mapping between the Data Model and the Business Model, such as with a blogging or a forum engine; it's also a good pattern to use if you have an existing database model or tend to build applications with a "data first" approach. Because the business objects have a one-to-one mapping to the tables in the database and all have the same CRUD (create, read, update, and delete) methods, it's possible to use code generation tools to auto-generate your business model for you. Good code gen tools will also build in all of the database validation logic to ensure that you are allowing only valid data to be persisted. We will look more at automatically generating your business objects and frameworks that use the Active Record pattern in the next chapter when we discuss how to persist your business objects. As with the transaction script pattern, Active Record is similarly straightforward and easy to grasp.

However, the Active Record pattern is no silver bullet. It excels with a good underlying Data Model that maps to the business model, but when there is a mismatch, sometimes called an impedence mismatch, the pattern can struggle to cope. This is the result of complex systems sometimes having a very different conceptual business models than the Data Model. When there is a rich business domain with lots of complex rules, logic, and workflow, this favors going with the Domain Model approach.

Domain Model Pattern

You can think of a Domain Model as a conceptual layer that represents the domain you are working in. Things exist in this model and have relationships to other things. What do I mean by things? Well, for example, if you were building an e-commerce store, the "things" that would live in the model would represent a Basket, Order, and Order Item, and the like. If you were creating a loan application, you would have representations for a Borrower, Loan, Assets, and Debts. It's these things that have data and, more importantly, behavior. Not only would an order have properties that represent a creation date, status, and order number, but it would also contain the business logic to apply a voucher to, including all of the domain rules that surround it — Is the voucher valid? Can the voucher be used with the products in the basket? Are there any other offers in place that would render the voucher invalid, and so forth. The closer your Domain Model represents the real domain the better, as it will be easier for you to understand and replicate the complex business logic, rules, and validation process.

The main difference between the Domain Model and the Active Record pattern is that the business entities that live in the Domain Model have no knowledge of how to persist themselves, and there doesn't necessarily need to be one-to-one mapping between the Data Model and the Business Model. Figure 7-3 shows the impedence mismatch between an order business entity and the order table.

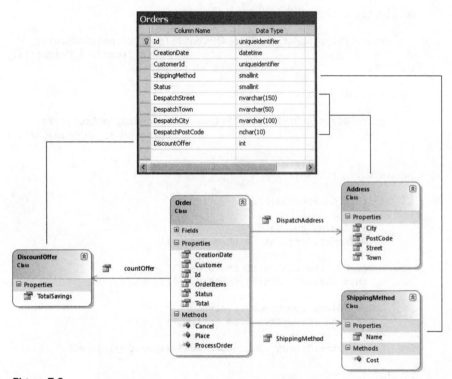

Figure 7-3

Each business object is rich with behavior such as validation and state-altering logic. The following code shows an implementation of the Domain Model pattern again, using the e-commerce domain used in the previous demos.

```
public class Order
{
    private Guid _id;

    ...

    public Guid Id
    {
        get { return _id;}
        set { _id = value; }
    }

    ...

    public float ShippingCost()
    {
        return ShippingMethod.ShippingCostTo(this.DispatchAddress,
                                    this.ItemsTotalWeight());
    }

    public float Total()
    {
        return DiscountOffer.TotalPriceWithDiscountOfferAppliedTo(
                                    this.Items, ShippingCost());
    }

    public void Process()
    {
        if (this.CanProcess())
        {
            // Charge the card
            Customer.Card.Charge(this.Total());

            // Set the status of the order
            this.Status = Status.Shipped;

            // Adjust the stock levels
            foreach (OrderItem item in Items)
            {
                item.Product.DecreaseStockBy(item.QtyOrdered);
            }
        }
        else
        {
            throw new InvalidOrderStateForOperationException(
                String.Formt(
                "Order {0} cannot be processed in its current state {1}",
                this.Id, this.Status.ToString());
        }
    }

    public bool CanProcess()
    {
        if (!this.Status == Status.Shipped && !this.Status = Status.Cancelled)
        {
            return (this.HasEnoughStockFor(me.Items) &&
```

```
                              GetBrokenRules.Count() == 0);
            }
            else
            {
                return false;
            }

        }

        public List<BrokenBusinessRule> GetBrokenRules()
        {
            List<BrokenBusinessRule> brokenRules = new List<BrokenBusinessRule>();

            if (Customer == null)
                brokenRules.Add(new BrokenBusinessRule() {
                  Property = "Customer", Rule = "An Order must have a Customer" });
            else if (Customer.GetBrokenRules().Count > 0)
            {
                AddToBrokenRulesList(brokenRules, Customer.GetBrokenRules());
            }

            if (DispatchAddress == null)
                brokenRules.Add(new BrokenBusinessRule() {
                  Property = "DispatchAddress",
                  Rule = "An Order must have a Dispatch Address" });
            else if (DispatchAddress.GetBrokenRules().Count > 0)
            {
                AddToBrokenRulesList(brokenRules,
                                  DispatchAddress.GetBrokenRules());
            }

            // ......

            return brokenRules;
        }

    }
```

Although this is only a small section from the complete order business entity, you should get a feel for the rich domain logic encapsulated within it. If you take a look at the `Process` method, it should be obvious as to the workflow:

1. A call to the CanProcess method verifies that:

    a. The order is in a valid state to be processed.

    b. There is enough stock to fulfill the items ordered.

2. The customer's credit card is charged; the logic again is encapsulated with the card object itself. The method to obtain the total order amount uses other classes associated with the order, namely the `ShippingMethod` and `DiscountOffer` classes.

3. The `ShippingMethod` object calculates the cost of shipping given the `DispatchAddress` and total weight of products ordered, while the `DiscountOffer` object applies any discounts to the total value of the goods plus any shipping charge.

4. After a charge has been made the `Order` object internally updates its state to one of shipped.

5. Finally the product stock is adjusted to reflect the shipped items.

As you can see, a lot is going on, but because the Domain Model excels at being able to present complex business logic in a logical manner, it should be easy to understand from the developer and business expert perspectives alike.

As mentioned earlier, the Domain Model, unlike the Active Record pattern, has no knowledge of persistence. The term *persistence ignorant* (PI) has been coined for the plain nature of the POCO (plain old common runtime object) business entities. How then do you persist a business object with the Domain Model? Typically, the repository pattern is used. When you are employing the Domain Model pattern, it's the responsibility of the `Repository` object, along with a data mapper, to map a business entity and its object graph of associated entities to the Data Model. You will look into the details of this in the following chapter, so for now just be aware that business entities inside the Domain Model are PI.

Trying to solve complex business problems in software is difficult, but when using the Domain Model pattern, you first create an abstract model of the real business model. With this model in place, you can then model complex logic by following the real domain and recreating the workflow and processing in your Domain Model. Another advantage that a Domain Model holds over the Transaction Script and the Active Record patterns is that, because it contains no data access code, it can be easily unit tested without having to mock and stub out dependencies of such a data access layer.

Again, the Domain Model pattern may not always be a great fit for your application needs. One of its great strengths is dealing with complex business logic, but a full-blown Domain Model is architectural overkill when very little business logic is contained within the application. Another disadvantage of the pattern is the steep learning curve needed to become proficient in it compared to the Active Record and Transaction Script options. To use the pattern effectively takes time and experience and, most importantly, a sound knowledge of the business domain you are trying to model.

Which Pattern to Use?

Each pattern has its pros and cons, and there is no one method that will suit all of your development needs. Let's take a brief look at each pattern and see when it's most appropriate to use it.

❏ **Transaction Script:** If you have a simple application with little or no logic, then Transaction Script is a great choice as a straightforward solution that is easily understood by other developers picking up your code down the line.

❏ **Active Record:** If your business layer is simply a thin veil over the top of your database, then this is a great pattern to opt for. There are many code generation tools that can automatically create your business objects for you based on your database schema, and it's not too difficult to create your own.

❏ **Domain Model:** The Domain Model excels when you have an involved, rich complex business domain to model. It's a pure object-oriented approach that involves creating an abstract model of the real business domain and is very useful when dealing with complex logic and workflow. The Domain Model is persistence ignorant and relies on mapper classes and the Repository pattern to persist and retrieve business entities.

So, the strengths of each of these patterns are all dependent on your application needs.

Serving Your Business

When using the Active Record and Domain Model business patterns, not all of your business logic can easily be replicated within the business logic layer. Some business processes simply do not fit within the patterns of a Domain Model or an Active Record pattern. For these business cases, the use of a service layer can be employed.

The Service Layer

As shown in Figure 7-4, the service layer fits between the business layer and the presentation or user interfaces or indeed other services that are using your application. The role of the service layer is on the face of it very similar to that of the Transaction Script pattern in that it typically maps to business use cases. Where it differs, however, is that unlike the Transaction Pattern the service layer simply coordinates the business use case transaction and delegates work to the business objects for all of the lower-level details. The service layer encapsulates the business model and acts as an interface into the application for all parties, rather like a business façade.

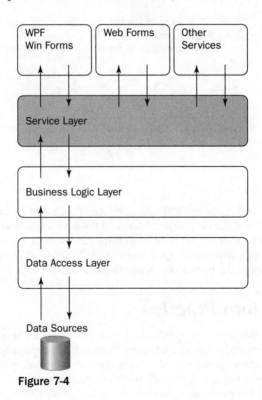

Figure 7-4

Let's take a look at a typical use of the service layer in the context of the e-commerce ordering workflow that you have used for the business patterns examples.

```
public class OrderService
{
    private IOrderRepository _orderRepository;
    private INotificationService _notificationService;

    public OrderService(IOrderRepository orderRepository,
                        INotificationService notificationService)
    {
        _orderRepository = orderRepository;
        _notificationService = notificationService;
    }

    public void ProcessOrderBy(Guid id)
    {
        Order orderToProcess = _orderRepository.FindBy(id);

        if (orderToProcess != null)
        {
            if (orderToProcess.CanProcess())
            {
                orderToProcess.Process();
                _orderRepository.Save(orderToProcess);
                _notificationService.ConfirmProcessOf(orderToProcess);
            }
        }
        else
        {
            throw new OrderNotFoundException(
                String.Format("Could not find an order with the Id '{0}'",
                              id.ToString()));
        }
    }
}
```

The `ProcessOrderBy` method maps to a business use case "Process an Order." The method coordinates the transaction, including the retrieval and persistence of the `Order` business object. Once the transaction has succeeded, the notification service is called to alert the customer of the order's dispatch. As you can see, the service method is simply delegating the work to the lower-level business objects; no state is held within the service method and the transaction is run in one atomic event.

Putting Patterns into Practice

They say the best way to learn is by example, so to demonstrate the business patterns you have just read about, let's take a real(ish)-world example and apply them to it. The application you will be developing in this chapter will be based on the domain of a mortgage loan approval system. The application will serve to demonstrate some of the concepts you have been reading about. In later chapters, you will expand on this example to demonstrate patterns found in the presentation and data access layers of an application.

Obviously, this will be a somewhat simplified version of the mortgage approval process you may encounter. But this example will give you a good overview of what to expect during the pre qualification, as well as the general process that takes place from start to finish.

Mortgage Loan Prequalification Application

The mortgage loan prequalification process is the procedure people go through when they want to borrow money to buy a house. The purpose of prequalification is for the potential borrower to establish how much money a bank is willing to lend them.

Prequalification follows a number of steps as detailed below:

1. A potential borrower(s) will provide a loan officer the following information:

    a. Gross monthly income

    b. All debts

    c. Bank account, address

    d. Address of property they are interested in buying

    e. Details of their employer

    f. The loan product they are applying for

2. After all information pertaining to the loan application has been submitted a loan officer will run a credit report to obtain a credit score.

3. With all the borrowers personal information and a credit score the loan officer will prequalify the application to determine if it satisfies the selected product requirements.

4. If the application satisfies all the rules for the product then an offer letter can be generated which is good for 6 months. This letter will guarantee that in principal the bank will offer the loan to the borrower subject to further checks and verification of all details.

5. If the application is unsuccessful all is not lost as the loan officer can use the same application for a different product and the process returns to step 3. Similarly if the situation changes for a borrower their details can be altered, any offers generated are void and the process recommences at step 3.

It is clear that the mortgage loan prequalification approval workflow involves complex business logic and, therefore, you will be employing the Domain Model pattern to organize the business logic.

Even though you have a good idea of the prequalification process, you still don't have enough information to start to build the application. What you need is a thorough understanding of the problem space, and to get this you need to talk to an expert.

Talking the Language of the Domain

To ensure that your Domain Model truly reflects the actual domain it's important to use the same language, concepts, and processes that are used by the domain experts; to ensure that you are all using the same terminology you need a shared language or a ubiquitous language. Your software development efforts will be sufficiently improved if you have a thorough understanding of the real business domain, which enables complex business processes to be easily modeled in your Domain Model.

The notion of a ubiquitous language is that it should act as a common vocabulary that is used by developers, domain experts, and anyone else involved in a project to describe the domain. A domain expert is someone with the knowledge and skills in a particular domain that will work closely with you as you develop the Domain Model, to ensure that you fully understand the business model before trying to represent it in code. In the example of a loan application, this could be an underwriter. Through listening to this person, you will build a vocabulary of all terminology used during the process of approving a loan. Your class, methods, and property names should all be based around the same ubiquitous language, this will enable you to talk to domain experts about code in a language that they understand, plus new developers working on the code should get a good grounding in what the domain is really all about. It will also enable them to talk to business experts about the smallest details of complex business logic with relative ease. When all parties involved in the development of an application are speaking the same language, problems and solutions can be conveyed easily, making the application quicker and easier to build.

You are probably thinking to yourself this is all common sense and something you probably are currently doing. The concept of a ubiquitous language comes from a Design methodology called Domain-Driven Design (DDD); as a whole Domain-Driven Design isn't a new idea. Think of it as a set of guidelines to remind you not to get carried away with infrastructure concerns and to keep your eyes set firmly on the business needs, and strive to keep those at the forefront of your mind.

A Little Bit about Domain-Driven Design

It's beyond the scope of this book to give you a complete introduction to the Domain-Driven design methodology, so for more information on Domain-Driven Design in .NET, check out the Wrox book, *.NET Domain Driven Design with C#: Problem – Design – Solution* by Tim McCarthy (ISBN 978-0-470-14756-6).

In a nutshell Domain-Driven Design is a collection of patterns and principles that aid you in your efforts to build applications that reflect an understanding of and meet the requirements of your business. Outside of that, it's a whole new way of thinking about your development methodology. DDD is about modeling the real domain by first fully understanding it and placing all of the terminology, rules, and logic into an abstract representation within your code, typically in the form of a Domain Model.

Domain-Driven Design is not a framework, but it does have a set of building blocks or concepts that you can incorporate into your solution. Let's look at these concepts one at a time.

Entities

Entities are the things we were talking about earlier, for example, the `Borrower`, `Loan`, `Assets`, and `Debts` objects in a Loan approval application. They encompass the data and behavior of the real entity in an abstract manner. Any logic pertaining to an entity should be contained within it. Entities are the things that require an identity, which will remain with it throughout its lifetime. Consider a borrower in terms of a loan application; a borrower has a name but names can change and also be duplicated, so you need to add a separate identity that will stay with the borrower through its life in the loan application regardless of a name, job, or address change. Typically, a system will use some kind of unique identifier or auto-numbering value for any entities that don't have a natural way to identity them. Sometimes entities do have natural keys, such as a Social Security number or an employee number.

Not all of the objects in your Domain Model will be unique and will require an identity. For some objects, it's the data that is of most importance and not identity; these objects are called *value objects*.

Value Objects

Value objects have no identity; they are of value because of their attributes only. Value objects generally don't live on their own; they are typically, but not always, attributes of an entity. Continuing with the loan approval domain, a borrower will have an address; the address is a value object because, in this context, it doesn't exist on its own. If a borrower were to move to a new house, you would simply overwrite that person's address with another, so it makes no sense to give the address an identity. If we were talking about an `Address` in terms of an e-commerce delivery address book, then the `Address` would be represented as an entity, because we care about its identity since you would have need to edit and delete specific addresses. Figure 7-5 shows the relationship between a `Borrower` entity and an `Address` value object. The address doesn't mean much on its own, but the fact that it is related to a borrower gives it an associated identity. In the database, the address could well be contained within the same Borrower table, but outside the Data Model these two are separate objects representing very different things.

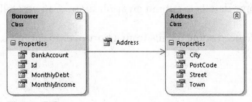

Figure 7-5

Aggregates and Aggregate Roots

Big systems or complex domains could have hundreds of entity and value objects, which have complex relationships; the Domain Model needs a method of managing these associations, and, more importantly, logical groups of entities and value objects need to define a interface that lets other entities work with them. Without such a structure, the interaction between groups of objects could be confusing and lead to problems later.

The notion of an aggregation is used to group logical entities and value objects. From the Domain-Driven Design definition, an aggregate is simply "a cluster of associated objects that are treated as a unit for the purpose of data changes." The aggregate root is an entity, which is the only member of the aggregate that any object outside the aggregate is allowed to hold a reference to. The reason why the idea of an aggregate exists in Domain-Driven Design is to ensure data integrity within the Domain Model. An aggregate root is a special entity that acts as the logical way into the aggregate. For example, if we take an order in the context of an e-commerce shop, we can regard it as the aggregate root, as we only want to be able to edit an order line or apply a voucher by going through the root of the aggregate; that is, the order entity. This enables complex object graphs to remain consistent and business rules to be adhered to. So, instead of an `Order` just exposing a collection of vouchers issued against it through a simple `List` property, it can have methods with complex rules that enable vouchers to be applied to it and expose the list of vouchers as a read-only collection for display purposes.

Talking with the Domain Expert

Now that you have had a quick introduction to the fundamentals of Domain-Driven Design, you can continue gathering the requirements for the mortgage loan prequalification application. You know about the workflow related to the prequalification process, but now it's time to start to get into the real details of the domain, and what better way to do that then by asking an expert, or in this case Bob.

Bob is a loan officer who, in the context of the mortgage loan prequalification world, is your domain expert. By talking to Bob, you will build up a common vocabulary to describe the business domain. It's important that you talk to the domain expert to fully understand the processes and workflows of the business domain that you are building an application for.

To get a feeling for the domain, you will walk through a conversation between you and Bob.

You: "Hi, Bob. I will be building the mortgage loan prequalification system. As I understand it, a borrower needs to fill in some details to submit an application. Can you tell what they are? "

Bob: "Yes, that's correct. We need some details from a borrower to submit a loan application. Here is a list of items:

- ❏ Borrower
    - ❏ First Name
    - ❏ Last Name
    - ❏ Age
    - ❏ Bank Account
    - ❏ Address
    - ❏ Credit Score
    - ❏ Employer (including monthly salary and address)
- ❏ A Mortgage Loan Product
- ❏ List of Debts
- ❏ List of Assets"

You: "OK, that makes sense. Shouldn't the list of debts and assets come under the borrower?"

Bob: "It does not matter who the debts and assets belong to; that's why they are attached to the loan."

You: "OK, so there can be more than one borrower?"

Bob: "Yes, that's correct, at least one borrower and a maximum of two."

You: "Thanks for that. Tell me about the process of prequalification; how does that work?"

Bob: "When a borrower submits a loan application, it immediately gets prequalified, as long as it is valid — i.e., has all of the details required. Prequalification is the process of ascertaining if, in principle, the borrower can be considered for a loan based on the information given. The prequalification checklist is as follows:

- ❑ Does the total monthly debt, including the calculated payment for the new loan amount, exceed 30% of the gross monthly income?

- ❑ Does the upfront down payment constitute at least 10% of the total value of the home?

- ❑ Do the mortgage payments conform to the basic rules of the calculator?

- ❑ Is the total loan amount within the thresholds of the chosen mortgage product?

- ❑ Will the loan be paid back before the borrower reaches retirement age of 65?

- ❑ Do both credit scores rate at least above 650?"

You: "OK, I understand all of that, but what's a mortgage calculator?"

Bob: "A mortgage calculator simply works out how much money a borrower will need to pay back each month for a given loan amount, interest rate, and loan term."

You: "I see. What do you mean when you are talking about a product's threshold? "

Bob: "We have many different mortgage products for different types of borrowers, and each has a different threshold and limit, but they all follow the same checks. For example, we may have a very low interest rate on one product, but we would only want to give this to low-risk borrowers, so we might set the loan-to-value low. That way, if the borrower were to default on the loan, it would be easy for us to get our money back. On the other hand, we will generally charge a greater interest rate for borrowers with a poorer loan-to-value ratio, reducing the equity margin in the property."

You: "I follow; so, you could say a product will only be applicable to a loan application that satisfies its specifications?"

Bob: "Yes, that's exactly the way we phrase it."

You: "Cool. Can you tell me all the attributes of a product? I am guessing interest rate must be one, and from what you have said there must be some kind of loan to value property?

Bob: "That's correct. Here are the all of the attributes of a product:

- ❑ Interest Rate
- ❑ Max Loan Amount
- ❑ Max Loan Term
- ❑ Max Loan to Value"

For the sake of brevity, we will leave the conversation here. However, in the real world, the conversation between you and Bob would carry on until you have a full understanding of the business process, and you and Bob could agree on the concepts and terminology.

Now that you have a better understanding of the problem domain, you can start to build the application, taking care to ensure that you use the language and concepts that you have learned from the approval workflow and the conversation with the domain expert.

Building the Domain Model

Based on the initial requirements of the application, the model in Figure 7-6 has been sketched out.

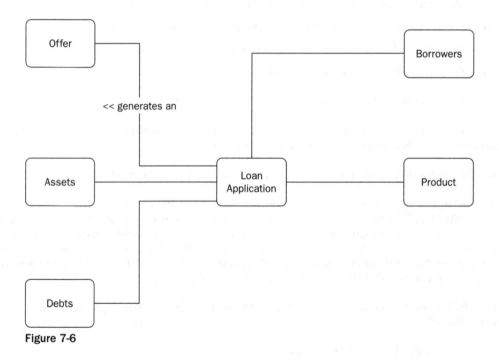

Figure 7-6

It's always a good idea to sketch out an initial model in front of the domain expert, so that he can verify that you have understood the domain and to get immediate feedback.

As you can see from Figure 7-6, a *loan application* is at the core of your Domain Model. A loan application must have at least a borrower, a list of debts, a list of assets, and a product. If the application satisfies the requirements of a product then prequalification is approved, an offer will be generated and can be printed for the borrower. A product represents the selected mortgage product that the borrower is applying for. A borrower itself is a representation of the real-life person applying for a loan.

Once you have designed the Domain Model, you can build your class diagram to see how it will look in code. Figure 7-7 shows the class diagram.

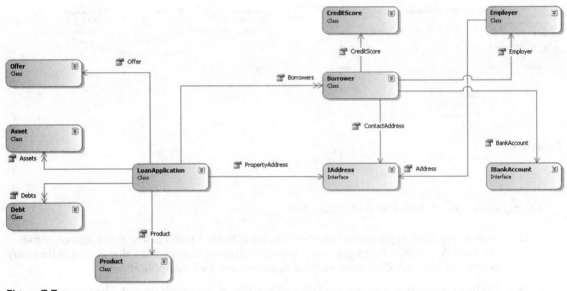

Figure 7-7

The entities that were identified in the Domain Model are still present in the class diagram, but there is a big difference in that value objects are used to represent objects that are shared throughout the Domain Model, such as `Address` and `BankAccount`.

Identifying the Aggregates

Now that you have built the Domain Model and class diagram, you need to identify the aggregate roots that will act as the entry points into the Domain Model, Figure 7-8 shows each of the aggregate boundaries circled.

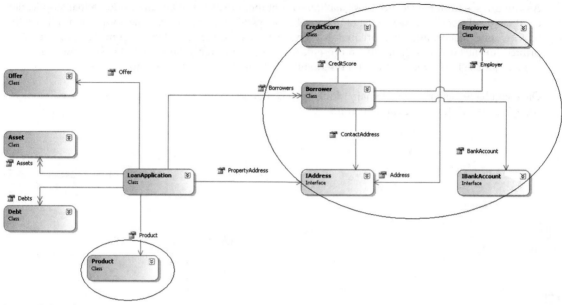

Figure 7-8

The aggregate roots that have been identified are:

❑ Loan Application Aggregation with the `LoanApplication` entity acting as the aggregate root. The Loan Application Aggregation encompasses all of the entities and value objects in the entire Domain Model, and all of them working together form the loan application.

❑ Product Aggregation with the `Product` entity acting as the aggregate root. The reason a `Product` has its own aggregation is that you will want to work with `Products` without having to go through the `Loan Application`. You can say that `Products` exist without a `Loan Application`.

❑ Borrower Aggregation with the `Borrower` entity acting as the aggregate root. As with the Solicitor Aggregation, it makes sense to be able to work with a `Borrower` without having to go through a `Loan Application`.

Building the Application

Now that you have mapped out the Domain Model and identified the aggregates, it's time to flesh out the model with all the behavior and data that it needs to represent.

1. Create a new blank solution named `ProEnt.LoanApproval` by selecting Other Projects Types ⇨ Visual Studio Solutions from the New Project dialog box, as shown in Figure 7-9.

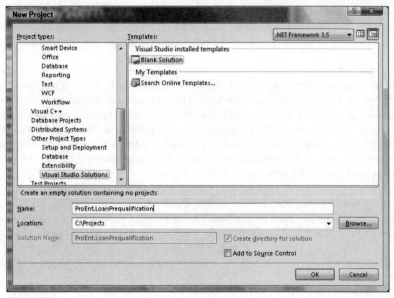

Figure 7-9

2. Now add a new class library project to the solution by selecting File ⇨ Add ⇨ New Project, and name it `ProEnt.LoanPrequalification.Model`.

3. Once the project is built, add a folder for each of the aggregates in the model. The folders to add are: `Borrowers`, `LoanApplications`, and `Products`. Your solution should now look like Figure 7-10.

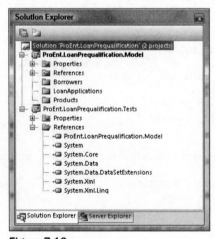

Figure 7-10

4. Finally add a new class library project to the solution by selecting File ⇨ Add ⇨ New Project, name it `ProEnt.MortgageBroker.ModelTests`, and add a reference to the model project. This will hold tests that verify your model and will also help you with the design of your system.

Now that you have set up your project, you can start to build the application. If you take a look at the class diagram that you initially sketched out, there are two classes that are shared among many of the aggregates. These are `Address` and `BankAccount`. These two classes are both value objects and don't require an identity, because it's the values of the attributes that are important. The `Address` and `BankAccount` objects will contain little business logic apart from a method call in the constructor to ensure that the object is created in a valid state. You need to add the validation at this point, as the `Address` and `BankAccount` are immutable and cannot be changed once created. The `BankAccount` will have a single method that enables money to be transferred.

To make it easy to identify if an object is valid or not, you are going to create a standalone object that will be used to hold any broken business or validation rules relating to an entity or value object. This `BrokenBusinessRule` object will be consistently used across all of your entities and value objects.

Now that you understand the roles of `Address`, `BankAccount`, and `BrokenBusinessRule`, you can start to build your Domain Model.

1. Create a new class called `BrokenBusinessRule` in the root of the model project with the following code:

```
namespace ProEnt.LoanPrequalification.Model
{
    public class BrokenBusinessRule
    {
        private string _property;

        public string Property
        {
            get { return _property; }
            set { _property = value; }
        }

        private string _rule;

        public string Rule
        {
            get { return _rule; }
            set { _rule = value; }
        }

        public BrokenBusinessRule(string property, string rule)
        {
            this._property = property;
            this._rule = rule;
        }
    }
}
```

2. Add a new interface to the root of the Model project, named IAddress:

```
using System.Collections.Generic;

namespace ProEnt.LoanPrequalification.Model
{
    public interface IAddress
    {
        string City { get; }
        List<BrokenBusinessRule> GetBrokenRules();
        string PostCode { get; }
        string Street { get; }
        string Town { get; }
    }
}
```

3. Add a new class to the root of the Model project, named Address, that implements the interfaces with the following code listing:

```
using System.Collections.Generic;
using System.Text;

namespace ProEnt.LoanPrequalification.Model
{
    /// <summary>
    /// This is a value object and has no identity
    /// </summary>
    public class Address : IAddress
    {
        private string _street;
        private string _town;
        private string _city;
        private string _postcode;

        public Address(string street, string town, string city, string postcode)
        {
            _street = street;
            _town = town;
            _city = city;
            _postcode = postcode;

            if (GetBrokenRules().Count > 0)
            {
                throw new Exception(String.Format(
                    "The Address you are trying to create is invalid.{0}",
                                        GetBrokenRulesToString()));
            }
        }

        public string Street
        {
            get { return _street; }
        }
```

```csharp
        public string Town
        {
            get { return _town; }
        }

        public string City
        {
            get { return _city; }
        }

        public string PostCode
        {
            get { return _postcode; }
        }

        private string GetBrokenRulesToString()
        {
            StringBuilder sbBrokenRules = new StringBuilder();

            foreach (BrokenBusinessRule br in GetBrokenRules())
            {
                sbBrokenRules.Append(br.Rule);
            }

            return sbBrokenRules.ToString();
        }

        public List<BrokenBusinessRule> GetBrokenRules()
        {
            List<BrokenBusinessRule> brokenRules = new List<BrokenBusinessRule>();

            if (String.IsNullOrEmpty(Street))
                brokenRules.Add(new BrokenBusinessRule(
                    "Street", "A Street must be defined for an address."));

            if (String.IsNullOrEmpty(Town))
                brokenRules.Add(new BrokenBusinessRule(
                    "Town", "A Town must be defined for an address."));

            if (String.IsNullOrEmpty(City))
                brokenRules.Add(new BrokenBusinessRule(
                    "City", "A City must be defined for an address."));

            if (String.IsNullOrEmpty(PostCode))
                brokenRules.Add(new BrokenBusinessRule(
                    "PostCode", "A PostCode must be defined for an address."));

            return brokenRules;
        }
    }
}
```

4.   Add a second interface, again to the root of the project, named `IBankAccount`:

```
using System.Collections.Generic;

namespace ProEnt.LoanPrequalification.Model
{
    public interface IBankAccount
    {
        string AccountNumber { get; }
        string BankName { get; }
        void Credit(float Amount);
        List<BrokenBusinessRule> GetBrokenRules();
        string Name { get; }
        string SortCode { get; }
    }
}
```

5.   Add a new class to the root of the Model project, named `BankAccount`, with the following code listing:

```
using System;
using System.Collections.Generic;
using System.Text;

namespace ProEnt.LoanPrequalification.Model
{
    /// <summary>
    /// This is a value object and has no identity
    /// </summary>
    public class BankAccount : IBankAccount
    {
        private string _accountNumber;
        private string _name;
        private string _bankName;
        private string _sortCode;

        public BankAccount(string accountNumber, string name,
                           string sortCode, string bankName)
        {
            _accountNumber = accountNumber;
            _name = name;
            _sortCode = sortCode;
            _bankName = bankName;

            if (GetBrokenRules().Count > 0)
            {
                throw new Exception(String.Format(
                "The bank account you are trying to create contains invalid
                data.{0}",
```

```
                    GetBrokenRulesToString()));
        }
    }

    public string AccountNumber
    {
        get { return _accountNumber; }
    }

    public string Name
    {
        get { return _name; }
    }

    public string SortCode
    {
        get { return _sortCode; }
    }

    public string BankName
    {
        get { return _bankName; }
    }

    private string GetBrokenRulesToString()
    {
        StringBuilder sbBrokenRules = new StringBuilder();

        foreach (BrokenBusinessRule br in GetBrokenRules())
        {
            sbBrokenRules.Append(br.Rule);
        }

        return sbBrokenRules.ToString();
    }

    public List<BrokenBusinessRule> GetBrokenRules()
    {
        List<BrokenBusinessRule> brokenRules = new List<BrokenBusinessRule>();

        if (String.IsNullOrEmpty(SortCode))
            brokenRules.Add(new BrokenBusinessRule(
                "SortCode", "A SortCode must be defined for an Bank Account."));

        if (String.IsNullOrEmpty(AccountNumber))
            brokenRules.Add(new BrokenBusinessRule(
                "AccountNumber",
                "An AccountNumber must be defined for an Bank Account."));
```

```
            if (String.IsNullOrEmpty(BankName))
                brokenRules.Add(new BrokenBusinessRule(
                    "Bank", "Please specify the name of the bank."));

            if (String.IsNullOrEmpty(Name))
                brokenRules.Add(new BrokenBusinessRule(
                    "Name", "Please specify the name of the account holder."));

            return brokenRules;
        }
    }
}
```

The reason why interfaces have been used for the `BankAccount` and `Address` is that they will help to keep the code loosely coupled and will enable you to easily swap out the implementations if you need to create a different type of `Address` or `BankAccount` down the line without danger of the Domain Model being broken. Another side effect of loosely coupled code is that it makes it easier to test, as you can substitute real implementation of the `Address` and `BankAccount` classes for stubs or mocks, as was discussed in Chapter 4.

Both the `BankAccount` and the `Address` classes are very simple and contain only minimal validation logic; however, you could further expand on the validation for the `BankAccount` class by adding a regular expression check to verify that the sort code and account number were in the correct format.

The next entity you will tackle is the `Product` class, which represents the actual mortgage product.

Create a new class in the Products folder of the Model class named `Product` with the following code:

```
using System;
using System.Collections.Generic;

namespace ProEnt.LoanPrequalification.Model.Products
{
    public class Product
    {
        private Guid _id;
        private string _name;
        private float _interestRate;
        private float _maximumLTV;
        private float _maximumLoan;
        private int _maximumLoanTerm;

        public Guid Id
        {
            get { return _id; }
            set { _id = value; }
        }
        public string Name
        {
            get { return _name; }
```

```
            set { _name = value; }
    }

    public float InterestRate
    {
        get { return _interestRate; }
        set { _interestRate = value; }
    }

    public float MaximumLTV
    {
        get { return _maximumLTV; }
        set { _maximumLTV = value; }
    }

    public float MaximumLoan
    {
        get { return _maximumLoan; }
        set { _maximumLoan = value; }
    }

    public int MaximumLoanTerm
    {
        get { return _maximumLoanTerm; }
        set { _maximumLoanTerm = value; }
    }

    public List<BrokenBusinessRule> GetBrokenRules()
    {
        List<BrokenBusinessRule> brokenRules = new List<BrokenBusinessRule>();

        if (String.IsNullOrEmpty(Name))
            brokenRules.Add(new BrokenBusinessRule(
                            "Name", "A product must have a name."));

        if (!IsValidInterestRate())
            brokenRules.Add(new BrokenBusinessRule(
                    "InterestRate",
                    " product's interest rate must be a multiple of 0.25."));

        return brokenRules;
    }

    private bool IsValidInterestRate()
    {
        bool valid = true;

        if (InterestRate > 0)
        {
            if (InterestRate % 0.125 != 0)
```

```
            {
                valid = false;
            }
        }
        else
        {
            valid = false;
        }

        return valid;
    }
}
}
```

Again this is a very simple class; the only logic used is the IsValidInterestRate method that is used to verify that interest rates are in multiples of 0.25%.

The penultimate aggregation you need to create is the Borrower aggregation. You have already created both the BankAccount and Address value objects, but you need to create two more value objects to represent the borrower's employer and the borrower's credit score.

1. Create a new class within the Borrowers folder of the Model project called Employer with the following code:

```
using System;
using System.Collections.Generic;
using System.Text;

namespace ProEnt.LoanPrequalification.Model.Borrowers
{
    public class Employer
    {
        private float _monthlyIncome;
        private IAddress _address;
        private string _name;

        public Employer(float MonthlyIncome, IAddress EmployerAddress,
                        string EmployerName)
        {
            _monthlyIncome = MonthlyIncome;
            _employerAddress = EmployerAddress;
            _employerName = EmployerName;

            if (GetBrokenRules().Count > 0)
            {
                throw new Exception(String.Format(
                "The Employer you are trying to create contains invalid data.{0}",
                                                GetBrokenRulesToString()));
            }
        }

        public string Name
        {
```

```csharp
        get { return _name; }
    }

    public float MonthlyIncome
    {
        get { return _monthlyIncome; }
    }

    public IAddress Address
    {
        get { return _address; }
    }

    private string GetBrokenRulesToString()
    {
        StringBuilder sbBrokenRules = new StringBuilder();

        foreach (BrokenBusinessRule br in GetBrokenRules())
        {
            sbBrokenRules.Append(br.Rule);
        }

        return sbBrokenRules.ToString();
    }

    public List<BrokenBusinessRule> GetBrokenRules()
    {
        List<BrokenBusinessRule> brokenRules = new List<BrokenBusinessRule>();

        if (String.IsNullOrEmpty(Name))
            brokenRules.Add(new BrokenBusinessRule(
                    "Name", "A name must defined for an employer."));

        if (MonthlyIncome <= 0)
            brokenRules.Add(new BrokenBusinessRule(
                    "MonthlyIncome",
                    "A Monthly Income must be greater than 0."));

        if (Address == null)
            brokenRules.Add(new BrokenBusinessRule(
                    "Address",
                    "An address must defined for an employer."));
        else if (Address.GetBrokenRules().Count > 0)
        {
            AddToBrokenRulesList(brokenRules, Address.GetBrokenRules());
        }

        return brokenRules;
    }

    private void AddToBrokenRulesList(
                List<BrokenBusinessRule> currentBrokenRules,
                List<BrokenBusinessRule> brokenRulesToAdd)
    {
```

```
            foreach (BrokenBusinessRule brokenRule in brokenRulesToAdd)
            {
                currentBrokenRules.Add(brokenRule);
            }
        }
    }
}
```

2.   Create a credit score value object within the Borrowers folder with the following code definition:

```
using System;
using System.Collections.Generic;
using System.Text;

namespace ProEnt.LoanPrequalification.Model.Borrowers
{
    public class CreditScore
    {
        private int _score;
        private string _creditAgency;

        public CreditScore(string creditAgency, int score)
        {
            _creditAgency = creditAgency;
            _score = score;

            if (GetBrokenRules().Count > 0)
            {
                throw new Exception(String.Format(
                    "The Credit score has been created with invalid data. {0}",
                                        GetBrokenRulesToString()));
            }
        }

        public string CreditAgency
        {
            get { return _creditAgency; }
        }

        public int Score
        {
            get { return _score; }
        }

        public override string ToString()
        {
            return string.Format("{0},  Score: {1}", CreditAgency, Score);
        }
```

```
public List<BrokenBusinessRule> GetBrokenRules()
{
    List<BrokenBusinessRule> brokenRules = new List<BrokenBusinessRule>();

    if (string.IsNullOrEmpty(CreditAgency))
        brokenRules.Add(new BrokenBusinessRule(
            "CreditAgency",
            "You must enter a valid credit agency for this credit score."));

    if (Score < 400 || Score > 900)
        brokenRules.Add(new BrokenBusinessRule(
            "Score",
            "You must enter a valid credit score between 400 and 900."));

    return brokenRules;
}

private string GetBrokenRulesToString()
{
    StringBuilder sbBrokenRules = new StringBuilder();

    foreach (BrokenBusinessRule br in GetBrokenRules())
    {
        sbBrokenRules.Append(br.Rule);
    }

    return sbBrokenRules.ToString();
}
    }
}
```

3. Finally, create the `Borrower` entity itself with its associations to `Employer`, `Address`, and `BankAccount`. The code listing that follows shows the definition of a `Borrower`:

```
using System;
using System.Collections.Generic;

namespace ProEnt.LoanPrequalification.Model.Borrowers
{
    public class Borrower
    {
        private Guid _id;
        private int _age;
        private string _firstName;
        private string _lastName;
        private IAddress _contactAddress;
        private IBankAccount _bankAccount;
        private CreditScore _creditScore;
        private Employer _employer;
        private LoanApplication _loanApplication;

        public Guid Id
        {
```

```
        get { return _id; }
        set { _id = value; }
    }

    public LoanApplication LoanApplication
    {
        get { return _loanApplication; }
        set { _loanApplication = value; }
    }

    public int Age
    {
        get { return _age; }
        set { _age = value; }
    }

    public string FirstName
    {
        get { return _firstName; }
        set { _firstName = value; }
    }

    public string LastName
    {
        get { return _lastName; }
        set { _lastName = value; }
    }

    public IAddress ContactAddress
    {
        get { return _address; }
        set { _address = value; }
    }

    public Employer Employer
    {
        get { return _employer; }
        set { _employer = value; }
    }

    public IBankAccount BankAccount
    {
        get { return _bankAccount; }
        set { _bankAccount = value; }
    }

    public CreditScore CreditScore
    {
        get { return _creditScore; }
        set { _creditScore = value; }
    }

    public List<BrokenBusinessRule> GetBrokenRules()
    {
```

```
List<BrokenBusinessRule> brokenRules = new List<BrokenBusinessRule>();

if (Age < 18)
    brokenRules.Add(new BrokenBusinessRule(
        "Age", "A borrower must be over 18 years of age."));

if (String.IsNullOrEmpty(FirstName))
    brokenRules.Add(new BrokenBusinessRule(
        "FirstName", "A borrower must have a first name."));

if (String.IsNullOrEmpty(LastName))
    brokenRules.Add(new BrokenBusinessRule(
        "LastName", "A borrower must have a last name."));

if (CreditScore == null)
    brokenRules.Add(new BrokenBusinessRule(
        "CreditScore", "A borrower must have a credit score."));
else if (CreditScore.GetBrokenRules().Count > 0)
{
    AddToBrokenRulesList(brokenRules,
                        CreditScore.GetBrokenRules());
}

if (BankAccount == null)
    brokenRules.Add(new BrokenBusinessRule("BankAccount",
        "A borrower must have a bank account defined."));
else if (BankAccount.GetBrokenRules().Count > 0)
{
    AddToBrokenRulesList(brokenRules,
                        BankAccount.GetBrokenRules());
}

if (Employer == null)
    brokenRules.Add(new BrokenBusinessRule("Employer",
        "A borrower must have an employer."));
else if (Employer.GetBrokenRules().Count > 0)
{
    AddToBrokenRulesList(brokenRules, Employer.GetBrokenRules());
}

if (ContactAddress == null)
    brokenRules.Add(new BrokenBusinessRule("ContactAddress",
        "A borrower must have a bank account defined."));
else if (ContactAddress.GetBrokenRules().Count > 0)
{
    AddToBrokenRulesList(brokenRules,
                ContactAddress.GetBrokenRules());
}

return brokenRules;
}
```

```
        private void AddToBrokenRulesList(
                List<BrokenBusinessRule> currentBrokenRules,
                List<BrokenBusinessRule> brokenRulesToAdd)
    {
        foreach (BrokenBusinessRule brokenRule in brokenRulesToAdd)
        {
            currentBrokenRules.Add(brokenRule);
        }
    }
    }
    }
}
```

The last aggregate group you need to add to the Domain Model is the loan application. You have already created most of this aggregation during the creation of the other aggregations, so this will be a short exercise.

1. Add a new class to the LoanApplications folder named Asset with the following listing. An Asset will represent the combined assets that the borrowers to put up against the loan. You will be creating both the Asset and Debt objects as entities, because you are interested in the identity of these objects, as the borrowers may want to update the state of their assets and debts throughout the lifetime of a loan application.

```
using System;
using System.Collections.Generic;

namespace ProEnt.LoanPrequalification.Model.LoanApplications
{
    public class Asset
    {
        private Guid _id;
        private float _balance;
        private string _accountNumber;
        private string _description;
        private LoanApplication _loanApplication;

        public Guid Id
        {
            get { return _id; }
            set { _id = value; }
        }
        public LoanApplication LoanApplication
        {
            get { return _loanApplication;  }
            set {  _loanApplication = value;  }
        }

        public string Description
        {
            get { return _description; }
            set { _description = value; }
        }
```

```
          public string AccountNumber
          {
              get { return _accountNumber; }
              set { _accountNumber = value; }
          }

          public float Balance
          {
              get { return _balance; }
              set { _balance = value; }
          }

          public List<BrokenBusinessRule> GetBrokenBusinessRules()
          {
              List<BrokenBusinessRule> brokenRules = new List<BrokenBusinessRule>();

              if (string.IsNullOrEmpty(Description))
                  brokenRules.Add(new BrokenBusinessRule(
                      "Description",
                      "You must enter a valid description for this asset."));

              if (Balance <= 0)
                  brokenRules.Add(new BrokenBusinessRule("Balance",
                      "You must enter a valid amount for the balance of this asset." +
                      " Do not use commas."));

              return brokenRules;
          }
      }
  }
```

2. Add a new class to the LoanApplications folder named Debt with the following code definition. A Debt will represent the combined debts of the borrowers to be taken into consideration when verifying if the borrowers can afford the loan payments.

```
using System.Collections.Generic;

namespace ProEnt.LoanPrequalification.Model.LoanApplications
{
    public class Debt
    {
        private string _id;
        private string _description;
        private string _creditorName;
        private float? _balanceOwed;
        private float? _monthlyPayment;
        private LoanApplication _loanApplication;

        public string Id
        {
            get { return _id; }
```

```
        set { _id = value; }
    }

    public LoanApplication LoanApplication
    {
        get { return _loanApplication; }
        set { _loanApplication = value; }
    }

    public string Description
    {
        get { return _description; }
        set { _description = value; }
    }

    public string CreditorName
    {
        get { return _creditorName; }
        set { _creditorName = value; }
    }

    public float? BalanceOwed
    {
        get { return _balanceOwed; }
        set { _balanceOwed = value; }
    }

    public float? MonthlyPayment
    {
        get { return _monthlyPayment; }
        set { _monthlyPayment = value; }
    }

    public List<BrokenBusinessRule> GetBrokenBusinessRules()
    {
        List<BrokenBusinessRule> brokenRules = new List<BrokenBusinessRule>();

        if (string.IsNullOrEmpty(Description))
            brokenRules.Add(new BrokenBusinessRule("Description",
                "You must enter a valid description for this debt."));

        if (string.IsNullOrEmpty(CreditorName))
            brokenRules.Add(new BrokenBusinessRule("CreditorName",
                "You must enter a valid name for the creditor."));

        if (BalanceOwed == null ||
            BalanceOwed <= 0)
            brokenRules.Add(new BrokenBusinessRule("BalanceOwed",
                "You must enter a valid balance for this debt. "+
                " Do not use commas."));

        if (MonthlyPayment == null ||
            MonthlyPayment <= 0)
```

```
            brokenRules.Add(new BrokenBusinessRule("MonthlyPayment",
                "You must enter a valid monthly payment for this debt. "+
                " Do not use commas."));

            return brokenRules;
        }
    }
}
```

3. Add a new class to the LoanApplications folder named `Offer` with the following code. The offer entity will represent the real offer amount given to borrowers after they have been approved for a loan.

```
using System;
using System.Collections.Generic;
using System.Text;

namespace ProEnt.LoanPrequalification.Model.LoanApplications
{
    public class Offer
    {
        private DateTime _expirationDate;
        private int _loanAmount;
        private float _interestRate;
        private int _loanTerm;

        public Offer()
        { }

        public Offer(int loanAmount, int loanTerm,
                    float interestRate, DateTime expirationDate)
        {
            _loanAmount = loanAmount;
            _loanTerm = loanTerm;
            _interestRate = interestRate;
            _expirationDate = expirationDate;

            if (GetBrokenRules().Count > 0)
            {
                throw new Exception(
        String.Format("The offer is trying to be created with invalid data.{0}",
                        GetBrokenRulesToString()));
            }
        }

        public float InterestRate
        {
            get { return _interestRate; }
        }

        public int LoanAmount
        {
            get { return _loanAmount; }
```

```
    }

    public DateTime ExpirationDate
    {
        get { return _expirationDate; }
    }

    public int LoanTerm
    {
        get { return _loanTerm; }
    }

    public bool HasExpired()
    {
        return ExpirationDate < DateTime.Now.AddMonths(-6);
    }

    private string GetBrokenRulesToString()
    {
        StringBuilder sbBrokenRules = new StringBuilder();

        foreach (BrokenBusinessRule br in GetBrokenRules())
        {
            sbBrokenRules.Append(br.Rule);
        }

        return sbBrokenRules.ToString();
    }

    public List<BrokenBusinessRule> GetBrokenRules()
    {
        List<BrokenBusinessRule> brokenRules = new List<BrokenBusinessRule>();

        if (InterestRate <= 0)
            brokenRules.Add(new BrokenBusinessRule
                ("InterestRate",
                 "An Offer must have an interest rate greater than zero."));

        if (LoanAmount <= 0)
            brokenRules.Add(new BrokenBusinessRule
                ("LoanAmount",
                 "An Offer must have a Loan Amount greater than zero."));

        if (LoanAmount <= 0)
            brokenRules.Add(new BrokenBusinessRule
                ("LoanTerm",
                 "An Offer must have a Loan Term greater than zero."));

        return brokenRules;
    }
    }
}
```

4. Before you create the `LoanApplication` itself, there are two more supporting classes that need to be created. One is an enumeration that will be used to identify the status of a loan application. The second is a custom exception, which will be thrown when methods are called on a `LoanApplication` when it is in an invalid state. It's a good idea to use custom exceptions so that client code can handle exceptions that represent errors in the workflow as opposed to exceptions thrown by the .NET Framework. Create both of these classes within the LoanApplications folder, with the following code:

```
namespace ProEnt.LoanPrequalification.Model.LoanApplications
{
    public enum Status
    {
        AwaitingPrequalification = 0,
        OfferGiven = 1,
        Declined = 2,
        Expired = 3     }
}

namespace ProEnt.LoanPrequalification.Model.LoanApplications
{
    public class InvalidLoanApplicationException : Exception
    {
        public InvalidLoanApplicationException() { }
        public InvalidLoanApplicationException(string message) : base(message) { }
    }
}
```

5. Finally add a new class to represent the loan application itself, name the class `LoanApplication`, and again create this within the `LoanApplications` folder with the following code:

```
using System;
using System.Collections.Generic;
using System.Collections.ObjectModel;
using System.Text;
using ProEnt.LoanPrequalification.Model.Borrowers;
using ProEnt.LoanPrequalification.Model.Products;
using ProEnt.LoanPrequalification.Model.Solicitors;

namespace ProEnt.LoanPrequalification.Model.LoanApplications
{
    public class LoanApplication
    {
        private Guid _id;
        private int _deposit;
        private Status _status;
        private IList<Borrower> _borrowers;
        private IAddress _property;
        private Products.Product _product;
        private Offer _offer;
        private int _propertyValue;
        private int _loanAmount;
        private int _loanTerm;
        private Solicitors.Solicitor _solicitor;
```

```csharp
private IList<Asset> _assets;
private IList<Debt> _debts;

public LoanApplication()
{
    _borrowers = new List<Borrower>();
    _assets = new List<Asset>();
    _debts = new List<Debt>();
}

public Guid Id
{
    get { return _id; }
    set { _id = value; }
}

public int Deposit
{
    get { return _deposit; }
    set { _deposit = value; }
}

public Status Status
{
    get { return _status; }
    set { _status = value; }
}

public ReadOnlyCollection<Borrower> Borrowers
{
    get { return new ReadOnlyCollection<Borrower>(_borrowers); }
}

public void Add(Borrower borrower)
{
    if (Borrowers.Count != 2)
    {
        _borrowers.Add(borrower);
    }
    else
    {
        throw new InvalidLoanApplicationException(
            "No more than two borrowers can apply for a loan.");
    }
}

public void Remove(Borrower borrower)
{
    _borrowers.Remove(borrower);
}

public IAddress PropertyAddress
{
```

```csharp
        get { return _property; }
        set { _property = value; }
    }

    public int PropertyValue
    {
        get { return _propertyValue; }
        set { _propertyValue = value; }
    }

    public int LoanAmount
    {
        get { return _loanAmount; }
        set { _loanAmount = value; }
    }

    public int LoanTerm
    {
        get { return _loanTerm; }
        set { _loanTerm = value; }
    }

    public Product Product
    {
        get { return _product; }
        set { _product = value; }
    }

    public Solicitor Solicitor
    {
        get { return _solicitor; }
        set { _solicitor = value; }
    }

    public Offer Offer
    {
        get { return _offer; }
    }

    public List<Asset> Assets
    {
        get { return _assets; }
        set { _assets = value; }
    }

    public List<Debt> Debts
    {
        get { return _debts; }
        set { _debts = value; }
    }

    public float BorrowerTotalMonthlyIncome()
    {
```

```csharp
        float totalJoinedMonthlyIncome = 0;

        foreach (Borrower b in Borrowers)
        {
            totalJoinedMonthlyIncome += b.Employer.MonthlyIncome;
        }
        return totalJoinedMonthlyIncome;
    }

    public float BorrowerTotalMonthlyDebts()
    {
        float totalMonthlyDebt = 0;

        foreach (Debt d in Debts)
        {
            totalMonthlyDebt += d.MonthlyPayment.Value;
        }
        return totalMonthlyDebt;

    }

    public List<BrokenBusinessRule> GetBrokenRules()
    {
        List<BrokenBusinessRule> brokenRules = new List<BrokenBusinessRule>();

        if (Borrowers.Count == 0)
            brokenRules.Add(new BrokenBusinessRule("Borrower",
                    "A loan application must have at least one borrower."));
        else
        {
            foreach (Borrower borrower in this.Borrowers)
            {
                if (borrower.GetBrokenRules().Count > 0)
                {
                    AddToBrokenRulesList(brokenRules,
                                    Borrowers[0].GetBrokenRules());
                }
            }
        }

        if (Solicitor == null)
            brokenRules.Add(new BrokenBusinessRule("Solicitor",
                    "A loan application must have an acting Solicitor."));
        else if (Solicitor.GetBrokenRules().Count > 0)
        {
            AddToBrokenRulesList(brokenRules, Solicitor.GetBrokenRules());
        }

        if (PropertyAddress == null)
            brokenRules.Add(new BrokenBusinessRule("PropertyAddress",
                    "A loan application must have a property address."));
        else if (PropertyAddress.GetBrokenRules().Count > 0)
        {
```

```
                    AddToBrokenRulesList(brokenRules,
                                    PropertyAddress.GetBrokenRules());
        }

        if (Deposit < 0)
            brokenRules.Add(new BrokenBusinessRule("Deposit",
                    "A deposit must be a non negative number."));

        if (PropertyValue <= 0)
            brokenRules.Add(new BrokenBusinessRule("PropertyValue",
                    "A property must have a value gretaer than zero."));

        if (LoanAmount <= 0)
            brokenRules.Add(new BrokenBusinessRule("LoanAmount",
                    "A loan amount must be greater than zero."));

        if (LoanTerm <= 0)
            brokenRules.Add(new BrokenBusinessRule("LoanTerm",
                    "A loan term must be greater than zero."));

        if (Product == null)
            brokenRules.Add(new BrokenBusinessRule("Product",
                    "A loan application must have a loan product selected."));
        else if (Product.GetBrokenRules().Count > 0)
        {
            AddToBrokenRulesList(brokenRules, Product.GetBrokenRules());
        }

        return brokenRules;
    }

    private void AddToBrokenRulesList(
            List<BrokenBusinessRule> currentBrokenRules,
            List<BrokenBusinessRule> brokenRulesToAdd)
    {
        foreach (BrokenBusinessRule brokenRule in brokenRulesToAdd)
        {
            currentBrokenRules.Add(brokenRule);
        }
    }
}
}
```

6. Your solution should resemble Figure 7-11.

Figure 7-11

Up to now, you have simply built the framework for the Domain Model. The model itself is looking very anemic at the moment and doesn't really do a lot, so it's time to add some behavior to the entities.

To ensure that you stay focused on the job at hand, you are going to create some tests that will drive your development of the business logic involved in the approval of a loan.

1. Before you create any tests, you need to add a reference to the NUnit framework. Navigate to the folder structure by right-clicking on the solution name and selecting Open Folder in Windows Explorer. Add a new folder called lib, and copy the NUnit.Framework.dll file from C:\Program Files\NUnit 2.4.8\bin into the newly created lib folder. Refer to Chapter 3 for where to download the NUnit framework.

2. Add a new solution folder to the solution called Lib. To do this, right-click on the solution root, then select Add ⇨ Add New Solution Folder.

3. Add the NUnit.Framework.dll to your solution by right-clicking on the lib solution folder and selecting Add ⇨ Add Existing Item, then navigating to the NUnit.Framework.dll file in the lib folder at the root of your application.

4. Add a reference to the NUnit.Framework.dll from the ProEnt. LoanPrequalification.Tests Project by right-clicking on the ProEnt.LoanPrequalification.Tests Project name and selecting Add Reference. In the dialog window that appears, select the Browse tab, navigate to the Lib folder, and select NUnit.Framework.dll.

5. Now that you have the NUnit framework in place, you can start to write your tests. Add a new class to the Test project called `LoanApplicationTests`, with the following definition, which includes your first test:

```
using NUnit.Framework;
using ProEnt.LoanPrequalification.Model.LoanApplications;

namespace ProEnt.LoanPrequalification.Tests
{
    [TestFixture]
    public class LoanApplicationTests
    {
        [Test]
        [ExpectedException(typeof(InvalidLoanApplicationException))]
        public void
A_Loan_Application_Will_Throw_An_Error_If_It_Is_In_An_Invalid_State_When_
Prequalifiying()
        {
            LoanApplication loanApp = new LoanApplication();

            loanApp.Prequalify();
        }
    }
}
```

If you try to build the solution, it won't compile because of the missing `Prequalify` method, so the first thing to do is to create this method. The only job the method needs to do to get this test to pass is determine if the loan is in a valid state.

```
        public class LoanApplication
        {
            ...

            public void Prequalify()
            {
                ThrowExceptionIfLoanAppIsInvalid("Prequalification");
            }

            private void ThrowExceptionIfLoanAppIsInvalid(string Process)
            {
                if (GetBrokenRules().Count > 0)
                {
                    StringBuilder sbBrokenRules = new StringBuilder();

                    foreach (BrokenBusinessRule br in GetBrokenRules())
                    {
                        sbBrokenRules.Append(br.Rule);
                    }

                    throw new InvalidLoanApplicationException(
                        String.Format(
                            "The '{0}' process cannot be started because"+
```

```
                            " the loan application is in an invalid state. {1}",
                            Process, sbBrokenRules.ToString()));
            }
        }

        ...
    }
```

A second method has been created, as this check on an application's validity will be called before any attempt is made to call a method on it. If you rebuild the solution and run the test, it will pass.

Before we write the next test you are going to create a helper method within the test class that will return a valid loan application. This is necessary because nearly all of the subsequent tests are going to need a valid loan application, and it will be easier to have a ready-made one than to clog up the test case itself with setup code. You are also going to make two stub classes to create the valid loan application faster.

1. Create a folder called Stubs within the Test project.

2. Add two classes into the Stubs folder, named StubBankAccount and StubAddress, with the following class listings:

```
using System.Collections.Generic;
using ProEnt.LoanPrequalification.Model;

namespace ProEnt.LoanPrequalification.Tests.Stubs
{
    public class StubAddress : IAddress
    {
        public string City
        {
            get { return ""; }
        }

        public List<BrokenBusinessRule> GetBrokenRules()
        {
            return new List<BrokenBusinessRule>();
        }

        public string PostCode
        {
            get { return ""; }
        }

        public string Street
        {
            get { return ""; }
        }

        public string Town
        {
```

```
            get { return ""; }
        }
    }
}

using System.Collections.Generic;
using ProEnt.LoanPrequalification.Model;

namespace ProEnt.LoanPrequalification.Tests.Stubs
{
    public class StubBankAccount : IBankAccount
    {
        public string AccountNumber
        {
            get { return "AccountNumber"; }
        }

        public string BankName
        {
            get { return "BankName"; }
        }

        public void Credit(float Amount)
        {
        }

        public List<BrokenBusinessRule> GetBrokenRules()
        {
            return new List<BrokenBusinessRule>();
        }

        public string Name
        {
            get { return "Name"; }
        }

        public string SortCode
        {
            get { return "SortCode"; }
        }
    }
}
```

3. Now you can create the helper method on the test class to generate a valid loan application. Add the following code to the `LoanApplicationTests` class:

```
using NUnit.Framework;
using ProEnt.LoanPrequalification.Model;
using ProEnt.LoanPrequalification.Model.Borrowers;
using ProEnt.LoanPrequalification.Model.LoanApplications;
using ProEnt.LoanPrequalification.Model.Products;
```

```csharp
using ProEnt.LoanPrequalification.Tests.Stubs;

namespace ProEnt.LoanPrequalification.Tests
{
    [TestFixture]
    public class LoanApplicationTests
    {
        ...

        public LoanApplication
            CreateAValidLoanApplicationAwaitingPrequalification()
        {
            LoanApplication loanApp = new LoanApplication();

            Product product = new Product();
            product.InterestRate = 1.25f;
            product.Name = "Tracker A";
            product.MaximumLTV = 95;
            product.MaximumLoan = 200000;
            product.MaximumLoanTerm = 35;

            IAddress address = new StubAddress();
            IBankAccount bankAccount = new StubBankAccount();

            loanApp.Product = product;
            loanApp.PropertyAddress = address;
            loanApp.LoanAmount = 80000;
            loanApp.PropertyValue = 100000;
            loanApp.LoanTerm = 30;
            loanApp.Deposit = 20000;


            Borrower borrower = new Borrower();

            Employer employer = new Employer(3000, address, "IBM");
            CreditScore creditScore = new CreditScore("Experian", 800);

            borrower.Employer = employer;
            borrower.CreditScore = creditScore;
            borrower.BankAccount = bankAccount;
            borrower.ContactAddress = address;
            borrower.Age = 21;
            borrower.FirstName = "Scott";
            borrower.LastName = "Millett";

            loanApp.Add(borrower);

            loanApp.Status = Status.AwaitingPrequalification;

            return loanApp;

        }
    }
}
```

The next test requires a valid loan application that will not pass the prequalification process. You can use the new helper method, but you will need to swap the employer implementation for a new employer object that has a very low borrower monthly income to ensure that prequalification is not passed.

```
[Test]
public void A_Loan_Applications_Status_Will_Change_To_Declined_If_Valid_But_Does_
Not_Pass_Prequalification()
{
        LoanApplication loanApp =
            CreateAValidLoanApplicationAwaitingPrequalification();

        // Ensure the loan applicaiton will not pass prequalification by
        // altering the borrowers monthly salary
        IAddress exisitngAddress = loanApp.Borrowers[0].Employer.Address;
        Employer emp = new Employer(100, exisitngAddress, "My Employer");

        loanApp.Borrowers[0].Employer = emp;

        loanApp.Prequalify();

        Assert.AreEqual(loanApp.Status, Status.Declined);
}
```

The test will fail because the `Prequalify` method lacks any real business logic. From the conversation with the domain expert, you know that the prequalification process needs to perform a number of steps to ensure that a loan application for a given product is within the thresholds of the product as well as being affordable to the borrower. This check is common to all products but varies as the products' attributes vary. You are going to create a class that will be used by the product to verify all of these rules.

Before you can add a class to check for prequalification, you need a way to calculate the monthly cost of a mortgage loan. The reason for keeping this class separate from the prequalification verifier is that it will be able to be reused elsewhere in your application. Create a class named `LoanMonthlyPaymentCalculator` in the Products folder of the Model Project with the following listing:

```
namespace ProEnt.LoanPrequalification.Model.Products
{
    public class LoanMonthlyPaymentCalculator
    {
        public float LoanPaymentsPerMonthFor(float LoanAmount,
                                             float InterestRate,
                                             int LoanTerm)
        {
            double int_trm = Math.Pow(1 + InterestRate / 1200, LoanTerm * 12);
            double mrt_year =
                (LoanAmount * InterestRate * int_trm) / (1200 * (int_trm - 1));
            double payments = (mrt_year * 12 / 12);
            double p = Math.Round(payments * 100) / 100;
            return (float)Math.Round(p * 1, 2);
        }
    }
}
```

The `LoanMonthlyPaymentCalculator` simply works out a monthly repayment amount based on a loan amount, interest rate, and loan term.

Now you can add a new class to the Products folder of the Model project, named `ProductIsAvailableSpecification`. This class will use the `LoanMonthlyPaymentCalculator` class and do all the hard work of verifying that a loan application passes all of the prequalification steps against a product's attributes. Add the following definition for the class:

```
using ProEnt.LoanPrequalification.Model.Borrowers;
using ProEnt.LoanPrequalification.Model.LoanApplications;

namespace ProEnt.LoanPrequalification.Model.Products
{
    public class ProductIsAvailableSpecification
    {
        private Product _product;
        private LoanMonthlyPaymentCalculator _loanMonthlyPaymentCalculator;

        public ProductIsAvailableSpecification(Product product,
                        LoanMonthlyPaymentCalculator loanMonthlyPaymentCalculator)
        {
            _product = product;
            _loanMonthlyPaymentCalculator = loanMonthlyPaymentCalculator;
        }

        public bool IsSatisfiedBy(LoanApplication loanApplication)
        {
            bool PreQualifiesForProduct = true;

            if (!IsValidLoanAmount(loanApplication.LoanAmount))
                PreQualifiesForProduct = false;

            if (!PropertyValueGreaterThanLoan(
                    loanApplication.LoanAmount, loanApplication.PropertyValue))
                PreQualifiesForProduct = false;

            if (!LoanWillCoverPropertyValue(loanApplication.LoanAmount,
                            loanApplication.PropertyValue,
                            loanApplication.Deposit))
                PreQualifiesForProduct = false;

            if (!WithinMaximumLTV(loanApplication.LoanAmount,
                            loanApplication.Deposit))
                PreQualifiesForProduct = false;

            foreach (Borrower borrower in loanApplication.Borrowers)
            {
                if (!WillPayLoanOffBeforeRetirement(borrower.Age,
                                        loanApplication.LoanTerm))
                PreQualifiesForProduct = false;
            }

            foreach(Borrower borrower in loanApplication.Borrowers)
```

```
        {
            if (!HasGoodEnoughCreditScore(borrower.CreditScore.Score ))
                PreQualifiesForProduct = false;
        }

        if (!IsAffordable(loanApplication.LoanAmount, loanApplication.LoanTerm,
                        loanApplication.BorrowerTotalMonthlyIncome(),
                        loanApplication.BorrowerTotalMonthlyDebts()))
            PreQualifiesForProduct = false;

        return PreQualifiesForProduct;
    }

    public bool HasGoodEnoughCreditScore(int creditScore)
    {
        return creditScore > 650;
    }

    public bool PropertyValueGreaterThanLoan(int LoanAmount, int propertyValue)
    {
        return propertyValue > LoanAmount;
    }

    public bool IsAffordable(float loan, int term,
                            float borrowerMonthlyIncome,
                            float borrowerMonthlyDebt)
    {
        float TotalMonthlyDebt =
          TotalMonthlyDebtWithLoanPaymentsFor(loan, term, borrowerMonthlyDebt);

        return MonthlyDebtExceedsThirtyPC(borrowerMonthlyIncome,
                                          TotalMonthlyDebt);
    }

    public float TotalMonthlyDebtWithLoanPaymentsFor(
                                    float loan,
                                    int term,
                                    float borrowerMonthlyDebts)
    {
        return _loanMonthlyPaymentCalculator.LoanPaymentsPerMonthFor(
                        loan, _product.InterestRate, term) +
                        borrowerMonthlyDebts;
    }

    private bool MonthlyDebtExceedsThirtyPC(float borrowerMonthlyIncome,
                                            float TotalMonthlyDebt)
    {
        decimal percentageOfIncomeSpentOnDebt =
        (decimal.Divide((decimal)TotalMonthlyDebt,
                    (decimal)borrowerMonthlyIncome) * 100);

        return percentageOfIncomeSpentOnDebt < 31;
    }
```

```
    private bool LoanWillCoverPropertyValue(float loan, float propertyValue,
                                            float deposit)
    {
        return loan >= (propertyValue - deposit);
    }

    private bool WithinMaximumLTV(float LoanAmount, float deposit)
    {
        return _product.MaximumLTV >=
                (int)(100 * (1 - deposit / (LoanAmount + deposit)));
    }

    private bool WillPayLoanOffBeforeRetirement(int borrowerAge, int term)
    {
        int retirmentAge = 65;
        int ageOfBorrowerWhenLoanPaidBack = borrowerAge + term;

        return ageOfBorrowerWhenLoanPaidBack <= retirmentAge;
    }

    private bool IsValidLoanAmount(float LoanAmount)
    {
        return LoanAmount <= _product.MaximumLoan;
    }
  }
}
```

Because of space limitations, we won't be showing the many tests for this method, but any object you create with complex logic must be unit tested to ensure that it's doing the job you think it is.

Now that you have the class in place that will verify if a loan passes the prequalification process of a given product, you need to use it. From your conversation with the domain expert, you may remember that a Product will be able to ascertain if a loan application satisfies its prequalification checks, so it makes sense that a product should contain a method that takes a `LoanApplication` as an argument and then uses `ProductIsAvailableSpecification` to determine if a loan application satisfies all of the prequalification checks.

Edit the `Product` class in the Model project to include the following constructor and method:

```
using ProEnt.LoanPrequalification.Model.LoanApplications;

namespace ProEnt.LoanPrequalification.Model.Products
{
    public class Product
    {
        ...

        private ProductIsAvailableSpecification _productIsAvailable;

        public Product()
        {
            _productIsAvailable = new ProductIsAvailableSpecification(
                        this, new LoanMonthlyPaymentCalculator());
```

```
        }

        public bool IsAvailableFor(LoanApplication loanApplication)
        {
            return _productIsAvailable.IsSatisfiedBy(loanApplication);
        }

        ...


    }
}
```

Finally, you can now edit the LoanApplication's Prequalify method to use the new Product methods and get the test to pass. Add the following method to the LoanApplication class within the Model project:

```
public class LoanApplication
{
    ...

    public void Prequalify()
    {
        ThrowExceptionIfLoanAppIsInvalid("Prequalification");

        if (Product.IsAvailableFor(this))
            _status = Status.OfferGiven;
        else
            _status = Status.Declined;          }
    }
```

If you build the solution and run all of the tests, they should now pass.

The last test you will create is simply to test that a valid loan application passes the prequalification check and has its status updated. Add the following test to your LoanApplicationTests class within the Test project, then build the solution and run the tests to verfiy that they produce the expected behavior.

```
[Test]
public void
  A_Loan_Applications_Status_Will_Change_To_OfferGiven_After_Prequalification ()
    {
        LoanApplication loanApp =
            CreateAValidLoanApplicationAwaitingPrequalification();

        loanApp.Prequalify();

        Assert.AreEqual(loanApp.Status, Status.OfferGiven);
    }
```

The next set of tests you need to create are for verifying the behavior of the offer generated.

Add the following code to the `LoanApplicationTests` class:

```
[Test]
public void
  An_Offer_That_Is_First_Generated_Must_Match_The_Application_Amount()
{
    LoanApplication loanApp =
       CreateAValidLoanApplicationAwaitingPrequalification();

    loanApp.Prequalify();

    Offer offer = loanApp.GetOfferInPrincipal();

    Assert.AreEqual(offer.LoanAmount, loanApp.LoanAmount);
}
```

The solution will not compile, so you will need to add the the logic to generate an offer when an application passes Prequalification and a method to retrieve that offer. Amend the `Prequalify` method of the `LoanApplication` class like so:

```
public void Prequalify()
{
    ThrowExceptionIfLoanAppIsInvalid("Prequalification");

    if (Product.IsAvailableFor(this))
    {
        _status = Status.OfferGiven;
        GenerateOffer();
    }
    else
        _status = Status.Declined;
}
```

The logic is straightforward enough: when an application passes prequalification an offer is generated. The `GenerateOffer` method does not exist yet so go ahead and add it to the LoanApplication class; the code for the method is displayed below.

```
private void GenerateOffer()
{
    _offer = new Offer(LoanAmount, LoanTerm,
                       Product.InterestRate,
                       DateTime.Now.AddMonths(6));
}
```

You now need to add a method so that the `Offer` can be retrieved. Amend the `LoanApplication` class to include this method:

```
public Offer GetOfferInPrincipal()
{
    return Offer;
}
```

As you don't want to really expose the Offer as a property that can be edited you will need to mark it as private. Go ahead and amend the visibility on the Offer property as shown in the code below.

```
public class LoanApplication
{
    ...

    private Offer Offer
    {
        get { return _offer; }
    }
    ...
}
```

After you have added the methods and amended the property, rebuild the solution and run the tests. When all tests are verified, you are going to add one further test to triangulate the behavior of generating an offer to ensure that it isn't generated if a loan does not pass prequalification. For more information on triangulating tests, refer to Chapter 3 on test driven development.

Add the following test to your list of tests:

```
[Test]
[ExpectedException(typeof(AnOfferInPrincipalHasNotBeenGenerated))]
public void
An_Exception_Will_Be_Thrown_If_An_Offer_Attempted_To_Be_Retrieved_Before_
Prequalification()
{
    LoanApplication loanApp =
        CreateAValidLoanApplicationAwaitingPrequalification();

    Assert.AreEqual(loanApp.GetOfferInPrincipal().LoanAmount,
                    loanApp.LoanAmount);
}
```

This test is going to verify that an exception will be thrown if the GetOfferInPrincipal method is called before the loan application has been prequalified. You are going to throw a custom exception as there is no other sensible way to let the client know that the offer has not been generated and a custom exception is more intention-revealing than just returning a null value.

To get the test to compile you will need to create the custom exception, so add the following class to the LoanApplications folder of the ProEnt.LoanPrequalification.Model Project.

```
using System;

namespace ProEnt.LoanPrequalification.Model.LoanApplications
{
    public class AnOfferInPrincipalHasNotBeenGenerated : Exception
    {
        public AnOfferInPrincipalHasNotBeenGenerated() { }
        public AnOfferInPrincipalHasNotBeenGenerated(string message) :
                                                base(message) { }
    }
}
```

The test will now compile but it will fail when run with a `NullReferenceException`; this exception doesn't really give the client much to go on. By using the custom exception the client will be able to understand what the problem is. With that in mind amend the `GetOfferInPrincipal` as below.

```
public Offer GetOfferInPrincipal()
{
    if (Offer == null)
        throw new AnOfferInPrincipalHasNotBeenGenerated();

    return Offer;
}
```

Now you need to test that the behavior of the `GetOfferInPrincipal()` when it's called and the offer has expired. You can't wait around for 6 months for the offer to expire so you will have to set the date yourself. The problem however is that the `Offer` is a private property and cannot be directly set. To get around this you can use reflection to set the property. Add the test and reflection helper method shown below to your suite of tests.

```
[Test]
[ExpectedException(typeof(AnOfferInPrincipalHasExpired ))]
public void
An_Exception_Will_Be_Thrown_If_An_Offer_Is_Attempted_To_Be_Retrieved_If_It_Is_
Expired()
{
    LoanApplication loanApp =
        CreateAValidLoanApplicationAwaitingPrequalification();

    loanApp.Prequalify();

    Offer expiredOffer = new Offer(100000, 35, 1.25f,
                                DateTime.Now.AddYears(-1));

    // Set by reflection
    SetPrivateFieldUsingReflection(loanApp, "_offer", expiredOffer);

    loanApp.GetOfferInPrincipal();
}

public static void SetPrivateFieldUsingReflection
        (object instance, string fieldName, object newValue)
{
    Type t = instance.GetType();
    System.Reflection.FieldInfo f = t.GetField(fieldName
        , BindingFlags.Instance | BindingFlags.Public
        | BindingFlags.NonPublic);
    f.SetValue(instance, newValue);
}
```

Again you will not be able to compile the test project because the custom exception does not exist, so create this in the LoanApplications folder first.

```
using System;

namespace ProEnt.LoanPrequalification.Model.LoanApplications
{
    public class AnOfferInPrincipalHasExpired : Exception
    {
        public AnOfferInPrincipalHasExpired() { }
        public AnOfferInPrincipalHasExpired(string message) : base(message) { }
    }
}
```

Now the test will compile but it will fail because the exception is not thrown. Amend the `GetOfferInPrincipal` method as shown below and add the new `HasOfferExpired` method.

```
public Offer GetOfferInPrincipal()
{
    if (Offer == null)
        throw new AnOfferInPrincipalHasNotBeenGenerated();

    if (HasOfferExpired())
        throw new AnOfferInPrincipalHasExpired();

    return Offer;
}

public bool HasOfferExpired()
{
    if (Offer == null)
        throw new AnOfferInPrincipalHasNotBeenGenerated();

    return Offer.HasExpired();
}
```

After a rebuild your test will now pass, verify that all of the tests pass before moving on.

The core Domain Model is now complete; however, because of space limitations, you didn't look at testing all parts of the Domain Model that exposed business logic. In a real application it would be strongly advisable to ensure that you test anything that contains any reasonable amount of business logic. If you download the source code, you will find the full suite of tests that verify all business logic. Now that the Domain Model is complete, you can focus your efforts on the services that will be used to coordinate the logic and persist changes to the entities.

Creating the Repositories

To enable the entities and value objects to be persisted, you need to create some repositories. A `Repository` is an object that allows your entities to be persisted and retrieved from your data store, be that an XML file or an SQL database. It is an abstraction separate from the underlying technology used to store your Domain Model objects; typically, you would have a `Repository` for every aggregate root. Martin Fowler describes a `Repository` in this way: "Mediates between the domain and data mapping layers using a collection-like interface for accessing domain objects." (*Patterns of Enterprise Application Architecture*, Addison-Wesley, 2002).

For this chapter, you will just create the interfaces for the repositories. In the next chapter, you will look at some data access patterns used to create the actual repository implementations.

Each aggregate root will require a corresponding repository, so by looking at your aggregate groupings, you can see that you will require:

- ProductRepository
- BorrowerRepository
- LoanRepository

Because each of the repositories does the same basic job, you can create a base repository interface and have all of the individual repositories inherit from it.

1. Create a new interface named IRepository in the root of the Model project with the following code:

```
using System;
using System.Collections.Generic;

namespace ProEnt.LoanPrequalification.Model
{
    public interface IRepository<T>
    {
        void Save(T obj);
        void Add(T obj);
        T FindBy(Guid id);
        List<T> FindAll();
    }
}
```

2. Create a repository for each of the aggregates, and place the interface in each of the folders:

```
namespace ProEnt.LoanPrequalification.Model.Borrowers
{
    public interface IBorrowerRepository :IRepository<Borrower>
    {
    }
}
namespace ProEnt.LoanPrequalification.Model.LoanApplications
{
    public interface ILoanApplicationRepository : IRepository<LoanApplication>
    {
    }
}
namespace ProEnt.LoanPrequalification.Model.Products
{
    public interface IProductRepository :IRepository<Product>
    {
    }
}
```

Now that the model is complete and the repository interfaces have been created, you only have a simple service layer left to build to finish this stage of the application.

Creating the Domain Services

You will create a service for each of the aggregate roots to coordinate the persistence and business transactions, such as creating a new loan product. First off is the LoanApplicationService. The LoanApplicationService is a very simple service that coordinates the transcriptions involved in all of the steps of the approval workflow.

Add a new class to the LoanApplications folder of the Model project, named LoanApplicationService, with the following definition:

```
using System;
using System.Collections.Generic;
using System.Text;

namespace ProEnt.LoanPrequalification.Model.LoanApplications
{
    public class LoanApplicationService
    {
        private ILoanApplicationRepository loanApplicationRepository;

        public LoanApplicationService(
                ILoanApplicationRepository loanApplicationRepository)
        {
            this.loanApplicationRepository = loanApplicationRepository;
        }

        #region Loan Application WorkFlow

        /// <summary>
        ///Loan Appliction Is Submitted and Prequalified
        /// </summary>
        public void SubmitForPrequalification(LoanApplication loanApplication)
        {
            if (loanApplication.GetBrokenRules().Count == 0)
                throw new InvalidLoanApplicationException(
                    String.Format(
                    "This loan is invalid and cannot be submmitted. {0}",
                    GetBrokenRulesToStringFor(loanApplication.GetBrokenRules())));

            loanApplication.Prequalify();
            loanApplicationRepository.Save(loanApplication);

        }

        /// <summary>
        /// Retrieving an offer in principal
        /// </summary>
        public Offer GetOfferInPrincipalFor(Guid loanApplicationId)
        {
            LoanApplication loanApp = FindLoanApplicationBy(loanApplicationId);
```

```
            return loanApp.GetOfferInPrincipal();
        }

        #endregion

        public LoanApplication FindLoanApplicationBy(Guid loanApplicationId)
        {
            LoanApplication loanApp =
                loanApplicationRepository.FindBy(loanApplicationId);
            if (loanApp == null)
                throw new Exception(
                 String.Format("Cannot find a loan application with the ID '{0}'.",
                               loanApplicationId.ToString()));

            return loanApp;
        }

        public void Save(LoanApplication loanApplication)
        {
            if (loanApplication.GetBrokenRules().Count > 0)
            {
                throw new InvalidLoanApplicationException(
                    String.Format("This loan application is invalid and"+
                                " cannot be saved in its present state. '{0}'",
                                GetBrokenRulesToStringFor(
                                    loanApplication.GetBrokenRules())));
            }
            loanApplicationRepository.Save(loanApplication);
        }

        public List<LoanApplication> FindAll()
        {
            return loanApplicationRepository.FindAll();
        }

        private string
            GetBrokenRulesToStringFor(List<BrokenBusinessRule> brokenRules)
        {
            StringBuilder sbBrokenRules = new StringBuilder();

            foreach (BrokenBusinessRule br in brokenRules)
            {
                sbBrokenRules.Append(br.Rule);
            }

            return sbBrokenRules.ToString();
        }
    }
}
```

As you can see in the code listing, you are using Dependency Injection to inject the loan application repository into the constructor of the service class. This, if you remember, was discussed in great detail back in Chapter 3. By using interfaces for the repositories and injecting them into the service layer, you are keeping your code loosely coupled and are making it easy on yourself if you ever want to change your data access strategy.

The main methods of the service class all map to the business use case of the mortgage application; these are:

1. `SubmitForPrequalification(LoanApplication loanApplication)`: A loan application is submitted, prequalification is performed, and the application is saved by the repository.

2. `GetOfferInPrincipalFor(Guid loanApplicationId)`: Used to obtain the offer for a given loan application ID.

3. `FindLoanApplicationBy(Guid loanApplicationId)`: Used to retrieve a specified loan application by its ID.

4. `Save(LoanApplication loanApplication)`: Used to save changes to a loan application, only valid loan applications can be saved.

5. `List<LoanApplication> FindAll()`: Used to retrieve all of the loan applications.

Next is the turn of the `ProductService` class, which will be added to the Products folder. This is a very simple service class with methods similar to the `LoanApplicationService` class to find all Products and save a Product.

```
using System;
using System.Collections.Generic;
using System.Text;

namespace ProEnt.LoanPrequalification.Model.Products
{
    public class ProductService
    {
        private IProductRepository productRepository;

        public ProductService(IProductRepository productRepository)
        {
            this.productRepository = productRepository;
        }


        public Product FindLoanApplicationBy(Guid productId)
        {
            Product product = productRepository.FindBy(productId);
            if (product == null)
                throw new Exception(
                String.Format("Cannot find a product with the ID '{0}'.",
                        productId.ToString()));

            return product;
        }
    }
```

```
        public void Save(Product product)
        {
            if (product.GetBrokenRules().Count > 0)
            {
                throw new ArgumentException(
                  String.Format(
                        "This product is invalid and cannot"+
                        " be saved in its present state. '{0}'",
                        GetBrokenRulesToStringFor(product.GetBrokenRules())));
            }
            productRepository.Save(product);
        }

        public List<Product> FindAll()
        {
            return productRepository.FindAll();
        }

        private string
            GetBrokenRulesToStringFor(List<BrokenBusinessRule> brokenRules)
        {
            StringBuilder sbBrokenRules = new StringBuilder();

            foreach (BrokenBusinessRule br in brokenRules)
            {
                sbBrokenRules.Append(br.Rule);
            }

            return sbBrokenRules.ToString();
        }
    }
}
```

The BorrowerService class, which will be created in the Borrowers folder, is identical to the ProductService class but deals with Borrowers rather than Products.

```
using System;
using System.Collections.Generic;
using System.Linq;
using System.Text;

namespace ProEnt.LoanPrequalification.Model.Borrowers
{
    public class BorrowerService
    {
        private IBorrowerRepository borrowerRepository;

        public BorrowerService(IBorrowerRepository borrowerRepository)
        {
            this.borrowerRepository = borrowerRepository;
        }
```

```
public Borrower FindLoanApplicationBy(Guid borrowerId)
{
    Borrower borrower = borrowerRepository.FindBy(borrowerId);
    if (borrower == null)
        throw new Exception(
          String.Format(
            "Cannot find a borrower with the ID '{0}'.",
            borrowerId.ToString()));

    return borrower;
}

public void Save(Borrower borrower)
{
    if (borrower.GetBrokenRules().Count > 0)
    {
        throw new ArgumentException(
            String.Format(
                "This borrower is invalid and"+
                " cannot be saved in its present state. '{0}'",
                GetBrokenRulesToStringFor(borrower.GetBrokenRules())));
    }
    borrowerRepository.Save(borrower);
}

public List<Borrower> FindAll()
{
    return borrowerRepository.FindAll();
}

private string
  GetBrokenRulesToStringFor(List<BrokenBusinessRule> brokenRules)
{
    StringBuilder sbBrokenRules = new StringBuilder();

    foreach (BrokenBusinessRule br in brokenRules)
    {
        sbBrokenRules.Append(br.Rule);
    }
    return sbBrokenRules.ToString();
}
    }
}
```

This completes the creation of the mortgage loan prequalification application, Figure 7-12 shows the complete solution.

Figure 7-12

Hopefully, you should now understand a little bit about the process of creating an application using some of the techniques that you have read about in this chapter, namely the Domain Model business pattern and also techniques from earlier chapters such as Test Driven Development and Dependency Injection.

In subsequent chapters, you will learn about patterns designed to keep code in your presentation and data access layer modular, testable, and loosely coupled. After reading about and understanding this pattern, you will add to the mortgage loan approval application until you have a full-blown working application.

Summary

In this chapter, you learned to focus your attention on the business domain so that you would be better equipped to resolve complex business logic and processes in an application. You looked at three of the popular solutions for organizing and structuring your business logic and evaluated the strengths and weaknesses of each. The three middleware patterns you looked at were:

❑ **Transaction Script:** Transaction Script is a procedural pattern that handles business transactions typically in a single method, directly interfacing with the presentation layer. The pattern is very simple and straightforward but can lead to the duplication of business logic when used on anything but very simple applications with little or no logic.

❑ **Active Record:** The Active Record pattern is used when the underlying Data Model is the same as your business model. Code generation software can be used to automatically build the business objects by analyzing the database schema. Each business object represents a row in the database and is responsible for its own persistence. The pattern does not fit well when there is a discrepancy between the Data Model and the business model.

❑ **Domain Model:** The Domain Model pattern is used for complex business domains where a full abstract representation of the domain is needed in code to help to solve difficult problems. The Domain Model has a longer learning curve than the previous two patterns and a deep knowledge of the business domain is needed to make full effect of it.

However, as you learned, not everything can be modeled with business objects; sometimes a business transaction needs to work with many different modules and doesn't seem to belong to any one business object. For these cases, you employ a service layer to coordinate the transaction. A service layer acts as a thin layer that sits between the business logic and your client code. The role of the service layer is to simply coordinate the transactions and define a set of business use cases in the form of methods, so that the client has a simple entry point into the application, rather like a business façade.

To demonstrate using the Domain Model, you were introduced to the domain of mortgage loan approvals. By utilizing some of the concepts from Domain-Driven Design, you were able to talk to the domain expert and model your solution using the same terms and concepts as used in the business world. By using a common language, also referred to as the ubiquitous language, you were able to talk to a business expert about the application in a way that he would understand and at the same time increase your knowledge of the business you were building software for.

The mortgage loan prequalification application was built using a combination of upfront design in the form of Domain Model sketches and Test Driven Development, as described in Chapter 4.

In the next chapter, you will tackle the problem of the impedance mismatch between the Domain Model and the relational database. You will also see how frameworks can get you started quickly with the Active Record pattern, and implement the repository interfaces that you created for the mortgage loan approval application.

8

"Mining" Your Own Business

With your business logic layer now in place it's time to turn your thoughts to how you are going to store the state of your business objects. In this chapter, you will learn about the various methods and patterns at your disposal that will enable you to seamlessly save the state of your business model via a data access layer.

You will learn about two data access patterns, namely the very simple Data Access Object pattern and a pattern that you have read about in the previous chapter, called the Repository pattern. To demonstrate these patterns, you will learn the basics of three popular object relational mappers: Microsoft's LinqToSQL, the Entity Framework, and the open source NHibernate.

Before we explore these frameworks, it's important to define the role of the data access layer. Then, you will find out what an object relational mapper is and what problems it can help you with in your development efforts.

What Is the Data Access Layer?

The data access layer, as shown in Figure 8-1, is the layer in your application that is solely responsible for talking to the data store (note the reference to a data store and not a database; you don't always have to have a database — sometimes an XML file will be sufficient) and persisting and retrieving your business objects. It typically includes all of the CRUD (create, read, update, and delete) methods as well as a querying mechanism to enable your business logic layer to retrieve objects for any given criteria.

The data access layer should not contain any business logic at all and should be accessed via the business logic layer through interfaces; this adheres to the separation of concerns principle that you read about back in Chapter 3. By communicating via an interface, you will easily be able to swap out data access layer implementations without having a negative impact on the legitimacy of your software.

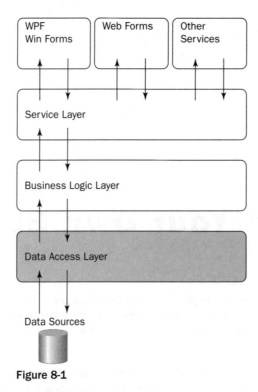

Figure 8-1

Rolling Your Own Data Access Layer

Traditional Microsoft developers have built their own data access layer by hand in order to map the business objects to their corresponding database tables. There is nothing inherently bad about this, it's just that it can be a little, dare we say, boring? Not only that, but hand rolling your own DAL can be error prone, as ADO.NET is not type safe, and can be difficult to maintain when changes are needed in the schema of the application as similar code is duplicated. With large projects, the amount of plumbing code needed can quickly engulf the project and developers can lose sight of the end goal — that is, getting the business processes and logic right — because of hours spent writing stored procedures and low-level ADO.NET objects.

Why do we need to do all of this plumbing code?

Object Relation Mapping

Object relational mappers (ORMs) have been around for a long time, but with Microsoft producing two ORMs of its own, the whole idea of ORMs is starting to pick up speed as a solution to enterprise-level persistence needs.

The Role of ORMs

The role of an ORM is to bridge the gap between the relational model (the database) and the object-oriented model. This problem is often referred to as the *impedance mismatch issue*. Using mapping files or attributes on a business object, an ORM framework can be used to persist business objects to the database and retrieve them simply via the ORM framework's API with no or little SQL needed.

So, what else do you get in the box when you opt for an ORM rather than rolling your own?

❏ The Unit of Work pattern: A Unit of Work is used to maintain a list of business objects that have been changed during a business transaction whether that be adding, removing or updating. The Unit of Work will coordinate the saving of the changes into the data store in one atomic action if an error occurs all changes roll back.

❏ Identity Map: An Identity Map "Ensures that each object gets loaded only once by keeping every loaded object in a map. Looks up objects using the map when referring to them." (Quoted from Martin Folwer, *Patterns of Enterprise Application Architecture*, Addison-Wesley, 2002.)

❏ Lazy loading: Lazy loading is the term often referred to as the ability to defer the loading of a resource until it's needed. Think of a customer and her orders: a customer may have 100s of orders but you wouldn't want to load them each time you wanted to view the customer's details. By using lazy loading the list of orders would only be loaded when they were needed.

❏ Business object–focused querying language: Instead of writing stored procedures over relational data, an ORM will allow you to write object oriented queries that the ORM will translate into the SQL dialect of your database. Strongly typed querying language is kept with your code.

❏ Caching: Loading from memory will generally be a lot faster than loading from a database. A good ORM will cache data until it is changed, giving you a nice performance boost.

❏ Abstraction from underlying database: An ORM will completely abstract away from your underlying database. This will enable you to change database implementations as your application grows.

The Data Context

All of the functions described in the previous section that make up an ORM need to be coordinated and that is the role of the class that acts as the DataContext. The DataContext, shown in Figure 8-2, is responsible for changing tracking along with managing the Identity Map and concurrency concerns; it is the manager for all entry points into the database.

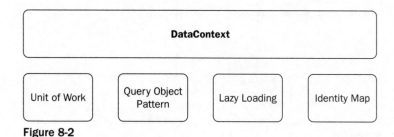

Figure 8-2

Now let's have a look at how three ORMs can be used with two different data access patterns.

Data First and the Data Access Object Pattern

The Data First, or Bottom Up, approach to software development starts with the creation of a relational database schema design: then, in turn, the rest of the application is built around the database. As you will find out in a moment, both LinqToSQL and the Entity Framework have great support for generating a model from a database schema.

The Data Access pattern that you will be using with the Data First approach, and both LinqToSQL and the Entity Framework, are called the Data Access Object pattern. The DAO pattern is a very straightforward design that simply provides an interface to persist and retrieve business objects, typically with a separate DAO for each table in the database.

The Data Access Object pattern is a good fit for the Transaction Script and Active Record business patterns that were discussed in the previous chapter.

LinqToSQL

Microsoft's LinqToSQL was released as part of the .NET 3.5 Framework; it provides a framework for generating and managing a conceptual model of your relational data model. LinqToSQL contains a DataContext as described previously that tracks changes and keeps an identity map of all objects pulled from the database. The easiest way to generate a model is by using the object designer to drag and drop database objects, such as tables, views, and stored procedures. Business objects are created that match the database objects to an object-oriented type. Behind the scenes, the framework will build an XML mapping metadata file, which will map the database columns and relationships to the auto-generated business, as shown in Figure 8-3.

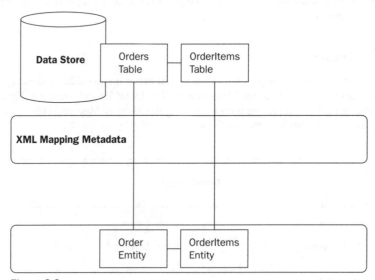

Figure 8-3

A DataContext is also created which is your entry point for retrieving and persisting the business objects. You can use standard Linq to retrieve business objects, and the DataContext will translate this into raw SQL. The benefit is that you get type-safe querying built into your application, removing the need to have masses of stored procedures in the database.

You don't have to use the built-in designer to generate your business objects, although it is the easiest method. LinqToSQL also supports attribute-based mapping of business objects to the database tables, as well as an XML configuration done by hand for times when you have an existing entities, which you will learn about a little later.

LinqToSQL uses Linq to query against the DataContext. Linq stands for Language Integrated Query, and gives you an object-oriented view of your relational data. It enables you to create strongly typed queries, which are then translated into the low-level SQL commands that MS SQL Server can understand.

To demonstrate LinqToSQL, the Entity Framework, and NHibernate, you are going to build a very simple bug-tracking system. Users will be able to add applications and add bugs to them; the system will also allow bugs to be marked as fixed when they have been eradicated from the application.

Let's start with creating the application using LinqToSQL and following the Data Access Object pattern:

1. Open Visual Studio and create a new web application named `ProEnt.Chap8.LinqBugTracker`, as shown in Figure 8-4.

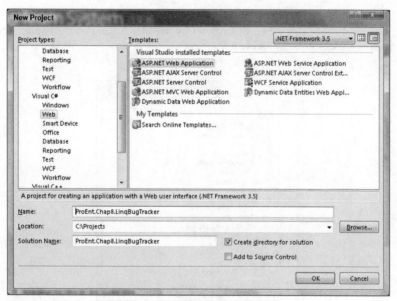

Figure 8-4

2. As mentioned, LinqToSQL works best when being generated from a database, so add a new SQL Server database to the application by right-clicking on the project name and selecting Add ➪ New Item, then select SQL Server Database and name the database `BugTrackerDB.mdf`, as shown in Figure 8-5. Confirm that you would like the database to be created in the default `App_Data` folder when prompted.

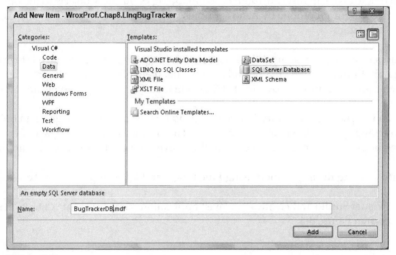

Figure 8-5

3. Open the `BugTrackerDB` in Server Explorer by double-clicking on the name; Server Explorer will then open, as shown in Figure 8-6.

Figure 8-6

4. Right-click on the `Tables` folder and select Add New Table. The Table definition window will appear. Enter these column names and types:

Column Name	Data Type	Allow Nulls
ApplicationId	Int IDENTITY, Primary Key	False
Name	nvarchar(50)	False

Save the table with the name Applications.

5. Right-click on the `Tables` folder again, and select Add New Table. The Table Definition window will appear once more. Enter these definitions:

Column Name	Data Type	Allow Nulls
BugId	Int IDENTITY, Primary Key	False
Description	nvarchar(50)	False
Fixed	Bit	False
ApplicationId	int	False

Save the table with the name Bugs.

6. Back in your database server explorer window right-click on the `Database Diagrams` folder and select Add New Database Diagram. Click Yes when prompted to create the all of the necessary objects required to create database diagrams. Add the two newly created tables to the diagram and select and drag the `ApplicationId` from the Applications table onto the `ApplicationId` of the Bugs Table. After you have created the connection, two dialog boxes will confirm the details of the relationship. Click OK in both of these, and save the diagram with the default `diagram1` name, and click OK at the prompt that warns of changes to the tables. Your diagram should resemble Figure 8-7.

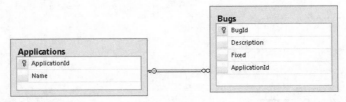

Figure 8-7

7. Switch back to Solution Explorer, and create a new folder named `Model` by right-clicking the project and selecting New Folder. Now you will create the LINQ to SQL classes that will build a conceptual model of the database. Right-click on the `Model` folder, select Add New Item, from the pop-up dialog select Linq to SQL Classes, and save the item as `BugTracker.dbml`, as shown in Figure 8-8.

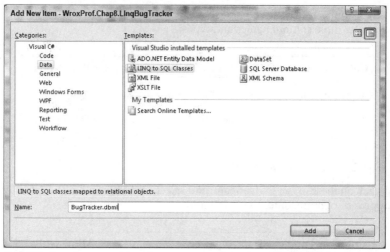

Figure 8-8

8. After Visual Studio creates all the files for your LinqToSQL class, you will be presented with the LINQ to SQL Designer, as shown in Figure 8-9.

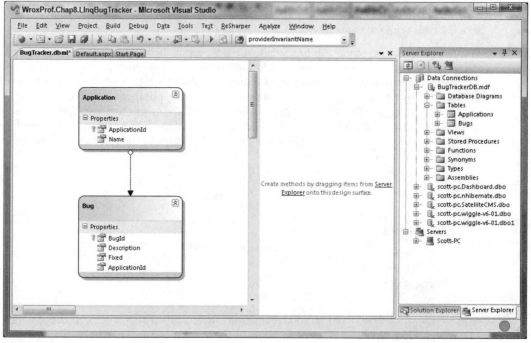

Figure 8-9

9. The LINQ to SQL Designer is a graphical interface that allows you to build object models from your database in a very easy manner. To work with the Designer, first view your database by clicking the server explorer tab, then drag and drop the Applications table and the Bugs table onto the left-hand side of the Designer, which is the ObjectRelational Designer. As you do this, LinqToSQL automatically generates the classes and associations to match your database tables and relationships, as well as building an XML mapping file, which you will inspect next.

Your solution should now resemble Figure 8-10.

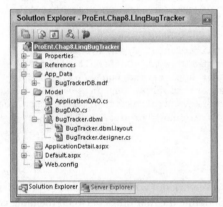

Figure 8-10

Right-click on the BugTracker.dbml file, select Open With, and choose the XML Editor; the following XML will be loaded.

```xml
<?xml version="1.0" encoding="utf-8"?>
<Database Name="BugTrackerDB"
          Class="BugTrackerDataContext"
          xmlns="http://schemas.microsoft.com/linqtosql/dbml/2007">
  <Connection
      Mode="WebSettings"
      ConnectionString="Data Source=.\SQLEXPRESS;
          AttachDbFilename=|DataDirectory|\BugTrackerDB.mdf;
          Integrated Security=True;User Instance=True"
      SettingsObjectName="System.Configuration.ConfigurationManager.
ConnectionStrings"
      SettingsPropertyName="BugTrackerDBConnectionString"
      Provider="System.Data.SqlClient" />
  <Table Name="dbo.Applications" Member="Applications">
    <Type Name="Application">
      <Column Name="ApplicationId" Type="System.Int32"
              DbType="Int NOT NULL IDENTITY" IsPrimaryKey="true"
              IsDbGenerated="true" CanBeNull="false" />
      <Column Name="Name" Type="System.String"
              DbType="NVarChar(50) NOT NULL" CanBeNull="false" />
      <Association Name="Application_Bug" Member="Bugs" ThisKey="ApplicationId"
                   OtherKey="ApplicationId" Type="Bug" />
```

```
        </Type>
      </Table>

    <Table Name="dbo.Bugs" Member="Bugs">
      <Type Name="Bug">
        <Column Name="BugId" Type="System.Int32"
                DbType="Int NOT NULL IDENTITY" IsPrimaryKey="true"
                IsDbGenerated="true"
                CanBeNull="false" />
        <Column Name="[Desc]" Member="Desc" Type="System.String"
                DbType="NVarChar(50) NOT NULL" CanBeNull="false" />
        <Column Name="Fixed" Type="System.Boolean"
                DbType="Bit NOT NULL" CanBeNull="false" />
        <Column Name="ApplicationId" Type="System.Int32"
                DbType="Int NOT NULL" CanBeNull="false" />
        <Association  Name="Application_Bug"
                      Member="Application" ThisKey="ApplicationId"
                      OtherKey="ApplicationId" Type="Application"
                      IsForeignKey="true" />
      </Type>
    </Table>
  </Database>
```

It should be fairly easy to work out what's going on in the XML mapping file. You have two table sections that each define the mappings between the table columns and the member properties. The other section of importance is the Association section that defines the relationship between the members or business objects.

Now expand the `BugTracker.dbml` file, and open the `BugTracker.designer.cs` file. This class file contains the generated partial classes that appeared on the Object Designer. Also contained in this file is the `DataContext` class, in this instance named `BugTrackerDataContext`. As mentioned, this class is the interface you will use to interact with the database.

10. Now that you have your business objects and DataContext in place, you can build the Data Access Objects. Switch back to Solution Explorer, right-click the Model folder, and add a new class named `ApplicationDAO` with the following definition:

```csharp
using System.Collections.Generic;
using System.Linq;

namespace ProEnt.Chap8.LinqBugTracker.Model
{
    public class ApplicationDAO
    {
        private BugTrackerDataContext dataContext;

        public ApplicationDAO()
        {
            dataContext = new BugTrackerDataContext();
        }

        public List<Application> FindAll()
        {
```

```
            return dataContext.Applications.ToList();
        }

        public Application FindBy(int Id)
        {
            Application application =
              dataContext.Applications.SingleOrDefault(a => a.ApplicationId == Id);
            application.Bugs.Load();
            return application;
        }

        public void Add(Application application)
        {
            dataContext.Applications.InsertOnSubmit(application);
            // NOTE: No work is done until SubmitChanges is called
        }

        public void Delete(Application application)
        {
            // Remove all bugs linked to the Application
            dataContext.Bugs.DeleteAllOnSubmit(application.Bugs);
            // Remove the application
            dataContext.Applications.DeleteOnSubmit(application);
            // NOTE: No work is done until SubmitChanges is called

        }

        public void SubmitChanges()
        {
            dataContext.SubmitChanges();
        }
    }
}
```

Let's have a look what's going on in this class. An instance of the `BugTrackerDataContext` is instantiated in the constructor. The `BugTrackerDataContext` is a lightweight class and only makes a connection to the database when a call to `SubmitChanges()` is made or objects are retrieved.

No work is done until the `SubmitChanges` method is called on the `DataContext` class: this enables a number of tasks to be completed as a single unit of work because if there is an error, all work is rolled back.

1.   Create a second class within the `Model` folder, named BugDAO, with the following listing:

```
using System.Linq;
using System.Collections.Generic;

namespace ProEnt.Chap8.LinqBugTracker.Model
{
    public class BugDAO
    {
        private BugTrackerDataContext dataContext;

        public BugDAO()
```

```
        {
            dataContext = new BugTrackerDataContext();
        }

        public List<Bug> FindAll()
        {
            return dataContext.Bugs.ToList();
        }

        public Bug FindBy(int Id)
        {
            Bug bug = dataContext.Bugs.SingleOrDefault(b => b.BugId == Id);
            return bug;
        }

        public void Add(Bug bug)
        {
            dataContext.Bugs.InsertOnSubmit(bug);
            dataContext.SubmitChanges();
        }

        public void Delete(Bug bug)
        {
            dataContext.Bugs.DeleteOnSubmit(bug);
            dataContext.SubmitChanges();
        }

        public void Save(Bug bug)
        {
            dataContext.SubmitChanges();
        }
    }
}
```

Now that you have the Repository and model created, to test out the functionality you will create a very simple front end consisting of two Web Forms.

2. Open default.aspx in source view and edit the file to match the following definition:

```
<%@ Page Language="C#" AutoEventWireup="true"
    CodeBehind="Default.aspx.cs"
    Inherits="ProEnt.Chap8.LinqBugTracker._Default" %>

<!DOCTYPE html PUBLIC "-//W3C//DTD XHTML 1.0 Transitional//EN"
    "http://www.w3.org/TR/xhtml1/DTD/xhtml1-transitional.dtd">
<html xmlns="http://www.w3.org/1999/xhtml">
<head runat="server">
    <title></title>
</head>
<body>
    <form id="form1" runat="server">
    <div>
        <p>
            <b>Bug Tracker</b>
```

```
            </p>
            <fieldset>
                <legend>Applications</legend>
                <asp:Repeater ID="rptApplications" runat="server">
                    <HeaderTemplate>
                        <ul>
                    </HeaderTemplate>
                    <ItemTemplate>
                        <li>
                         <a href="ApplicationDetail.aspx?ApplicationId=
                                    <%# Eval("ApplicationId") %>">
                         <%# Eval("Name") %></a>
                        </li>
                    </ItemTemplate>
                    <FooterTemplate>
                        </ul>
                    </FooterTemplate>
                </asp:Repeater>
            </fieldset>
            <fieldset>
                <legend>Add Application</legend>
                <p>
                    <asp:TextBox ID="txtApplicationName" runat="server"></asp:TextBox>
                     
                    <asp:Button ID="btnAddApplication"
                                runat="server"
                                Text="Add Application"
                                OnClick="btnAddApplication_Click" />
                </p>
            </fieldset>
        </div>
        </form>
    </body>
</html>
```

3. Now open the code view of `default.aspx`, and update it with the following listing:

```csharp
using System;
using ProEnt.Chap8.LinqBugTracker.Model;

namespace ProEnt.Chap8.LinqBugTracker
{
    public partial class _Default : System.Web.UI.Page
    {
        ApplicationDAO _applicationDAO;

        protected void Page_Load(object sender, EventArgs e)
        {
            if (! this.IsPostBack)
            {
                ShowAllApplications();
            }
        }
```

```
            private void ShowAllApplications()
            {
                this.rptApplications.DataSource = ApplicationDAO.FindAll();
                this.rptApplications.DataBind();
            }

            private ApplicationDAO ApplicationDAO
            {
                get {
                    if (_applicationDAO == null)
                        _applicationDAO = new ApplicationDAO();

                    return _applicationDAO;
                }
            }

            protected void btnAddApplication_Click(object sender, EventArgs e)
            {
                Application application = new Application();
                application.Name = this.txtApplicationName.Text;
                ApplicationDAO.Add(application);
                ShowAllApplications();
            }

        }
    }
```

4.   Create a second Web Form by right-clicking on the project, select Add New Item, then select a
Web Form and name it `ApplicationDetails.aspx`. Again, update the markup with the
following listing:

```
<%@ Page Language="C#" AutoEventWireup="true"
    CodeBehind="ApplicationDetail.aspx.cs"
    Inherits="ProEnt.Chap8.LinqBugTracker.ApplicationDetail" %>

<!DOCTYPE html PUBLIC "-//W3C//DTD XHTML 1.0 Transitional//EN"
   "http://www.w3.org/TR/xhtml1/DTD/xhtml1-transitional.dtd">
<html xmlns="http://www.w3.org/1999/xhtml">
<head runat="server">
    <title></title>
</head>
<body>
    <form id="form1" runat="server">
    <div>
        <p>
            <b>Bug Tracker</b>
        </p>
        <fieldset>
            <legend>Bugs for the
                <asp:Literal ID="litApplicationName" runat="server"></asp:Literal>
                application</legend>
            <p>
```

```
                    <asp:GridView DataKeyNames="BugId"
                            AutoGenerateColumns="False"
                            OnRowDeleting="grdBugs_RowDeleting"
                            ID="grdBugs" runat="server"
                            OnRowCommand="grdBugs_ItemCommand">
                    <Columns>
                        <asp:BoundField DataField="Desc"
                            HeaderText="Bug Description" />
                        <asp:BoundField DataField="Fixed"
                            HeaderText="Has Bug Been Fixed?" />
                        <asp:CommandField ShowDeleteButton="True" />
                        <asp:TemplateField ShowHeader="False">
                            <ItemTemplate>
                                <asp:LinkButton
                                    Visible='<%# IsNotFixed((bool)Eval("Fixed")) %>'
                                    ID="lnkMarkAsFixed"
                                    runat="server" CausesValidation="false"
                                    CommandArgument='<%# Eval("BugId") %>'
                                    CommandName="MarkAsFixed"
                                    Text="Mark as Fixed"></asp:LinkButton>
                            </ItemTemplate>
                        </asp:TemplateField>
                    </Columns>
                </asp:GridView>
            </p>
        </fieldset>
        <fieldset>
            <legend>Add Bug</legend>
            <p>
                <asp:TextBox ID="txtBugDesc" runat="server"></asp:TextBox>
                 
                <asp:Button ID="btnAddBug" runat="server" Text="Add Bug"
                                            OnClick="btnAddBug_Click" />
            </p>
        </fieldset>
    </div>
    </form>
</body>
</html>
```

5.   Again, flip over to the code view and fill in the following details:

```
using System;
using System.Linq;
using System.Web.UI.WebControls;
using ProEnt.Chap8.LinqBugTracker.Model;

namespace ProEnt.Chap8.LinqBugTracker
{
    public partial class ApplicationDetail : System.Web.UI.Page
```

```
{
    ApplicationDAO _applicationDAO;
    BugDAO _bugDAO;

    protected void Page_Load(object sender, EventArgs e)
    {
        if (!this.IsPostBack)
        {
            ShowApplication();
        }
    }

    protected void grdBugs_RowDeleting(object sender,
                                    GridViewDeleteEventArgs e)
    {
        int bugId = (int)grdBugs.DataKeys[e.RowIndex].Values[0];

        Bug bugToRemove = BugDAO.FindBy(bugId);

        if (bugToRemove != null)
            BugDAO.Delete(bugToRemove);

        ShowApplication();
    }

    private void ShowApplication()
    {
        Application application =
            ApplicationDAO.FindBy(CurrentApplicationId());
        this.litApplicationName.Text = application.Name;

        this.grdBugs.DataSource = application.Bugs;
        this.grdBugs.DataBind();
    }

    private ApplicationDAO ApplicationDAO
    {
        get
        {
            if (_applicationDAO == null)
                _applicationDAO = new ApplicationDAO();

            return _applicationDAO;
        }
    }

    private BugDAO BugDAO
    {
        get
```

```
        {
            if (_bugDAO == null)
                _bugDAO = new BugDAO();

            return _bugDAO;
        }
    }

    public int CurrentApplicationId()
    {
        int applicationId;
        applicationId = Int32.Parse(Request.QueryString["ApplicationId"]);
        return applicationId;
    }

    public Boolean IsNotFixed(Boolean isFixed)
    {
        return !isFixed;
    }

    protected void btnAddBug_Click(object sender, EventArgs e)
    {
        Application application =
            ApplicationDAO.FindBy(CurrentApplicationId());
        Bug newBug = new Bug();
        newBug.Desc = this.txtBugDesc.Text;
        application.Bugs.Add(newBug);

        ApplicationDAO.Save(application);

        ShowApplication();
    }

    protected void grdBugs_ItemCommand(object sender,
                                    GridViewCommandEventArgs e)
    {
        if (e.CommandName == "MarkAsFixed")
        {
            int bugId =  Int32.Parse((string)e.CommandArgument);

            Bug bugToMarkAsFixed = BugDAO.FindBy(bugId);

            if (bugToMarkAsFixed != null)
                bugToMarkAsFixed.Fixed = true;

            BugDAO.Save(bugToMarkAsFixed);

            ShowApplication();
        }
    }
}
```

Before we get into the details of what's happening in the code, let's see the application in action. Click Run or press F5 to start the web application in debug mode. The first page that is loaded is the `default.aspx` page, and this page lists all of the applications you have in the database as well as giving you the option of creating some more. Figure 8-11 shows the page with some dummy data. Go ahead and enter some data of your own to verify that the `DataContext` class is doing what it's supposed to do.

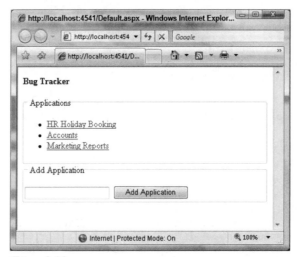

Figure 8-11

After you have created some applications, click on one of the names to be taken to the `ApplicationDetails.aspx` page; from there, you can manage the application as shown in Figure 8-12.

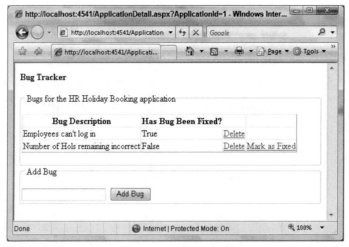

Figure 8-12

Entity Framework

The Entity Framework is being touted as Microsoft's enterprise-level object relational mapper. It differs from LinqToSQL in a number of ways. The Entity Framework can be used by more than just a MS SQL Server database. It can also map business entities to far more complex relational data models. This is because of the three layers of mapping, which you will learn about as you step through a simple exercise in a moment.

The Entity Framework's strength lies in the mapping of relational data models that don't have a one-to-one mapping to the business model, as shown in Figure 8-13.

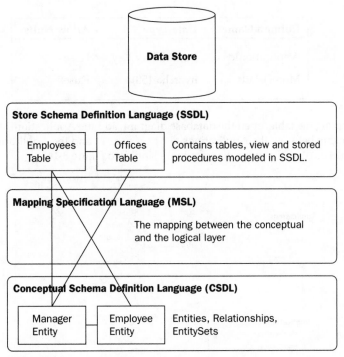

Figure 8-13

The Entity Framework isn't just limited to databases. You can pull data from a number of different sources in a single entity model, including using services for your data source.

Querying is achieved using LINQ to Entities, which is very similar to the LinqToSQL querying mechanism, using strongly typed objects or the literal-based Entity SQL.

In this example, you will build the same basic bug-tracking application as you did in the LinqToSQL example, but this time you will add to the relational data model to show how the Entity Framework can handle more than the simple one-to-one mapping between the domain and data models.

1. To work with Entity Framework, you will need to download the Visual Studio 2008 Service Pack 1 and the .NET Framework 3.5 Service Pack 1.

2. Once the service packs have been installed, open Visual Studio and create a new web application named `ProEnt.Chap8.EFBugTracker`. You now need a database with the same schema as the database you created in the LinqToSQL project. There are two ways you can do this. One is to copy the database you were using in the previous project by right-clicking on the `App_Data` folder name and selecting Add Existing Item, then navigating to the `App_Data` folder of the LinqToSQL Project. The second way is to create it again from scratch following steps 2 to 7.

3. With the database in place, it's time to add a third table. Add a new table to the database, named ApplicationDetails, with the following schema:

Column Name	Data Type	Allow Nulls
ApplicationId	Int, Primary Key	False
MoreDetails	nvarchar(50)	False

After creating the table, open the database diagram, add the ApplicationDetails table, and make a relationship between the Applications `ApplicationId` and the ApplicationDetails `ApplicationId` so that your diagram looks similar to Figure 8-14.

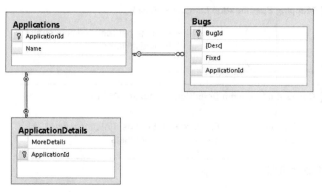

Figure 8-14

4. Now that you have your database with an extra table, you can map it to a conceptual model by using the Entity Framework. To do this, first create a folder named `Model`, then right-click on the folder and click Add New Item: then as shown in Figure 8-15, select the ADO.NET entity data model and name it `BugTracker.edmx`.

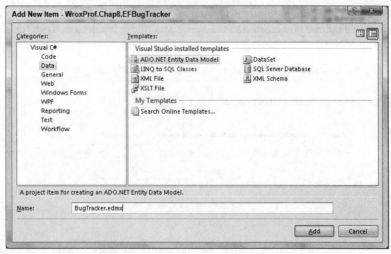

Figure 8-15

5. After you click the Add button, you are taken through a series of steps to build your model. Step one, as shown in Figure 8-16, gives you a choice between generating a model from the database or creating one yourself. As you already have an existing database, you can select Generate From Database and click Next.

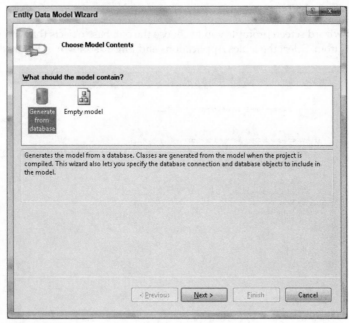

Figure 8-16

6. The next screen, shown in Figure 8-17, enables you to specify the location of your database. By default, the database you created in the `App_Data` folder is selected. Keep the settings as they are and click Next.

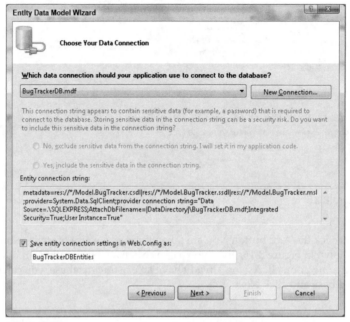

Figure 8-17

7. The third wizard screen prompts you to choose the database objects that you want your model to be created from. Select the tables Applications and Bugs, as shown in Figure 8-18, and click Finish.

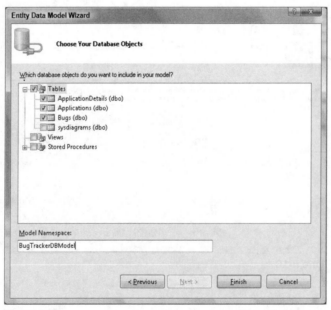

Figure 8-18

8. Visual Studio will now start to build your entity data model, and after a while you will be presented with the Entity Designer, as shown in Figure 8-19.

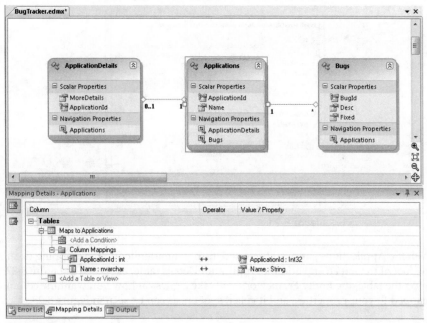

Figure 8-19

Like LinqToSQL, Entity Framework has built an entity for each of the tables you selected and has added the relationships between the entities based on the schema of the tables.

9. The Entity Framework has done a good job at guessing the relationships between the entities, but from the domain model point of view, the data in the Applications and ApplicationDetails belongs in one entity, so you will need to edit the model a little.

Right-click on the Applications entity and add a new scalar property, as shown in Figure 8-20; name this property MoreDetails.

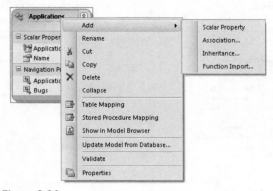

Figure 8-20

Next right-click on the MoreDetails property you just created, and select properties from the context menu. As shown in Figure 8-21, set the properties type to String and Nullable to False.

Figure 8-21

10. With the Applications entity still selected, turn your attention to the mapping details section at the foot of the screen and add the ApplicationDetails table, as shown in Figure 8-22. After you select the table, the Entity Framework will take a guess at how you want the columns to be mapped to your properties, and it gets it spot on, as can be seen in Figure 8-23.

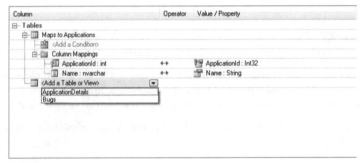

Figure 8-22

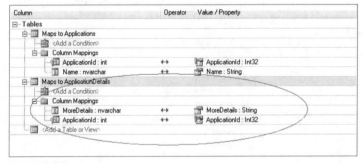

Figure 8-23

With the Applications and ApplicationDetails table now both mapped to the one entity, you can delete the `ApplicationDetails` entity by selecting it and clicking Delete. Your entity model will now look like Figure 8-24.

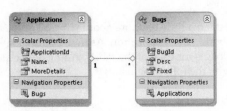

Figure 8-24

11. The Entity Framework has done a good job at guessing the names for the classes, but it's not quite right. Fear not though, as you can simply edit the class names and properties straight from the designer as highlighted in Figure 8-25. To do this, double-click on the `Applications` class name and rename it `Application`. Rename the `Bugs` class to `Bug`, and rename the `Applications` property of `Bug` to `Application`.

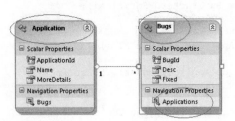

Figure 8-25

Before going any further, let's take a look at the other files generated by the Entity Framework. Close the EF Designer window, right-click on the `BugTracker.edmx` file, and select Open With. From the dialog box that appears, select XML Editor and hit OK. You are now presented with the XML metadata that represents the three layers of the Entity Framework.

❑ Stored Schema Definition Language (SSDL)

The SSDL maps the database structure including tables and relationships, views, and stored procedures. This is your logic layer.

❑ Conceptual Schema Definition Language (CSDL)

The CSDL maps the conceptual view detailing your entities and their relationships. This is the conceptual layer.

❑ Mapping Specification Language (MSL)

The MSL maps the logical layer to the conceptual layer. It maps your business entities to the underlying database.

12. The second file created by the Entity Framework is `BugTracker.Designer.cs`. This can be found by expanding `BugTracker.edmx`. Do this and double-click it to bring up the class definition. The `BugTracker.Designer.cs` file is similar to the LinqToSQL designer class in that it contains all of the generated classes plus the `DataContext` class that you can use to retrieve and persist your entities.

13. Now that you understand a little bit more about what all of the magically generated files do, you can continue to build your application. As in the LinqToSQL example, you are going to create Data Access Objects for each of the tables. Add a new class to the `Model` folder, named `ApplicationDAO`, with the following listing:

```
using System.Collections.Generic;
using System.Linq;

namespace ProEnt.Chap8.EFBugTracker.Model
{
    public class ApplicationDAO
    {
        private BugTrackerDBEntities _db;

        public ApplicationDAO()
        {
            _db = new BugTrackerDBEntities();
        }

        public List<Application> FindAll()
        {
            return (_db.ApplicationSet).ToList();
        }

        public Application FindBy(int Id)
        {
            return (_db.ApplicationSet).First(a => a.ApplicationId == Id);
        }

        public void Add(Application application)
        {
            _db.AddToApplicationSet(application);
            _db.SaveChanges();
        }

        public void Save(Application application)
        {
            _db.SaveChanges();
        }
    }
}
```

14. Add a second class to the `Model` folder, named `BugDAO`:

```
using System.Collections.Generic;
using System.Data.Objects;
using System.Linq;

namespace ProEnt.Chap8.EFBugTracker.Model
```

```
{
    public class BugDAO
    {
        private BugTrackerDBEntities _db;

        public BugDAO()
        {
            _db = new BugTrackerDBEntities();
        }

        public List<Bug> FindAll()
        {
            return (_db.BugSet).ToList();
        }

        public Bug FindBy(int Id)
        {
            return (_db.BugSet).First(a => a.BugId == Id);
        }

        public void Save(Bug bug)
        {
            _db.SaveChanges();
        }

        public List<Bug> FindAllByApplication(int Id)
        {
            ObjectQuery<Bug> Allbugs = _db.BugSet;

            var bugs = from bug in Allbugs
                        where bug.Application.ApplicationId == Id
                         select bug;

            return bugs.ToList();
        }

        public void Add(Bug bug)
        {
            _db.AddToBugSet(bug);
            _db.SaveChanges();
        }

        public void DeleteBy(int BugId)
        {
            Bug bugToDelete = FindBy(BugId);
            _db.DeleteObject(bugToDelete);
            _db.SaveChanges();
        }
    }
}
```

The syntax for the DAO is so close to that of the LinqToSQL implementation that you should be able to understand it fairly easily.

15. As with the LinqToSQL sample, you need to add some Web Forms to complete the application. Open the `Default.aspx` page, and update the HTML source view with the following definition:

```
<%@ Page Language="C#" AutoEventWireup="true"
    CodeBehind="Default.aspx.cs"
    Inherits="ProEnt.Chap8.EFBugTracker._Default" %>

<!DOCTYPE html PUBLIC "-//W3C//DTD XHTML 1.0 Transitional//EN"
  "http://www.w3.org/TR/xhtml1/DTD/xhtml1-transitional.dtd">
<html xmlns="http://www.w3.org/1999/xhtml">
<head runat="server">
    <title></title>
</head>
<body>
    <form id="form1" runat="server">
    <div>
        <p>
            <b>Bug Tracker</b></p>
        <fieldset>
            <legend>Applications</legend>
            <asp:Repeater ID="rptApplications" runat="server">
                <HeaderTemplate>
                    <ul>
                </HeaderTemplate>
                <ItemTemplate>
                    <li>
                    <a href="ApplicationDetail.aspx?ApplicationId=
                        <%# Eval("ApplicationId") %>">
                    <%# Eval("Name") %></a> (<%# Eval("MoreDetails") %>) </li>
                </ItemTemplate>
                <FooterTemplate>
                    </ul>
                </FooterTemplate>
            </asp:Repeater>
        </fieldset>
        <fieldset>
            <legend>Add Application</legend>
            <p>
                  Application Name
                <br />
                 <asp:TextBox ID="txtApplicationName" runat="server">
                    </asp:TextBox>
                <br />
                 More Details<br />
                 <asp:TextBox ID="txtApplicationMoreDetails" runat="server">
                    </asp:TextBox>
                <br />
                 
            <asp:Button ID="btnAddApplication" runat="server"
                        Text="Add Application"
                        OnClick="btnAddApplication_Click" />
            </p>
        </fieldset>
```

```
        </div>
        </form>
</body>
</html>
```

16. Flip over to the code behind, and add the following code listing:

```
using System;
using ProEnt.Chap8.EFBugTracker.Model;

namespace ProEnt.Chap8.EFBugTracker
{
    public partial class _Default : System.Web.UI.Page
    {
        private ApplicationDAO _applicationDAO;

        protected void Page_Load(object sender, EventArgs e)
        {
            if (! this.IsPostBack)
            {
                ShowAllApplications();
            }
        }

        private void ShowAllApplications()
        {
            this.rptApplications.DataSource = ApplicationDAO.FindAll();
            this.rptApplications.DataBind();
        }

        private ApplicationDAO ApplicationDAO
        {
            get {
                if (_applicationDAO == null)
                    _applicationDAO = new ApplicationDAO();

                return _applicationDAO;
            }
        }

        protected void btnAddApplication_Click(object sender, EventArgs e)
        {
            Application application = new Application();
            application.Name = this.txtApplicationName.Text;
            application.MoreDetails = this.txtApplicationMoreDetails.Text;
            ApplicationDAO.Add(application);
            ShowAllApplications();
        }
    }
}
```

17. Add a second Web Form to the project, named `ApplicationDetails.aspx`, with the following markup:

```
<%@ Page Language="C#" AutoEventWireup="true"
    CodeBehind="ApplicationDetail.aspx.cs"
    Inherits="ProEnt.Chap8.EFBugTracker.ApplicationDetail" %>

<!DOCTYPE html PUBLIC "-//W3C//DTD XHTML 1.0 Transitional//EN"
 "http://www.w3.org/TR/xhtml1/DTD/xhtml1-transitional.dtd">
<html xmlns="http://www.w3.org/1999/xhtml">
<head runat="server">
    <title></title>
</head>
<body>
    <form id="form1" runat="server">
    <div>
        <p>
            <b>Bug Tracker</b></p>
        <fieldset>
            <legend>Application Details</legend> App Name<br />
             <asp:TextBox ID="txtApplicationName" runat="server">
                </asp:TextBox>
            <br />
             More Details<br />
             <asp:TextBox ID="txtApplicationMoreDetails" runat="server">
                </asp:TextBox>
            <br />
             
          <asp:Button ID="btnUpdateApplication" runat="server" Text="Save"
                    OnClick="btnUpdateApplication_Click" />
        </fieldset>
        <fieldset>
            <legend>Bugs </legend>
            <p>
                <asp:GridView DataKeyNames="BugId"
                            AutoGenerateColumns="False"
                            OnRowDeleting="grdBugs_RowDeleting"
                    ID="grdBugs" runat="server" OnRowCommand="grdBugs_ItemCommand">
                    <Columns>
                        <asp:BoundField DataField="Desc"
                                        HeaderText="Bug Description" />
                        <asp:BoundField DataField="Fixed"
                                        HeaderText="Has Bug Been Fixed?" />
                        <asp:CommandField ShowDeleteButton="True" />
                        <asp:TemplateField ShowHeader="False">
                            <ItemTemplate>
                              <asp:LinkButton
                                    Visible='<%# IsNotFixed((bool)Eval("Fixed")) %>'
                                    ID="lnkMarkAsFixed"
                                    runat="server"
                                    CausesValidation="false"
                                    CommandArgument='<%# Eval("BugId") %>'
                                    CommandName="MarkAsFixed"
                                    Text="Mark as Fixed"></asp:LinkButton>
```

```
                         </ItemTemplate>
                    </asp:TemplateField>
                </Columns>
            </asp:GridView>
        </p>
    </fieldset>
    <fieldset>
        <legend>Add Bug</legend>
        <p>
              Bug Description<br />
             <asp:TextBox ID="txtBugDesc" runat="server"></asp:TextBox>
             <br />
             <asp:Button ID="btnAddBug" runat="server"
                            Text="Add Bug" OnClick="btnAddBug_Click" />
        </p>
    </fieldset>
</div>
</form>
</body>
</html>
```

18. Again, flip over to the code view, and amend it to the following:

```csharp
using System;
using System.Web.UI.WebControls;
using System.Collections.Generic;
using ProEnt.Chap8.EFBugTracker.Model;

namespace ProEnt.Chap8.EFBugTracker
{
    public partial class ApplicationDetail : System.Web.UI.Page
    {
        private ApplicationDAO _applicationDAO;
        private BugDAO _bugDAO;

        protected void Page_Load(object sender, EventArgs e)
        {
            if (!this.IsPostBack)
            {
                ShowApplication();
            }
        }

        protected void grdBugs_RowDeleting(object sender,
                                    GridViewDeleteEventArgs e)
        {
            int bugId = (int)grdBugs.DataKeys[e.RowIndex].Values[0];

            BugDAO.DeleteBy(bugId);

            ShowApplication();
        }

        private void ShowApplication()
```

```
    {
        Application application =
            ApplicationDAO.FindBy(CurrentApplicationId());
        this.txtApplicationName.Text = application.Name;
        this.txtApplicationMoreDetails.Text = application.MoreDetails;

        List<Bug> bugs =
            BugDAO.FindAllByApplication(application.ApplicationId);

        this.grdBugs.DataSource = bugs;
        this.grdBugs.DataBind();
    }

    private ApplicationDAO ApplicationDAO
    {
        get
        {
            if (_applicationDAO == null)
                _applicationDAO = new ApplicationDAO();

            return _applicationDAO;
        }
    }

    private BugDAO BugDAO
    {
        get
        {
            if (_bugDAO == null)
                _bugDAO = new BugDAO();

            return _bugDAO;
        }
    }

    public int CurrentApplicationId()
    {
        int applicationId;
        applicationId = Int32.Parse(Request.QueryString["ApplicationId"]);
        return applicationId;
    }

    public Boolean IsNotFixed(Boolean isFixed)
    {
        return !isFixed;
    }

    protected void btnAddBug_Click(object sender, EventArgs e)
    {
        Application application =
            ApplicationDAO.FindBy(CurrentApplicationId());

        Bug newBug = new Bug();
        newBug.Desc = this.txtBugDesc.Text;
```

```
            newBug.Application = application;
            application.Bugs.Add(newBug);

            ApplicationDAO.Save(application);

            ShowApplication();
        }

        protected void grdBugs_ItemCommand(object sender,
                                    GridViewCommandEventArgs e)
        {
            if (e.CommandName == "MarkAsFixed")
            {
                int bugId =  Int32.Parse((string)e.CommandArgument);

                Bug bugToMarkAsFixed = BugDAO.FindBy(bugId);

                if (bugToMarkAsFixed != null)
                    bugToMarkAsFixed.Fixed = true;

                BugDAO.Save(bugToMarkAsFixed);

                ShowApplication();
            }
        }

        protected void btnUpdateApplication_Click(object sender, EventArgs e)
        {
            Application application =
                ApplicationDAO.FindBy(CurrentApplicationId());

            application.Name = this.txtApplicationName.Text;
            application.MoreDetails = this.txtApplicationMoreDetails.Text;

            ApplicationDAO.Save(application);

            ShowApplication();
        }
    }
}
```

19. Now simply press F5 or start the debugger to launch the application, and the Entity Framework will handle the mapping and persistence for you when you persist your applications and bugs.

Although this example was fairly trivial, hopefully it showed you the power of the Entity Framework, and even though it may have a fairly steep learning curve, if you have a legacy database with an obscure relational model, it may be just the thing to enable you to easily map it to your business entities.

So, now that you have seen two object relational mapping solutions from Microsoft, which one should you go with?

LinqToSQL or the Entity Framework?

You wait ages for an object relational mapper from Microsoft, then two come along at the same time! So, why the need for two ORMs and what's the difference between LinqToSQL and EF?

One of the first major differences between LinqToSQL and the Entity Framework is that LinqToSQL is only compatible with MS SQL Server, whereas the Entity Framework can be used with a multitude of databases. LinqToSQL works very well if you have a normalized database that has one-to-one mapping between tables and business objects, rather like the Active Record pattern you learned about in the previous chapter. If you want to build a business object that spans more than one table in LinqToSQL, you will have to build a view in the database first. However, once you do this you are unable to persist any changes to this data when using the business object mapped to the view. The Entity Framework, on the other hand, has the notion of a conceptual layer that allows complex mappings that can span more than one table and can handle updates from a business object created from joined tables, which you saw in the code sample.

So, with all that in mind, it depends on what you need, how your database is set up, and what your business model looks like. If you are looking for a quick object-oriented data model to program against and your business model matches your data model, then LinqToSQL is a good match. On the other hand, if you are working against a legacy database or you are pulling your data from more than one source, then the Entity Framework is going to be much more useful to you.

Just because LinqToSQL and Entity Framework are made by Microsoft, it doesn't mean that they are the only players in town when it comes to ORM. Next you will look at an open source product called NHibernate, but before we look at this, let's take a look at a different perspective when it comes to the point where you need to persist your business objects.

Model First

The Model First or Top Down approach to development starts with the business domain model. From there a database schema is built to accommodate the persistence of the model's state. Domain Driven Design purists will argue that the domain model should be built without a second thought for how it will be persisted, but it's always a good idea to be a little more practical to make life a little easier on yourself.

One of the benefits that the Model First approach has over the Data First approach is that you can build you application in a completely Test Driven Development manner. Also, it can be very liberating to build a complete idealist conceptual model of the problem space you are working in before having to meet infrastructure needs half way.

The Model First approach suits the domain model business pattern that you learned about in the previous chapter and is favored by developers following a Domain Driven Design approach to software development.

Repository Pattern

The Repository pattern was mentioned briefly in the previous chapter, as it is a popular choice for persistence and retrieval needs for those applications that use the domain model business pattern. The Repository pattern differs from the DAO pattern in that a repository will typically correspond to an aggregate root as opposed to the Data Access Object pattern corresponding to a single table.

POCO and Persistence Ignorance

Another feature popular with the domain model pattern is the concept of PI (Persistence Ignorance) or POCO. POCO is an acronym for "Plain Old CLR Object." The term is used to contrast an object with one that is used with a complicated, special object framework that needs to inherit from certain base classes or implement certain types of interfaces. The idea is to keep your business objects decoupled from your data access layer so that they contain code only specific to business logic.

Even though you generated your business entities via the LinqToSQL designer and there was an awful lot of infrastructure code intertwined with the business entities, PI is achievable using the LinqToSQL framework, although at the cost of lazy loading, as lazy or deferred loading is achieved by using the LinqToSQL `EntityRef` and `EntitySet` specific types. One method of allowing an existing model to be persisted by LinqToSQL is to use attributes to decorate properties so that the DataContext knows how they should be stored. A second way is by using the XML mapping metadata file to specify the mappings between the business entities properties and the database columns. A third way to use LinqToSQL and keep your business model free from persistence concerns is to use the generated model as an object-oriented database and manually map your POCO business entities to the LinqToSQL-generated one.

The Entity Framework, on the other hand, is not very PI-friendly, at least not in the current version, which at the time of writing was version 3.0. After a vote of no confidence, in the form of a number of blog posts from the Domain Driven Design community, Microsoft has promised to tackle the issues of having to implement set base classes and is planning to release version 4.0 with the .NET 4.0 Framework, with a PI Entity Framework implementation.

One of the best PI ORMs currently available to the .NET community is an open source solution called NHibernate, and that's what you are going to learn about next.

NHibernate

NHibernate is a port of the popular open source Hibernate framework for Java. Hibernate has been around for years, and it's a proven and robust piece of software. ORM has had a slow take-up in the .NET world, but with the release of LinqToSQL and the beta of the Entity Framework, many developers are starting to see the benefit of automating their data access layer.

One of the best features of NHibernate, is the support for persistence ignorance — this means that your business objects don't have to inherit from any base classes or implement any framework interfaces.

NHibernate uses an instance of an `ISession` as its DataContext; it is very similar to the DataContexts of LinqToSQL and the Entity Framework in that it acts as your persistence manger and gateway into the database, allowing you to query against it, as well as saving, deleting, and adding entities.

There are a number of ways to map business objects to database tables in NHibernate. One of the most popular is via an XML configuration file (shown in Figure 8-26), but the use of attributes and a fluent code mapping option are also available.

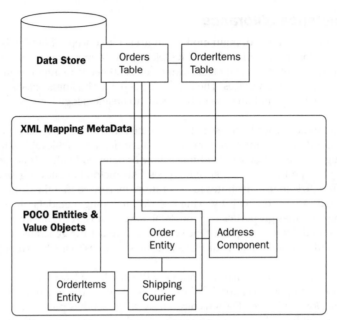

Figure 8-26

Like Microsoft's offerings, NHibernate has two methods of querying for entities. These include an implementation of Martin Fowlers Query Object pattern and a literal base query language called HQL.

As with the Entity Framework demo, you are going to build the same basic bug tracker application, but you will add some more columns to the Applications table to hold data for a value object so that you can see how this is mapped as a component in NHibernate.

1. To work with NHibernate, you'll first need the framework, so navigate to www.nhibernate.org and click on the latest release, as shown in Figure 8-27, (at the time of writing this is version 2.0.1.GA). You will be redirected to SourceForge — once there, click Download, as shown in Figure 8-28, to display all of the downloads for this release. Select the project named, at the time of this writing, NHibernate-2.1.0.Beta2-bin.zip, as shown in Figure 8-29. When this download has completed, extract all of the containing folders and files to C:\NHibernate.

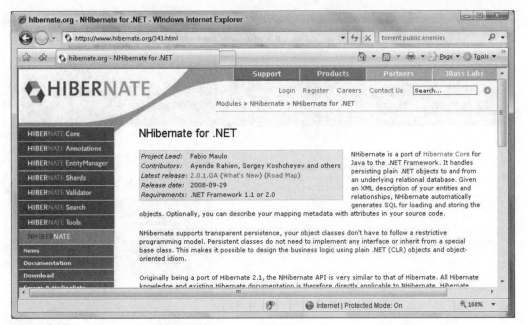

Figure 8-27

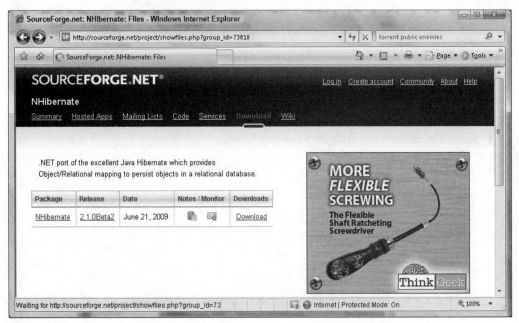

Figure 8-28

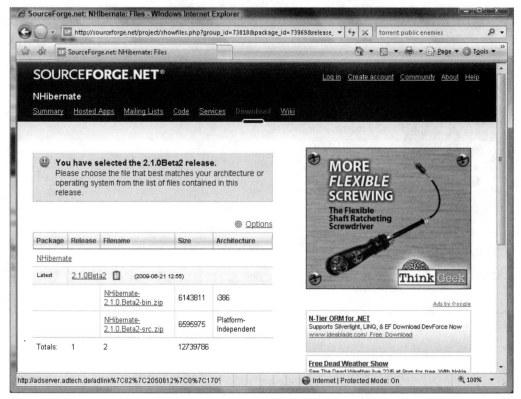

Figure 8-29

2. Fire up Visual Studio and create a new web application named `ProEnt.Chap8.NHibernateBugTracker`.

3. Add a new folder to the project, named `Model`, then add the following three classes: `Developer`, `Application`, and `Bug` with the following listing:

```
namespace ProEnt.Chap8.NHibernateBugTracker.Model
{
    public class Developer
    {
        private string _firstName;
        private string _secondName;

        public Developer()
        { }

        public Developer(string FirstName, string SecondName)
        {
            _firstName = FirstName;
            _secondName = SecondName;
        }
    }
```

```csharp
        public string FirstName
        {
            get { return _firstName; }
        }

        public string SecondName
        {
            get { return _secondName; }
        }
    }
}


using System.Collections.Generic;

namespace ProEnt.Chap8.NHibernateBugTracker.Model
{
    public class Application
    {
        private string _name;
        private Developer _developer;
        private int _id;
        private List<Bug> _bugs;

        public Application()
        {
            _bugs = new List<Bug>();
        }

        public int ApplicationId
        {
            get { return _id; }
            set { _id = value; }
        }

        public Developer Developer
        {
            get { return _developer; }
            set { _developer = value; }
        }

        public string Name
        {
            get { return _name; }
            set { _name = value; }
        }

        public List<Bug> Bugs
        {
            get { return _bugs; }
            set { _bugs = value; }
        }
    }
}
```

```
namespace ProEnt.Chap8.NHibernateBugTracker.Model
{
    public class Bug
    {
        private int _id;
        private string _desc;
        private bool _fixed;
        private Application _application;

        public int BugId
        {
            get { return _id; }
            set { _id = value; }
        }

        public string Desc
        {
            get { return _desc; }
            set { _desc = value; }
        }

        public bool Fixed
        {
            get { return _fixed; }
            set { _fixed = value; }
        }

        public Application Application
        {
            get { return _application; }
            set { _application = value; }
        }
    }
}
```

4. With your domain model built, you now need a database with the same schema as the database you created in the LinqToSQL project. There are two ways you can do this. One is to copy the database you were using in the previous project by right-clicking on the App_Data folder name and selecting Add Existing Item, then navigating to the App_Data folder of the LinqToSQL Project. The second way is to create it again from scratch following steps 2 to 7 from the LinqToSQL exercise.

5. With the database in place, it's time to amend the Applications table. If you have copied the database from the LinqToSQL exercise go in and remove all of the records from the Bugs table and then the Applications table. With the tables all clear, amend the Applications table so it includes the two columns defined here:

Column Name	Data Type	Allow Nulls
DeveloperFirstName	nvarchar(50)	False
DeveloperSecondName	nvarchar(50)	False

6. Now you need to add the reference to the NHibernate framework. Right-click on the project and click Add Reference, select the Browse tab, and navigate to the location that you extracted the NHibernate download to. If you have been following along, the location will be `C:\NHibernate\NHibernate-2.1.0.Beta2-bin`. From the folder `C:\NHibernate\NHibernate-2.1.0.Beta2-bin\Required Bins`, add these files.

   ❑ `Iesi.Collections.dll`

   ❑ `log4net.dll`

   ❑ `NHibernate.dll`

   From the folder `C:\NHibernate\NHibernate-2.1.0.Beta2-bin\Required For LazyLoading\LinFu`, add these files as references.

   ❑ `LinFu.DynamicProxy.dll`

   ❑ `NHibernate.ByteCode.LinFu.dll`

7. There is no graphical designer with NHibernate, so you will need to map the business objects to your Data tables manually. Add a new XML file to the `Models` folder, named `Application.hbm.xml`, with the following markup:

```xml
<?xml version="1.0" encoding="utf-8" ?>
<hibernate-mapping xmlns="urn:nhibernate-mapping-2.2"
    namespace="ProEnt.Chap8.NHibernateBugTracker.Model"
        assembly="ProEnt.Chap8.NHibernateBugTracker">

        <class name="Application" table="Applications" lazy="false">
id name="ApplicationId" column="ApplicationId" type="int" unsaved-value="0">
                    <generator class="native" />
            </id>

            <property name="Name" column="Name"/>

            <component access="field.camelcase-underscore"
                    name="Developer" class="Developer">
                <property access="field.camelcase-underscore"
                        column="DeveloperFirstName" name="FirstName"/>
                <property access="field.camelcase-underscore"
                        column="DeveloperSecondName" name="SecondName"/>
            </component>

            <bag
                    cascade="all-delete-orphan"
                    inverse="true"
                    name="Bugs"
                    lazy="false"
                    access="field.camelcase-underscore">
                <key column="ApplicationId" />
                <one-to-many class="Bug" />
            </bag>

        </class>
</hibernate-mapping>
```

```xml
<?xml version="1.0" encoding="utf-8" ?>
<hibernate-mapping xmlns="urn:nhibernate-mapping-2.2"
                   namespace="ProEnt.Chap8.NHibernateBugTracker.Model"
                   assembly="ProEnt.Chap8.NHibernateBugTracker">

    <class name="Application" table="Applications" lazy="false">

        <id name="ApplicationId" column="ApplicationId" type="int"
            unsaved-value="0">
            <generator class="native" />
        </id>

        <property name="Name" column="Name"/>

        <component access="field.camelcase-underscore" name="Developer"
                   class="Developer">
            <property access="field.camelcase-underscore"
                      column="DeveloperFirstName" name="FirstName"/>
            <property access="field.camelcase-underscore"
                      column="DeveloperSecondName" name="SecondName"/>
        </component>

        <bag
            cascade="all-delete-orphan"
            inverse="true"
            name="Bugs"
            lazy="false"
            access="field.camelcase-underscore">
            <key column="ApplicationId" />
            <one-to-many class="Bug" />
        </bag>

    </class>
</hibernate-mapping>
```

8. Add a second XML file to the Model folder, named Bug.hbm.xml.

```xml
<?xml version="1.0" encoding="utf-8" ?>
<hibernate-mapping xmlns="urn:nhibernate-mapping-2.2"
    namespace="ProEnt.Chap8.NHibernateBugTracker.Model"
        assembly="ProEnt.Chap8.NHibernateBugTracker">

    <class name="Bug" table="Bugs" lazy="false">

        <id name="BugId" column="BugId" type="int" unsaved-value="0">
            <generator class="native" />
        </id>

        <property name="Desc" column="Description"/>

        <property name="Fixed" column="Fixed"/>

        <many-to-one name="Application"
                     class="Application"
```

```
                            column="ApplicationId"
                            cascade="all"
                            not-null="true"/>
        </class>
    </hibernate-mapping>
```

9. After you have created both of the XML files, you will need to embed them as resources in your project. Right-click on each of the XML files in turn, select Properties, and choose Embedded Resource for the build action, as shown in Figure 8-30.

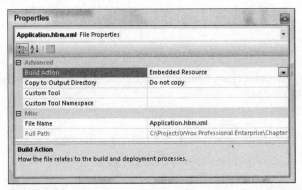

Figure 8-30

10. Add a new class to the Model folder, named SessionProvider, with the following definition:

```
namespace ProEnt.Chap8.NHibernateBugTracker.Model
{
    public class SessionProvider
    {
        private static NHibernate.ISessionFactory _SessionFactory;

        private static void Init()
        {

            NHibernate.Cfg.Configuration config;

            config = new NHibernate.Cfg.Configuration();
            config.AddAssembly("ProEnt.Chap8.NHibernateBugTracker");
            config.Configure();


            _SessionFactory = config.BuildSessionFactory();
        }

        public static NHibernate.ISessionFactory GetSessionFactory()
        {
            if (_SessionFactory == null)
```

```
        {
            Init();
        }

        return _SessionFactory;
    }

    public static NHibernate.ISession GetSession()
    {


        return GetSessionFactory().OpenSession();
    }
  }
}
```

11. Now you can add a new class, named `ApplicationRepository`, to the `Model` folder with the following code listing:

```
using System.Collections.Generic;
using NHibernate;

namespace ProEnt.Chap8.NHibernateBugTracker.Model
{
    public class ApplicationRepository
    {
        public List<Application> FindAll()
        {
            using (ISession NSession = SessionProvider.GetSession())
            {
                NHibernate.ICriteria CriteriaQuery =
                        NSession.CreateCriteria(typeof(Application));

                return (List<Application>) CriteriaQuery.List<Application>();

            }
        }

        public Application FindBy(int Id)
        {
            using (ISession NSession = SessionProvider.GetSession())
            {
                return NSession.Get<Application>(Id);
            }
        }

        public void Add(Application application)
        {
            using (ISession NSession = SessionProvider.GetSession())
```

```
                    {
                        using (ITransaction Transaction = NSession.BeginTransaction())
                        {
                            NSession.Save(application);
                            Transaction.Commit();
                        }
                    }
                }

                public void Delete(Application application)
                {
                    using (ISession NSession = SessionProvider.GetSession())
                    {
                        using (ITransaction Transaction = NSession.BeginTransaction())
                        {
                            NSession.Delete(application);
                            Transaction.Commit();
                        }
                    }
                }

                public void Save(Application modifiedApplication)
                {
                    using (ISession NSession = SessionProvider.GetSession())
                    {
                        using (ITransaction Transaction = NSession.BeginTransaction())
                        {
                            NSession.SaveOrUpdate(modifiedApplication);
                            Transaction.Commit();
                        }
                    }
                }
            }
        }
    }
}
```

12. As with LinqToSQL and the Entity Framework projects, you will add a very simple front end for the application. Open up the `default.aspx` page that was created by Visual Studio when you first created the project, and add the following markup:

```
<%@ Page Language="C#" AutoEventWireup="true"
    CodeBehind="Default.aspx.cs"
    Inherits="ProEnt.Chap8.NHibernateBugTracker._Default" %>

<!DOCTYPE html PUBLIC "-//W3C//DTD XHTML 1.0 Transitional//EN"
 "http://www.w3.org/TR/xhtml1/DTD/xhtml1-transitional.dtd">
<html xmlns="http://www.w3.org/1999/xhtml">
<head runat="server">
    <title></title>
</head>
<body>
    <form id="form1" runat="server">
    <div>
        <p>
```

```
            <b>Bug Tracker</b></p>
    <fieldset>
        <legend>Applications</legend>
        <asp:Repeater ID="rptApplications" runat="server">
            <HeaderTemplate>
                <ul>
            </HeaderTemplate>
            <ItemTemplate>
                <li>
                <a href="ApplicationDetail.aspx?ApplicationId=
                    <%# Eval("ApplicationId") %>">
                    <%# Eval("Name") %></a> (<%# Eval("Developer.FirstName") %>
                    <%# Eval("Developer.SecondName") %>)</li>
            </ItemTemplate>
            <FooterTemplate>
                </ul>
            </FooterTemplate>
        </asp:Repeater>
    </fieldset>
    <fieldset>
        <legend>Add Application</legend>
        <p>
              Application Name
            <br />
             <asp:TextBox ID="txtApplicationName" runat="server">
                </asp:TextBox>
            <br />
             Developer First Name
            <br />
             <asp:TextBox ID="txtDeveloperFirstName" runat="server">
                </asp:TextBox>
            <br />
             Developer Second Name<br />
             <asp:TextBox ID="txtDeveloperSecondName" runat="server">
                </asp:TextBox>
            <br />
             <asp:Button ID="btnAddApplication" runat="server"
                        Text="Add Application"
                        OnClick="btnAddApplication_Click" />
        </p>
    </fieldset>
</div>
</form>
</body>
</html>
```

13. Flip over to the code-behind view, and add the following code listing:

```
using System;
using ProEnt.Chap8.NHibernateBugTracker.Model;

namespace ProEnt.Chap8.NHibernateBugTracker
```

```
{
    public partial class _Default : System.Web.UI.Page
    {
        ApplicationRepository _applicationRepository;

        protected void Page_Load(object sender, EventArgs e)
        {
            if (! this.IsPostBack)
            {
                ShowAllApplications();
            }
        }

        private void ShowAllApplications()
        {
            this.rptApplications.DataSource = ApplicationRepository.FindAll();
            this.rptApplications.DataBind();
        }

        private ApplicationRepository ApplicationRepository
        {
            get {
                    if (_applicationRepository == null)
                        _applicationRepository = new ApplicationRepository();

                    return _applicationRepository;}
        }

        protected void btnAddApplication_Click(object sender, EventArgs e)
        {
            Application application = new Application();
            application.Name = this.txtApplicationName.Text;
            Developer developer = new Developer(this.txtDeveloperFirstName.Text,
                                                this.txtDeveloperSecondName.Text);
            application.Developer = developer;
            ApplicationRepository.Add(application);
            ShowAllApplications();
        }

    }
}
```

14. Now add a new Web Form to the project, named `ApplicationDetail.aspx`, with the markup shown here:

```
<%@ Page Language="C#" AutoEventWireup="true"
    CodeBehind="ApplicationDetail.aspx.cs"
    Inherits="ProEnt.Chap8.NHibernateBugTracker.ApplicationDetail" %>

<!DOCTYPE html PUBLIC "-//W3C//DTD XHTML 1.0 Transitional//EN"
  "http://www.w3.org/TR/xhtml1/DTD/xhtml1-transitional.dtd">
<html xmlns="http://www.w3.org/1999/xhtml">
<head runat="server">
    <title></title>
</head>
```

```
<body>
    <form id="form1" runat="server">
    <div>
        <p>
            <b>Bug Tracker</b></p>
        <fieldset>
            <legend>Bugs for the
                <asp:Literal ID="litApplicationName" runat="server"></asp:Literal>
                application</legend>
            <p>
                <asp:GridView DataKeyNames="BugId" AutoGenerateColumns="False"
                             OnRowDeleting="grdBugs_RowDeleting"
                    ID="grdBugs" runat="server" OnRowCommand="grdBugs_ItemCommand">
                    <Columns>
                        <asp:BoundField DataField="Desc"
                                        HeaderText="Bug Description" />
                        <asp:BoundField DataField="Fixed"
                                        HeaderText="Has Bug Been Fixed?" />
                        <asp:CommandField ShowDeleteButton="True" />
                        <asp:TemplateField ShowHeader="False">
                            <ItemTemplate>
                                <asp:LinkButton
                                  Visible='<%# IsNotFixed((bool)Eval("Fixed")) %>'
                                  ID="lnkMarkAsFixed"
                                  runat="server"
                                  CausesValidation="false"
                                  CommandArgument='<%# Eval("BugId") %>'
                                  CommandName="MarkAsFixed"
                                  Text="Mark as Fixed"></asp:LinkButton>
                            </ItemTemplate>
                        </asp:TemplateField>
                    </Columns>
                </asp:GridView>
            </p>
        </fieldset>
        <fieldset>
            <legend>Add Bug</legend>
            <p>
                <asp:TextBox ID="txtBugDesc" runat="server"></asp:TextBox>
                 <asp:Button ID="btnAddBug" runat="server"
                                Text="Add Bug" OnClick="btnAddBug_Click" />
            </p>
        </fieldset>
    </div>
    </form>
</body>
</html>
```

15. Finally, open the web.config file and add the following sections so that NHibernate knows what your database is and where to find it:

```
<?xml version="1.0"?>
<configuration>

        <configSections>
```

```xml
            <section
       name="hibernate-configuration"
       type="NHibernate.Cfg.ConfigurationSectionHandler, NHibernate"/>

       ...

       </configSections>

   <hibernate-configuration xmlns="urn:nhibernate-configuration-2.2">
       <session-factory name="NHibernate.Test">
           <property name="connection.driver_class">
               NHibernate.Driver.SqlClientDriver</property>
           <property name="connection.connection_string">
               Data Source=.\SQLEXPRESS;
               AttachDbFilename=|DataDirectory|\BugTrackerDB.mdf;
               Integrated Security=True;
               User Instance=True
           </property>
           <property name="adonet.batch_size">10</property>
           <property name="show_sql">true</property>
           <property name="dialect">NHibernate.Dialect.MsSql2005Dialect</property>
           <property name="use_outer_join">true</property>
           <property name="command_timeout">60</property>
           <property name="query.substitutions">
               true 1, false 0, yes 'Y', no 'N'</property>
           <property name="proxyfactory.factory_class">
             NHibernate.ByteCode.LinFu.ProxyFactoryFactory,
             NHibernate.ByteCode.LinFu</property>
       </session-factory>
   </hibernate-configuration>

   ...

</configuration>
```

16. Now, simply press F5 or start the debugger to launch the application, and watch how you can persist and retrieve your business entities and value objects without their having any knowledge of the infrastructure that supports this; in other words, they are persistence-ignorant, POCO business entities.

As with the LinqToSQL and Entity Framework exercises, this example was very simple. However, it should give you another option if you have an existing domain model that requires persistence and you are not too keen to start decorating your objects with attributes or to have them inherit from some persistence framework base class.

Mapping the Mortgage Application with NHibernate

Using an Object Relational Mapper for small applications is fine for learning the pattern. However, the real test of ORMs' power comes when you apply them to larger, complex applications. With this in mind, you are going to use NHibernate to build the repository layer for the model of the mortgage loan prequalification application built in the previous chapter. NHibernate has been chosen because you have already created a domain model and do not yet have a database, so you are taking a Model First approach.

Take a look at Figure 8-31 to remind yourself what entities and value objects make up the domain model.

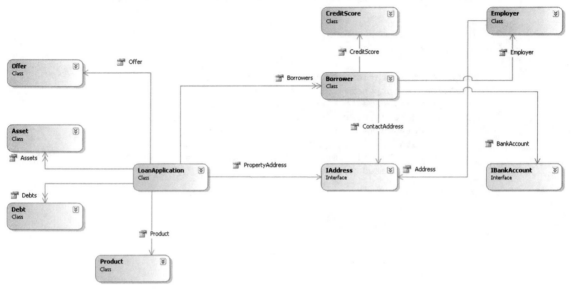

Figure 8-31

Keeping in mind the domain model, take a look at Figure 8-32, which shows the database you will be using to store the state of your business entities and value objects.

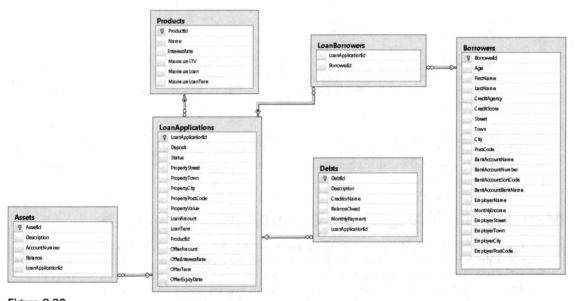

Figure 8-32

Notice how the domain model differs from the relational data model.

1. Open up the project solution you were using for the mortgage loan prequalification application from the previous chapter and add a new class library project, named `ProEnt.LoanPrequalification.IntegrationTests`. You are creating a second test project because you want to keep these long-running tests separate from your business logic tests.

2. After adding the project, add a reference to the `NUnit.dll` file found in the `Lib` folder in the root of the solution.

3. Now add you need to add the reference to the NHibernate framework. It's a good idea to add all of the dependant assemblies to the `Lib` folder to keep them altogether. Navigate to the folder where you extracted the NHibernate files. If you have been following along, the location will be `C:\NHibernate\NHibernate-2.1.0.Beta2-bin`. From the folder `C:\NHibernate\NHibernate-2.1.0.Beta2-bin\Required Bins`; add these files to the `Lib` folder of the solution:

- ❑ `Iesi.Collections.dll`
- ❑ `log4net.dll`
- ❑ `NHibernate.dll`

4. From the folder `C:\NHibernate\NHibernate-2.1.0.Beta2-bin\Required For LazyLoading\LinFu`, add these files to the `Lib` folder:

- ❑ `LinFu.DynamicProxy.dll`
- ❑ `NHibernate.ByteCode.LinFu.dll`

5. Once all the files have been added to the `Lib` folder, switch back to Visual Studio and add the files as references to the `ProEnt.LoanPrequalification.IntegrationTests` project.

6. Next, you need to add a project for your NHibernate implementation of the repositories that you created interfaces for in the previous chapter. Add a new Project to the solution named `ProEnt.LoanPrequalification.Repositories.NHibernate`. Add references to these assemblies located in the `Lib` folder:

- ❑ `Iesi.Collections.dll`
- ❑ `log4net.dll`
- ❑ `NHibernate.dll`
- ❑ `LinFu.DynamicProxy.dll`
- ❑ `NHibernate.ByteCode.LinFu.dll`

7. Add a project reference to the `ProEnt.LoanPrequalification.model` from the `ProEnt.LoanPrequalification.Repositories.NHibernate` project. You do this so that you can get a hold of the repository interfaces that you created in the previous chapter.

8. Finally, right-click on the `ProEnt.LoanPrequalification.IntegrationTests` project and add a reference to the `ProEnt.LoanPrequalification.Repositories.NHibernate` project. You have now set your solution up, and it should look like Figure 8-33.

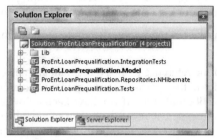

Figure 8-33

9. The next step is to create the database. Add a new folder to the `ProEnt.LoanPrequalification.IntegrationTests` project, named `App_Data`, then add a new database to this folder, named `LoanDB.mdf`. Once the database has been created double-click on it to be taken to the Server Explorer.

Add the following tables as defined in the figures:

❑ Figure 8-34: Assets

❑ Figure 8-35: Borrowers

❑ Figure 8-36: Debts

❑ Figure 8-37: LoanApplications

❑ Figure 8-38: LoanBorrowers

❑ Figure 8-39: Products

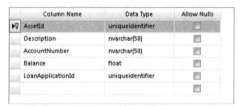

Column Name	Data Type	Allow Nulls
AssetId	uniqueidentifier	☐
Description	nvarchar(50)	☐
AccountNumber	nvarchar(50)	☐
Balance	float	☐
LoanApplicationId	uniqueidentifier	☐
		☐

Figure 8-34

Column Name	Data Type	Allow Nulls
🔑 BorrowerId	uniqueidentifier	☐
Age	int	☐
FirstName	nvarchar(50)	☐
LastName	nvarchar(50)	☐
CreditAgency	nvarchar(50)	☐
CreditScore	nvarchar(50)	☐
Street	nvarchar(50)	☐
Town	nvarchar(50)	☐
City	nvarchar(50)	☐
PostCode	nvarchar(50)	☐
BankAccountName	nvarchar(50)	☐
BankAccountNumber	nvarchar(50)	☐
BankAccountSortCode	char(9)	☐
BankAccountBankName	nvarchar(50)	☐
EmployerName	nvarchar(50)	☐
MonthlyIncome	float	☐
EmployerStreet	nvarchar(50)	☐
EmployerTown	nvarchar(50)	☐
EmployerCity	nvarchar(50)	☐
EmployerPostCode	nvarchar(50)	☐
		☐

Figure 8-35

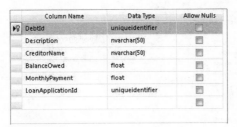

Column Name	Data Type	Allow Nulls
🔑 DebtId	uniqueidentifier	☐
Description	nvarchar(50)	☐
CreditorName	nvarchar(50)	☐
BalanceOwed	float	☐
MonthlyPayment	float	☐
LoanApplicationId	uniqueidentifier	☐
		☐

Figure 8-36

Column Name	Data Type	Allow Nulls
🔑 LoanApplicationId	uniqueidentifier	☐
Deposit	int	☐
Status	int	☐
PropertyStreet	nvarchar(50)	☐
PropertyTown	nvarchar(50)	☐
PropertyCity	nvarchar(50)	☐
PropertyPostCode	nvarchar(50)	☐
PropertyValue	int	☐
LoanAmount	int	☐
LoanTerm	int	☐
ProductId	uniqueidentifier	☐
OfferAmount	int	☑
OfferInterestRate	float	☑
OfferTerm	int	☑
OfferExpirationDate	datetime	☑
		☐

Figure 8-37

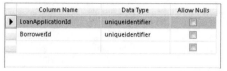

Column Name	Data Type	Allow Nulls
▶ LoanApplicationId	uniqueidentifier	☐
BorrowerId	uniqueidentifier	☐
		☐

Figure 8-38

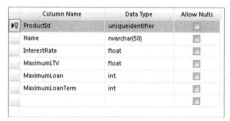

Column Name	Data Type	Allow Nulls
▶🔑 ProductId	uniqueidentifier	☐
Name	nvarchar(50)	☐
InterestRate	float	☐
MaximumLTV	float	☐
MaximumLoan	int	☐
MaximumLoanTerm	int	☐
		☐

Figure 8-39

10. Once the tables have been constructed you will need to create the relationships between them. Create a new database diagram and add the relationships as shown in Figure 8-40.

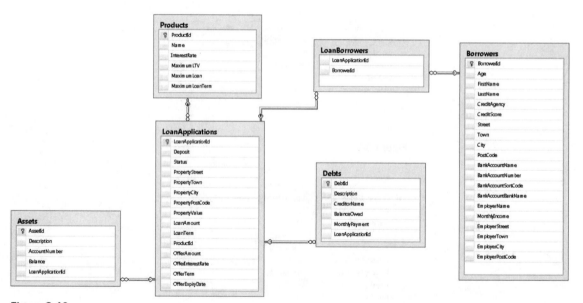

Figure 8-40

11. Now that you have you database set up, you can build the NHibernate repositories. Add a new class to the `ProEnt.LoanPrequalification.Repositories.NHibernate` project, named `SessionProvider`. This class is the same as the one you created for the NHibernate bug tracker application earlier.

```
using NHibernate;
using NHibernate.Cfg;
using System.Web;

namespace ProEnt.LoanPrequalification.
                                    Repositories.NHibernate
{
    public class SessionProvider
    {
        private static ISessionFactory _SessionFactory;
        private static ISession _session;

        private static void Init()
        {
            Configuration  config = new Configuration();
            config.AddAssembly(
              "ProEnt.LoanPrequalification.Repositories.NHibernate");

            log4net.Config.XmlConfigurator.Configure();

            config.Configure();

            _SessionFactory = config.BuildSessionFactory();
        }

        public static ISessionFactory GetSessionFactory()
        {
            if (_SessionFactory == null)
                Init();

            return _SessionFactory;
        }

        public static ISession GetNewSession()
        {
            return GetSessionFactory().OpenSession();
        }

        public static ISession GetCurrentSession()
        {
            if (HttpContext.Current != null)
            {
                if (HttpContext.Current.Items["NHibernateSession"] == null)
                    HttpContext.Current.Items["NHibernateSession"] =
                                                GetNewSession();
                return (ISession)HttpContext.Current.Items["NHibernateSession"];
            }
            else
```

```
            {
                if (_session == null)
                    _session = GetNewSession();

                return _session;
            }

        }

    }
}
```

12. Your next job is to create the mapping metadata that will map the entities and value object to the database tables. Add a new folder to the project, named `MappingFiles`, and add a new XML file, named `Asset.hbm.xml`, with the following markup:

```xml
<?xml version="1.0" encoding="utf-8" ?>
<hibernate-mapping xmlns="urn:nhibernate-mapping-2.2"
    namespace=
    "ProEnt.LoanPrequalification.Model.LoanApplications"
    assembly="ProEnt.LoanPrequalification.Model">

    <class name="Asset" table="Assets" lazy="false">

        <id name="Id" column="AssetId" type="guid">
            <generator class="guid" />
        </id>

        <property name="Description">
            <column name="Description" sql-type="nvarchar(50)" not-null="true" />
        </property>

        <property name="AccountNumber">
            <column name="AccountNumber" sql-type="nvarchar(50)" not-null="true" />
        </property>

        <property name="Balance">
            <column name="Balance" sql-type="float" not-null="true" />
        </property>

        <many-to-one name="LoanApplication"
                     class="LoanApplication"
                     column="LoanApplicationId"
                     not-null="true"
                                        />

    </class>
</hibernate-mapping>
```

13. Add a second XML file to the `MappingFiles` folder, named `Debt.hbm.file`:

```xml
<?xml version="1.0" encoding="utf-8" ?>
<hibernate-mapping xmlns="urn:nhibernate-mapping-2.2"
    namespace=
    "ProEnt.LoanPrequalification.Model.LoanApplications"
    assembly="ProEnt.LoanPrequalification.Model">

        <class name="Debt" table="Debts" lazy="false">

                <id name="Id" column="DebtId" type="guid">
                        <generator class="guid" />
                </id>

                <property name="Description">
                        <column name="Description" sql-type="nvarchar(50)"
                                not-null="true" />
                </property>

                <property name="CreditorName">
                        <column name="CreditorName" sql-type="nvarchar(50)"
                                not-null="true" />
                </property>

                <property name="BalanceOwed">
                        <column name="BalanceOwed" sql-type="float"
                                not-null="true" />
                </property>

                <property name="MonthlyPayment">
                        <column name="MonthlyPayment" sql-type="float"
                                not-null="true" />
                </property>

            <many-to-one name="LoanApplication"
                    class="LoanApplication"
                    column="LoanApplicationId"
                    not-null="true"/>

        </class>
</hibernate-mapping >
```

14. Add a third XML file to the `MappingFiles` folder, named `Product.hbm.xml`, with the markup defined here:

```xml
<?xml version="1.0" encoding="utf-8" ?>
<hibernate-mapping xmlns="urn:nhibernate-mapping-2.2"
    namespace=
    "ProEnt.LoanPrequalification.Model.Products"
     assembly="ProEnt.LoanPrequalification.Model">

        <class name=
"ProEnt.LoanPrequalification.Model.Products.Product"
```

```
        table="Products" lazy="false">

                <id name="Id" column="ProductId" type="guid">
                        <generator class="guid" />
                </id>

                <property name="Name">
                        <column name="Name" sql-type="nvarchar(50)"
                                not-null="true" />
                </property>

                <property name="InterestRate">
                        <column name="InterestRate" sql-type="float"
                                not-null="true" />
                </property>

                <property name="MaximumLTV">
                         <column name="MaximumLTV" sql-type="float"
                                not-null="true" />
                </property>

                <property name="MaximumLoan">
                        <column name="MaximumLoan" sql-type="integer"
                                not-null="true" />
                </property>

                <property name="MaximumLoanTerm">
                        <column name="MaximumLoanTerm" sql-type="integer"
                                not-null="true" />
                </property>

        </class>
</hibernate-mapping>
```

15. Add the penultimate mapping file, named `Solicitor.hbm.xml`, with the following code:

```
<?xml version="1.0" encoding="utf-8" ?>
<hibernate-mapping xmlns="urn:nhibernate-mapping-2.2"
    namespace=
    "ProEnt.LoanPrequalification.Model.Solicitors"
    assembly="ProEnt.LoanPrequalification.Model">

        <class name="Solicitor" table="Solicitors" lazy="false">

                <id name="Id" column="SolicitorId" type="guid">
                        <generator class="guid" />
                </id>

                <component name="BankAccount"
class=
"ProEnt.LoanPrequalification.Model.BankAccount">
                        <property access="field.camelcase-underscore"
                                column="BankAccountName" name="Name"/>
```

```
                            <property access="field.camelcase-underscore"
                                    column="BankAccountNumber" name="AccountNumber"/>
                            <property access="field.camelcase-underscore"
                                    column="BankAccountSortCode" name="SortCode"/>
                            <property access="field.camelcase-underscore"
                                    column="BankAccountBankName" name="BankName"/>
                </component>

                <component name="Address"
    class=
    "ProEnt.LoanPrequalification.Model.Address">
                            <property access="field.camelcase-underscore"
                                    column="Street" name="Street"/>
                            <property access="field.camelcase-underscore"
                                    column="Town" name="Town"/>
                            <property access="field.camelcase-underscore"
                                    column="City" name="City"/>
                            <property access="field.camelcase-underscore"
                                    column="PostCode" name="PostCode"/>
                </component>

                <property name="Name">
                        <column name="Name" sql-type="nvarchar(50)"
                                not-null="true" />
                </property>

                <property name="PhoneNumber">
                        <column name="PhoneNumber" sql-type="nvarchar(50)"
                                not-null="true" />
                </property>

        </class>

</hibernate-mapping>
```

16. Finally add the metadata for the mapping of the LoanApplication class itself. Add LoanApplication.hbm.xml to the mapping files folder with the following code:

```
<?xml version="1.0" encoding="utf-8" ?>
<hibernate-mapping xmlns="urn:nhibernate-mapping-2.2"
    namespace=
 "ProEnt.LoanPrequalification.Model.LoanApplications"
        assembly="ProEnt.LoanPrequalification.Model">

        <class name=
"ProEnt.LoanPrequalification.Model.
LoanApplications.LoanApplication"
                table="LoanApplications" lazy="false">

                <id name="Id" column="LoanApplicationId" type="guid">
                        <generator class="guid" />
                </id>
```

```xml
<component access="field.camelcase-underscore" name="PropertyAddress"
    class="ProEnt.LoanPrequalification.Model.Address">
    <property access="field.camelcase-underscore"
            column="PropertyStreet" name="Street"/>
    <property access="field.camelcase-underscore"
            column="PropertyTown" name="Town"/>
    <property access="field.camelcase-underscore"
            column="PropertyCity" name="City"/>
    <property access="field.camelcase-underscore" column="PropertyPostCode"
            name="PostCode"/>
</component>

<component access="field.camelcase-underscore" name="Offer" class="Offer">
    <property access="field.camelcase-underscore"
            column="OfferInterestRate"
            name="InterestRate"/>
    <property access="field.camelcase-underscore" column="OfferAmount"
            name="LoanAmount"/>
    <property access="field.camelcase-underscore" column="OfferExpiryDate"
            name="ExpiryDate"/>
    <property access="field.camelcase-underscore" column="OfferTerm"
            name="LoanTerm"/>
    <property access="field.camelcase-underscore"
            column="OfferFundsReleased"
            name="FundsReleased"/>
</component>

<property name="Deposit">
    <column name="Deposit" sql-type="integer" not-null="true" />
</property>

<property name="PropertyValue">
    <column name="PropertyValue" sql-type="integer" not-null="true" />
</property>

<property name="LoanAmount">
    <column name="LoanAmount" sql-type="integer" not-null="true" />
</property>

<property name="LoanTerm">
    <column name="LoanTerm" sql-type="integer" not-null="true" />
</property>

<property name="Status">
    <column name="Status" sql-type="integer" not-null="true" />
</property>

<many-to-one name="Product"
            class="ProEnt.
                    LoanPrequalification.Model.Products.Product"
            column="ProductId"
            cascade="none"
            not-null="true"
                                /> 
```

```
            <many-to-one name="Solicitor"
                    class="ProEnt.
                        LoanPrequalification.Model.Solicitors.Solicitor"
                    column="SolicitorId"
                    cascade="none"
                                    not-null="true"
                                    />

        <bag name="Borrowers" table="LoanBorrowers"
            access="field.camelcase-underscore" inverse="true"
            cascade="all" lazy="true" >
                    <key column="LoanApplicationId"/>
                    <many-to-many
                        class="ProEnt.
                        LoanPrequalification.Model.Borrowers.Borrower"
                            column="BorrowerId"></many-to-many>
            </bag>

        <bag name="Assets" access="field.camelcase-underscore"
            inverse="true"
            cascade="all" lazy="true" >
                <key column="LoanApplicationId"/>
                <one-to-many class="Asset"></one-to-many>
            </bag>

        <bag name="Debts" access="field.camelcase-underscore"
                inverse="true"
            cascade="all" lazy="true" >
                <key column="LoanApplicationId"/>
                <one-to-many class="Debt"></one-to-many>
            </bag>
    </class>
</hibernate-mapping>
```

17. For all of the mapping files, ensure that you right-click on each and select Embedded Resource as the build action form the Properties window, as shown in Figure 8-41.

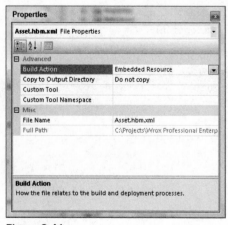

Figure 8-41

18. As all of the repositories for the aggregate groups contain the same basic methods, it makes sense to create a generic base class, so that is exactly what you are going to do. Create a new class named `BaseRepository` with the following definition.

```
using System;
using System.Collections.Generic;
using NHibernate;
using ProEnt.LoanPrequalification.Model;

namespace ProEnt.LoanPrequalification.Repositories.NHibernate
{
    public abstract class BaseRepository<T> : IRepository<T>
    {
        public void  Save(T obj)
        {
                using (ITransaction transaction =
                 SessionProvider.GetCurrentSession().BeginTransaction())
                {
                    SessionProvider.GetCurrentSession().SaveOrUpdate(obj);

                    try
                    {  transaction.Commit();    }
                    catch (Exception)
                    {
                        transaction.Rollback();
                        throw;
                    }
                }
        }

        public void  Add(T obj)
        {
            using (ITransaction transaction =
                SessionProvider.GetCurrentSession().BeginTransaction())
            {
                SessionProvider.GetCurrentSession().Save(obj);

                try
                { transaction.Commit(); }
                catch (Exception)
                {
                    transaction.Rollback();
                    throw;
                }
            }
        }

        public T  FindBy(Guid id)
```

```
        {
            return SessionProvider.GetCurrentSession().Get<T>(id);
        }

        public List<T>  FindAll()
        {
            ICriteria CriteriaQuery =
                    SessionProvider.GetCurrentSession().CreateCriteria(typeof(T));

            return (List<T>)CriteriaQuery.List<T>();
        }
    }
}
```

19. Because all of the work of each repository has been taken care of in the base class, the actual concrete implementations can be kept very simple and added to when extra functionality is needed. Add a new class to the project, named BorrowerRepository, with the following code:

```
using ProEnt.LoanPrequalification.Model.Borrowers;

namespace ProEnt.LoanPrequalification.Repositories.NHibernate
{
    public class BorrowerRepository : BaseRepository<Borrower>
    {

    }
}
```

20. You will now add the remaining repository classes to the project in the same manner; create two class files with the names LoanApplicationRepository, and ProductRepository, and the following class definitions:

```
using ProEnt.LoanPrequalification.Model.LoanApplications;

namespace ProEnt.LoanPrequalification.Repositories.NHibernate
{
    public class LoanApplicationRepository : BaseRepository<LoanApplication>
    {
    }
}
using ProEnt.LoanPrequalification.Model.Products;

namespace ProEnt.LoanPrequalification.Repositories.NHibernate
{
    public class ProductRepository : BaseRepository<Product>
    {
    }
}
```

Your solution should now resemble Figure 8-42.

Figure 8-42

21. With the repositories, mapping metadata files, and their accompanying `SessionProvider` class created, you need to turn your attention to testing to ensure that everything is as it needs to be. Add an `App.Config` file to the `ProEnt.LoanPrequalification.IntegrationTests` project with the following definition:

```
<?xml version="1.0" encoding="utf-8" ?>
<configuration>
    <configSections>
        <!-- NHibernate Section -->
        <section name="hibernate-configuration"
                type="NHibernate.Cfg.ConfigurationSectionHandler, NHibernate"/>
        <!-- NHibernate Section End -->
    </configSections >


    <connectionStrings>
        <add name="LoanDBConnectionString"
            connectionString=
"Data Source=.\SQLEXPRESS;AttachDbFilename=|DataDirectory|\App_Data\LoanDB.mdf;
Integrated Security=True;User Instance=True;User Instance=True"
            providerName="System.Data.SqlClient" />
    </connectionStrings>


    <hibernate-configuration xmlns="urn:nhibernate-configuration-2.2">
        <session-factory>
            <property name="connection.provider">
                NHibernate.Connection.DriverConnectionProvider
            </property>
            <property name="dialect">
                NHibernate.Dialect.MsSql2005Dialect
            </property>
            <property name="connection.driver_class">
                NHibernate.Driver.SqlClientDriver
            </property>
```

```
        <property name="connection.connection_string">
            Data Source=.\SQLEXPRESS;AttachDbFilename=|DataDirectory|\App_Data\
LoanDB.mdf;
Integrated Security=True;User Instance=True
        </property>
        <property name="show_sql">true</property>
    </session-factory>
</hibernate-configuration>
</configuration>
```

This is the same NHibernate configuration that you used in the NHibernate bug tracker project.

22. Now to write some tests. Create a new class file in the `ProEnt.LoanPrequalification. IntegrationTests` project, named `NHibernateProductTests`. Amend the class so that it has an initial test, as shown in the following listing:

```csharp
using System.Configuration;
using System.Data;
using System;
using System.Data.SqlClient;
using NUnit.Framework;
using ProEnt.LoanPrequalification.Model.LoanApplications;
using ProEnt.LoanPrequalification.Model.Products;
using ProEnt.LoanPrequalification.Repositories.NHibernate;

namespace ProEnt.LoanPrequalification.IntegrationTests
{
    [TestFixture]
    public class ProductTests
    {

        [Test]
        public void Can_Add_Product_To_Repository()
        {
            ProductRepository productRepository = new ProductRepository();

            productRepository.Add(new Product
                                  {
                                      InterestRate = 1.25f,
                                      MaximumLoan = 10000,
                                      MaximumLoanTerm = 35,
                                      MaximumLTV = 98f,
                                      Name = "Test Product"
                                  });


            Assert.AreEqual(1, productRepository.FindAll().Count);
        }
    }
}
```

23. If you run the class, it should pass with flying colors. All is good with the world … or is it? Run the test again, and you will find that it fails. This happens because the database is not in a known state before the test is run. If you remember back to the chapter on Test Driven Development, one of the facets of a good unit test is that it must be able to run without relying on the state of outside dependencies. Put another way — you need to ensure that the database is clean of products so that you can be sure that the test is functioning correctly. Add a new stored procedure to the database with the following code:

```
CREATE PROCEDURE sClearDB

AS

        DELETE Assets

        DELETE Debts

        DELETE LoanBorrowers

        DELETE Borrowers

        DELETE LoanApplications


        DELETE Products
```

You are going to run this before each test so that the database is in a known state on which you can base your unit tests.

24. Add a setup method to the `NHibernateProductTests` class, as shown here:

```
[TestFixture]
public class ProductTests
{
    [SetUp]
    public void SetUp()
    {
        // Clear the database to put into a known state
        string connectionString =
          ConfigurationManager.ConnectionStrings["LoanDBConnectionString"].
          ConnectionString;

        using (SqlConnection connection = new SqlConnection(connectionString))
        {
            using (SqlCommand cmd = new SqlCommand("sClearDB", connection))
            {
                cmd.CommandType = CommandType.StoredProcedure;
                connection.Open();
                cmd.ExecuteNonQuery();
            }
        }
    }

    ...
}
```

This method will be run before each test in the class. To test this, run the `Can_Add_Product_To_Repository()` test a number of times.

25. To finish the project, you will add the remaining tests for the persistence related to the Products. Download the full solution from the Wrox site to inspect the full suite of tests.

Add the following methods to the `NHibernateProductTests` class:

```
[TestFixture]
    public class ProductTests
    {
        ...

        [Test]
        public void Can_Find_A_Product_By_Id()
        {
            Guid productId;
            float interestRate = 1.25f;
            int maximumLoan = 10000;
            int maximumLoanTerm = 35;
            float maximumLTV = 98f;
            string name = "Test Product";

            ProductRepository productRepository = new ProductRepository();

            Product productToAdd = new Product
            {
                InterestRate = interestRate,
                MaximumLoan = maximumLoan,
                MaximumLoanTerm = maximumLoanTerm,
                MaximumLTV = maximumLTV,
                Name = name
            };

            productRepository.Add(productToAdd);
            productId = productToAdd.Id;

            productRepository = new ProductRepository();
            Product productToFind = productRepository.FindBy(productId);

            Assert.AreEqual(interestRate, productToFind.InterestRate);
            Assert.AreEqual(maximumLoan, productToFind.MaximumLoan);
            Assert.AreEqual(maximumLoanTerm, productToFind.MaximumLoanTerm);
            Assert.AreEqual(maximumLTV, productToFind.MaximumLTV);
            Assert.AreEqual(name, productToFind.Name);


        }

        [Test]
        public void Can_Save_Changes_To_A_Product()
        {
            Guid productId;
            ProductRepository productRepository;
```

```
        string originalProductName = "Test Product";
        string amendedProductName = "Amended Test Product";

        productRepository = new ProductRepository();
        Product productToAdd = new Product
            {
                InterestRate = 1.25f,
                MaximumLoan = 10000,
                MaximumLoanTerm = 35,
                MaximumLTV = 98f,
                Name = originalProductName
            };

        productRepository.Add(productToAdd);
        productId = productToAdd.Id;
        Assert.AreEqual(1, productRepository.FindAll().Count);

        productRepository = new ProductRepository();
        Product productToAmend = productRepository.FindBy(productId);
        Assert.AreEqual(originalProductName, productToAmend.Name);
        productToAmend.Name = amendedProductName;
        productRepository.Save(productToAmend);

        productRepository = new ProductRepository();
        Product productAmended = productRepository.FindBy(productId);
        Assert.AreEqual(amendedProductName, productAmended.Name);

    }
}
```

That completes the creation of the repositories to persist the state of all entities and value objects within the domain model. Hopefully, you can see how a product like NHibernate can seriously reduce the time it takes to create the infrastructure code. In the upcoming chapters, you will be look at adding a front end to the mortgage loan approval application.

Summary

In this chapter, you have been introduced to the concept of an object relational mapper (ORM) and how one can be applied to your application to fulfill all of you persistence needs. An object relational mapper bridges the gap between the database's relational data model and your object-oriented domain model, better known as the impedance mismatch. Using an ORM framework gives you a lot of functionality straight out of the box, including:

- ❏ Unit of Work
- ❏ Identity Map
- ❏ Lazy loading
- ❏ Strongly typed querying language
- ❏ Caching

The three ORMs that you looked at were MS LinqToSQL, the MS Entity Framework, and the open source NHibernate.

❏ LinqToSQL: LinqToSQL works best when generating a conceptual model from the database and when the relational model and object-oriented model have a one-to-one mapping. It's a great fit for use with the Transaction Script and especially the Active Record patterns, as existing Active Record business objects can be decorated with attributes and handled by LinqToSQL.

❏ Entity Framework: The Entity Framework is Microsoft's enterprise-level object relational mapper capable of very complex mappings spanning different databases and other forms of data sources. It's a great product when it comes to working with legacy databases that don't map easily to the business model because of its three conceptual mapping layers. The only downside is that it doesn't offer a PI experience or good Model First development, both of which are being addressed in the next version, so invest now and reap the rewards later, as this could be a contender for the best ORM.

❏ NHibernate: NHibernate is an open source ORM that has been around for years and that is based on the Java port of Hibernate, which has been around even longer. What you are getting is a wealth of lessons learned and a mature product. It has great support for PI/POCO models and is very simple to come to grips with. The only downside is that it doesn't have a native designer for a graphical representation of your model, but this is only a very small issue. The query language is not as good as Linq, but because it is open source. A Linq provider has already been built for it, so at the moment it's your best bet for enterprise-level ORM needs.

In this chapter, you also took a look at two popular data access patterns that you could put to use in your data access layer.

❏ Data Access Object Pattern: This is a very simple pattern designed to separate the elements of your data access layer form the rest of the application. Typically, a DAO will exist for each table and will contain all of the CRUD methods, which makes it an ideal DAL pattern for the Transaction Script and Active Record business patterns.

❏ Repository Pattern: The Repository pattern, by and large, is used with logical collections of objects, or aggregates as they are better known. The CRUD methods take an instance of the aggregate root and delete all of the associated objects in the object graph. This works really well if you are taking a Domain-Driven Design approach to development, and it is a good fit with the domain model business pattern.

During the exercises to demonstrate the three object relational mappers, you needed to create a web front end. To keep things simple, you placed all of the logic for accessing the DAOs and repositories in the code behind. This was fine for the small bug tracker application. When your applications grow in size and complexity, just placing all of the code in the page behind a web form simply won't do, and some organization needs to take place in the form of design patterns.

The next three chapters will introduce you to some patterns and practices for organizing the presentation layer. You will learn about patterns designed keep your user interface code separate from your presentation logic, and in doing so will take a look at the new ASP.NET MVC Framework.

9

Organizing Your Front End

Moving away from middleware and persistence layers, we will now begin to explore how enterprise systems handle the user interface. The next few chapters take a step back and address the individual front end design patterns commonly found within enterprise systems. In this chapter, we will explore the background of user interface design, and its supporting conceptual layers. In this chapter, we will:

❑ Discuss some of the history of the UI and the evolution of front-end patterns

❑ Review the early model of Model-View-Controller (MVC) and how it applied to legacy systems

❑ Explore the use of MVC on other platforms, including Java Struts

❑ Discuss the difference between ASP.NET and traditional web applications

❑ Review an example of MVP in a simple ASP.NET web page

❑ Discuss the emergence of web MVC and the difference between it and MVP

The Neglected Front End

Programming a user interface is nothing new. People have been developing interactive interfaces for literally decades, conforming to new platforms and technologies as they've come down the pike. A user interface, or UI, can provide a number of different types of experiences. Older legacy systems delivered their UIs in the form of command line terminals, allowing users to enter only text or limited system commands. The proliferation of the Windows paradigm inevitably led to the design of graphical user interfaces, or GUIs, which allow the user to interact with an application via a mouse or other keyboard alternative. The Internet age saw the GUI evolve even further, with developers eventually embracing the web browser and HTML as the primary vehicles of GUI design. Although the technologies have changed and the UIs have become more powerful, they remain one of the most ignored portions of a system when it comes to the subject of well-designed code. The screens got flashier and the controls much slicker, yet the code that drives those applications hasn't enjoyed the same degree of evolution.

There are a number of reasons for this disparity. Originally, the UI was the slimmest section of code, conceptually speaking. Legacy systems with terminal, text-based interfaces simply didn't require much orchestration. The programmer relied on a thin layer of procedural code to control text output and invoke functions within the system. There was little state management available, and the entirety of the UI code existed within the same physical tier as the core system code. The simplicity of the UI never warranted much thought to its design. Therefore, the culture of UI design grew more slowly than that of core system design.

All of that changed with the advent of the graphical user interface. GUIs increased the flexibility of an application's interface, enabling users to interact with the core application in ways that were far more intuitive than simple text commands. Things like windows, buttons, images, slider controls, drop-down lists, and even animations have added a whole new dimension to the way we approach the user experience. Over time, there grew a strong culture of UI design, eventually becoming its own sector of the IT marketplace. However the design culture concentrated mostly on layout and the physical artifacts that compose a screen interface. The main focus of UI designers was to make sure that the screens *looked* good and that the general composition intuitively matched the intent of their underlying features. Little thought was given to the design of the UI code. In fact, as the presence of the Microsoft platform grew in the business world and Windows programs became the technology of choice for business applications, much of the code that powered the GUI was packaged into pluggable components. Enter rapid application development (RAD). Recall that back in the first chapter we discussed the era of RAD programming and its effect on enterprise development. One of the core facets of RAD-powered suites was the ability to snap together canned components and widgets for the quick generation of graphical user interfaces. The need to produce visible results quickly eclipsed the need to balance the code that drove the screens. As a result, a vast number of client applications created over the last 10 or 15 years are powered by poorly designed software.

Over time, many companies started to feel the pinch of poor design. As businesses became more dependent upon the interfaces they used, they naturally needed to scale and extend them. Yet a great number of terrific-looking user interfaces were simply not built to accommodate that sort of change. Business logic mixed in with UI behaviors made it difficult to isolate the right portions of an application on which to build. State management was spread throughout the screens, which made scalability somewhat cumbersome to code. This sobering set of conflicts has forced many IT shops to rethink their approaches to their user interfaces. Still, much of the software industry is still plagued by this issue.

Early Front-End Patterns

Not all areas of the IT world ignored the design of their user interfaces. Although the business world has yet to adopt a uniform approach to front-end design, there have been many software shops using well-known patterns and frameworks for the better part of 20 years. Perhaps the first well-known and widely accepted front-end pattern was the Model-View-Controller pattern, or MVC. First described in 1979 by Trygve Reenskaug, who was then working on Smalltalk at Xerox PARC, MVC has since become one of the most widely adopted frameworks used in software today. MVC endeavors to break the front end of an application into three conceptual layers. The Model represents the data of the application. The View represents the visible components of the UI, and the Controller handles the communication of data and business rules between the Model and the View. Those readers familiar with MVC or MVC-like patterns are certain to claim that this is a somewhat oversimplified explanation of the pattern. Still, at its core MVC strives first and foremost to separate data from UI in a manner that makes it easier to modify either the UI or the data and business rules without affecting the other.

Implementation of the MVC framework varies from platform to platform. Traditional MVC typically employed what is known as an *Observer pattern*. In the Observer pattern, objects maintain relationships with various dependencies and notify them of changes in state. Notification can be done through the use of eventing, abstract typing, or indirect method invocation. MVC uses this pattern to enable direct communication between the Model and the View for the purpose of automatic UI updating. The Controller is still used to initialize state and, in many implementations, to handle some of the business logic. Yet once the runtime state has been established, the Model can directly convey changes in data to the visible interface through the View. A simple example of this mechanism is a small client application that monitors changes in temperatures. When the application starts up, the Controller initializes the View and its corresponding controls, such as the buttons, checkboxes, labels, and the like. The Controller also initializes the Model, making the requisite connections to other parts of the system to populate the Model with data and to keep receiving new data as it becomes available. At this point, the Controller is still on the hook for communication between the layers. If new data becomes available in the Model, the Controller has to communicate that to the View. However, in an Observer pattern the Controller establishes an indirect relationship between the Model and the View directly. In this example, let's assume that the View subscribes to an event on the Model named `TemperatureChanged`. When this event is raised, the View is passed the new temperatures directly from the Model and updates its own controls with the new values. This simple event frees the Controller from the responsibility of constant data communication between layers, while still supporting a loosely coupled pattern. Figure 9-1 depicts this relationship explicitly.

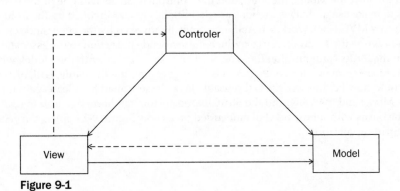

Figure 9-1

The solid lines seen in the diagram depict direct relationships between layers. These relationships are typically achieved through the use of composition or simple object-oriented aggregation. The dotted lines represent indirect relationships. These are abstract, loosely coupled relationships that are achieved using events, callbacks, or abstract typing. Note that this diagram shows an indirect relationship between the

Model and the View, as well as between the View and the Controller. This second connection is typically used to invoke actions on the Controller when the user interacts physically with the UI.

Other frameworks have emerged from this popular pattern, some of which use only portions of the original model. Microsoft Foundation Classes, or MFC, was a set of C++ classes that wrapped the core Windows API. It used a pattern known as Document/View to maintain a separation of the state-based data from the front-end interface. MFC has since evolved into the more mature .NET Winforms model; however, developers can still build legacy applications using the older model. Cocoa, Apple Computer's native API for developing applications for the Mac OS X operating system, uses a flavor of MVC that provides high-level View classes but lacks a strong vehicle for the Model. The Model was expanded upon greatly as Apple transitioned more of its systems to the Mac OS X system, adding many predefined Model classes with built-in functionality commonly found in desktop applications. As these types of MVC patterns matured, so did the use of the Web as the primary vehicle for UI delivery. MVC models vary greatly between thick client and Web-based models. Enterprise developers should familiarize themselves with at least a few of these before choosing the framework that best suits their systems.

Java Struts

There have been a number of variations on the MVC pattern in the Web world. On the Java platform, Java and J2EE servlets employ the use of Model/View separation. However, neither of these models is considered to be a full-bodied framework. Rather, they are sets of APIs used to build clients that provide for degrees separation to be embraced at the developer's discretion. The J2EE servlet model was later wrapped within a popular MVC pattern called *Struts*. Created by Craig McClanahan and donated to the Apache Foundation in May of 2000, Struts is an open source web application framework that builds on the use of J2EE constructs. The Struts model provides some out-of-the-box components for implementing MVC objects and makes use of a standard XML configuration file (`struts-config.xml`) to bind together the Model, the View, and the Controller. Struts was one of the first MVC frameworks to make use of *Actions*. Actions are definitions of tasks invoked by the front-end UI and sent into the core MVC framework. An Action is typically invoked by the client and sent to the Controller, known as the `ActionServlet` which in turn sends the action to the associated `Action` class as defined in the Struts configuration file. The `Action` class interacts with the Model, which in turn returns an `ActionForward`. `ActionForward` is a string containing the name, URI, or URL, to which the client should now be directed. Special reusable Java classes called JavaBeans pass information between the Model and the View, and the Struts-based custom tag library is used to read and write the content of the beans without the need of embedded Java code. Figure 9-2 depicts the generalized flow of a typical Struts application.

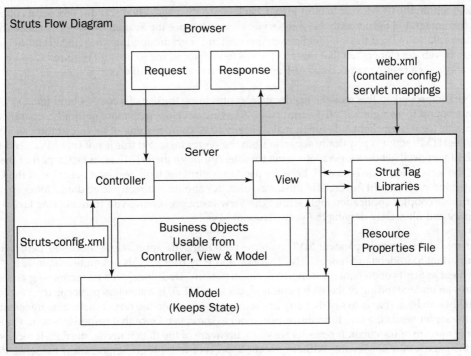

Figure 9-2

Struts has become an increasingly popular framework for web applications over the last few years. It standardizes the MVC implementation in a manner that's tailored specifically for the Web paradigm. Yet there are many who feel that Struts is a notably heavy framework, ideal for large applications but not always suitable for smaller, agile systems. This book doesn't cover the specifics of Struts or other Apache Java projects.

ASP.NET

On the Microsoft side of the Web fence the majority of web applications have been built using the ASP.NET framework. Originally known simply as ASP (Active Server Pages) and expanded considerably with the release of the .NET 1.0 Framework, ASP.NET is Microsoft's model for building intelligent, stateful web applications. A common misconception in the web development community is that ASP.NET is an MVC-inspired pattern. This is fundamentally untrue, and requires some explaining. Classic ASP mixed server-side script with client script and HTML in a single document. Like JSP (Java Server Pages), embedded tagging was used to convey to the interpreter when code should be executed on the server, and when it should be ignored and delivered to the client. The mixed code became tiresome after too long, and many found it difficult to follow and maintain. Java applications typically minimized embedded code through use of the Java servlet model, which provided code-only classes that worked seamlessly with the web server. The Microsoft web platform provided similar web classes, though they didn't integrate with the web server as seamlessly as Servlets. VB programmers could create web server-accessible COM objects using ActiveX, but the integration was awkward. The object had to be instantiated from a script call in the ASP page, and then intermediary COM libraries had to be invoked within the COM class to emit HTML back out to the page. Microsoft did provide a code-only class that integrated tightly with the web server. However since the available code-only classes on the Windows platform used the Internet Server Application Programming Interface (ISAPI) model, most Microsoft web developers felt that this model was too cumbersome to use and required C++ knowledge to leverage. As a result, many classic ASP applications remained in mixed script files.

ASP.NET improved on this model considerably by providing the use of a code-behind file. Code-behind files are bound to a single ASP.NET script page, allowing developers to more naturally separate their server-side logic from client-side functionality. Many have come to think of this separation as MVC-like, since the HTML script is physically separate from the server logic. Yet this is not true MVC, and thinking so might very well get developers into some trouble. Although the HTML is, in fact, a part of the View layer, the server-side code is as well. Both are used to control the look, feel, and behavior of the UI. The code-behind page should not contain business rules, nor should it directly store data. Doing so inextricably couples application logic within the View layer, preventing you from altering layers with impunity and ultimately defying the very nature of MVC.

There are valid ways to implement MVC patterns with ASP.NET applications; however, before doing so it's important to understand how ASP.NET works, and why true MVC is not quite as simple to implement as Struts or an equivalent non-Windows pattern. Traditional web programming generally requires an understanding of the Web paradigm. Because HTTP is a stateless protocol, the Web itself is implicitly stateless. That is to say that any one request coming into the server maintains transient state until the server sends the synchronous response out to the caller. Once that response is sent, the server is no longer aware of the client. It remains blissfully unaware of the data it needs, the data it received, or even the page it may be viewing. Although some aspects of web programming allow for some state management, such as session variables and cookies, the core mechanism that drives all things Web is built to receive requests, send responses, and go about its merry way. This can be a difficult model to understand if you are a thick client programmer. Thick client applications maintain their own state implicitly. Developers can take advantage of application global variables, connection management, data sharing, or any other feature that has some form of state.

ASP.NET is a programming model that emulates thick client functionality within the Web model. It is built directly on top of the same features that drive any other web application, such as HTML and client scripting. Yet the ASP.NET API uses these features to imitate state, ultimately faking what looks like thick client functionality. Most of ASP.NET's magic is in the client scripts emitted by the core engine. Using a strong postback model and a client-aware caching mechanism known as the ViewState, ASP.NET applications can be created with the same programmatic patterns as a thick client program. For the developer, these tools are transparent to them. Like other client application IDE's in the past, the ASP.NET IDE allows developers to drop buttons, textboxes, checkboxes, and other simple UI components onto a page, and respond to the user-initiated events through components' events, such as a button's `Click` event or a checkbox's `CheckChanged` event. What many ASP.Net developers don't realize, however, is that this is a little bit of a smoke-and-mirrors routine. The events consumed imply state management on the server (i.e., imply that the server is aware of the client's button and raised its `Click` event directly). In fact, the truth is that a button's `Click` event is simply a request to the server like any other web page. Through use of the client scripts emitted by the engine and a rigid event model, the request re-creates the page's state on the fly, executing the code in the `Click` event's handler only after the page has been reassembled on the server. Figure 9-3 depicts the event lifecycle of a typical ASP.NET page.

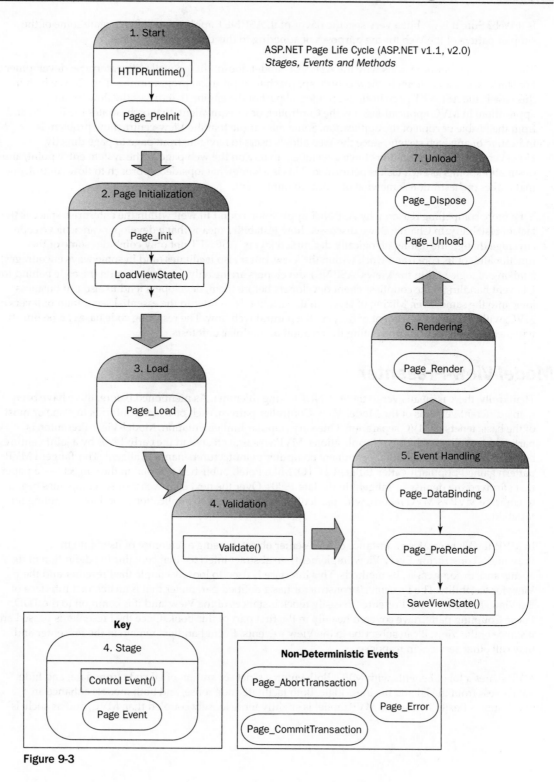

ASP.NET Page Life Cycle (ASP.NET v1.1, v2.0)
Stages, Events and Methods

Figure 9-3

Is it Web? Sure it is . . . but a very specific flavor of it. ASP.NET applications often negate some of the simpler patters of the Web for the purposes of adhering to this development model.

There are a number of reasons why the ASP.NET model doesn't fit too well with enterprise development. For starters, it is an extremely View-centric approach to application programming. The View, which in this case is the ASP.NET page itself, is an integral part of the engine that drives the flow for an application. In MVC applications, it is the Controller, or its equivalent, that orchestrates the flow to and from the visible portion of the application. Some may argue that the View-centric flow problem is indicative of any web system, since the Web allows users to navigate from page to page directly. However, ASP.NET applications force developers to rely on the web page as the system entry point, and destination points as each task is performed. This is a somewhat lopsided approach to flow control, one that makes orchestration somewhat of a bear to implement.

Yet a more compelling reason why ASP.NET applications don't fit well within the enterprise space is the lack of testability. In Chapter 3, we discussed how testability means that a developer can achieve code coverage though the testing of logically decoupled layers. ASP.NET not only combines some of the functionality of its core framework within the View, but it also facilitates (and in some ways encourages) a mixing of logic within the Views. ASP.NET developers are heavily dependent upon the code behind for UI event handling. Like countless client developers before them, developers tend to also put business logic into the same layer. Mixing of layers in this fashion is counter to the essential separation of layers in MVC, with the added detriment of defying the natural web flow. The resulting code base can be unruly, with heavy dependencies preventing the creation of modular unit tests.

Model-View-Presenter

Thankfully, there is an answer to the ASP.NET testing dilemma. As mentioned before, there have been many different versions of the Model-View-Controller pattern, each of which conforms to some or most of the basic tenets of MVC separation. One very popular implementation, Model-View-Presenter, is particularly well suited for web applications. MVP was first created in the early 1990s by a joint venture between IBM, Apple, and other prominent computer manufacturers named Taligent. The Taligent MVP pattern gained popularity after Taligent's CTO, Mike Potel, published a paper on the subject — a paper that survived the demise of Taligent in the late 1990s. Over the next eight years or so, companies began to embrace MVP as MVC reborn, with particular emphasis on web applications and loose coupling for testability.

In MVP, the View creates an instance of a Presenter object, passing a reference of itself into the Presenter's constructor. Every View implements an abstract interface that contains the definition of its events and, in some cases, its methods. This interface is used to loosely couple the Presenter and the View for testability. The Presenter's constructor has a defined parameter that is an abstract Interface of the View. This allows the Presenter to easily mock instances of the View, and it is common to the TDD Loose Coupling pattern we covered heavily in the first part of this book. Once the Presenter is passed an instance of the View, it can subscribe to the View's events. Event handlers remain in the Presenter and may call other services in response.

MVP shares a lot of benefits with MVC. Both enforce strict separation of UI code from data, and hide data access from the UI and business logic. Both facilitate code reuse, and both models enhance an application's flexibility. Yet the MVP model is slightly more loosely coupled than MVC, and as such, is particularly suited for unit testing. Unfortunately there is a lot of confusion about the differences between MVC and MVP. Since there are many variations of both, it's tough to say that any one group of rules applies definitively to one or the other. The fundamental difference is the way the two models relate layers to one another. MVC tightly couples each of its layers, often aggregating concrete instances of one into another. MVC patterns may also employ a one-to-many relationship between the Controller and Views, allowing the Controller to handle user navigation, as well as View-initiated actions that might invoke the logic of another View. MVP patterns tend to be more modular, typically employing a one-to-one relationship between the View and its Presenter. Presenters are used more frequently for testability of UI behaviors than for overall flow control.

MVP's View-driven flow makes it ideal for testing ASP.NET applications. The ASP.NET engine abstracts users from the base web patterns that drive application flow, and places navigation squarely on the web pages. Since a web page is the natural destination for most ASP.NET requests, the MVP pattern fits naturally into the code-behind model. Each code-behind page essentially defines a class, or rather, a type, within the application's namespace. This type can be further abstracted by defining an interface containing the definitions of the web page's attributes. This should be a simple one-to-one mapping of the page's UI components to public properties. For example, a public string property mapped to a label's Text property. A Presenter is then defined, with a constructor accepting an instance of the interface defining the page's abstract type. The Presenter is then provisioned with public (or accessible) methods that can be called within the Page's event handlers, removing the logic from the UI event. When a web page is called the page's *Page_Load* event is invoked. From there the MVP pattern takes over, instantiating the View's Presenter and passing in an instance of itself to the constructor. It is the job of the Presenter to respond to the page's UI events, decoupling the logic of the requested task from the View in which it was invoked. As users navigate from page to page, the MVP pattern repeats itself, using each page's code behind as an instance of its View, and passing it abstractly into the page's specifically designed Presenter.

Let's take a look at a small example of MVP in ASP.NET. The following is the markup for the simplest of web pages. It contains a form, a <div> element, a button, and a label.

```
<html xmlns="http://www.w3.org/1999/xhtml" >
<head runat="server">
    <title></title>
</head>
<body>
    <form id="MainForm" runat="server">
    <div style="width:100%">
        <asp:Button runat="server" ID="btnGetDate" Width="178px"
            Text="What time is it?" />
            <br />
            <asp:Label runat="server" ID="lblTime" Width="178px" />
    </div>
    </form>
</body>
</html>
```

This should look simple enough, even if your ASP.NET experience is limited. When the button is clicked, the application should post the page back to the server, which in turn will raise a button `Click` event that will post the current time into the label defined directly below the button. Without an MVP pattern, the code behind might look something like this:

```
public partial class WebTimePage: System.Web.UI.Page
    {
        protected void Page_Load(object sender, EventArgs e)
        {

        }

        protected override void OnInit(EventArgs e)
        {
            base.OnInit(e);
            this.btnGetDate.Click += new EventHandler(btnGetDate_Click);
        }

        void btnGetDate_Click(object sender, EventArgs e)
        {
            this.lblTime.Text = DateTime.Now.ToShortTimeString();
        }
    }
```

The pattern here is quite simple. The page's Init event is overridden and an extra event handler is defined for the `btnGetDate` button's Click event. In the event handler, we set the `Text` property of the `lblTime` label to short time format of the .NET `DateTime` object's Now property. Compile and run the application and you'll see the label print the current time each time you click the button that reads "What time is it?"

An MVP approach would require some slight modifications. First, an abstract type should be defined containing the definition of properties that will map to the page's UI controls.

```
public interface IWebTime
    {
        string CurrentTime { get; set; }
    }
```

Next, we will need to create a Presenter that handles the page logic. It should contain a field defined as the page's interface. The Presenter's constructor accepts an instance of the interface and sets the value of its field to the incoming parameter. Public methods are then defined to get or set values on the interface.

```
public class WebTimePresenter
    {
        private IWebTime _view;

        public WebTimePresenter(IWebTime view)
        {
            _view = view;
        }

        public void GetTheCurrentTime()
```

```
        {
            _view.CurrentTime = DateTime.Now.ToShortTimeString();
        }
    }
```

The interface should then be implemented by the web page, which in turn should define public properties that get or set the values of its UI components to the values of the interface properties. A field is then defined as the Presenter, which is instantiated in the Load event. When instantiated the constructor receives an instance of the page itself since it now implements the interface in the constructor's definition. Finally, the page's UI events invoke methods on the Presenter, which in turn gets and sets values on the page through the concrete instance of the interface, which maps to properties on the page itself.

```
public partial class WebTimePage : System.Web.UI.Page, IWebTime
    {
        private WebTimePresenter _presenter;

        public string CurrentTime
        {
            get
            {
                return this.lblTime.Text;
            }

            set
            {
                this.lblTime.Text = value;
            }
        }

        protected void Page_Load(object sender, EventArgs e)
        {
            _presenter = new WebTimePresenter(this);
        }

        protected override void OnInit(EventArgs e)
        {
            base.OnInit(e);
            this.btnGetDate.Click += new EventHandler(btnGetDate_Click);
        }

        void btnGetDate_Click(object sender, EventArgs e)
        {
        _presenter.GetTheCurrentTime();
        }
    }
```

Compile and run this code and the page behaves just as it did prior to the MVP implementation. The difference now is that the View is now testable. The page logic is no longer coupled to the page's control events and, therefore, can be tested without running the ASP.NET engine. Likewise, the View is now an abstract type, allowing View mocking in a manner that conforms to the tenets of TDD.

Admittedly this is an overly simplified example of MVP in an ASP.NET application — one that doesn't really reflect a real-life use of the pattern. This, of course, was dumbed down for demonstrative purposes. However, it helps to show the application of base enterprise concepts inside of the popular Microsoft web programming platform. Through MVP we can achieve better code coverage, separation of concerns, and overall flexibility for code maintenance. We will dig deeper into MVP and its uses in both ASP.NET, as well as in thick client applications, later in this book.

Back to MVC . . . the Rails Way

Of course, not everyone loves ASP.NET. Although the platform has enjoyed immense popularity among seasoned Windows developers, many feel it is a gross departure from traditional web programming. The API and its supporting scripts abstract the developer from the older Internet patterns that make web programming straightforward and simple. The View-centric flow of an ASP.NET application makes it difficult to separate UI behaviors from business logic without the use of a contrived pattern such as MVP. In fact, a large number of Web "traditionalists" are turning back to the patterns of old as they implicitly divide UI from the underlying logic. To this end, the Ruby on Rails model is one of the most influential MVC patterns of the last 5 years.

Ruby on Rails, or RoR for short, is an open source web application framework for the Ruby programming language.

> The term Ruby on Rails is the trademarked term of David Heinemeier Hansson, and will be referred to solely as RoR from here on in.

Originally implemented into the Basecamp project of the 37signals website, it was later released for open source by Basecamp's creator, David Heinemeier Hansson in July 2004. The RoR model is a stark break from many of the design patterns used on the Java and Windows platforms. Unlike ASP.NET, it embraces older, cleaner web programming tenets, marrying its core feature to simple HTTP and URL-driven patterns. It uses a powerful MVC model for separation of concerns, yet unlike other MVC models prevalent on the Java platform such as Struts, RoR does not rely on cumbersome configurations, nor does it use an unwieldy number of objects to communicate between layers. RoR is rooted strongly on the notion of *Convention over Configuration*, a programming approach in which names, types, and values can be inferred from common usages and in which developers need only specify unconventional aspects of their system or application. RoR also employs the use of packaged utilities and auto-generating scripts to quickly get developers up and running (known commonly as *Action PackI*). The combination of these tools and the MVC design resulted in a happy marriage of RAD and sound enterprise patterns. Figure 9-4 shows the RoR home page, available publically at `http://rubyonrails.org`. This book does not cover RoR specifically as an enterprise programming platform.

Figure 9-4

The benefit of the Rails pattern was not lost on Microsoft developers. Many seasoned Windows programmers interested in a cleaner, more modular approach to web programming gravitated to its straightforward, yet robust design. However RoR has a few notable hits against it. For starters, it is based primarily on the Ruby programming language. Ruby is an object-oriented interpreted language that supports multiple programming paradigms and provides a dynamic type system and automatic memory management. To developers it is somewhat of a cross between a scripted language and a compiled language. Like a compiled language Ruby makes use of a runtime interpreter, which performs some debugging and translates the code into machine language. Yet like a script Ruby does a lot of acrobatics at runtime, switching types and even injecting code when specified. RoR makes use of these language features, passing code blocks and weaving dynamic behavior directly into to core API. For programmers rooted in traditional C-based languages like C# and Java, Ruby isn't that easy to swallow. Although the syntax is straightforward, the behavioral patterns are quite different from those of a compiled language in a managed environment like .NET or the Java Runtime Environment (JRE). Still, the Rails model is a powerful MVC pattern for web applications. Some open source projects have become available emulating Rails, chief among them being Monorail by the Castle Project, and more recently ASP.NET MVC by Microsoft.

Monorail is an open source web application framework built by the Castle Project and specifically designed to run on top of ASP.NET. Similarly to RoR before it, Monorail uses an MVC pattern that makes use of simple web programming tenets. Monorail comes with utilities for quickly generating code, and has been tailored to work with various View engines that integrate with ASP.NET. Figure 9-5 shows the Monorail home page on the Castle Project website at `www.castleproject.org/MonoRail`.

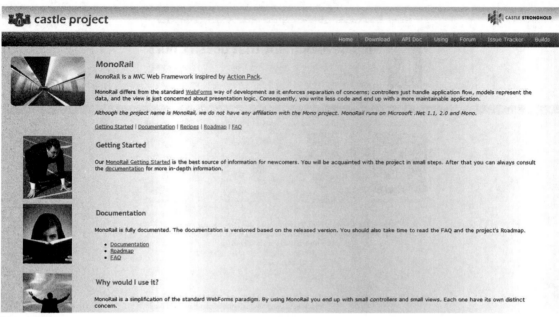

Figure 9-5

Out of Monorail came ASP.NET MVC, Microsoft's answer to the web MVC pattern. ASP.NET MVC and Monorail are very similar in behavior and feature set. Both use an MVC pattern that implicitly decouples the view from the application flow, and both rely on URL-driven commands rather than the traditional ASP.NET postback model. ASP.NET MVC makes use of native ASP.NET Routing, a mechanism released with the 3.5 version of the .NET framework. Monorail, on the other hand, makes use its own homegrown URL processor using custom-built `HttpModules`. Likewise, ASP.NET MVC makes use of utilities bundled within the .NET Framework and designed specifically for it. The MVC model used by both is a dramatic departure from older ASP and ASP.NET programming. The first, most notable difference is in the use of URLs. Traditional ASP.NET applications employ a one-to-one relationship between a URL and a physical web page. A URL usually ends with something like `MyHomePage.aspx`, which directs a user to a file on the hard drive named `MyHomePage.aspx`. The Web MVC model does not map to any one web page. Instead the URL is broken down into three distinct sections: the Controller, the Action, and the Parameter. The Controller invokes a class logically coupled to a subset of the application. The Action maps to a method on the Controller, and the Parameter is a value passed to the Action. Controllers are implicitly associated with one or more Views, located in a subdirectory of the root View folder that is named after the controller itself. The MVC engine then processes the action and, through the use of a configured View engine (ASP.NET and nVelocity being the two popular choices), renders the HTML accordingly. Figure 9-6 depicts the flow of an incoming request using this pattern.

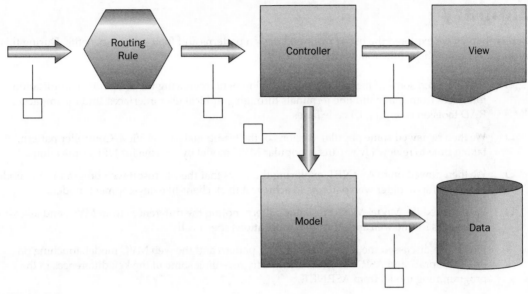

Figure 9-6

Again, this is a gross oversimplification of the pattern, yet it demonstrates the departure from older View-based web applications.

Both Monorail and ASP.NET MVC are available for free download and can be installed with an Add-on that integrates directly with the latest editions of Visual Studio.net. Since so many facets of the base MVC model are shared between both Monorail and ASP.NET MVC, this book won't be referencing each separately. Instead, this book concentrates solely on ASP.NET MVC as the available web MVC framework for enterprise development. Readers can assume that most of the features of ASP.NET MVC are applicable in some fashion to Monorail, and should reference the Castle Project's online API for details.

MVC and MVP both have their place in the software development community. Both have enjoyed a certain amount of maturing as they have evolved to support the needs of contemporary application development patterns. As we dig deeper into both in the coming chapters, readers should note that neither one should be considered "right" or "better," but rather right or better for the application for which they are intended. Remember, our goal isn't to unify the development world behind one all mighty, all-powerful design. Our goal is to build applications that are secure, stable, and flexible enough to scale and grow in functionality. Just as Microsoft takes care to emphasize that ASP.NET MVC is an alternative to ASP.NET Web Forms and not a replacement, both web MVC and MVP have their place relative to the platform and engines they need to implement.

Summary

In this chapter, we explored the use of front-end design patterns and their relative benefits. During this process we accomplished the following:

❑ We discussed some of the history of UI development, reviewing the evolution of application interfaces from command line terminals through graphical user interfaces, and the impact of RAD tools on emerging UI code bases.

❑ We then reviewed some popular versions of the traditional Model-View-Controller pattern, taking time to review Java Struts, a popular MVC model by Apache for J2EE applications.

❑ We then moved on to ASP.NET, exploring the ways that the Microsoft web programming model builds on top of older web patterns to achieve a thick client-like development model.

❑ We explored the Model-View-Presenter pattern, noting the differences from MVC, and assessing its benefits for the web and ASP.NET applications specifically.

Finally we discussed the Rails programming pattern and the web MVC model, touching on RoR, Monorail, and ASP.NET MVC and briefly revealing some of the key differences in the programming model from ASP.NET.

Chapter 10 moves away from the theoretical discussion of front end patterns and takes a deep dive into the Model-View-Presenter design pattern.

10

Model-View-Presenter

Of all the design patterns and code methodologies we will cover in this book, perhaps the most pervasive of these is the Model-View-Presenter pattern. Model-View-Presenter, or MVP, represents the latest evolution of front-end orchestration code. It is lightweight, allowing for its application within a large number of varying platforms and programming models. It is loosely coupled, enabling enterprise developers to quickly create unit tests and deploy them easily. Most importantly, it separates code in a predictable manner, ultimately facilitating the development of a more flexible code base. Once developers become accustomed to the MVP pattern, most find that jumping in and out of other MVP projects is quite simple.

In this chapter, we will:

❑ Review a brief overview of the MVP pattern and what it's like today

❑ Discuss the application of MVP in different platforms

❑ Build an MVP example in ASP.NET using the previously developed mortgage calculator code

❑ Refactor the mortgage calculator example into a thick client application

The MVP Pattern — Simplified

OK, so back to this whole front-end orchestration thing. By this point, we hope the benefits of using an orchestration pattern within your front end is evident to you, but we would be remiss not to quickly review the core benefits these patterns offer. To begin with, a good front-end orchestration pattern should facilitate the separation of concerns. This is a really important concept when handling this conceptual layer. The mixing of business logic with UI code is found all too often in business applications. Separating the logic that drives the View from that which drives the business rules makes the entirety of the program simpler to follow and much easier to maintain. Next, a good orchestration pattern should facilitate testability. As you'll see when we create the MVP sample later in this chapter, MVP is a loosely coupled design pattern. Each layer is appropriately abstracted from the other layers in a manner that fits nicely with Test Driven Development methodologies. Since the actual user interfaces cannot be tested, separation is critical in this portion of an enterprise system. Finally, MVP provides a predictable model for front-end code for the purposes of maintainability and extensibility. Often large systems are quickly modified for new needs and new features. These quick changes can lead to miles of tangled code as different developers jump in and out of the code base. Applications adhering to the MVP pattern isolate code on purpose in a manner that is entirely predictable to all coders familiar with the pattern.

Before digging too deeply into MVP, it's worth mentioning that, as a pattern, MVP has a number of different implementations. Do a quick search for MVP online, and you're bound to find a veritable cornucopia of varying flavors of MVP, each providing some modicum of improvement in various areas, depending on the needs of an application. Readers will find articles and blogs on the Supervising Controller pattern, which breaks the Presenter down into two or more objects for handling input and synchronizing the View and the Model. Readers will also find articles on the Presentation Model, which aims to simplify the View through a more powerful `Presenter` class. Looking even deeper, readers will find materials on the Model-View-ViewModel pattern (perhaps the least creatively named of them all, but we digress), which may or may not diminish the usefulness of the `Presenter` class and boil it down to a set of mappings between the View and the Model. All of these patterns have their merits, and all are valid flavors of the Model-View-Presenter pattern. In this book, however, we're going to keep things real simple. Rather than wax geek-intellectual on the finer points of MVP glory, we'll just boil things down to the bare minimum. For more information on these different implementations of MVP, feel free to refer to the following online resources:

```
http://www.martinfowler.com/
```

```
http://en.wikipedia.org/wiki/Model_View_Presenter
```

The MVP pattern that we'll be using a somewhat akin to the Presentation Model pattern, but don't hold us to that. Our goal is to quickly and intuitively convey the spirit of simplified MVP without conjuring a holy war on implementations.

The Model

At the core of the MVP pattern lies the Model, or rather, the logic portion of the code that handles the business rules and logic. The Model typically houses the meat of the system's data and base business methods. Functionality such as data retrieval, checking business rules, and performing business calculations always take place in this layer. Depending on the version of MVP being used, this code can be isolated into a single class, or can exist as a loose confederation of services that work interchangeably with each other and other portions of the code.

The View

The View is the topmost layer of code exposed by your application. Depending on the framework in which you are working, this layer can consist of web pages, server-side scripts, HTML, XML, or any other UI-specific code. The conceptual limit of the View can become confusing and should be carefully controlled by the developer. Put simply, the View code contains all functionality that handles the physical display, or the behavior of that display, to the end user. Code that manipulates bindings;

changes colors, fonts, or backgrounds; performs animations; or handles any manner of executable behavior in the user interface lives in this layer.

The Presenter

At the heart of this pattern lies the Presenter — the glue that holds it all together. Think of this piece as the Geneva of the pattern, carefully balancing the exchange between the View and the Model. Older design patterns referred to this piece as the Controller, although the implementation of MVP demands a notable difference in the way the Presenter is used. In most cases, the Presenter acts as a testable abstraction from the View, facilitating the invocation of methods on the Model while passing values back to the View's UI. Unfortunately, the definitions of MVP alone don't really convey how they work or how to effectively implement them. The example in the next section will demonstrate how to take a simple ASP.NET web page and break it up into a predictable, simple, MVP pattern.

The MVP Mortgage Calculator — Web Sample

It's time to get your hands dirty with a little code again. The best way to understand MVP is to build an example of an MVP page. To do this, you will create a small, interactive calculator for generating monthly mortgage payments based on some small amount of user input. This sample will be a similar mortgage calculator class that you created in Chapter 7. You first have to pick which platform you want to use: web or thick client. Since most UIs nowadays are built for the web, let's begin with web example. MVP is well designed for both web and client applications; however, there is particularly good use for MVP in the ASP.NET world. Recall from the last chapter that ASP.NET is a break from traditional web tenets. Although the ASP.NET API and Event Model are terrific tools for building RAD-type applications, the plumbing inherent to its design makes the ASP.NET flow very View-centric. That is, the View or UI portion of an ASP.NET page is the main point of entry for a single post to or from the web server. Counter to traditional web? Yes, but MVP fits in well with the ASP.NET flow. As we will cover in later chapters, traditional web applications can benefit from a broader pattern known as web MVP (also referred to as ASP.NET MVP or Rails MVP).

Since the purpose of MVP is to facilitate better testing, you'll likely want to provision your projects with NUnit again, just as you did in Chapter 4. Here are the steps again for downloading and installing NUnit:

1. Go to `http://www.nunit.org` and download version 2.4.8.

2. Run the downloaded `msi` installer.

3. Verify that the installation completed successfully by confirming that the NUnit folder is present under your program files directory.

Next, you'll need a new Visual Studio .NET solution to host your MVP project, along with the eventual tests you'll be writing:

1. Open Visual Studio and create a new blank solution called `ProfEnt.Chap10` under `C:\Projects\`, as shown in Figure 10-1.

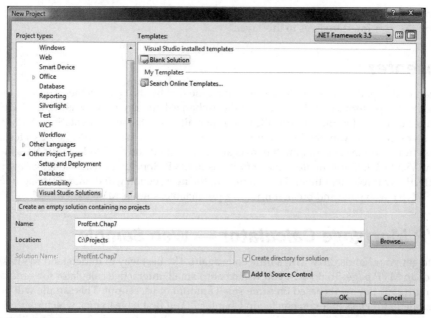

Figure 10-1

2. Add a new ASP.NET Project to your solution by right-clicking on the `ProfEnt.Chapter10` solution in Solution Explorer and selecting New Project from the popup menu.

3. Create a new ASP.NET web application from the dialog box, and name it `SimpleMortgageCalculator`, as shown in Figure 10-2.

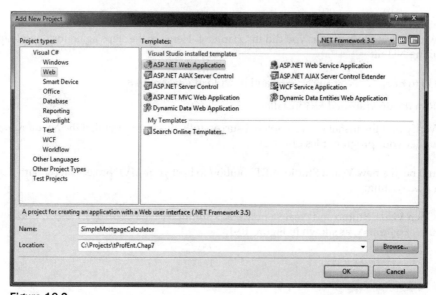

Figure 10-2

4. Now create the test projects just as you did in Chapter 4 by right-clicking the `WroxProfEnt` `.Chapter10` solution in the Solution Explorer and adding a new Class Library test project named `SimpleMortgageCalculator_Tests`.

Your Solution Explorer window should now look similar to the image in Figure 10-3.

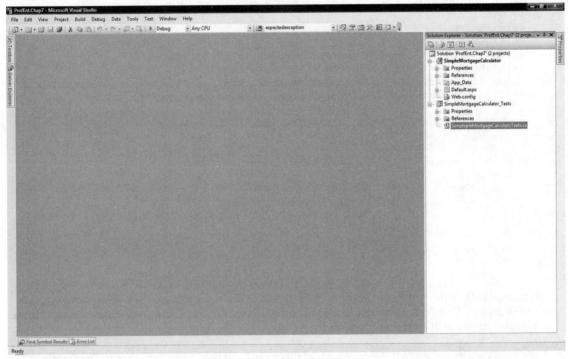

Figure 10-3

You'll also need to create a couple of new directories to help separate the individual objects you'll be creating.

1. Right-click on the `SimpleMortgageCalculator` web project in the Solution Explorer window, and select Add ➤ New Folder from the popup menu. Name this folder `Views`.

2. Repeat the previous step and create a folder named `Presenters`.

Finally, you'll need to remove the Default.aspx page at the root of the `SimpleMortgageCalculator` project by right-clicking on the file in Solution Explorer and selecting Delete. We won't be using it for this example.

Okay, we're ready to begin. Time to start thinking in terms of MVP. Recall that back in the first portion of the book we changed the way we approached our projects in terms of requirements and tests. Rather than jumping in with code, we first listed what we wanted the application to accomplish, creating tests to effectively ensure that all rules are maintained. The approach is the same here. In this example, we want to allow users to enter three criteria: the loan amount, the interest rate of the loan, and the number of years for the loan. Since the basic business rules of loan calculations have already been built into the Mortgage Calculator Model, our sample has only one new requirement — all three values must be supplied in order to execute a calculation. Let's provision your solution with some quick stub code. Remember to add a project reference to the NUnit library like you did in Chapter 4. Rename the default file .cs file (Class1.cs) to "SimpleMortgageCalculatorPresenter_Test" and replace the code in the file with the following:

```
using System;
using NUnit.Framework;
using WroxProfEnt.Chapt10.SimpleMortgageCalculator.Presenters;
using WroxProfEnt.Chapt10.SimpleMortgageCalculator.Views;
using WroxProfEnt.Chapt10.SimpleMortgageCalculator;
using WroxProfEnt.Chapt10.SimpleMortgageCalculator.Tests.Mocks;

namespace WroxProfEnt.Chapt10.SimpleMortgageCalculator.Tests
{
    [TestFixture]
    public class SimpleMortgageCalculatorPresenter_TestFixture
    {
        [Test]
        public void will_succeed_with_valid_data()
        {            //...TODO
        }
    }
}
```

We will get back to this test a little later on. The purpose of this demonstration is to show how to create an MVP project. Therefore, the sample has little business logic outside of the previously coded Mortgage Calculator library to distract from that end.

Let's think for a moment about the three parts of this model and how you can use them. The Simple Mortgage Calculator example has a single entry page for collecting user input and providing results. That means that you'll have at least one View object. Yet before you rush headlong into web objects and HTML you need to think about the data the View needs to collect or display. This information needs to be defined in some sort of a contract that other parts of the system can see. Using an abstract contract allows other classes to interact with the web page's data without actually needing a full instance of the page itself.

Our View consists of four fields:

1. The loan amount to be financed

2. The interest rate of the loan

3. The number of years the user intends to pay on the loan

4. The monthly payment

You need to define this collection of data in an interface that can be abstractly consumed and referenced throughout the project. Right-click on the SimpleMortgageCalculator web project in Solution Explorer,

and select Add ➢ New Item. Select an Interface file from the dialog, and name it
ISimpleMortgageCalculatorView.cs.

Open the file and replace the default code with the following:

```
using System;
using System.Collections.Generic;
using System.Linq;
using System.Web;

namespace WroxProfEnt.Chapt10.SimpleMortgageCalculator
{
    public interface ISimpleMortgageCalculatorView
    {
        double LoanAmount { set; get; }
        double InterestRate { set; get; }
        int NumberOfYears { set; get; }
    }
}
```

This interface will come in handy in just a few minutes when you create your Presenter. Before that,
though, you should create the physical implementation of your web UI. Create that View by adding an
ASP.NET Web Form to the Views directory:

1. Right-click on the Views folder in the SimpleMortgageCalculator web project, and select
    Add ➢ New Item.

2. Select Web Form in the dialog window, and name the new form SimpleMortgageCalculatorView
    .aspx.

*Traditional MVP fans would suggest that a full ASP.NET Web Form might be slightly heavy for a
lightweight MVP Model. HTM/HTML pages would also work here, although server-side scripts would
be needed to facilitate the View-Presenter relationships. This example makes use of the ASP.NET Code-
Behind Model for this purpose.*

You really don't need too much in the View to make this sample work. The user interface needs only a
handful of fields and a Calculate button to make the magic happen. An ASP.NET script snippet containing
the UI artifacts you need is provided. Enter this code into the SimpleMortgageCalculatorView.aspx
page:

```
<%@ Page Language="C#" AutoEventWireup="true" CodeBehind="SimpleMortgageCalculator
View.aspx.cs" Inherits="WroxProfEnt.Chapt10.SimpleMortgageCalculator.Views
.SimpleMortgageCalculatorView" %>

<!DOCTYPE html PUBLIC "-//W3C//DTD XHTML 1.0 Transitional//EN" "http://www.w3.org/
TR/xhtml1/DTD/xhtml1-transitional.dtd">


<html xmlns="http://www.w3.org/1999/xhtml" >
<head id="Head1" runat="server">
    <title>Simple Mortgage Calculator</title>
    <script type="text/javascript">
```

```
        // <![CDATA[
        function Validate() {
            if (document.getElementById("loanAmount").value == "" ||
                document.getElementById("interestRate").value == "" ||
                document.getElementById("numberOfYears").value == "") {
                alert("You must eneter a value for Loan Amount, Interest Rate, and
the Number of Years to calculate a payment!");
                return false;
            }
            return true;
        }

        // ]]>
    </script>
</head>
<body>
    <form id="mortgageCalculatorForm" runat="server">
    <h1>Simple Mortgage Calulator</h1>
    <div style="position:fixed; top:100px; left:100px; width:550px; height:400px">
        <table width="100%">
            <colgroup>
                <col align="right" width="70%"/>
                <col align="left" width="30%"/>
            </colgroup>
            <tr>
                <td>Enter the Loan amount to finance:</td>
                <td><input type="text" rows="1" cols="30" runat="server"
                id="loanAmount"/></td>
            </tr>
            <tr>
                <td>Enter the interest rate if the loan:</td>
                <td><input type="text" rows="1" cols="30" runat="server"
                id="interestRate"/></td>
            </tr>
            <tr>
                <td>Enter the number of years on the loan:</td>
                <td><input type="text" rows="1" cols="30" runat="server"
                id="numberOfYears"/></td>
            </tr>
            <tr>
                <td>Mortgage Payment:</td>
                <td><label id="payment" style="width:100px" runat="server" /></td>
            </tr>
            <tr>
                <td colspan="2" align="center"><input type="button" value="Calculate
                Mortgage Payment" id="calculatePaymentButton" onclick=
                "if(!Validate()){return false;}" runat="server"/></td>
            </tr>
        </table>
    </div>
    </form>
</body>
</html>
```

Admittedly, this web page is intentionally plain. However it has the essential elements to make the Model work. Notice that the entry fields in this web page roughly match the same fields defined in the ISimpleMortgageCalculator interface. That's because the interface is meant to provide the requisite abstraction from the page, offering a reference to the entry fields without relying on an instance of the web page itself. Also note that all of the input fields are HTML objects with the runat attribute set to server. This allows you to take advantage of the ASP.NET plumbing and reference your UI fields from the View's code-behind page.

Of course, you must implement the ISimpleMortgageCalculator interface on the web page itself. That way, other classes can reference the web page's data without requiring hard instances of the page itself. In Solution Explorer find and open the file named SimpleMortgageCalculatorView.aspx.cs. Add the following reference to the using block at the top of the page

```
using WroxProfEnt.Chapt10.SimpleMortgageCalculator;
```

Now change the class declaration to read as follows:

```
public partial class SimpleMortgageCalculatorView : System.Web.UI.Page,
ISimpleMortgageCalculatorView
    {
```

If you try to compile and build the project now, you'll be dead in the water. You need to provision the View's code-behind page with the properties that will map the UI fields to the interface definitions. Add an explicit interface reference for the loan amount by typing the following below the class definition and above the Page_Load() method:

```
public double ISimpleMortgageCalculatorView.LoanAmount
        {
        set { this.loanAmount.Value = value.ToString(); }
        get { return double.Parse(this.loanAmount.Value) ;}
        }
```

The property defined here explicitly maps the loanAmount HTML field to the LoanAmount definition on the ISimpleMortgageCalculatorView interface, making some slight adjustments to translate the user-provided string to double and vice versa. Now each time the interface's LoanAmount field is referenced, the value of the web page element will bind accordingly. The following is the full interface implementation for the SimpleMortgageCalculatorView.aspx.cs file:

```
#region ISimpleMortgageCalculatorView Implementation

        double ISimpleMortgageCalculatorView.LoanAmount
        {
            set { this.loanAmount.Value = value.ToString(); }
            get { return double.Parse(this.loanAmount.Value) ;}
        }

        double ISimpleMortgageCalculatorView.InterestRate
        {
            set { this.interestRate.Value = value.ToString(); }
            get {return double.Parse(this.interestRate.Value); }
        }
```

```
int ISimpleMortgageCalculatorView.NumberOfYears
{
    set { this.numberOfYears.Value = value.ToString(); }
    get { return int.Parse(this.numberOfYears.Value); }
}


#endregion
```

For now, let's keep both setters and getters in our properties to simplify our approach. As you'll see later in this chapter, you can slim down some accessibility to keep the code cleaner once you understand the full behavior of the code.

That's a good start on the View. We will revisit some of the code in this class when we need to handle formatting and UI behaviors, but it's good enough for now. As long as you have defined an abstract type for the data fields and implemented it by mapping the HTML controls to the properties, the basic plumbing is in place.

The next thing you need to do is define your Presenter. The Presenter can seem a little tricky at first, but once you understand how it interacts with the View and Model, the pattern is very repeatable.

In the Presenters folder in the `SimpleMortgageCalculator` project, right-click and select Add ➤ New Item. In the dialog box, select Class, and name it `SimpleMortgageCalculatorPresenter.cs`.

Now provision your Presenter with some code to scope out the correct namespaces and define your class by replacing the default code with the following:

```
using System;
using WroxProfEnt.Chapt10.SimpleMortgageCalculator.Views;
//using WroxProfEnt.Mortgage.Model.MortgageCalculators;
//using WroxProfEnt.Mortgage.Model;

namespace WroxProfEnt.Chapt10.SimpleMortgageCalculator.Presenters
{
    public class SimpleMortgageCalculatorPresenter
    {}
}
```

Ignore the commented-out `using` statements for the moment. They will be referenced when we begin talking about the Model portion of the code. Since the purpose of the Presenter is to handle the inputs and outputs to and from the View, it's going to need an instance of the `SimpleMortgage CalculatorView` within it to reference the data the user enters. You could define a reference to the web page within the Presenter, but that would defy all rules of loose coupling. Once the web page is required, the Presenter will be that much heavier when it comes time to test. It will also marry this Presenter to a Web Model . . . something you won't want to do when it comes to time use this example in a client application.

Instead, create a reference to the `ISimpleMortgageCalculatorView` interface as a field within the Presenter by adding the following field to the top of the class:

```
ISimpleMortgageCalculatorView _IView;
```

To get an instance of the View we are going to use a dependency injection pattern, allowing the View to pass an instance of itself at runtime into the Presenter's constructor. Therefore, the constructor should be changed to accept an injected instance of `ISimpleMortgageCalculatorView` and set it equal to the field instance:

```
public SimpleMortgageCalculatorPresenter(ISimpleMortgageCalculatorView iview)
    {
        this._IView = iview;
    }
```

Now let's look at this from the Model side of the project. The Model typically consists of the objects and services that handle the business rules and data manipulation. It's essentially the meat of the project. Unlike the Views and the Presenters, you may not always see dedicated Model objects within a project. That's usually because the Models are projects of their own, compiled into separate assemblies and invoked from within the Presenters directly. Such is the case with the mortgage calculator. If you created the sample in that chapter and separated out the models, you can create a reference to the assembly directly and reference the mortgage calculator accordingly.

As an alternative, you can quickly create your own Model objects within your project if you have not had the benefit of building the code in Chapter 3 (or if you skipped ahead to this chapter directly). Add another folder to your `SimpleMortgageCalculator` project, named `Models`. Add two class files to that folder, named `IMortgageCalculator.cs` and `SimpleMortgageCalculator.cs`, and add the following snippets of code to each, respectively:

IMortgageCalculator.cs

```
using System;

namespace WroxProfEnt.Mortgage.Model
{
    public interface IMortgageCalculator
    {
        double LoanPaymentsPerMonthFor(double LoanAmount, double InterestRate, int
        LoanTerm);
    }
}
```

(continued)

SimpleMortgageCalculator.cs *(continued)*

```
using System;

namespace WroxProfEnt.Mortgage.Model.MortgageCalculators
{

public class LoanMonthlyPaymentCalculator: IMortgageCalculator
    {
        public double LoanPaymentsPerMonthFor(double LoanAmount, double
        InterestRate, int LoanTerm)
        {
            double int_trm = Math.Pow(1 + InterestRate / 1200, LoanTerm * 12);
            double mrt_year = (LoanAmount * InterestRate * int_trm) / (1200 *
            (int_trm - 1));
            double payments = (mrt_year * 12 / 12);
            double p = Math.Round(payments * 100) / 100;
            return (float)Math.Round(p * 1, 2);
        }
    }}
```

Either approach should work fine for this sample, although keep in mind that you will be building on the Mortgage Calculator Model in the next chapter, so the shortcuts won't be so easy. Add a reference to an instance of IMortgageCalculator as a field variable in the SimpleMortgageCalculatorPresenter class directly above the View interface, as follows:

```
IMortgageCalculator _IMort;
```

Now change the constructor to receive an instance of IMortgageCalculator as you did with the ISimpleMortgageCalculatorView interface, setting it equal to the corresponding field variable. The constructor should now look like this:

```
public SimpleMortgageCalculatorPresenter(ISimpleMortgageCalculatorView iview,
IMortgageCalculator imort)
    {
        this._IView = iview;
        this._IMort = imort;
    }
```

The Presenter can now use the interfaces its receiving to handle the interaction between the web page and the calculator. Using the Dependency Injection pattern, you can rely on an external source to pass in the hard instances of the View and the Model instead of creating or obtaining those objects directly. The abstraction makes the Presenter much easier to build and, just as importantly, much easier to test.

This example requires the Presenter to facilitate one simple example — the mortgage calculation. You need to define a public method on the Presenter that will retrieve the user-supplied values from the View, pass them into the Model for calculation, and then pass the result back to the View for displaying. This sounds like a lot of work, but in fact it's really about four lines of code. Add the following method to your SimpleMortgageCalculatorPresenter class:

```
public double GetMortgagePayment()
    {
        double monthlyPayment = _IMort.LoanPaymentsPerMonthFor(_IView.LoanAmount,
                                                             _IView.InterestRate,
                                                             _IView.NumberOfYears);

        return monthlyPayment;
    }
```

Deceptively simple? Maybe so, but a closer look reveals some of the magic under the covers. The reference to _IMort assumes that a live instance of a mortgage calculator will eventually be present and will, therefore, execute accordingly. Same goes for the reference to _IView. Look back at the implementation of the SimpleMortgageCalculatorView class you created a few pages back. See how the code-behind for the web page implements the ISimpleMortgageCalculatorView interface by setting the Html control's values directly? Once you establish that the Presenter's reference to ISimpleMortgageCalculatorView (or _IView by the field name) is a direct instance of the web page that implements the interface, the rest sort of works itself out.

You now have everything you need to wire this sample up and bring this calculator to life. Since you are using an ASP.NET Web Form Model for the web application, the View is starting point for all incoming requests. Your goal now is to keep the code within the View specific to UI functionality only. Any other processing calls should be invoked through the Presenter. Therefore, the View is going to need to create an instance of the Presenter and provision it with the references it needs to operate.

Define a local field variable for the SimpleMortgageCalculatorPresenter in the SimpleMortgageCalculatorView.aspx.cs file like this:

```
SimpleMortgageCalculatorPresenter _presenter;
```

You will also need to add a using directive to the top of your code file in order to bring the presenter into scope:

```
using WroxProfEnt.Chapt10.SimpleMortgageCalculator.Presenters;
```

Now create a new instance of the Presenter in the Page_Load event. As the first argument, pass in an instance of the live running page by using the this keyword. As the second argument, create a new instance of the SimpleMortgageCalculator object, either the one created in Chapter 3 or the one defined in your Models folder (they should have the same namespace). Since you are mucking around in the Page_Load event, you should also create a delegate handler for the calculatePaymentButton defined in Html. The entire Page_Load event method should resemble the following:

```
protected void Page_Load(object sender, EventArgs e)
    {
        _presenter = new SimpleMortgageCalculatorPresenter(this,
                    new WroxProfEnt.Mortgage.Model.MortgageCalculators
                    . LoanMonthlyPaymentCalculator ());

        this.calculatePaymentButton.ServerClick += new EventHandler(calculate
        PaymentButton_ServerClick);
    }
```

Feel free to use whatever method name you wish for the calculatePaymentButton's event handler; we just went with the Visual Studio.NET–provided stub code to keep matters simple. Do note, however, that the event we are handling is the `ServerClick` event. This event is specific to `HtmlControls` with ASP.NET server-side state (i.e., `HtmlControl` objects with an attribute of "runat=server"). We chose this event because we are not using a native ASP.NET button, which exposes a `Click` event. The reason behind our choice of control is to try to make the `Html` portion of the code as platform independent as we can. Although any MVP example ultimately has to invoke a platform API once processing on the server begins, it's important to keep in mind that this is not an ASP.NET pattern exclusively. Any web page can, and often should, make use of this pattern.

You now have a live instance of a Presenter and can perform your calculations. The rest of your code is simple page processing. You want the Calculate button on the front page to read the user's inputs, execute the calculation, and display the results in the `monthlyPayment` label. Let's cut to the chase — add the following block of code to your `SimpleMortgageCalculatorView.aspx.cs` page below the `Page_Load` event:

```
void calculatePaymentButton_ServerClick(object sender, EventArgs e)
    {
        ExecutePaymentCalculation();
    }


    private void ExecutePaymentCalculation()
    {
        double payment = _presenter.GetMortgagePayment();

        this.payment.InnerHtml = GetPaymentLabel(payment);
    }

    private string GetPaymentLabel(double payment)
    {
        return string.Format("<span style=\"font-family:Verdana; color:Red;
        font-weight:bold\">${0}</span>", payment.ToString());
    }
```

If you have any experience with ASP.NET programming (or JSP programming for that matter) this should look uncomplicated. The `ServerClick` event is invoked through the framework when the user clicks the Calculate button. This event calls the `ExecutePaymentCalculation()` method, which calls directly into the Presenter's `GetMortgagePayment()` method. Remember, you don't need to pass in any user input. You have already passed an instance of the page into the Presenter's constructor by way of an `ISimpleMortgageCalculatorView` instance. The Presenter already knows how to extract those values implicitly, and the web page's implementation of the View maps the Presenter directly back to the `HtmlControls`' values. Finally, some simple formatting is done in the `GetPaymentLabel()` method, wrapping the payment value with some HTML to make it bold, red, and of a different font.

OK, you're ready to run our code, right? Not according to the rules of TDD . . . you haven't created your tests yet. You took all of the steps you needed to make your MVP Model testable, you might as well put your tests in, right? The calculator itself was already tested in Chapter 7, so you don't necessarily have to write those again. However, you should test the Presenter and the single function it performs. That means you'll need to test the Presenter in varying starts of the View. Considering the plainness of this sample, the tests are understandably simple:

❑ The `GetMortgagePayment` method should return a valid number greater than zero if the loan amount, interest rate, and number of years have been entered into the View.

❑ The `GetMortgagePayment` method should fail if the loan amount has not been supplied to the View.

❑ The `GetMortgagePayment` method should fail if the interest rate has not been supplied to the View.

❑ The `GetMortgagePayment` method should fail if the number of years has not been supplied to the View.

These tests have a notably different tack from the tests for the mortgage calculator. Rather than testing the math functions, they test the state of the View against the Presenter. Normally, any tests on or with the View are difficult to perform, since they are almost always written with UI code such as HTML. However, since you abstracted your View into an interface, you have the ability to easily mock instances of it to emulate various View states. So, you'll need to create a class that implements `ISimpleMortgageCalculatorView` to use as your mock and pass to your Presenter.

In the `SimpleMortgageCalculator.Tests` project add a new folder, named `Mocks`. Then add a new class file named `SimpleMortgageCalculatorView_Mock` and place the following code in the file:

```
using System;
using WroxProfEnt.Chapt10.SimpleMortgageCalculator.Presenters;
using WroxProfEnt.Chapt10.SimpleMortgageCalculator.Views;
using WroxProfEnt.Chapt10.SimpleMortgageCalculator;


namespace WroxProfEnt.Chapt10.SimpleMortgageCalculator.Tests.Mocks
{
    class SimpleMortgageCalculatorView_Mock : ISimpleMortgageCalculatorView
    {
        private double _loanAmount;

        public double LoanAmount
        {
            get { return _loanAmount; }
            set { _loanAmount = value; }
        }

        private double _interestRate;

        public double InterestRate
        {
            get { return _interestRate; }
            set { _interestRate = value; }
        }

        private int _numberOfYears;

        public int NumberOfYears
        {
```

```
            get { return _numberOfYears; }
            set { _numberOfYears = value; }
        }


    }
}
```

You can now use this class to emulate different states of the user input. Your tests seem to call for the user input in four distinct states. Therefore, let's create four functions that return the right mock in the right state for each test.

In the SimpleMortgageCalculatorPresenter_Test class, add the following methods:

```
private ISimpleMortgageCalculatorView CreateViewWithAllData()
        {
            ISimpleMortgageCalculatorView mockView = new
            SimpleMortgageCalculatorView_Mock();
            mockView.LoanAmount = 150000.00;
            mockView.InterestRate = 5.75;
            mockView.NumberOfYears = 30;
            return mockView;
        }

        private ISimpleMortgageCalculatorView CreateViewWithoutLoanAmount()
        {
            ISimpleMortgageCalculatorView mockView = new
            SimpleMortgageCalculatorView_Mock();
            mockView.InterestRate = 5.75;
            mockView.NumberOfYears = 30;
            return mockView;
        }

        private ISimpleMortgageCalculatorView CreateViewWithoutInterestRate()
        {
            ISimpleMortgageCalculatorView mockView = new
            SimpleMortgageCalculatorView_Mock();
            mockView.LoanAmount = 150000.00;
            mockView.NumberOfYears = 30;
            return mockView;
        }

        private ISimpleMortgageCalculatorView CreateViewWithoutNumberOfYears()
        {
            ISimpleMortgageCalculatorView mockView = new
            SimpleMortgageCalculatorView_Mock();
            mockView.LoanAmount = 150000.00;
            mockView.InterestRate = 5.75;
            return mockView;
        }
```

These are quick and dirty, but they get the job done. As you expand on this example, you can flush out some better, more detailed mocks. In the meantime, we can finally add some code to the very first test we stubbed out at the beginning of this chapter.

```
[Test]
public void will_succeed_with_valid_data()
{
    SimpleMortgageCalculatorPresenter presenter =
        new SimpleMortgageCalculatorPresenter(CreateViewWithAllData(),
        new WroxProfEnt.Mortgage.Model.MortgageCalculators
        .SimpleMortgageCalculator());
    Assert.Greater(presenter.GetMortgagePayment(), 0.0);
}
```

This seemingly mundane test is actually performing some pretty important validation. Using the abstract interface you defined for your View, you are able to pass a mock View, which is essentially a fake user interface, to your Presenter. The Presenter, not knowing or caring what the View is exactly, treats the mock the same as the web page and attempts to execute the mortgage calculation. Now you can perform tests on your Presenter without the heavy dependency of the web page! This is one of the most important and powerful tenets of the MVP Model. Here is the full code in the SimpleMortgageCalculator_Test class:

```
[Test]
    public void will_succeed_with_valid_data()
    {
        SimpleMortgageCalculatorPresenter presenter =
            new SimpleMortgageCalculatorPresenter(CreateViewWithAllData(),
            new WroxProfEnt.Mortgage.Model.MortgageCalculators
            .LoanMonthlyPaymentCalculator());
        Assert.Greater(presenter.GetMortgagePayment(), 0.0);
    }[Test]
    public void will_return_zero_without_a_loan_amount()
    {
        SimpleMortgageCalculatorPresenter presenter =
            new SimpleMortgageCalculatorPresenter(CreateViewWithoutLoanAmount(),
            new WroxProfEnt.Mortgage.Model.MortgageCalculators
            . LoanMonthlyPaymentCalculator ());
        Assert.AreEqual(presenter.GetMortgagePayment(), 0.0);
    }

    [Test]
    public void will_evaluate_to_infinity_wiuhout_number_of_years()
    {
        SimpleMortgageCalculatorPresenter presenter =
            new SimpleMortgageCalculatorPresenter(CreateViewWithoutNumberOf
            Years(), new WroxProfEnt.Mortgage.Model.MortgageCalculators.
            LoanMonthlyPaymentCalculator ());
        Assert.AreEqual(presenter.GetMortgagePayment(), double
        .PositiveInfinity);
```

```
    }

    [Test]
    public void will_evaluate_to_NaN_without_interest_rate()
    {
        SimpleMortgageCalculatorPresenter presenter =
            new SimpleMortgageCalculatorPresenter(CreateViewWithoutInterest
            Rate(), new WroxProfEnt.Mortgage.Model.MortgageCalculators.
            LoanMonthlyPaymentCalculator ());
        Assert.IsNaN(presenter.GetMortgagePayment());
    }

    private ISimpleMortgageCalculatorView CreateViewWithAllData()
    {
        ISimpleMortgageCalculatorView mockView = new
        SimpleMortgageCalculatorView_Mock();
        mockView.LoanAmount = 150000.00;
        mockView.InterestRate = 5.75;
        mockView.NumberOfYears = 30;
        return mockView;
    }


    private ISimpleMortgageCalculatorView CreateViewWithoutLoanAmount()
    {
        ISimpleMortgageCalculatorView mockView = new
        SimpleMortgageCalculatorView_Mock();
        mockView.InterestRate = 5.75;
        mockView.NumberOfYears = 30;
        return mockView;
    }

    private ISimpleMortgageCalculatorView CreateViewWithoutInterestRate()
    {
        ISimpleMortgageCalculatorView mockView = new
        SimpleMortgageCalculatorView_Mock();
        mockView.LoanAmount = 150000.00;
        mockView.NumberOfYears = 30;
        return mockView;
    }

    private ISimpleMortgageCalculatorView CreateViewWithoutNumberOfYears()
    {
        ISimpleMortgageCalculatorView mockView = new
        SimpleMortgageCalculatorView_Mock();
        mockView.LoanAmount = 150000.00;
        mockView.InterestRate = 5.75;
        return mockView;
    }
```

You should now have everything you need to run your sample and execute your tests. Set the SimpleMortgageCalculator project as your startup project by right-clicking on the project in Solution Explorer and selecting Set as StartUp Project from the popup menu, then run the project. Enter some values in the expected fields, and click Calculate to get a monthly payment. Use the NUnit client to run your unit tests and make sure they are functional. You should see output similar to the screenshots in Figures 10-4 and 10-5.

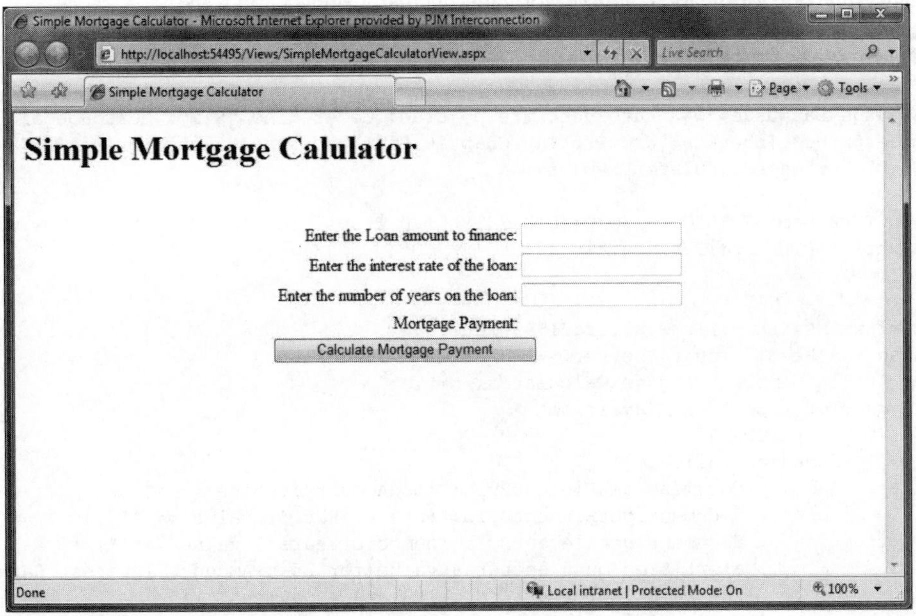

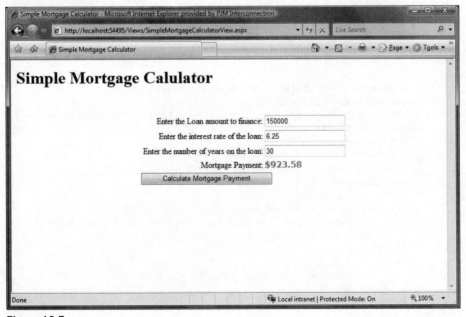

Figure 10-4

Figure 10-5

We didn't spend much time on the details of the data entry. If this were a live site, you'd likely want to add some more simple validation to make sure the data entered is numeric, and possibly some formatters to remove dollar signs or commas associated with the load amount.

Here is the full code for the MVP SimpleMortgageCalculator project and tests:

SimpleMortgageCalculatorView.aspx

```
<%@ Page Language="C#" AutoEventWireup="true" CodeBehind="SimpleMortgageCalculatorV
iew.aspx.cs" Inherits="WroxProfEnt.Chapt10.SimpleMortgageCalculator.Views
.SimpleMortgageCalculatorView" %>

<!DOCTYPE html PUBLIC "-//W3C//DTD XHTML 1.0 Transitional//EN" "http://www.w3.org/
TR/xhtml1/DTD/xhtml1-transitional.dtd">


<html xmlns="http://www.w3.org/1999/xhtml" >
<head id="Head1" runat="server">
    <title>Simple Mortgage Calculator</title>
    <script type="text/javascript">
        // <![CDATA[
        function Validate() {
            if (document.getElementById("loanAmount").value == "" ||
                document.getElementById("interestRate").value == "" ||
                document.getElementById("numberOfYears").value == "") {
                alert("You must eneter a value for Loan Amount, Interest Rate, and
                the Number of Years to calculate a payment!");
                return false;
            }
            return true;
        }

        // ]]>
    </script>
</head>
<body>
    <form id="mortgageCalculatorForm" runat="server">
    <h1>Simple Mortgage Calulator</h1>
    <div style="position:fixed; top:100px; left:100px; width:550px; height:400px">
        <table width="100%">
            <colgroup>
                <col align="right" width="70%"/>
                <col align="left" width="30%"/>
            </colgroup>
            <tr>
                <td>Enter the Loan amount to finance:</td>
                <td><input type="text" rows="1" cols="30" runat="server"
                id="loanAmount"/></td>
            </tr>
            <tr>
                <td>Enter the interest rate of the loan:</td>
```

```
                <td><input type="text" rows="1" cols="30" runat="server"
                id="interestRate"/></td>
            </tr>
            <tr>
                <td>Enter the number of years on the loan:</td>
                <td><input type="text" rows="1" cols="30" runat="server"
                 id="numberOfYears"/></td>
            </tr>
            <tr>
                <td>Mortgage Payment:</td>
                <td><label id="payment" style="width:100px" runat="server" /></td>
            </tr>
            <tr>
                <td colspan="2" align="center"><input type="button" value="Calculate
                Mortgage Payment" id="calculatePaymentButton" onclick="if(!Validate())
                {return false;}" runat="server"/></td>
            </tr>
        </table>
    </div>
    </form>
</body>
```

SimpleMortgageCalculatorView.aspx.cs

```
using System;
using System.Web;
using System.Web.UI;
using System.Web.UI.WebControls;
using WroxProfEnt.Chapt10.SimpleMortgageCalculator;
using WroxProfEnt.Chapt10.SimpleMortgageCalculator.Presenters;


namespace WroxProfEnt.Chapt10.SimpleMortgageCalculator.Views
{
    public partial class SimpleMortgageCalculatorView : System.Web.UI.Page,
ISimpleMortgageCalculatorView
    {


        #region ISimpleMortgageCalculatorView Implementation

        double ISimpleMortgageCalculatorView.LoanAmount
        {
            set { this.loanAmount.Value = value.ToString(); }
            get { return double.Parse(this.loanAmount.Value) ;}
        }

        double ISimpleMortgageCalculatorView.InterestRate
        {
```

(continued)

SimpleMortgageCalculatorView.aspx.cs *(continued)*

```
            set { this.interestRate.Value = value.ToString(); }
            get {return double.Parse(this.interestRate.Value); }
        }

        int ISimpleMortgageCalculatorView.NumberOfYears
        {
            set { this.numberOfYears.Value = value.ToString(); }
            get { return int.Parse(this.numberOfYears.Value); }
        }



        #endregion

        SimpleMortgageCalculatorPresenter _presenter;

        protected void Page_Load(object sender, EventArgs e)
        {
            _presenter = new SimpleMortgageCalculatorPresenter(this,
                        new WroxProfEnt.Mortgage.Model.MortgageCalculators.
                        LoanMonthlyPaymentCalculator ());

            this.calculatePaymentButton.ServerClick += new EventHandler(calculate
            PaymentButton_ServerClick);
        }

        void calculatePaymentButton_ServerClick(object sender, EventArgs e)
        {
            ExecutePaymentCalculation();
        }

        private void ExecutePaymentCalculation()
        {
            double payment = _presenter.GetMortgagePayment();

            this.payment.InnerHtml = GetPaymentLabel(payment);
        }

        private string GetPaymentLabel(double payment)
        {
            return string.Format("<span style=\"font-family:Verdana; color:Red;
            font-weight:bold\">${0}</span>", payment.ToString());
        }

    }
}
```

ISimpleMortgageCalculatorView.cs

```
using System;
using System.Collections.Generic;
```

```
using System.Linq;
using System.Web;

namespace WroxProfEnt.Chapt10.SimpleMortgageCalculator
{
    public interface ISimpleMortgageCalculatorView
    {
        double LoanAmount { set; get; }
        double InterestRate { set; get; }
        int NumberOfYears { set; get; }
    }
}
```

SimpleMortgageCalculatorPresenter.cs

```
using System;
using WroxProfEnt.Chapt10.SimpleMortgageCalculator.Views;
using WroxProfEnt.Mortgage.Model.MortgageCalculators;
using WroxProfEnt.Mortgage.Model;

namespace WroxProfEnt.Chapt10.SimpleMortgageCalculator.Presenters
{
    public class SimpleMortgageCalculatorPresenter
    {
        ISimpleMortgageCalculatorView _IView;
        IMortgageCalculator _IMort;

        public SimpleMortgageCalculatorPresenter(ISimpleMortgageCalculatorView
        iview, IMortgageCalculator imort)
        {
            this._IView = iview;
            this._IMort = imort;
        }

        public double GetMortgagePayment()
        {
            double monthlyPayment = _IMort.LoanPaymentsPerMonthFor(_IView.LoanAmount,
                                                _IView.InterestRate,
                                                _IView.NumberOfYears);

            return monthlyPayment;
        }
    }
}
```

SimpleMortgageCalculator.cs

```csharp
using System;

namespace WroxProfEnt.Mortgage.Model.MortgageCalculators
{
    public class LoanMonthlyPaymentCalculator: IMortgageCalculator
    {
        public double LoanPaymentsPerMonthFor(double LoanAmount, double
        InterestRate,
        int LoanTerm)
        {
            double int_trm = Math.Pow(1 + InterestRate / 1200, LoanTerm * 12);
            double mrt_year = (LoanAmount * InterestRate * int_trm) / (1200 *
            (int_trm - 1));
            double payments = (mrt_year * 12 / 12);
            double p = Math.Round(payments * 100) / 100;
            return Math.Round(p * 1, 2);
        }
    }
}


namespace WroxProfEnt.Mortgage.Model
{
    public interface IMortgageCalculator
    {
        double LoanPaymentsPerMonthFor(double LoanAmount, double InterestRate, int
        LoanTerm);
    }
}
```

Switching Platforms — Thick Client Sample

Now that you've gotten your head around a little web MVP code, let's switch gears and take a stab at a thick client example. This sample provides a terrific opportunity to demonstrate the practical benefits of separation of concerns. As we discussed previously, The Model-View-Presenter pattern is platform agnostic. Partitioning the presentation code from the business logic is beneficial to all applications, allowing for increased flexibility and ease of maintenance. That means that portions of the code you just wrote should be reusable, right? So they are! In fact, the Model and Presenter stay 100% intact. There are differences in the two communications models as well, but that is somewhat orthogonal to the goal of the pattern. MVP is a front-end orchestration pattern. In most client applications all three layers live within the client application, with some extra connectivity built into the Model for database operations, services calls, FTP connections, and so forth. The only notable difference in the MVP pattern occurs within the View. As the natural representative for all things user interface, the View needs to be able to convey user inputs and relay outputs to the end user. Yet the View needs to remain abstractly defined so that the Presenter can exist in a testable state. That means you will need to define an abstract View interface, implement it on a client user interface, and pass it explicitly to the Presenter's constructor. Sound familiar?

The client application can be built on any platform that allows for object-oriented design, but since you are working with the latest version of the .NET platform, let's create a small Windows Presentation Foundation application for this sample. Windows Presentation Foundation, or WPF, is the most recent SDK provided by Microsoft for designing and building behaviorally rich client user interfaces. WPF uses a relatively new markup language, XAML (Extensible Application Markup Language), to define the interface itself, which makes the transition from a web UI to a client UI easy to follow.

Setting Up the WPF Application

1. In your solution explorer window, right-click on the `ProfEnt.Chap10` solution, and select Add ➤ New Project from the popup menu.

2. In the dialog window, select Windows from the Project Type panel and WPF Application from the Templates panel, as shown in Figure 10-6.

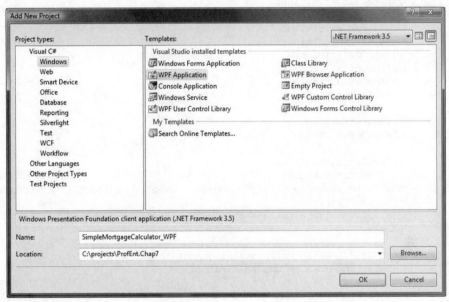

Figure 10-6

3. Name the project `SimpleMortgageCalculator_WPF`, and save the project.

4. Following the steps outlined when we created the ASP.NET application, create three folders in your project, named `Models`, `Views`, and `Presenters`, respectively.

5. Add a new window to your application by right-clicking the `Views` folder, selecting Add ➤ New item, and selecting a new WPF window. Name it "`SimpleMortgageCalculator_WPF`".

6. In the other folders, add the files we used for the Presenter and the Model in the ASP.NET application. If you referenced the code in Chapter 7, then you should feel free to do so again for this example. If you are pasting any code into new `.cs` files be sure that the namespaces match

(if you are only copying over the class definitions and not the namespaces and `using` statements, you're bound to have referencing errors).

7. Add the `ISimpleMortgageCalculatorView` interface to the `Views` folder with the new WPF window.

Now you'll need the new interface for the user to enter their figures and execute the calculation. In the `SimpleMortgageCalculator_View.xaml` file add the following markup:

```
<Window x:Class=" WroxProfEnt.Chapt10.SimpleMortgageCalculator_WPF
.SimpleMortgageCalculator_View"
    xmlns="http://schemas.microsoft.com/winfx/2006/xaml/presentation"
    xmlns:x="http://schemas.microsoft.com/winfx/2006/xaml"
    Title="SimpleMortgageCalculator_View" Height="229" Width="550" Background="Blan
    chedAlmond" >
    <Grid HorizontalAlignment="Center" Width="548" Height="190">
        <Grid.ColumnDefinitions>
            <ColumnDefinition/>
            <ColumnDefinition/>
        </Grid.ColumnDefinitions>
        <Grid.RowDefinitions>
            <RowDefinition/>
            <RowDefinition/>
            <RowDefinition/>
            <RowDefinition/>
            <RowDefinition/>
            <RowDefinition/>

            <RowDefinition/>
        </Grid.RowDefinitions>
        <Label Grid.ColumnSpan="2" FontWeight="bold" FontSize="14" Horizontal
        Alignment="Center">
            Simple Mortgage Calculator
        </Label>

        <Label Grid.Row="1" HorizontalAlignment="Right">
            Enter the Loan amount to finance:
        </Label>
        <TextBox x:Name="loanAmount" Grid.Row ="1" Grid.Column="1" Width="200"
        HorizontalAlignment="Left"/>

        <Label Grid.Row="2" HorizontalAlignment="Right">
            Enter the interest rate of the loan:
        </Label>
        <TextBox x:Name="interestRate" Grid.Row ="2" Grid.Column="1" Width="200"
        HorizontalAlignment="Left"/>

        <Label Grid.Row="3" HorizontalAlignment="Right">
            Enter the number of years on the loan:
        </Label>
        <TextBox x:Name="numberOfYears" Grid.Row ="3" Grid.Column="1" Width="200"
        HorizontalAlignment="Left"/>

        <Label Grid.Row="4" HorizontalAlignment="Right">
```

```
        Monthly Payment:
    </Label>
    <Label x:Name="monthlyPayment" Grid.Row="4" Grid.Column="2" Horizontal
    Alignment="Left" Width="200" FontWeight="bold" Foreground="Red"/>

    <Button Grid.Row="6" x:Name="calculatePayment" Grid.ColumnSpan="2" Horizontal
    Alignment="Center" Width="100" Content="Calculate" Click="calculatePayment_Click" />
    </Grid>
</Window>
```

If you're new to XAML it may seem a bit sensitive the first few times you use it. Be very sure that the x: Class attribute in the Window definition matches the fully qualified name of the class defined in your SimpleMortgageCalculator_View.xaml.cs file.

In the SimpleMortgageCalculator_View.cs file, replace the default class code with the following:

```
public partial class SimpleMortgageCalculator_View : Window,
ISimpleMortgageCalculatorView
    {

    private SimpleMortgageCalculatorPresenter _presenter;

    #region ISimpleMortgageCalculatorView Implementation
    double ISimpleMortgageCalculatorView.LoanAmount
    {
        get
        {
            return double.Parse(this.loanAmount.Text);
        }
        set { }
    }

    double ISimpleMortgageCalculatorView.InterestRate
    {
        get
        {
            return double.Parse(this.interestRate.Text);
        }
        set { }
    }

    int ISimpleMortgageCalculatorView.NumberOfYears
    {
        get
        {
            return int.Parse(this.numberOfYears.Text);
        }
        set { }
    }

    #endregion

    public SimpleMortgageCalculator_View()
```

```
    {
        InitializeComponent();
        _presenter = new SimpleMortgageCalculatorPresenter(this, new
        LoanMonthlyPaymentCalculator ());
    }

    private void calculatePayment_Click(object sender, RoutedEventArgs e)
    {
        ExecutePaymentCalculation();
    }

    private void ExecutePaymentCalculation()
    {
        this.monthlyPayment.Content = string.Format("${0}", _presenter.
        GetMortgagePayment().ToString());
    }
}
```

This should look very similar to the web example. The Xaml class acts just like the code-behind page for the ASP.NET application, implementing ISimpleMortgageCalculatorView and mapping the interface's properties to the UI elements. The class contains a field variable referencing the Presenter and initializes it in the constructor, passing in an instance of itself as a valid reference to ISimpleMortgageCalculatorView. The rest of the code is identical to the web sample. The View contains a method named ExecutePaymentCalculation(), which calls into the fully provisioned Presenter to get the monthly mortgage payment. The Presenter, using its reference to ISimpleMortgageCalculatorView, calls back into the WPF window implicitly and extracts the values entered by the user. The Model objects are then invoked by the Presenter though its handle to IMortgageCalculator, which in turn performs the math to determine the figure for the monthly payment. By separating out the business logic and testable Presenter from View, you have effectively cleaved your dependency on the Web Model and facilitated reuse of other testable portions of code. Run the application; the output should look like Figure 10-7.

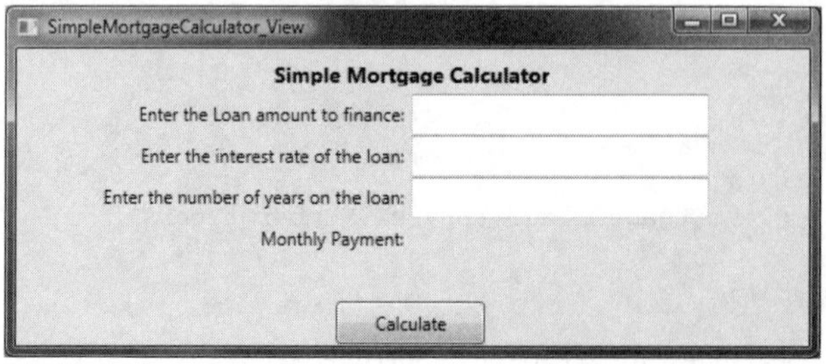

Figure 10-7

Hopefully, by now you're beginning to see the practical merits of front-end orchestration and separation. The MVP pattern has a wide range of uses and has been embraced by developers in many different development communities. If this was your first exposure to MVP, the pattern may take some getting used to. However, once you get the hang of it, your projects will become surprisingly flexible and easy to manage.

Summary

In this chapter, we took a deeper look into the Model-View-Presenter pattern first introduced in Chapter 9. We defined the individual components within the pattern, and the purpose each of them served. We then built an example of a simple MVP application, walking through the individual components as we put them into the project. Through this process we covered the following areas:

❑ We revisited the Model-View-Presenter pattern, taking time to review some of its design benefits and underlying concepts.

❑ We created an ASP.NET web application and began provisioning it with our individual conceptual layers.

❑ We created our HTML user interface, including three fields for entering data for a mortgage calculation. Our abstract View definition was then defined separately and implemented in the web page class, mapping the interface properties to their corresponding user interface elements.

❑ We created a Presenter class with a reference to that View definition, along with either a reference to an existing Model class or a newly provided Model.

❑ We then completed the MVP pattern by instantiating the Presenter from the View and calling the Presenter methods accordingly.

❑ We completed the chapter by going back to our test harness, and running the tests in the NUnit client application to ensure that all business rules had been met.

❑ Finally, we reused portions of the MVP web example in a WPF application to demonstrate the use of MVP on a thick client platform.

In the next chapter we will explore newer web-based Model-View-Controller pattern. Web MVC bears some of the same tenets as MVP, allowing for increased flexibility and testability. Yet Web MVC is a more rigid framework, delivering a stronger paradigm within which the developer must work. This framework is more rigid than the MVP model, but provides a different set of features for larger, ground-up enterprise web applications.

11

The Model-View-Controller Pattern

The Model-View-Presenter pattern is fine for small client applications or for migrating older Web Form applications into a new, testable platform. However, MVP falls short of providing developers a solid framework for cogent separation of concerns. To this end, the Model-View-Controller (MVC) pattern is an ideal framework for delivering a structured, testable UI model. In Chapter 9 we reviewed the evolution of MVC, beginning with the initial design by Small Talk, and exploring its most recent incarnation within the Ruby on Rails framework. This chapter explores the web MVC designed Microsoft applications, focusing on the March 2009 release for ASP.NET.

In this chapter, we will:

❑   Discuss the merits of web MVC and how it compares to other models

❑   Begin exploring the ASP.NET MVC framework

❑   Build a UI front end for a mortgage loan application using ASP.NET MVC

Back to Basics

Let's face it, if you've had the opportunity to examine a few different MVP programs, you've likely found that they can be unpredictable. That's because MVP is a pattern, not really a framework. The Model-View-Presenter pattern is popular as much for its flexibility as it is for its testability. However, flexibility has its costs. Since each developer makes their own decisions about how and where their entities should be developed, you inevitably find that each MVP-driven program has its own flavor and its own quirks. What the user interface world really needs is a *less* flexible front end framework . . . a framework that enforces patterns and conventions in a manner that makes all programs using framework easy to follow. Enter web MVC. Recall back in Chapter 9 that web MVC, as we have come to know it today, was first conceived in the world of Ruby. The Rails web framework implements a tight Model-View-Controller pattern that leverages the power of classic web architecture to deliver a platform that combines sound architecture with rapid application development.

Of course, that's not the easiest thing for all web programmers to understand. A good number of web developers have become accustomed to one or more of the technologies that sit on top of the traditional HTML/HTTP model to facilitate a more client-like user experience. Although there are many such technologies like this, perhaps one of the most popular is ASP.NET. ASP.NET provides developers with the means to create user forms that simulate the UI of a client application. Programmers can add UI elements to their design panel such as buttons, grids, and text fields, and implement logic on their respective events without getting their hands dirty with the underlying scripted plumbing. The merits of this model are debatable; most feel that Web Forms still have their place. However, to understand the power of web MVC, it is important for readers to first reacquaint themselves with the original model that still drives all browser-based applications.

The web in its truest form is entirely stateless. With each request to a server, a single response is delivered and forgotten. Disregarding for a moment the eventual use of sessions and session variables, old-fashioned HTTP consisted of simple HTML forms with actions and methods. The body of the HTML was for display purposes only, delivering design-based markup for the browser to render text, images, tables, and so forth. For the interactive portions of the page, a form was declared. Forms consisted of actions and methods that communicated to the browser where to send the form's data once the page had been submitted. Let's take a look at a simple HTML form declaration:

```
<form id="sampleForm" action="/samplewebsite/process" method="GET">
```

This declaration consists of three attributes. The first is the unique ID of the form itself (that is, unique to the page). The second is the "action" attribute. This tells the browser that when this form is submitted an HTTP request should be sent to the URL provided. The third attribute is the "method." The method tells the browser how to deliver the user-entered data within the page to the URL provided in the action. Typically, there are two types of methods: GET and POST. A GET tells the browser to assemble the form variables into a querystring appended to the action's URL. The querystring will consist of key/value pairs defining the form elements and values, each separated by an ampersand. If the form had three textboxes with IDs of firstName, lastName, and favoriteColor, respectively, the URL to which the browser would post might look something like this:

```
http://www.mysamplewebsite.com/samplewebsite/process?firstName=Jon&lastName=
Arking&favoriteColor=hotpink
```

GET posts are used for small posts, often to different URLs within the same website. They are easy to use but not very practical. Aside from the fact that our favorite color is *not* hotpink, this example is unrealistic for larger data entry pages. Most HTML entry forms are composed of many more fields. Exposing all of them within the URL is both cumbersome and not very private. For larger forms, developers can use the POST method. This option assembles the key/values pairs into the actual message buffer, making the URL easier to read, while still delivering all of the data the user entered. If you have worked with a web platform before you have likely seen forms, actions, and methods before. However, what most don't realize is that once the post is made, the user state resets. The server receives the data and sends a response back to the browser, usually in the form of a redirect. A new page is loaded and the last page is forgotten. Unless you use a technology that sits on top of the HTTP model, the web page is simply a thin veneer for showing simple UI from post to post.

Of course, that was then. The last 15 years since the advent of the Internet have produced a lot of state-enabling frameworks to make web development a bit less cumbersome. JSP, ColdFusion, PHP, and classic ASP all implement utilities and scripts that empower the developer to maintain relevant information about a user's session as they navigate though an application. These tools are still relevant; no self-respecting business is going to force their customers to use a cumbersome application. Nowadays people are used to sessions, shopping carts, favorites lists, and lots of other features that show web state. Yet as the technologies that sit on top of the HTTP model have become more popular, the original patterns have gotten somewhat diluted. The result of these tools has been a market flush with web developers who understand how to build web-enabled systems without really understanding how the underlying communication model functions.

Web MVC is a throwback to the web days of old. Like other web development platforms, web MVC provides developers with tools and utilities to make web programming easier. However, unlike the multitude of competing platforms, web MVC relies on the original stateless model that drives the Internet. That may seem like a simple statement, but try not to oversimplify what it means. Moving from an intricate framework like ASP.NET to web MVC is a big task. Most don't realize the amount of plumbing built into ASP.NET Web Forms in order to emulate page state. The very concept of the same-page post is somewhat alien to the web MVC developer. In fact, the concept of a web *page* doesn't even really fit. ASP.NET Web Forms utilize files consisting of an .aspx extension as the target of an intended navigation. Within that page lives an event lifecycle that simulates the loading and unloading of a client Windows Form. Working with a set of hidden fields and DHMTL scripts that are placed in the user's web page when the page loads, the ASP.NET engine manipulates the stateless HTTP communication model to make the application function like a client executable.

The web MVC model is quite different. There are no state-holding web pages used, at least not the kind of pages you might find in an ASP or even JSP or PHP system. Web MVC separates the incoming request from the intended output, routing the request to the appropriate method on a server-side object. This pattern has been used in other well-known MVC web models such as Java Struts (the pattern emulated is the Action Bean pattern); however, web MVC couples the incoming request with the controllers in a pattern that closely aligns the MVC components with the default HTTP communication model.

Models

At the heart of an MVC application lies the model class. This class or classes represent the business logic of your application. They are the closest objects in your MVC project to your system's domain model, and in some cases, may be an actual part of it. Models can be found as components or members of the MVC project itself, or they may be components of other classes or conceptual layers. Most ASP.NET

MVC applications use one or more `Model` classes as at least a service container, invoking or requesting data from services in other parts of your system. This helps to keep the MVC patter predictable. As you will see in this chapter's example, local models help the ASP.NET templates derive the views and populate them with bindable HTML elements.

Controllers

Controllers are the coordinating entities of the MVC application. They expose public methods that receive incoming data from an HTTP post and pass that information to a model or view, depending on the action being performed. No portion of a model is ever invoked directly from a view, nor is any view ever displayed or invoked directly from a model. The controller handles the management of the two at runtime. Public methods on a controller are known as *actions*. Actions are directly accessible through an HTTP post via the format of an MVC-specific URL. The URL follows the routing mechanism inherent to web MVC, which is fundamentally different from traditional page-targeting URLs. There is typically one controller declared for each model on the application, although that is not always the way ASP.NET MVC applications function. The MVC framework provides built-in navigation utilities for moving from controller to controller without having to specify web pages by physical location.

Views

The view is the physical display of any one part of an MVC application. Views are usually constructed using common HTML and DHTML, along with some server-side scripting tags to dynamically load data. Views in MVC are markedly different than those found in a traditional ASP.NET application. On their own, they have no inherent lifecycle or state. There is no concept of the code-behind class, postbacks, or ViewStates. They are simply dynamically loaded HTML displays that can be bound to a model based on the action the user intends to perform. In most cases, each controller action has a view with which it is associated and after which the view is named. All MVC views are placed in the project's View folder, under a subfolder named after the controller with which it is coupled. For example, say that you have a model named `Borrower`, and a controller named `BorrowerController` with three methods: `Create`, `Edit`, and `Details`. The views for each of these actions would be placed in Views/Borrower and named `Create.aspx`, `Edit.aspx`, and `Details.aspx`, respectively (assuming that we are using the ASP.NET view engine, but we'll get to that later). It is important to place the views in their correct location. The MVC engine uses conventions that rely on this project structure to navigate to the right view for the right action.

Routing

Routing is an important aspect of ASP.NET MVC, and likely a new topic for many web developers. If your experience with web programming has been limited to ASP.NET, you have likely become accustomed to a URL system that is location-specific. Users making a request to `myapplication/games/tictactoe.aspx` would normally be taken to a web paged named `TicTacToe.aspx` physically located on the web server under the project's Games folder. MVC is entirely different. URLs are made up of elements that communicate to the engine which classes and methods to invoke and what data to pass in. Web MVC URLs are broken into three distinct portions under the root application name. The first is the name of the controller that contains the action to be performed. The second is the name of the action on the controller being invoked. The third element is the parameter being passed to the action. This last item is usually an ID of some sort and more often than not a single value. However, in some cases this element may be null (if viewing a list on an index page), or it can consist of multiple parameters. Most MVC developers try to avoid multiple parameter passing as it may indicate a nesting of scope that conflicts with the otherwise strict MVC pattern. However, every application is different; the ASP.NET MVC framework allows for flexibility in this area.

There is obviously much more to ASP.NET MVC than can be covered in one chapter of a book on enterprise development. These points highlight the most salient features of the MVC model for people just beginning to explore it. As we move through the example in the next section, we will discuss other nuances and points of interest along the way; however, the topic can be quite comprehensive. For more information on ASP.NET MVC and the web MVC model, readers should feel encouraged to explore the online documentation located at `http://www.asp.net/mvc`.

The Mortgage Loan Application

As with all new things, seeing is believing. With that in mind it's time to get our hands dirty with ASP.NET MVC and write a little code. Continuing with our mortgage loan theme, we are going to build a front-end web interface used to apply for a mortgage. The sample should be kept simple enough to easily follow the ASP.NET MVC pattern. So, we will begin by creating a standalone web façade, complete with its own models and simplified logic. However, we will take the time to maintain the application process workflow. The implementation of the mortgage process within the rubric of the MVC stateless model will prove to be a good first stab at web MVC. Keep in mind, though, that this sample will follow the spirit of the mortgage domain model we built in Chapter 7 without following it to the letter. Full integration with the domain model will take place when we get to Chapter 12.

Before we begin, you'll want to be sure that you have downloaded and installed the ASP.NET MVC project from Microsoft, as well as its prerequisites. At the time of this writing, the framework can be downloaded from the following URL: `www.asp.net/mvc/download`.

Note that ASP.NET MVC requires at least Visual Studio .NET 2008 with Service Pack 1 installed. Alternatively, you can download Visual Web Developer with SP1. Visual Web Developer can be found at the following URL: `www.microsoft.com/express/vwd`.

Since most readers will be using Visual Studio .NET 2008, the sample diagrams for this chapter will reflect screens in that IDE; however, the differences between Visual Web Developer and the full version of Visual Studio.Net 2008 are nominal.

Begin by opening Visual Studio and creating a new ASP.NET MVC project. You should be able to find this option by selecting Create ➪ Project, selecting Web from the Project Types pane, and selecting ASP.NET MVC Web Application from the project templates. Name the project `ProEnt.Chap11` and place it in the `C:\Projects` folder, as shown in Figure 11-1.

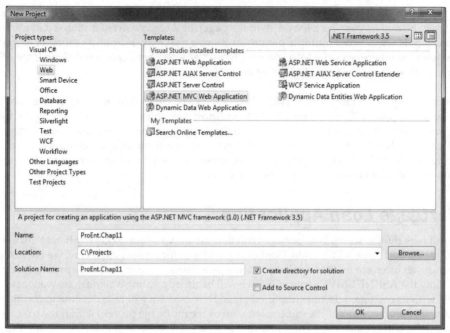

Figure 11-1

You will see a popup dialog window asking if you would like to create a unit test project along with your web application project, as shown in Figure 11-2.

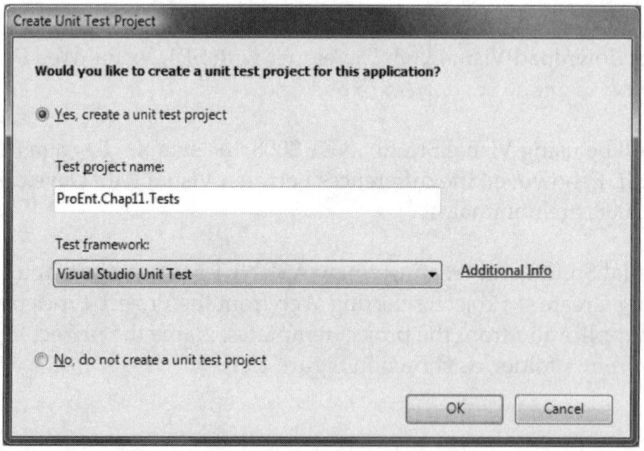

Figure 11-2

Select the option that reads Yes, create a unit test project and leave the drop-down list selected on Visual Studio Unit Test; finally, click OK. If you have installed nUnit in previous chapters and have configured VS.NET to use it, you may be inclined to change the test framework. However, for the benefit of readers who might be skipping to this chapter's sample before the others, we are going to use the VS.NET test framework. This chapter's sample includes unit tests but does not focus on unit testing as a subject. Since the template comes with VS.NET unit test framework preconfigured, let's not muddy the waters by reconfiguring it.

As you'll find once the template finishes loading, the project comes flush with a staple diet of scripts and sample files. Have a look at the expanded Solution Explorer shown in Figure 11-3.

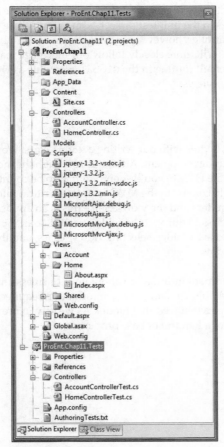

Figure 11-3

The template loads two projects — an MVC website project and its corresponding unit test project. The web project loads with some of the same features you might see in a regular ASP.NET web project, such as a content folder with a `site.css` style sheet, and an `APP_Data` folder. It also loads with a set of scripts to simplify basic scripting tasks such as using jQuery or implementing Ajax calls. Most importantly, you'll find three folders, for Controllers, Models, and Views, respectively. The MVC engine requires developers to separate their code into these folders in order to function properly. The Models folder is empty as the application logic has not been implemented. Yet the Controller and View folders have already been populated with sample Home and Account code files. Note that the Controllers for each are named `HomeController` and `AccountController`; however, the subfolders in the Views directory are named Home and Account. The web MVC convention refers to these two items by their proper names, Home and Account, appending them with the word Controller as a means of common identification. As you will soon see, the MVC engine expects these naming conventions to navigate from action to action.

The first thing you'll want to do is remove the existing sample code. Find the `HomeController` and `AccountController` in Solution Explorer, right-click on each, and select Delete. Click OK on the confirmation dialog to commit the action. Repeat this step for the Home and Account View folders, as well as for the two test fixtures in the unit test project. Some may debate whether a web MVC application should consist of a Home Controller; however, we are going to create a base Loan Controller instead as our default set of actions. This will more closely follow our mortgage loan pattern and it will give us a chance to take a look at the default routing in the `Global.asax` file as well. Your project should now have no controllers, models, or views.

The Model

Our application development begins with our writing a `Model` class. Working with a web MVC model requires a certain order to your development. Although you might be inclined to jump into the Views folder and starting writing some HTML, you'll soon find that to be counter to the MVC development flow. The models typically help convey to the MVC templates critical information that is then used to stub out the code for the controllers and the views. Since this is an application for creating mortgage loan applications, let's add a new class to our `Models` folder, named `LoanApplication`. You can do this by simply right-clicking on the `Models` folder, selecting Add ⇨ Class, and then entering `LoanApplication` as the name in the dialog window.

Models should contain the pertinent information about your business and business entities. In this case, the `LoanApplication` class should contain the key information required to apply for a mortgage, as well as references to other objects that feed that model. As we saw in previous chapters, a mortgage loan application typically consists of a handful of base properties:

- ❑ Loan Amount
- ❑ Interest Rate
- ❑ Loan Term
- ❑ Down Payment

These fields will define the financial particulars of this loan, which we can later use for simple validation. We will also need to provide an Application ID, along with a readable Application Name, to further identify any one loan from another. However a handful of primitive `int`s and floats won't be enough to build a real application. We will need to have some references to other model classes as well, such as borrowers, debts, assets, and credit scores. However let's ignore those properties for the time being. As we build on our application we will refactor the `LoanApplication` class accordingly. Your class should look something like this:

```
public class LoanApplication
    {
        #region properties
        private int _applicationID;

        public int ApplicationID
        {
            get { return _applicationID; }
            set { _applicationID = value; }
        }

        private string _applicationName;

        public string ApplicationName
        {
            get { return _applicationName; }
            set { _applicationName = value; }
        }

        private float? _loanAmount;

        public float? LoanAmount
        {
            get { return _loanAmount; }
            set { _loanAmount = value; }
        }

        private float? _downPayment;

        public float? DownPayment
        {
            get { return _downPayment; }
            set { _downPayment = value; }
        }

        private float? _interestRate;

        public float? InterestRate
        {
            get { return _interestRate; }
            set { _interestRate = value; }
        }


        private int? _loanTerm;

        public int? LoanTerm
        {
            get { return _loanTerm; }
            set { _loanTerm = value; }
        }
```

```
    #endregion

    public LoanApplication()
    {
        //Init Collections

    }
}
```

There is a lot of code missing from this class, but at the moment it's got enough to move forward. One of the quirks of the ASP.NET MVC model is that you will need the ability to compile and build the source code from time to time, even if you don't intend to run the code. There will be more on this in just a bit.

The Controller

Now we will need to create the controller for this class. Remember that each conceptual entity in our system typically consists of one model, one controller, and *n* number of views. Go to the `Controllers` folder in the Solution Explorer, right-click and select Add ⇨ Controller. You will see a popup window asking you to put in a controller name, as shown in Figure 11-4.

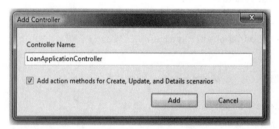

Figure 11-4

Put in the name "LoanApplicationController." The web MVC engine relies on a specific naming convention when navigating objects within the site. Controllers that correspond to models should share the same model name, appended with the word "Controller." You will want to check the box that reads Add Action Methods to allow the MVC templates to stub out the basic CRUD (Create, Read, Update, Delete) operations. The MVC templates will automatically build the core actions required for most basic web operations. Let's take a look at the generated code:

```
public class LoanApplicationController : Controller
    {
        //
        // GET: /LoanApplication/

        public ActionResult Index()
        {
            return View();
        }

        //
        // GET: /LoanApplication/Details/5

        public ActionResult Details(int id)
        {
```

```
        return View();
    }

    //
    // GET: /LoanApplication/Create

    public ActionResult Create()
    {
        return View();
    }

    //
    // POST: /LoanApplication/Create

    [AcceptVerbs(HttpVerbs.Post)]
    public ActionResult Create(FormCollection collection)
    {
        try
        {
            // TODO: Add insert logic here

            return RedirectToAction("Index");
        }
        catch
        {
            return View();
        }
    }

    //
    // GET: /LoanApplication/Edit/5

    public ActionResult Edit(int id)
    {
        return View();
    }

    //
    // POST: /LoanApplication/Edit/5

    [AcceptVerbs(HttpVerbs.Post)]
    public ActionResult Edit(int id, FormCollection collection)
    {
        try
        {
            // TODO: Add update logic here

            return RedirectToAction("Index");
        }
        catch
        {
            return View();
        }
    }
}
```

The first method applied, Index, is typically used as the default action for a controller. In our case, it will take the user to a list of loans in progress and display some simple information about them. The Details method is used to view more specific information about a model's or models' data. We will use this later to expand the entire loan's data prior to submission for approval. The two Create methods are for creating new instances of the models. The method is overloaded to accommodate for the initial post, which takes the user to a data entry page, and the submission of that page for processing and persisting the data entered. Notice that the second Create method is declared with an attribute labeled "AcceptVerbs ... " This attribute conveys to the MVC engine which HTTP verbs the method should expect to accept. The most common implementations of this attribute are used to accept GET and POST methods.

> ASP.NET MVC doesn't completely conform to the well-known semantics of Representational State Transfer (REST). The AcceptVerbs attribute does not automatically provide all of the HTTP methods needed for a REST application.

The second Create method also accepts a FormCollection object as a means of delivering the user-provided data. However, as you will see in a few moments, you can change that code to more closely couple it to your model objects. The final two methods are for editing existing records or model objects. Like the Create methods, there are two Edit methods, for the initial request and for the submission of data. All of these methods are public, ultimately exposing themselves as URL actions on the controller itself.

The View

With each of these controller actions, a corresponding view can be created. The Views all live in the controller's View folder, located under the main View directory and named for the controller itself. The LoanApplicationController class has four distinct actions. Therefore, we will eventually implement four views in the View/LoanApplication directory, one each named Index.aspx, Details.aspx, Create.aspx, and Edit.aspx. It's important to note that the ASP.NET MVC framework does not force the user to use the ASP.NET view engine. In fact, many developers using ASP.NET MVC have configured their projects to use other popular web MVC view engines, such as Spark and nVelocity. A discussion of the merits of these engines falls outside of the scope of this chapter; however, readers should investigate some of these options. Unlike traditional ASP.NET, ASP.NET MVC was designed with configuration in mind. Even though the ASP.NET view engine comes out of the box with the MVC framework, a few simple steps can easily allow for the use of other view utilities and patterns. For more information on either Spark or nVelocity, refer to their online configuration notes.

Keeping matters simple, we will continue using the ASP.NET view engine. That means that each view will be implemented as a scripted web page with the .aspx extension. The scripting elements found within an .aspx page should look familiar to readers with ASP.NET experience. Yet keep in mind that only a portion of the ASP.NET plumbing is used with web MVC. All manner of ViewState management, as well as the core ASP.NET lifecycle, have been pushed aside.

Adding views to an ASP.NET MVC is an interesting task. You could just write your views by hand (We're sure the diehard geeks out there insist upon it even for the simple tasks). Yet recall that we previously discussed that the power of web MVC lies in its ability to combine sound architectural patterns with rapid application development. Creating views is a compelling example of this compromise. Now that you have spent the time getting to understand the MVC pattern, you can take advantage of its shortcuts. The ASP.NET view template is analogous to the RoR tool known as scaffolding. By interrogating the properties of the model with which the view is associated, the scaffolding engine is able to generate web pages that perform the basic functions needed for simple model persistence. In other words, scaffolding generates web pages for adding model-based records to a data store. Although the persistence is not a requirement of the tool, most developers who use scaffolding are also likely using the Rails ActiveRecord model, which maps models to tables in a relational database such as MySQL.

The ASP.NET view templates work the same way scaffolding works. Selecting an action within a controller and directly associating it with a strongly typed model enables the templates to create web pages that allow you to create and display instances of your models. To see this in action, first compile and build the application as is. If you don't do so, the templating system won't be able to see the LoanApplication model and, therefore, won't be able to build the web pages. Now go into your newly generated `LoanApplicationController` class and right-click on the method named `Index`. Select Add View from the popup menu to get the View template helper window to come up. The name defaults to Index since that's the action you're generating this for. Click the second checkbox, labeled Create Strongly-typed View, and expand the drop-down menu labeled View Data Class: you should see a single option available that reads `ProEnt.Chap11.Models.LoanApplication`. Select that from the menu then expand the View Content menu. Here you'll find the various options from which to choose for your intended view. Look familiar? With the exception of the Empty option, these options correspond to the same default actions automatically stubbed out in the `LoanApplicationController` class. Select List, as you will be using this for the loan index page, and leave all other options alone. Since we are using the ASP.NET view engine, we have the ability to use master pages, as well as to create `.ascx` user controls. Both fall outside of the scope of this example; however, these features do blend nicely with the web MVC model. If you are unfamiliar with these features of ASP.NET, feel free to experiment with them later. Make sure your selection reflects the options shown in Figure 11-5.

Figure 11-5

Click Add at the bottom of the window to complete the process.

A few things just happened. First, the template added a new folder under your Views directory, named `LoanApplication`. Using the standard conventions inherent to web MVC, the templates will always provide (or rather, the engine will expect) a distinct view directory for each controller. Next, a web page was added, named `Index.aspx`. This is the default vehicle for your views. Finally, the web page was provisioned with a limited but effective amount of HTML and ASP.NET scripting to build a fully functional view that matches the like-named action on the controller. Let's take a moment to examine the code that was created:

```
<%@ Page Title="" Language="C#" MasterPageFile="~/Views/Shared/Site.Master"
Inherits="System.Web.Mvc.ViewPage<IEnumerable<ProEnt.Chap11ProEnt.Chap11Chap11.
Models.LoanApplication>>" %>

<asp:Content ID="Content1" ContentPlaceHolderID="TitleContent" runat="server">
        Index
</asp:Content>

<asp:Content ID="Content2" ContentPlaceHolderID="MainContent" runat="server">

    <h2>Index</h2>

    <table>
        <tr>
            <th></th>
            <th>
                ApplicationID
            </th>
            <th>
                ApplicationName
            </th>
            <th>
                LoanAmount
            </th>
            <th>
                DownPayment
            </th>
            <th>
                InterestRate
            </th>
            <th>
                LoanTerm
            </th>
        </tr>

    <% foreach (var item in Model) { %>

        <tr>
            <td>
                <%= Html.ActionLink("Edit", "Edit", new { /* id=item.PrimaryKey */ }) %> |
                <%= Html.ActionLink("Details", "Details", new { /* id=item.PrimaryKey */ })%>
            </td>
            <td>
```

```
        <%= Html.Encode(item.ApplicationID) %>
    </td>
    <td>
        <%= Html.Encode(item.ApplicationName) %>
    </td>
    <td>
        <%= Html.Encode(item.LoanAmount) %>
    </td>
    <td>
        <%= Html.Encode(item.DownPayment) %>
    </td>
    <td>
        <%= Html.Encode(item.InterestRate) %>
    </td>
    <td>
        <%= Html.Encode(item.LoanTerm) %>
    </td>
</tr>

<% } %>

</table>

<p>
    <%= Html.ActionLink("Create New", "Create") %>
</p>

</asp:Content>
```

You may first notice the common ASP.NET scripting tags used to register the page and couple it to the application's object model. Here we see some of the more standard ASP.NET patterns working nicely within our MVC view. Also, some tags were added to associate this page with the application's master page, an option that we elected to keep when generating the view. From there, the code begins to map out a table that will display all of the public fields exposed in the LoanApplication model class. We find a scripted foreach loop that then adds a row for every instance of a model object found in the collection named Model. Each ASP.NET MVC view has a reference named Model that serves as a handle to the model objects the page references. Since we elected to create a List of models when we defined our view, our Index page's Model is a reference to a collection of items. You will no doubt also wonder what the HTML reference is doing all over the place. This variable references an instance of the HTMLHelper class found within the ASP.NET MVC namespaces. This class emits various bits of HTML markup to help you quickly and uniformly define common web page artifacts, such as buttons, textfields, menus, and forms. The HTMLHelper class has a lot of great features built into it. For more information about how it works and what you can do with it, read some of the ASP.NET MVC online documentation found at its home website: www.asp.net/mvc.

You now have a model, a controller, and a view. We would suggest running the application and watching the site come to life, but you've got one big problem — no data. You created the model; however, you never created any database or repositories to which it should persist. If you followed the online tutorials available on the ASP.NET MVC website you would have created a database for your application first, then defined a set of object-relational maps for your models that can be saved to the database. This chapter distinctly avoided those steps. ASP.NET MVC is an ideal model for building data-centric applications; however, that's not really what this book is about. You are attempting to build a user interface for an enterprise system. That means that you should endeavor to create our UI abstract from our data source, which may be any number different platforms or technologies, depending on the way you designed your middleware. What you really need is an abstract repository into which you can persist and extract our model data.

A Simple Repository

Thinking back to Chapter 7, a repository is simply an abstract contract through which a system or set of services can persist and extract data. Depending on the tool or technology you choose, the contract may be simple or extremely intricate. Since simplicity is the name of the game in this sample, you are going to define a repository with three simple functions: `Save`, `Find`, and `GetAllLoans`. The interface should look something like this:

```
public interface ILoanApplicationRepository
    {
        void Save(LoanApplication loanApplication);
        LoanApplication Find(int id);
        List<LoanApplication> GetAllLoans();
    }
```

Using this simple contract, we can bind our controllers to any number of database platforms without having to alter our application logic. You may be inclined at this point to try and work in an nHibernate repository, as it is one of the preferred ORM platforms in the .NET enterprise community. nHibernate can be difficult to use in simple applications though. If we attempt to use nHibernate in this example, we can easily become distracted with the nuances of the ORM tool, and lose focus on the MVC patterns. Likewise, if we elect to use the preferred tool in the ASP.NET MVC community, Microsoft's Entity Framework, we couple ourselves to a data-centric solution that might not provide the degree of abstraction our code will need. Therefore, let's take the cheap way out. Instead of an ORM or RDBMS-based technology, we will write a quick and dirty XML serializer to turn our C# models into XML files. XML serialization is a tried-and-true feature of the .NET platform that dates all the way back to the original 1.0 release. It's an ideal pattern for simple persistence, and since it reflects against C# classes just like the MVC templates do, it is one that fits well with the MVC pattern. Those familiar with this feature have probably had some experience using the C# attributes that help to map class properties to XML elements and attributes. Our model will be even simpler. Since we don't have the need to read the XML in its raw form, we are going to let the .NET serializer figure out its own mapping. As long as we save and extract based on the same model definition, the pattern should prove to be adequate for this example.

Create a new folder at the root of your project named `Utilities`. Add an empty class to this folder named `LoanApplicationRepository`. Delete the code the IDE automatically stubbed out and replace it with the following:

```
using System;
using System.Collections.Generic;
using System.Web;
using System.Web.Mvc;
using System.Xml.Serialization;
using System.Xml;
using System.IO;
using System.Configuration;
using ProEnt.Chap11.Models;
```

```
namespace ProEnt.Chap11ProEnt.Chap11Chap11.Utilities
{
    public class LoanApplicationRepository : ILoanApplicationRepository
    {
        private XmlSerializer _serializer = new XmlSerializer(typeof(List<Loan
        Application>));
        private string _repository = ConfigurationSettings.AppSettings
        ["RepositoryUri"].ToString();


        public void Save(LoanApplication loanApplication)
        {
            List<LoanApplication> loans;

            if (!File.Exists(_repository))
                loans = new List<LoanApplication>();
            else
            {
                loans = DeserializeLoans();
                LoanApplication oldLoan = Find(loanApplication.ApplicationID);
                if(oldLoan != null)
                loans.Remove(loans.FindLast(x=>x.ApplicationID == loanApplication
                .ApplicationID));
            }

            loans.Add(loanApplication);
            SerializeLoans(loans);

        }

        public LoanApplication Find(int id)
        {
            return DeserializeLoans().FindLast(x=>x.ApplicationID == id);
        }


        public List<LoanApplication> GetAllLoans()
        {
            return DeserializeLoans();
        }


        private void SerializeLoans(List<LoanApplication> loans)
        {
            TextWriter write = new StreamWriter(_repository, false);
            _serializer.Serialize(write, loans);
            write.Close();
        }
```

```
            private List<LoanApplication> DeserializeLoans()
            {
                TextReader read = new StreamReader(_repository);
                List<LoanApplication> loans = (List<LoanApplication>)_serializer
                .Deserialize(read);
                read.Close();
                return loans;

            }

        }




        public interface ILoanApplicationRepository
        {
            void Save(LoanApplication loanApplication);
            LoanApplication Find(int id);
            List<LoanApplication> GetAllLoans();
        }
    }
```

If you are unfamiliar with C# XML serialization techniques, you may want to take a few moments to do a search on Google and find some articles on the subject. Essentially the pattern requires the use of an IO stream, a C# object with public properties, and an XML serializer instance. The serializer inspects the C# object using reflection and then writes out the instance to an XML file through the IO stream. When saving, we use a StreamWriter. When reading, a StreamReader. When an XML file is deserialized the StreamReader parses the file, passing the data to the XML serializer, which then repackages the data into instances of the same C# class it used for persisting. It isn't rocket science, but it gets the job done. Notice that the Serialize and Deserialize functions are private. These contain the internals of our repository about which the application doesn't need to know. The Save, Find, and GetAllLoans methods wrap these calls, adding some logic to overwrite old data when replacing it or filtering out the data that doesn't match the Find's search criteria. The location of the XML file is arbitrary so that it is referenced in a private field that pulls the value from a configuration setting. Add the following appSetting element to your Web.config file directly above the <connectionStrings> element:

```
<appSettings>
    <add key="RepositoryUri"
value="C:\projects\ProEnt.Chap11\ProEnt.Chap11\Loans.xml"/>
  </appSettings>
```

So, we've got a repository; now, let's use it. Since you don't have a loader class yet (we'll get to that later), you can cheat and just write some XML to load into your application. Create a new XML file in Notepad and save it as Loans.xml in the location you provided in the Web.config file. Add the following content:

```xml
<?xml version="1.0" encoding="utf-8" ?>
<ArrayOfLoanApplication xmlns:xsi="http://www.w3.org/2001/XMLSchema-instance"
xmlns:xsd="http://www.w3.org/2001/XMLSchema">
  <LoanApplication>
    <ApplicationID>1001</ApplicationID>
    <ApplicationName>Arking</ApplicationName>
    <LoanAmount>150000</LoanAmount>
    <DownPayment>30000</DownPayment>
    <InterestRate>6.25</InterestRate>
    <LoanTerm>30</LoanTerm>
    </LoanApplication>
</ArrayOfLoanApplication>
```

This is just a sample of what one loan might look like in your application. As you build more functionality into the application the data will get a bit more complex. To load this data, go back to the `LoanApplicationController` class. At the top of the class, declare a variable of type `ILoanApplicationRepository` and assign it a new instance of the `LoanApplicationRepository` class, as shown here:

```
private ProEnt.Chap11.Utilities.ILoanApplicationRepository _repository =
new ProEnt.Chap11.Utilities.LoanApplicationRepository();
```

Be sure to declare the `_repository` as a type of the abstract contract you defined earlier. This way when we need to switch to something more robust than XML, we need only to change the live instance to a class that implements the contract.

When refactoring loosely coupled object models many use an Inversion of Control container such as Spring.Net. However since IoC containers are typically used for domain models and not UI frameworks, we forego these tools in this sample. For more information on IoC containers, refer to Chapter 5.

Now replace the `Index` method with the following code:

```
public ActionResult Index()
        {
              return View(_repository.GetAllLoans());
        }
```

The `GetAllLoans` method returns a generic list of `LoanApplication` model instances. Remember when I said that each generated MVC view has its own reference to a variable named Model? That allows us to pass model objects from our controllers directly to our views. The template already provisioned the view with the code it needs to read this array.

The last step you need to take is to set the default routing to the `LoanController` class. We deleted the `HomeController` when we started the project, so if you try running the code now, the default routing won't know where to begin. Open the `Global.asax` file found at the root of your application in Solution Explorer. You will find a method named `RegisterRoutes` that configures the application to use the default routing convention most popular with web MVC. In this method is a call to `RouteCollection.MapRoute`. Since you want to keep the same routing pattern we discussed in the first section of this chapter, leave the code as is, and just replace the name of the controller with `LoanApplication`. The resulting `MapRoute` call should look like the following:

```
routes.MapRoute(
                "Default",                                              // Route name
                "{controller}/{action}/{id}",                           // URL with
                parameters
                new { controller = "LoanApplication", action = "Index", id = "" }
                // Parameter defaults
            );
```

Notice that you do not set the name of the controller property to `LoanApplicationController`, even though that is the name of your class. The web MVC convention refers to the `LoanApplication` as a single concept complete with model, controller, and views. The ASP.NET MVC engine will know how to find the controller.

Compile and run the application now. The MVC engine will begin by loading the `LoanApplication`'s controller class and invoking the action named Index. The controller will call the repository's `GetAllLoans` method to access the loan data you put in your XML file, which will package that data into `LoanApplication` model instances and pass them back to the controller in the form of a generic list. The view then receives the list and builds the HTML page accordingly. The resulting page should look like the page shown in Figure 11-6.

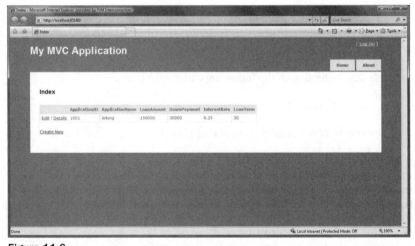

Figure 11-6

Creating and Editing

The `Index` action from the `LoanApplication` controller showed us the basic underpinnings of the MVC engine, along with some of the shortcuts that the templates provide. We should now build on our model a bit and flush out the rest of the interface. When applying for a mortgage loan, there are a handful of common tasks that need be accomplished to provision the application with enough relevant information for underwriting approval. These steps include:

❑   Creating a new mortgage loan application

❑   Adding one or more borrowers to the loan

❑   Adding employer information to the loan

❑   Adding one or more Assets to the loan to show a means of payment

❑   Adding any Debts that should be used when calculating full monthly debt payments

This is just a high-level list of course-grained tasks that need be performed, but it's a good starting point. Each of the items mentioned constitutes a class in the domain model. Since you are working within just the parameters of an ASP.NET MVC application, each domain class would, therefore, be a model in the MVC project. We can assume then that the list of model classes would be a simplified cross-section of the domain model we established in Chapter 7. Figure 11-7 shows the slimmed-down class diagram:

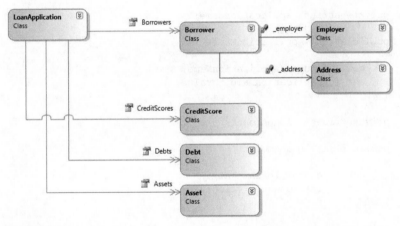

Figure 11-7

Again, remember that you are building a simplified version of a front end for entering a mortgage application. As you work the MVC project into the comprehensive project in Chapter 12, it will conform more closely to the flush domain model we established previously.

You can see from the diagram that all things center around the parent LoanApplication object. Therefore the use of the LoanApplication controller as the application's default controller was correct. Now you need to beef up the LoanApplication class to accommodate the addition of Borrowers, Employers, Assets, Debts, and CreditScores. In addition, you are going to add some properties to the

LoanApplication to help quickly derive some important mortgage calculations that you will need when submitting this for approval. Replace the LoanApplication model class you wrote with the following code:

```
using System;
using System.Collections.Generic;
using System.Linq;
using System.Web;

namespace ProEnt.Chap11.Models
{
    public class LoanApplication
    {
        #region properties
        private int _applicationID;

        public int ApplicationID
        {
            get { return _applicationID; }
            set { _applicationID = value; }
        }

        private string _applicationName;

        public string ApplicationName
        {
            get { return _applicationName; }
            set { _applicationName = value; }
        }

        private float? _loanAmount;

        public float? LoanAmount
        {
            get { return _loanAmount; }
            set { _loanAmount = value; }
        }

        private float? _downPayment;

        public float? DownPayment
        {
            get { return _downPayment; }
            set { _downPayment = value; }
        }

        private float? _interestRate;

        public float? InterestRate
        {
            get { return _interestRate; }
            set { _interestRate = value; }
        }
```

```
private int? _loanTerm;

public int? LoanTerm
{
    get { return _loanTerm; }
    set { _loanTerm = value; }
}

private float? _taxesAndInsurance;

public float? TaxesAndInsurance
{
    get { return _taxesAndInsurance; }
    set { _taxesAndInsurance = value; }
}

//private List<Borrower> _borrowers;

//public List<Borrower> Borrowers
//{
//    get { return _borrowers; }
//    set { _borrowers = value; }
//}


//private List<Asset> _assets;

//public List<Asset> Assets
//{
//    get { return _assets; }
//    set { _assets = value; }
//}


//private List<Debt> _debts;

//public List<Debt> Debts
//{
//    get { return _debts; }
//    set { _debts = value; }
//}


private LoanStatus _status;

public LoanStatus Status
{
    get { return _status; }
    set { _status = value; }
}

public int LTV
{
```

```csharp
        get
        {
            return (int)(100 * (1 - DownPayment / (LoanAmount + DownPayment)));
        }
    }


    public double MonthlyPayment
    {
        get
        {
            SimpleMortgageCalculator calc = new SimpleMortgageCalculator();
            return calc.LoanPaymentsPerMonthFor(Convert.ToDouble(LoanAmount),
            Convert.ToDouble(InterestRate), (int)LoanTerm);
        }
    }

    public double PrincipleInterestTaxesAndInsurance
    {
        get
        {
            return Convert.ToDouble(MonthlyPayment + TaxesAndInsurance);
        }
    }

    //public int AverageCreditScore
    //{
    //    get
    //    {
    //        int averageScore = 0;
    //        for (int i = 0; i <= CreditScores.Count - 1; i++)
    //            averageScore = (int)(averageScore + CreditScores[i].Score) / i;

    //        return averageScore;


    //    }
    //}


    #endregion

    public LoanApplication()
    {
        //Init Collections
        //this.Borrowers = new List<Borrower>();
        //this.Debts = new List<Debt>();
        //this.Assets = new List<Asset>();

        this.Status = LoanStatus.In_Progress;
```

```
        }

        public void UpdateMe(LoanApplication app)
        {
            ApplicationName = app.ApplicationName;
            InterestRate = app.InterestRate;
            LoanAmount = app.LoanAmount;
            LoanTerm = app.LoanTerm;
            DownPayment = app.DownPayment;
        }

        public List<BrokenBusinessRule> GetBrokenRules()
        {
            List<BrokenBusinessRule> brokenRules = new List<BrokenBusinessRule>();

            if (string.IsNullOrEmpty(ApplicationName))
            {
                brokenRules.Add(new BrokenBusinessRule("ApplicationName", "Please
                enter a name for this application"));
            }
            if (LoanAmount == null ||
                LoanAmount < 30000)
            {
                brokenRules.Add(new BrokenBusinessRule("LoanAmount", "You must
                enter a valid amount above $30,000. Do not use commas"));
            }
            if (DownPayment == null ||
                DownPayment < 1000)
            {
                brokenRules.Add(new BrokenBusinessRule("DownPayment", "You must
                enter a valid downpayment amount greater than $1000.00. Do not use
                commas"));
            }
            if (InterestRate == null ||
                InterestRate < 3 ||
                (InterestRate % 0.125) != 0)
            {
                brokenRules.Add(new BrokenBusinessRule("InterestRate", "You must
                enter a valid interest rate in multiples of 0.125 above 3% "));
            }
            if (LoanTerm == null ||
                LoanTerm < 5)
            {
                brokenRules.Add(new BrokenBusinessRule("LoanTerm", "You must
                enter a valid loan term greater than 5 years"));
            }

            return brokenRules;
        }
```

```
        }


    public enum LoanStatus
    {
        In_Progress = 0,
        Declined = 1,
        Approved = 2
    }
}
```

There is a lot more going on in this class than the first one you wrote, so let's take a moment to look at the code. Much of the code in this snippet is commented out to make sure that the application can continue to compile. Since you haven't created all of the objects declared in here, you will have to uncomment them as you go. The same properties you had before remain, along with new properties for adding the other models found in the class diagram. Below those properties are the derived calculations for the mortgage. The first of these, LTV, is the mortgage's Loan-to-Value. This number is a ratio depicting the percentage of the total value of the home covered by the loan itself. We assume in this sample that the borrower's down payment plus the loan amount equals the value of the home, even though other applications allow the home value to be listed separately. We did this for convenience. The second calculation, MonthlyPayment, generates the monthly mortgage payment the user will have to pay for the principle and interest only. This value can either be derived using the SimpleMortgage Calculator class you used in Chapter 7 or by adding the following class to your Models folder:

```
using System;

namespace ProEnt.Chap11.Models
{
    public class SimpleMortgageCalculator : IMortgageCalculator
    {
        public double LoanPaymentsPerMonthFor(double LoanAmount, double
        InterestRate, int LoanTerm)
        {
            double int_trm = Math.Pow(1 + InterestRate / 1200, LoanTerm * 12);
            double mrt_year = (LoanAmount * InterestRate * int_trm) / (1200 *
            (int_trm - 1));
            double payments = (mrt_year * 12 / 12);
            double p = Math.Round(payments * 100) / 100;
            return Math.Round(p * 1, 2);
        }
    }

    public interface IMortgageCalculator
    {
        double  LoanPaymentsPerMonthFor(double LoanAmount, double InterestRate, int
        LoanTerm);
    }
}
```

The calculation immediately following `MonthlyPayment` is `PrincipleInterestTaxesAndInsurance`. This is the full monthly payment most borrowers pay, which sums the mortgage payment with a breakdown of taxes and homeowner's insurance payments. The last calculation is the `AverageCreditScore`, which as its name suggests, returns a mean average of all the credit scores entered. Some mortgage loan companies weigh some credit reporting agency scores higher than others. This example treats them all equally, so feel free to add any logic you prefer here. After the calculations, you added in a constructor that initializes the generic lists that hold your models, as well as a copy function for overwriting the simple properties of the mortgage. The copy function will come in handy when you edit your models.

The last method, `GetBrokenBusinessRules`, is used for validating for simple rules, such as checking for null values or proper formatting. In the world of DDD (Domain Driven Design) it is often the job of the domain model object to know its own rules and if they have been broken. A lot of ASP.NET MVC samples out there show this sort of validation added to the controller. We want to follow enterprise patterns, so you will leave the rule validation within the models themselves. As you perform more comprehensive loan validation prior to loan submission, those rules will live elsewhere. To use this pattern you'll need to add a definition for `BrokenBusinessRule` under the `Models` folder:

```
using System;

namespace ProEnt.Chap11.Models
{
    public class BrokenBusinessRule
    {
        private string _property;

        public string Property
        {
            get { return _property; }
            set { _property = value; }
        }

        private string _rule;

        public string Rule
        {
            get { return _rule; }
            set { _rule = value; }
        }


        public BrokenBusinessRule(string property, string rule)
        {
            this._property = property;
            this._rule = rule;
        }
    }
}
```

The final item you'll notice in the code is a small enumeration containing the various statuses as of the loan. All new loans are entered In_Progress, and then promoted to other statuses as the user traverses the workflow.

Make sure that the application can still compile and run. If so, you are ready to begin adding in the rest of your workflow. You will begin by allowing the user to add a new mortgage application to your system. The process you will follow for this will be almost identical for all models you need to create or modify. You can walk through one of them in detail. Then you can repeat the process for other models you add, taking care to make the minor changes they require to maintain the workflow.

Going back to the LoanApplication controller, recall that two Create methods were stubbed out for you already. The first requires no alterations. It is just an action called by the MVC engine to render the LoanApplication's Create.aspx view. Once the data is submitted, you will need to run validation and persist the new record. Find the second Create method in the LoanApplication controller and replace it with the following code:

```
[AcceptVerbs(HttpVerbs.Post)]
        public ActionResult Create(LoanApplication newApp)
        {
            try
            {
                List<BrokenBusinessRule> brokenRules = newApp.GetBrokenRules();

                if (brokenRules.Count <= 0)
                {
                    newApp.ApplicationID = GetNewApplicationID();
                    _repository.Save(newApp);
                    return RedirectToAction("Index");
                }
                else
                {
                    ModelState.AddRuleViolations(brokenRules);
                    return View();
                }

            }
            catch
            {
                return View();
            }
        }
```

This Create method accepts an instance of the model for which the controller was created. This type is automatically passed back to you from the view since you elected to create a strongly typed view earlier in the sample. You then call the model's GetBrokenRules method to see if any basic validation rules were broken. Simple validation is built right into the ASP.NET MVC framework. Every MVC controller comes with an instance of a ModelStateDictionary object for storing model-specific information such as validation messages. In a moment, you will see how this dictionary works with ASP.NET MVC, and how you can use some C# 3.0 sleight of hand to make the controller validation code a little cleaner.

The generic list of broken rules is inspected to see if there are any broken rules present. If not, the new model instance is provisioned with an application ID and persisted to our XML data store. The

GetNewApplicationID function loops through all of the existing applications with a valid ID, gets the last one, and then increments the count. You can use that logic as well by adding this function to your LoanApplicationController.cs file:

```
private int GetNewApplicationID()
        {
            int appID = ((List<LoanApplication>)_repository.GetAllLoans()).
FindLast(x => x.ApplicationID != null).ApplicationID;
            return++ appID;
        }
```

It might not be perfect, but it will keep your loan applications unique for now.

The ModelState object has a built-in method named AddModelError that accepts a property name on the model and an error message to associate with it. When the MVC engine reloads the view, this ModelStateDictionary binds with the view template to automatically produce validation messages directly next to the property's HTML entry field. You could loop through your generic List of BrokenBusinessRule objects and call ModelState.AddModelError directly in the Create method. However, since you will need to call this method many times from different controllers, you should take advantage of a C# 3.0 feature known as extension methods. Extension methods allow for developers to add functionality to an existing type without affecting its inheritance model. Think of it like snapping functions onto classes without have to derive them into subtypes. Implementing an extension method is simple. Refer to Appendix A for more information.

In your sample, you just need to add an extension method to the ModelStateDictionary class that accepts a generic enumeration of BrokenBusinessRule objects and calls ModelState.AddModelError for each. Add a new class named ControllerHelpers to the Controllers directory of your project and replace the code in the file with the following:

```
using System;
using System.Web;
using System.Web.Mvc;
using ProEnt.Chap11.Models;
using System.Collections.Generic;

namespace ProEnt.Chap11.Controllers
{
    public static class ControllerHelpers
    {
        public static void AddRuleViolations(this ModelStateDictionary modelState,
        IEnumerable<BrokenBusinessRule> brokenRules)
        {
            foreach (BrokenBusinessRule brokenRule in brokenRules)
            {
                modelState.AddModelError(brokenRule.Property, brokenRule.Rule);
            }
        }
    }
}
```

Since you are using the same namespace as all the other controllers, this extension method should be available to use once it is saved to the `ControllerHelper` class.

Next, we will add the `LoanApplication`'s Create view. Right-click on the `Create` method in the `LoanApplication` controller class and generate a new strongly typed view based on `ProEnt .Chap11ProEnt.Chap11.Models.LoanApplication`, only this time select the View Content option labeled Create. The `Create.aspx` page is placed in the Views/LoanApplication directory adjacent to your `Index.aspx` page. The only change you need to make to the file is to comment out the `ApplicationID` tags in the HTML. You will be generating the application ID in your controllers, so there is no need for the users to enter it themselves. The code for the `LoanApplication's Create .aspx` view should look like this:

```
<%@ Page Title="" Language="C#" MasterPageFile="~/Views/Shared/Site.Master"
Inherits="System.Web.Mvc.ViewPage<ProEnt.Chap11.Models.LoanApplication>" %>

<asp:Content ID="Content1" ContentPlaceHolderID="TitleContent" runat="server">
        Create
</asp:Content>

<asp:Content ID="Content2" ContentPlaceHolderID="MainContent" runat="server">

    <h2>Create</h2>

    <%= Html.ValidationSummary("Create was unsuccessful. Please correct the errors
and try again.") %>

    <% using (Html.BeginForm()) {%>

        <fieldset>
            <legend>Fields</legend>
            <%--<p>
                <label for="ApplicationID">ApplicationID:</label>
                <%= Html.TextBox("ApplicationID") %>
                <%= Html.ValidationMessage("ApplicationID", "*") %>
            </p>--%>
            <p>
                <label for="ApplicationName">ApplicationName:</label>
                <%= Html.TextBox("ApplicationName") %>
                <%= Html.ValidationMessage("ApplicationName", "*") %>
            </p>
            <p>
                <label for="LoanAmount">LoanAmount:</label>
                <%= Html.TextBox("LoanAmount") %>
                <%= Html.ValidationMessage("LoanAmount", "*") %>
            </p>
            <p>
                <label for="DownPayment">DownPayment:</label>
                <%= Html.TextBox("DownPayment") %>
                <%= Html.ValidationMessage("DownPayment", "*") %>
            </p>
            <p>
                <label for="InterestRate">InterestRate:</label>
```

```
        <%= Html.TextBox("InterestRate") %>
        <%= Html.ValidationMessage("InterestRate", "*") %>
    </p>
    <p>
        <label for="LoanTerm">LoanTerm:</label>
        <%= Html.TextBox("LoanTerm") %>
        <%= Html.ValidationMessage("LoanTerm", "*") %>
    </p>
    <p>
        <label for="TaxesAndInsurance">TaxesAndInsurance:</label>
        <%= Html.TextBox("TaxesAndInsurance") %>
        <%= Html.ValidationMessage("TaxesAndInsurance", "*") %>
    </p>
    <p>
        <input type="submit" value="Create" />
    </p>
    </fieldset>

<% } %>

<div>
    <%=Html.ActionLink("Back to List", "Index") %>
</div>

</asp:Content>
```

If you compile and run the application now you should be able to add new loan applications. The Index view you generated earlier already comes equipped with the required action link to load the Create view. Still, you won't be able to edit loans you've created. Since the code pattern is almost identical for the `Edit.aspx` view, let's go ahead and create that as well. Find the first `Edit` method in the `LoanApplication`'s controller. Replace the code with the following snippet:

```
public ActionResult Edit(int id)
{
    return View(_repository.Find(id));
}
```

All you are doing here is loading the desired `LoanApplicationrecord` from our XML data store. You stored it when you created the file. Remember that most web MVC applications are stateless. Once a post is made, be it a call for create, edit, details, or index, the goal of the engine is to pull data from or push data to the repository in a manner that does not require the web application to be aware of what the user is working on. As the example grows, you will make use of some state management within the web application, but these calls will be negligible to the overall framework.

To pass the correct ID to this method, you need to jump back into the `LoanApplication` Index view and set the right parameters. If you open the `Index.aspx` file for the `LoanApplication`, you'll find two calls to the `HtmlHelper.ActionLink` method for the Edit and the Details links, respectively:

```
<%= Html.ActionLink("Edit", "Edit", new { /* id=item.PrimaryKey */ }) %> |
<%= Html.ActionLink("Details", "Details", new { /* id=item.PrimaryKey */ })%>
```

These tags populate the first column in the HTML table, rendering hyperlinks that forward the user to the proper controller and action. These helper methods are extremely convenient for outputting <a> tags to your pages with Href attributes that follow the default ASP.NET MVC routing pattern. Recall that the pattern for MVC routing is typically controller/action/parameter where the controller is the controller class, the action is a public method on the controller, and the parameter is the value or values to be passed to the action. You can construct these hyperlinks yourself, of course, but the HtmlHelper class gives us a way to tell the MVC engine to render the correct tag at runtime. The ActionLink method has a few overloads, giving developers the ability to pass controller names, parameter values, a RouteValueDictionary, and other MVC-specific constructs. In this sample, we will be using only one version of this overloaded method for consistency, but feel free to peruse the online documentation for more information about this method. For now, all we need to do is invoke another action on the same controller we're using right now. That's why these calls to ActionLink pass in only three values. The first is the visible text you want to display in the hyperlink. The second is the name of the action you wish to invoke. The third value is an object that contains the actual parameters for your route. Just about all ASP.NET MVC templates make use of the object initialize pattern. If you are not familiar with C# 30 object initialize syntax, you may want to jump to Appendix A and give it a quick read. The MVC engine uses reflection to inspect the object values you put in and pass them to their proper destinations. See the commented-out id parameter? Now you need to put that back in. Change the first ActionLink to the following:

```
<%= Html.ActionLink("Edit", "Edit", new { id = item.ApplicationID}) %> |
```

You won't be using the Details link until much later, so you can either leave it in or delete it. If you leave it in, keep in mind that the ASP.NET MVC engine automatically produces one of those famous yellow screen ASP.NET errors when clicking an ActionLink that does not point to a fully-wired action.

Now you can generate the LoanApplication Edit view. Right-click on the Edit method in the LoanApplication controller and select Add View. Click the option for creating the strongly typed view. Then select the View data class labeled ProEnt.Chap11ProEnt.Chap11.Models.LoanApplication and the View content labeled Edit. As before, leave all other defaults. A new Edit.aspx page is generated in the Views/LoanApplication folder, completed with much of the same HTML fields and helper tags we saw in the Create view. The MVC templates don't know that our application IDs are being handled behind the scenes, so we'll need to go in and comment out those fields and replace them with a hidden field. The hidden field will maintain the application ID just as well as the visible code and pass it to the controller when the user submits the page. The resulting view should look like the following:

```
<%@ Page Title="" Language="C#" MasterPageFile="~/Views/Shared/Site.Master"
Inherits="System.Web.Mvc.ViewPage<ProEnt.Chap11.Models.LoanApplication>" %>

<asp:Content ID="Content1" ContentPlaceHolderID="TitleContent" runat="server">
        Edit
</asp:Content>

<asp:Content ID="Content2" ContentPlaceHolderID="MainContent" runat="server">

    <h2>Edit</h2>

    <%= Html.ValidationSummary("Edit was unsuccessful. Please correct the errors and
try again.") %>
```

```
<% using (Html.BeginForm()) {%>

    <fieldset>
        <legend>Fields</legend>
        <%--<p>
            <label for="ApplicationID">ApplicationID:</label>
            <%= Html.TextBox("ApplicationID", Model.ApplicationID) %>
            <%= Html.ValidationMessage("ApplicationID", "*") %>
        </p>--%>
        <%= Html.Hidden("ApplicationID", Model.ApplicationID) %>
        <p>
            <label for="ApplicationName">ApplicationName:</label>
            <%= Html.TextBox("ApplicationName", Model.ApplicationName) %>
            <%= Html.ValidationMessage("ApplicationName", "*") %>
        </p>
        <p>
            <label for="LoanAmount">LoanAmount:</label>
            <%= Html.TextBox("LoanAmount", Model.LoanAmount) %>
            <%= Html.ValidationMessage("LoanAmount", "*") %>
        </p>
        <p>
            <label for="DownPayment">DownPayment:</label>
            <%= Html.TextBox("DownPayment", Model.DownPayment) %>
            <%= Html.ValidationMessage("DownPayment", "*") %>
        </p>
        <p>
            <label for="InterestRate">InterestRate:</label>
            <%= Html.TextBox("InterestRate", Model.InterestRate) %>
            <%= Html.ValidationMessage("InterestRate", "*") %>
        </p>
        <p>
            <label for="LoanTerm">LoanTerm:</label>
            <%= Html.TextBox("LoanTerm", Model.LoanTerm) %>
            <%= Html.ValidationMessage("LoanTerm", "*") %>
        </p>
        <p>
            <label for="TaxesAndInsurance">TaxesAndInsurance:</label>
            <%= Html.TextBox("TaxesAndInsurance", Model.TaxesAndInsurance) %>
            <%= Html.ValidationMessage("TaxesAndInsurance", "*") %>
        </p>
        <p>
            <input type="submit" value="Save" />
        </p>
    </fieldset>

<% } %>

<div>
    <%=Html.ActionLink("Back to List", "Index") %>
</div>

</asp:Content>
```

Finally, you'll need to replace the second `Edit` method on your controller with one that contains the logic for persisting the changes back to your repository. Replace the second `Edit` method in your `LoanApplication` controller with the following snippet:

```
[AcceptVerbs(HttpVerbs.Post)]
        public ActionResult Edit(LoanApplication app)
        {
            try
            {
                List<BrokenBusinessRule> brokenRules = app.GetBrokenRules();

                if (brokenRules.Count <= 0)
                {
                    LoanApplication oldApp = _repository.Find(app.ApplicationID);

                    //Do not remove this parent object...All aggregate objects will
be lost!!
                    oldApp.UpdateMe(app);
                    _repository.Save(oldApp);
                    return RedirectToAction("Index");
                }
                else
                {
                    ModelState.AddRuleViolations(brokenRules);
                    return View(app);
                }

            }
            catch
            {
                return View();
            }
        }
```

This method is patterned after most of the `Create` method you put in your controller previously. The only big difference is the call to `LoanApplication.Update()`. This function accepts another instance of a `LoanApplication` (in this case, the app that you just altered) and updates the record that was previously created. You do this to preserve the aggregate collections you will be adding to the class in your next task. If you delete the object altogether and replace it with the altered object, you would also need to move all of the aggregate values into the new class. The `LoanApplication`'s `Update` method preserves those collections while updating the fields from the Edit view. Aside from this call, the `Edit` method extracts any broken business rules, redisplays the validation messages, or saves the changes to your repository in the same fashion as was done in your `Create` method.

At this point, you can compile and run your application again. The application defaults to the `LoanApplication` controller's Index view as you configured previously in the `Global.asax` file. You can create new loan applications by clicking the link in Create New Hyperlink at the bottom of the grid. This takes you to the generated Create view, which provides all of the entry fields required to populate your model. The styles are simple but clean and easily modified. The ASP.NET MVC project template comes with a style sheet named `Site.css` located in the folder named `Content`. Feel free to crack this file open and spice up the view a little bit. Try entering the wrong information for a loan application to get the validation messages to execute. For example, if you click Create New, enter Darwin for the Application name, and then click Save, you should get a screen that looks like Figure 11-8.

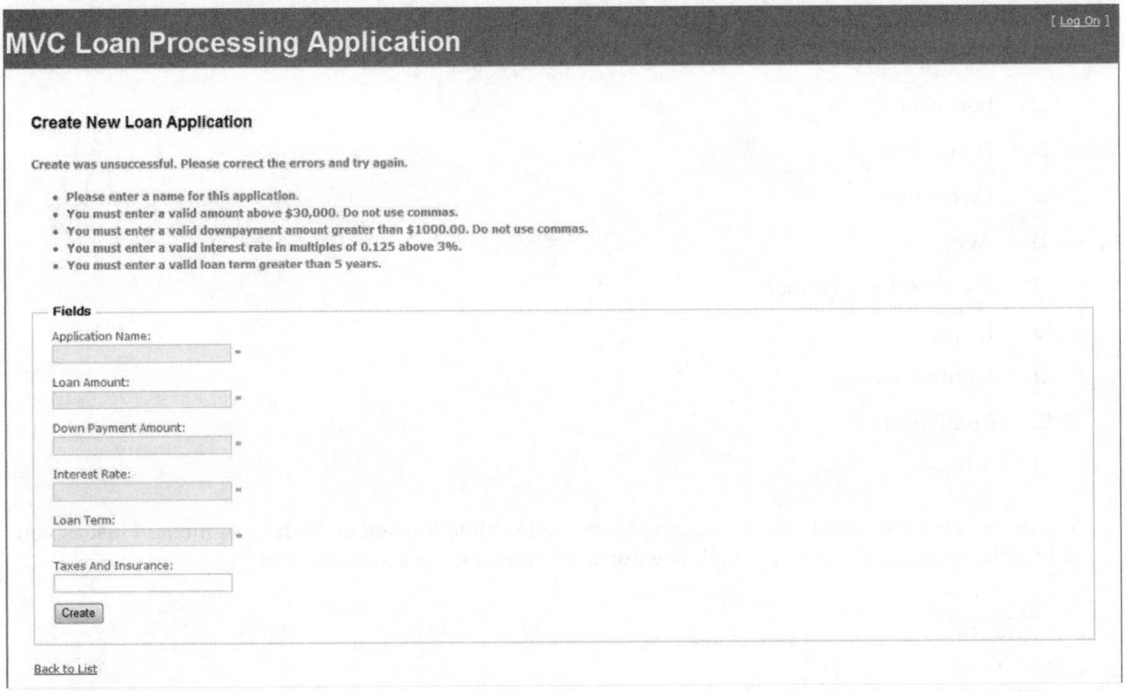

Figure 11-8

The validation messages were automatically associated with their corresponding data fields when you called the `ModelState.AddModelError` (which you placed into your `Controller Extension` method). The MVC engine, together with the generated templates, creates the red error messages based on the rule messages you passed in from your model's `GetBrokenRules` method. You may have noticed that some of the generated HTML needs to be fined-tuned. For instance, the labels on top of the data entry text fields are exact copies of the model property names to which they map. If you combined terms using camel casing, Pascal casing, or underscores, the MVC templates can't discern where or when to break apart the words. The same may go for some of your model. If you see zeros as default values for `ints` or floats it's likely because you did not mark these types as nullable. Therefore, the MVC engine forces a default value, making it difficult to validate when a user has physically entered a value of zero or skipped the field altogether. As we said earlier in this chapter, the HTML templates are meant to be a starting point only. It is up to the developer to make the necessary changes that work for their application.

Flushing Out the Model

Now that you have successfully created the components for adding and editing a loan application, you can continue to build in the rest of our model. If you refer back to the list of loan business tasks, you can see that the next bullet calls for you to add borrowers to the loan application. An application can have one or more borrowers, each one contributing to the household income, as well as to the overall assets and debts. That means that you need the ability to add and edit *n* number of borrowers per loan. We still want to keep the workflow simple and rely on the templates and conventions inherent to ASP.NET MVC.

401

A borrower will typically have a handful of simple properties to describe them to the LoanApplication. These fields include:

- Borrower ID
- First Name
- Last Name
- Age
- Social Security Number
- Employer
- Monthly Income
- Credit Score
- Address

You're also going to need to put in a method for simple validation and an UpdateMe method just as you did for the LoanApplication model. The Borrower model should look like this:

```csharp
using System;
using System.Collections.Generic;

namespace ProEnt.Chap11.Models
{
    public class Borrower
    {
        private string _borrowerID;

        public string BorrowerID
        {
            get { return _borrowerID; }
            set { _borrowerID = value; }
        }

        private string _firstName;

        public string FirstName
        {
            get { return _firstName; }
            set { _firstName = value; }
        }
        private string _lastName;

        public string LastName
        {
            get { return _lastName; }
            set { _lastName = value; }
        }

        private int? _age;
```

```csharp
public int? Age
{
    get { return _age; }
    set { _age = value; }
}

private long? _socialSecurityNumber;

public long? SocialSecurityNumber
{
    get { return _socialSecurityNumber; }
    set { _socialSecurityNumber = value; }
}

private float? _monthlyIncome;

public float? MonthlyIncome
{
    get { return _monthlyIncome; }
    set { _monthlyIncome = value; }
}

//private Employer _employer;

//public Employer Employer
//{
//    get { return _employer; }
//    set { _employer = value; }
//}

private int? _creditScore;

public int? CreditScore
{
    get { return _creditScore; }
    set { _creditScore = value; }
}

//private Address _address;

//public Address Address
//{
//    get { return _address; }
//    set { _address = value; }
//}


public override string ToString()
{
    string result;
```

```
        if (SocialSecurityNumber != null)
            result = string.Format("{0}, {1}. Age: {2}   SSN: {3}   Monthly
            Income: ${4}", LastName, FirstName, Age, SocialSecurityNumber,
            MonthlyIncome);
        else
            result = string.Format("{0}, {1}. Age: {2}   Monthly Income:
            ${3}", LastName, FirstName, Age, MonthlyIncome);
        return result;
    }

    public void UpdateMe(Borrower b)
    {
        Age = b.Age;
        FirstName = b.FirstName;
        LastName = b.LastName;
        SocialSecurityNumber = b.SocialSecurityNumber;
        MonthlyIncome = b.MonthlyIncome;
    }


    public List<BrokenBusinessRule> GetBrokenBusinessRules()
    {
        List<BrokenBusinessRule> brokenRules = new List<BrokenBusinessRule>();

        if (string.IsNullOrEmpty(FirstName))
            brokenRules.Add(new BrokenBusinessRule("FirstName", "You must enter
            a first name for this borrower."));


        if (string.IsNullOrEmpty(LastName))
            brokenRules.Add(new BrokenBusinessRule("LastName", "You must enter
            a last name for this borrower."));

        if (Age == null ||
            Age < 18)
            brokenRules.Add(new BrokenBusinessRule("Age", "You must enter valid
            age above 18 for this borrower."));


        if (MonthlyIncome == null ||
            MonthlyIncome <= 0)
            brokenRules.Add(new BrokenBusinessRule("MonthlyIncome", "You must
            enter a valid monthly income. Do not use commas."));


        if (CreditScore == null ||
            CreditScore <= 400)
```

```
brokenRules.Add(new BrokenBusinessRule("CreditScore", "You must
enter a valid credit score between 400 and 900."));

if (SocialSecurityNumber == null ||
    SocialSecurityNumber <= 0 ||
    SocialSecurityNumber.ToString().Length != 9)
    brokenRules.Add(new BrokenBusinessRule("SocialSecurityNumber",
    "You must enter a valid 9 digit SSN for this borrower. Do not use
    hyphens."));

return brokenRules;
        }
    }
}
```

Add that code as a class in the `Models` folder and you've got the second model. Just as with the `LoanApplication` model, comment out the objects you have not yet created so that you can compile the application prior to generating your strongly typed views. Borrowers are implicitly linked to `LoanApplications`. That's why if you look back at our `LoanApplication` model you'll notice a commented-out declaration of a generic list of Borrowers:

```
//private List<Borrower> _borrowers;

//public List<Borrower> Borrowers
//{
//    get { return _borrowers; }
//    set { _borrowers = value; }
//}
```

Before you uncomment, this let's walk through the same steps you did with the `LoanApplication` to generate the Create view and Edit view. The code pattern is almost identical, provided that you stick to the common MVC conventions. Create a `BorrowerController` class by right-clicking on the Controllers folder and selecting Add New ⇨ Controller. Be sure to name it `BorrowerController` and select the option for adding the `Create`, `Update`, and `Details` methods.

At this point, we need to address the issue of state management. The goal of a good web MVC model is to remain as stateless as possible. That is, as users post back and forth to and from the server, the application needs to know as little as possible about the user's session. However, there are times when some degree of state is needed, if for nothing more than a seamless user experience. In our sample, we need the ability to crack open a loan and add information to it without losing scope of the loan. The MVC operations by nature do not keep track of this. They just jump from action to action and render the correct views as if each request was the user's first. There are a lot of different ways to keep track of the loan ID on which you are working, many of which are hotly debated in the development community.

Therefore, let's abstract the model and use a state manager class to decouple the MVC code from whatever state managing tool you choose. In your utilities folder, add class named `StateManager` and replace the IDE-generated code with the following:

```
using System;
using System.Web;
using ProEnt.Chap11.Models;

namespace ProEnt.Chap11.Utilities
{
    public class StateManager : IStateManager
    {
        private ILoanApplicationRepository _repository = new
LoanApplicationRepository();

        public LoanApplication GetWorkingApplication()
        {
            return _repository.Find((int)HttpContext.Current.Session["workingID"]);
        }

        public void SetWorkingApplicationID(int ID)
        {
            HttpContext.Current.Session["workingID"] = ID;
        }
    }

    public interface IStateManager
    {
        LoanApplication GetWorkingApplication();
        void SetWorkingApplicationID(int ID);
    }
}
```

Like the abstract repository, this class implements a contract named `IStateManager`, which requires two methods: `GetWorkingApplication()` and `SetWorkingApplication()`. The `StateManager` class then implements these methods, utilizing the ASP.NET Session cache to hold the working ID of the loan. Some may not like the fact that we're using the session, but that's why this is abstract. Developers should be able to persist/handle state in whatever manner they choose without affecting the application code.

Now go back to the `BorrowerController` and replace the second `Create` method with the following:

```
[AcceptVerbs(HttpVerbs.Post)]
        public ActionResult Create(Borrower newBorrower)
        {
            try
            {
                List<BrokenBusinessRule> brokenRules = newBorrower
                .GetBrokenBusinessRules();

                if (brokenRules.Count <= 0)
                {
```

```
newBorrower.BorrowerID = Guid.NewGuid().ToString();
LoanApplication app = _stateManager.GetWorkingApplication();
app.Borrowers.Add(newBorrower);
_repository.Save(app);
return RedirectToAction("Edit", "LoanApplication", new
{ id = app.ApplicationID});
            }
            else
            {
                ModelState.AddRuleViolations(brokenRules);
                return View(newBorrower);
            }

        }
        catch
        {
            return View();
        }
    }
}
```

The code pattern here is almost identical to that which you implemented in the
LoanApplication controller's Create method. The only difference is the call to _statemanager
.GetWorkingApplication(). This gets you the ID of the loan you are working on currently, which will
set from the LoanApplication controller in just a few moments. You will need to add references to the
repository and state managers to your class:

```
private ILoanApplicationRepository _repository = new LoanApplicationRepository();
private IStateManager _stateManager = new StateManager();
```

And you will need to scope out the correct namespaces in the class's using block:

```
using ProEnt.Chap11ProEnt.Chap11.Models;
using ProEnt.Chap11ProEnt.Chap11.Utilities;
```

Go ahead and generate the Create view for this controller. Right-click on the Create method and choose
Add View. Make it a strongly typed view based on the ProEnt.Chap11.Models.Borrower class and
set the View Content to Create. Comment out the BorrowerID fields again and space out the names of
your fields. Delete the call to Html.ActionLink at the bottom. We won't be navigating back to the main
index page. Instead we will add a line for going back to the LoanApplication controller, which should
bring us back to the Edit view for the loan we are modifying. Replace the deleted ActionLink with the
following:

```
<div>
        <%=Html.ActionLink("Back to New Loan Form", "Edit", new { Controller =
        "LoanApplication", Action = "Edit", id = new ProEnt.Chap11
        .Utilities.StateManager().GetWorkingApplication().ApplicationID})%>
    </div>
```

The `ActionLink` method is almost the same as the one we declared previously, only this one has a few extra parameters and an extra object initializer field for the desired controller. The `LoanApplication` controller's `Edit` action needs the ID of the loan application, which we get by calling our `IStateManager` object. The full Create view should now look like this:

```
<%@ Page Title="" Language="C#" MasterPageFile="~/Views/Shared/Site.Master"
Inherits="System.Web.Mvc.ViewPage<ProEnt.Chap11.Models.Borrower>" %>

<asp:Content ID="Content1" ContentPlaceHolderID="TitleContent" runat="server">
        Create
</asp:Content>

<asp:Content ID="Content2" ContentPlaceHolderID="MainContent" runat="server">

    <h2>Create</h2>

    <%= Html.ValidationSummary("Create was unsuccessful. Please correct the errors
and try again.") %>

    <% using (Html.BeginForm()) {%>

        <fieldset>
            <legend>Fields</legend>
            <%--<p>
                <label for="BorrowerID">BorrowerID:</label>
                <%= Html.TextBox("BorrowerID") %>
                <%= Html.ValidationMessage("BorrowerID", "*") %>
            </p>--%>
            <p>
                <label for="FirstName">First Name:</label>
                <%= Html.TextBox("FirstName") %>
                <%= Html.ValidationMessage("FirstName", "*") %>
            </p>
            <p>
                <label for="LastName">Last Name:</label>
                <%= Html.TextBox("LastName") %>
                <%= Html.ValidationMessage("LastName", "*") %>
            </p>
            <p>
                <label for="Age">Age:</label>
                <%= Html.TextBox("Age") %>
                <%= Html.ValidationMessage("Age", "*") %>
            </p>
            <p>
                <label for="SocialSecurityNumber">Social Security Number:</label>
                <%= Html.TextBox("SocialSecurityNumber") %>
                <%= Html.ValidationMessage("SocialSecurityNumber", "*") %>
            </p>
            <p>
                <label for="MonthlyIncome">Monthly Income:</label>
                <%= Html.TextBox("MonthlyIncome") %>
                <%= Html.ValidationMessage("MonthlyIncome", "*") %>
            </p>
```

```
        <p>
            <label for="CreditScore">Credit Score:</label>
            <%= Html.TextBox("CreditScore") %>
            <%= Html.ValidationMessage("CreditScore", "*") %>
        </p>
        <p>
            <input type="submit" value="Create" />
        </p>
    </fieldset>

<% } %>

    <div>
<%=Html.ActionLink("Back to New Loan Form", "Edit", new { Controller =
"LoanApplication", Action = "Edit", id = new ProEnt.Chap11.Utilities
.StateManager().GetWorkingApplication().ApplicationID})%>
    </div>

</asp:Content>
```

Let's quickly jump back into the Borrower Controller and replace the next two `Edit` methods with the following code block:

```
public ActionResult Edit(string id)
    {
        LoanApplication app = _stateManager.GetWorkingApplication();
        Borrower b = app.Borrowers.Find(x => x.BorrowerID == id);
        return View(b);
    }


    [AcceptVerbs(HttpVerbs.Post)]
    public ActionResult Edit(Borrower b)
    {
        try
        {
            List<BrokenBusinessRule> brokenRules = b.GetBrokenBusinessRules();

            if (brokenRules.Count <= 0)
            {
                LoanApplication app = _stateManager.GetWorkingApplication();

                //Do not remove borrower or address will be lost
                Borrower existingBorrower = app.Borrowers.Find(x => x
                .BorrowerID == b.BorrowerID);
                app.Borrowers.Remove(existingBorrower);
                existingBorrower.UpdateMe(b);
                app.Borrowers.Add(existingBorrower);
                _repository.Save(app);
                return RedirectToAction("Edit", "LoanApplication", new
                { id = app.ApplicationID });
            }
            else
```

```
                    {
                        ModelState.AddRuleViolations(brokenRules);
                        return View(b);
                    }
                }
                catch
                {
                    return View();
                }
            }
        }
    }
```

Again, this is similar code to what you had before with a few adjustments. The first `Edit` method calls the `IStateManager`'s `GetWorkingApplication()` method to get a reference to the loan we're working on. It then uses a simple lambda expression to extract the right borrower from the `LoanApplication`'s Borrowers collection and passes that model instance to the view (which we haven't yet generated). The second `Edit` method checks for broken validation rules first. Then it extracts the record that exists currently, removes it from the Borrowers collection, updates the new object with all of the new information without overwriting the entire object, puts it back into the Borrowers collection, and saves the loan back into the repository.

Now generate the Edit view. Make it a strongly typed view based on the class `ProEnt.Chap11.Models.Borrower`, with a View Content of Edit. Once generated, comment out the HTML for the `BorrowerID` and replace it with hidden field just like we did with the `LoanApplication`'s Edit view. Replace the `ActionLink` at the bottom of the page with the same link you used in the Borrower's Create view to navigate back to the `LoanApplication`'s Edit view with the proper loan application ID. The page should now look like this:

```
<%@ Page Title="" Language="C#" MasterPageFile="~/Views/Shared/Site.Master"
Inherits="System.Web.Mvc.ViewPage<ProEnt.Chap11.Models.Borrower>" %>

<asp:Content ID="Content1" ContentPlaceHolderID="TitleContent" runat="server">
        Edit
</asp:Content>

<asp:Content ID="Content2" ContentPlaceHolderID="MainContent" runat="server">

    <h2>Edit</h2>

    <%= Html.ValidationSummary("Edit was unsuccessful. Please correct the errors and
    try again.") %>

    <% using (Html.BeginForm()) {%>

        <fieldset>
            <legend>Fields</legend>
            <%--<p>
                <label for="BorrowerID">BorrowerID:</label>
```

```
            <%= Html.TextBox("BorrowerID", Model.BorrowerID) %>
            <%= Html.ValidationMessage("BorrowerID", "*") %>
    </p>--%>
    <%=Html.Hidden("BorrowerID", Model.BorrowerID) %>
    <p>
        <label for="FirstName">FirstName:</label>
        <%= Html.TextBox("FirstName", Model.FirstName) %>
        <%= Html.ValidationMessage("FirstName", "*") %>
    </p>
    <p>
        <label for="LastName">LastName:</label>
        <%= Html.TextBox("LastName", Model.LastName) %>
        <%= Html.ValidationMessage("LastName", "*") %>
    </p>
    <p>
        <label for="Age">Age:</label>
        <%= Html.TextBox("Age", Model.Age) %>
        <%= Html.ValidationMessage("Age", "*") %>
    </p>
    <p>
        <label for="SocialSecurityNumber">SocialSecurityNumber:</label>
        <%= Html.TextBox("SocialSecurityNumber", Model
        .SocialSecurityNumber) %>
        <%= Html.ValidationMessage("SocialSecurityNumber", "*") %>
    </p>
    <p>
        <label for="MonthlyIncome">MonthlyIncome:</label>
        <%= Html.TextBox("MonthlyIncome", Model.MonthlyIncome) %>
        <%= Html.ValidationMessage("MonthlyIncome", "*") %>
    </p>
    <p>
        <label for="CreditScore">CreditScore:</label>
        <%= Html.TextBox("CreditScore", Model.CreditScore) %>
        <%= Html.ValidationMessage("CreditScore", "*") %>
    </p>
    <p>
        <input type="submit" value="Save" />
    </p>
    </fieldset>

<% } %>

<div>
    <%=Html.ActionLink("Back to New Loan Form", "Edit", new { Controller =
    "LoanApplication", Action = "Edit", id = new ProEnt.Chap11.Utilities
    .StateManager().GetWorkingApplication().ApplicationID})%>
</div>

</asp:Content>
```

OK, you are just about ready to run the sample again. You just need to make some adjustments to the LoanApplication's controller and Edit view to give us access to the Borrower views. Replace the first Edit method in the Loan Application's controller class with:

```
public ActionResult Edit(int id)
       {
              _stateManager.SetWorkingApplicationID(id);
              return View(_repository.Find(id));
       }
```

Then add the reference to the IStateManager object in your class, making sure to properly scope out the ProEnt.Chap11.Utilities namespace as well:

```
private IStateManager _stateManager = new StateManager();
```

The call to IStateManager.SetWorkingApplicationID will set the proper scope for this loan once we enter the Edit view. Lastly, we have to add some code to the bottom of the LoanApplication's Edit view to add some hyperlinks for adding and editing borrowers. Add the following code block to the LoanApplication Edit view directly above the Save button markup:

```
<%
                      if (Model.Borrowers.Count > 0)
                      {
            %>

            <p>
                <label for="Borrowers">Borrowers:</label>
            </p>

            <%      foreach (ProEnt.Chap11.Models.Borrower b in Model.Borrowers)
                       {
            %>
            <p>
<%=Html.ActionLink(string.Format("{0}, {1}", b.LastName, b.FirstName), "Edit",
new {Controller="Borrower", Action="Edit", id = b.BorrowerID })%>
                </p>
                <%       }
                    }
            %>

<br /><br />
            <p>
<% = Html.ActionLink("Create New Borrower", "Create", new { Controller = "Borrower",
Action = "Create" })%>
                </p>
```

This simple logic first checks to see if the `LoanApplication` being edited has any Borrowers added previously. If so, it creates `ActionLinks` for each that displays the Borrower's name and, when clicked, redirects the user to the Borrower Edit view, passing that borrower's ID. Then an `ActionLink` is added that takes the user to the Borrower's Create view for adding new borrowers to the loan.

You now have a working application for adding loans and borrowers to loans. Compile and run the application. Edit one of the loans you created previously and click the Create New Borrower link at the bottom, add a few people to the loan, and see how the `LoanApplication` Edit page stacks hyperlinks for each at the bottom of the page. Check your XML data store and verify that all of the information is being persisted. Once you become familiar with the ASP.NET MVC pattern, adding to the application becomes quite simple.

The Full Source Code

Hopefully, by this point you are starting to see a pattern developing. For each conceptual object you define in the ad hoc domain layer, a model and a controller class are declared, along with a set of views for each of the basic operations you need to perform. These classes help to separate business logic from application flow, using some of the basic MVC conventions we discussed earlier to move from task to task. As you build the rest of your website, the same patterns will be used to handle your debts, assets, employers, and so forth. Some readers may prefer slightly different web patterns than those used in this site, changing the way users flow through the application. The pattern for executing tasks is the same, however, requiring the same number of components. Therein lies one of the great benefits of ASP.NET MVC and web MVC patterns — predictability. No matter how you build you site, the separation of concerns remains roughly the same. Of course, some diehard techies may elect to alter the pattern, adding their own routing channels or even changing the source code for the ASP.NET templates, but take heed. The power of web MVC lies mostly in its known pattern. Changing that may yield some localized benefit to your application, but the cost may be a system that other MVC-savvy developers won't be able to easily support.

The full source code for the rest of the mortgage loan application is available on our book website at www.wrox.com.

Here you'll find all of the models, controller, and views needed to bring the site to life. We encourage readers to play around with this a bit. Change the repository to an nHibernate factory (or wait until the next chapter!). Change the domain model and add a collection of addresses to the borrower to account for primary address, secondary, vacation home, and the like. The more you use the ASP.NET MVC templates and familiarize yourself with the web MVC pattern the more you'll come to realize the power of its sober, logical flow.

Summary

In this chapter, we explored the web MVC framework. We reviewed some of the merits of web MVC as a pattern on many different platforms, identifying some of the key characteristics of the Model-View-Controller architecture. During this process we accomplished the following:

❑   We discussed some of the underpinnings of MVC, taking time to review the original features of older HTTP-based technology that drive the core MVC engines. By comparing web MVC with other popular web development platforms, we were able to recognize the key differences between current stateful models and the stateless model of MVC.

❑ We then jumped directly into Microsoft's web MVC platform, ASP.NET MVC, and explored the features and templates that help bridge rapid application development with sound architectural patterns.

❑ Finally, we walked through a portion of a comprehensive mortgage loan application developed using ASP.NET MVC and you familiarized yourself with the conventions and components that power an ASP.NET MVC web site.

In Chapter 12 we will take a step back and review all of the concepts we have covered in this book. We then explore a complete enterprise solution using the Mortgage Loan Application samples we've been using in other chapters, applying what we've learned.

12

Putting It All Together

We have covered a lot in this book. Starting with the basic principles of enterprise development and moving through methodologies and design patterns, we have reviewed a wide breadth of concepts that will help you design your systems for flexibility, durability, and testability. It is now time to put it all together. This final chapter fuses all of these enterprise concepts together, providing a loose roadmap for building powerful enterprise systems. This final chapter's sample code will consist of pieces of code from other chapters, culminating into one large, multifaceted system. In this chapter, we will:

❏ Review the basic principles of enterprise development

❏ Review each chapter's basic theme or concept and discuss how they apply to other areas of enterprise development

❏ Design a complex mortgage application system with multiple tiers and conceptual layers

❏ Explore some of the source code for this complex enterprise mortgage system

❏ Consider other areas of future development and how enterprise design will help to facilitate new features

One Step Back, Many Steps Forward

Often when a desired goal is difficult to achieve, it is best to take a step back and evaluate what you have done so far. In a book on this complex subject matter, nothing could be more true. Each of the chapters focuses on a very specific topic or theme. Each supplies important bits of information to help you become a more effective developer, providing you with a pattern, framework, or methodology, and a piece of focused sample code that demonstrates its purpose.

So, let's take a step back and review what this book has covered. Keep in mind as we review, that the goal here isn't just to educate you on the latest enterprise patterns and technologies but to help you understand how to think in terms of patterns and practices. As we review each part we've covered, take a moment to see how the principles discussed play a larger role in our development lifecycle.

The Concepts

In Chapters 1 and 2 of this book, we begin to explore the concepts of enterprise architecture and enterprise development. We review how enterprise architecture, by its nature, aims to provide software that supports core business needs at a comprehensive level. Enterprise architecture usually supports, or in some cases subsumes, many of the smaller applications used for business automation. It aims to unify their underlying data or processes in a manner that helps to them to share their processes as services with other members of the business. Enterprise development describes some of the core values that drive the building of enterprise systems. At the heart of these values lie four fundamental tenets:

Reliability

Writing reliable code means much more than just making sure that the code compiles and produces no runtime errors. It means breaking the code into modular pieces that can be tested with few or no dependencies on other pieces of code. This modularization ultimately increases testability, helping to expose potential bugs and exceptions as the code base augments.

Flexibility

Flexibility lies at the heart of enterprise development. Business requirements can change on a dime, and your code needs to accommodate these changes with relative ease. The structure of an enterprise code base should allow for changes in isolation, without the proverbial ripple affect often experienced when adding features or functions to a rapidly developed application.

Separation of Concerns

Supporting the need for reliability and flexibility requires a strong understanding of separation. Each unit of code should have a single, distinct purpose or value. This functionality should be testable on its own, embracing some of the tenets of the loose coupling and Test Driven Development (TDD) methodologies to emulate the behavior of the unit without creating or using other related objects.

Reusability

Sometimes a little upfront investment pays off handsomely as your system grows. Taking the time to separate your code into distinct, flexible units increases not only reliability and testability but also reusability. The more modular your code is, the better your chances are of being able to reuse portions of it when the same functionality is needed elsewhere in your system.

Maintainability

Perhaps the strongest argument for enterprise development is the ability to maintain your software after it has been released. Too often in the RAD world we find that a popular application or service cannot be grown, or even supported, because of the poor design of its internals. The mixing of features into different classes, as well as the mixing of logic in unrelated modules, makes maintenance a nightmare. As bugs arise and the code begins to act unpredictably, developers are not easily able to test the code and find the negative factors affecting it. Good enterprise design can help identify negative factors, as well as flush them out early through continuous unit testing.

The Big Picture

If you have been developing software for the last few years, chances are that you've heard of some of these concepts before. The goal of Part I was not only to define each of them correctly but also to codify them in a manner that can help you make design decisions at all levels of detail. By understanding the role that each value plays in the broad picture of software development, you should be better prepared for some of the concepts introduced in Parts II and III.

The Code

Chapters 3, 4, and 5 discussed the best ways to organize your code to better embrace the core values established in Chapters 1 and 2. Here, we explored the concepts of loose coupling and Test Driven Development patterns. You were exposed to some of the practices available for refactoring existing code as well. These practices aim to pry apart some of the dependencies that otherwise hamper testing efforts and lead to less maintainable code.

Chapter 3 began with the concept of decoupling classes. The vast majority of existing .NET code mixes dependencies from otherwise unrelated units of code. This stems from a strong culture of rapid application development (RAD) that encourages the quick writing or generation of .NET code using RAD-enabled tools. Platforms such as ActiveX and ASP.NET tend to encourage developers to add their code within the hooks and events of the framework itself, coupling tasks to areas of code specifically intended for the UI or some other portion of the framework. This chapter walked you through the concept of modularization, demonstrating how to first separate code into individual units of code, each designed for a specific goal or purpose. Once the code is more modular, developers can begin to isolate dependencies and separate out code in preparation for applying degrees of abstraction that enable testing.

Chapter 4 exposed you to the concept of Test Driven Development. While the previous chapter addressed the concepts of separating out existing code, this one focused on the concepts good code design from the beginning. Using a sample Tic Tac Toe game as a point of reference, it discussed the concept of defining requirements and then molding the code to the requirements, using the concepts defined in Chapter 3. Refactoring also plays a large role in this chapter, which explains how to alter the internals of the code without affecting its external behavior. The chapter then moved into the subject of testing for dependencies, focusing on the concept of mocking. Using abstract typing and a builder model that injects abstractly typed dependencies into class constructors, you were shown how to emulate instances of other classes for the purposes of testing units in varying conditions and states.

Chapter 5 focused on resimplifying the development process. Test Driven Development can be a lot of work for the developer. Although the added testability of code does increase the quality of the intended service or application, the development overheard is dramatically increased. Developers in need of consuming classes with complex dependencies and object graphs are forced to write a lot more code to put their objects in a valid state. Whereas developers once relied on constructors to abstract them from this work, TDD patterns forces them to be intimately aware of what an object needs and how to initialize them. There have been a handful of solutions to this problem. The first few are basic patterns that designers can implement to prevent consuming developers from having to know too much. The Factory pattern was introduced in this chapter, providing a point of reference for the creation of abstract preinitialized types. However, the consuming code is still tightly coupled to a type of class they need. Likewise, since the increase in dependencies requires a proliferation of factory creation methods, this pattern isn't always ideal. A second option, the Service Locator pattern, was also explored as a means of simplification. With this option, the consumer passes a string identifier to a service locator method, which in turn creates the correct instance of a class and passes it to the client. Yet the string identifier still tightly couples the caller to the service locator. As with the Factory pattern, as dependencies increase, both the Service Locator and the client need to change to accommodate the increased scope.

The last solution presented was the Inversion of Control, or IoC, container. Also referred to as the Dependency Injection (DI) container, this model places the responsibility of object creation and initialization on a container service. The service provides a single point of context, from which instances of objects are requested by name out of the container. The job of the container is to know what the object's dependencies are and attach them to the requested object implicitly. Different containers have different features to make both the object consumption and the object definitions easier to maintain. Many provide features for automatically wiring up objects by inspecting their constructors and public properties for objects that might also have definitions within the container. The chapter concluded with a brief exploration of popular IoC containers available.

The Big Picture

Chapters 1 and 2 of the book dealt mostly with theory and principle. Chapters 3, 4, and 5 jumped into the practical, exposing you to some of the basic code patterns that help to achieve the core tenets of enterprise development. These patterns may seem alien to seasoned Windows programmers. Many Microsoft developers are accustomed to a somewhat limited notion of object-oriented programming. While the notions of instancing, encapsulation, and even limited degrees of inheritance might be familiar, most have exposure to these concepts in their simplest form. To that end, the increased abstraction of types for testability, as well as strong modularization of code into individual units, may seem uncomfortable to use at first. Yet most agree that understanding these approaches and applying them early will not only facilitate better, more maintainable code but also fit nicely into many of the modern patterns and practices embraced by the enterprise community.

The Patterns

Chapters 6 through 12 delved deeply into the different patterns that drive many enterprise systems. In the second half of the book we explored different approaches to enterprise design and discussed some of the pros and cons of each. Each enterprise system has its own needs and requirements. Moreover, enterprise systems often encompass a few varying approaches for its many different facets. What works well for middleware might not work well for the UI. An MVP pattern well suited to a small web application might not provide enough separation for the persistence layer. It is important for developers to familiarize themselves with a number of different code patterns before making design decisions. If the system is well designed and meets the core values of enterprise architecture, developers will find increased flexibility as they add features or applications to their model.

Middleware

Chapter 7 took a deep dive into middleware patterns. Like the first half of the book, it began with some theory and principle. Sound enterprise design begins with a modeling of business processes. The idea of business modeling is a core concept when designing enterprise middleware. Too often developers jump quickly into code without first understanding the business demands. This can lead to confusing code that loses its focus on the core requirements. Understating not only what your business needs but also how it operates is paramount to the successful development of a system. Most business needs exist without any connection to technical features or frameworks. The need for a system to accomplish a business task has little or nothing to do with how a system stores its data or how the internals of a system execute business rules.

The chapter then walked through three common approaches to handling business logic. The first pattern is known as the Transactional or Transaction Script pattern. As its name suggests, it provides for the business requirements at the method level, implementing functions that relate to individual business tasks. The model typically employs one or more business managers or providers. Each manager contains methods relevant to the task grouping that a manager provides. An example is `OrderManager` with methods such as `ProcessOrder`, `AddItemToCart`, and `CheckOrderStatus`. Another example might be a `CustomerProvider`, with methods such as `GetCustomer`, `ChangeCustomerAddress`, or `DeleteCustomer`. The methods often satisfy specific use cases defined during the business-modeling process.

A use case is a description of system behavior as it responds to a request that originates externally.

The transaction model is useful when developing small systems or applications that may require quick delivery through multiple developers. The code is simple to follow and easy to implement, although it's not very flexible or extensible. The managers or providers provide a necessary layer of separation, allowing developers to keep their code modular and testable.

The next pattern discussed was the Active Record pattern. Active Record is a way of abstracting developers from the database design while providing a middleware model that remains closely aligned with data relationships. It is the first mention of what is known as object relational mapping, or ORM. In the Active Record pattern, business objects are created to match or emulate tables in the database. The business objects contain similar names and maintain many of the same connections to other objects that developers would find in the application's data store. Business objects also contain business rules, performing validation and changes to information as entered by users at runtime. Active Record objects almost always have a one-to-one relationship with the database entities to which they are related. Developers are relieved of the need to understand the database itself, and in many cases they do not need to write any database code to persist the data. Active Record is a popular pattern in many midsized applications. It is ideal for systems that are strongly data-centric by design, with middleware that exists as a thin veil over a strongly data-driven model.

The third pattern discussed is Domain Model pattern. In this pattern developers create business objects entirely separate from the persistence layer. Looking back to the beginning of the chapter, the business model itself becomes the entire focus of the middleware design, with objects and entities developed solely based on business behaviors and needs. The Domain Model is often broken into multiple conceptual tiers, with layers providing functionality for business tasks, persistence, and mapping between the domain and persistence layers. The Domain Model can employ ORMs for mapping middleware objects to database entities. However unlike the Active Record pattern, this model strongly separates the business logic from the code that persists. This introduces the concept of persistence ignorance, or PI.

There are other popular patterns for creating Enterprise Middleware; this only scratched the surface. When expanding your system into different business departments, you are encouraged to explore patterns akin to enterprise service buses and other widely served bus models. The purpose of Chapter 7 was not to box you into a limited range of choices but rather to demonstrate the differences among the popular patterns available. Lots of programmers assume that all enterprise patterns apply only to large systems serving thousands of users. In truth, some of the best enterprise applications feed a small group of users but still implement a design that provides for flexibility and maintainability. Ultimately, any model that accommodates for the core values of enterprise development is a viable option for one's system design.

Persistence

Chapter 8 continued where Chapter 7 left off, exploring some of the enterprise design patterns for persistence. As systems grow and become more intricate, developers often benefit from a strong separation of the business code from the code that stores and saves the data. Some of the design patterns commonly found in middleware couple these two layers for development simplicity. Yet these simplified patterns don't easily allow for extensibility of persistence and often forces the developer to become familiar with the technical details of database programming. Separation of the data layer helps to reduce the amount of database programming a developer needs to perform, while increasing the flexibility of persistence through the use of conceptual loose coupling.

A traditional approach to data separation provides for direct database calls from within (or conceptually close to) the business logic. This approach is loosely referred to as the data access layer, or DAL. DALs conveniently extend the Transaction Script pattern described in Chapter 7, providing for ADO.NET code that explicitly invokes database calls and directly handles cursors and recordsets. Ostensibly, this provides for a simple model that's easy to implement. However, development overhead is increased, as programmers are required to understand all of the requisite plumbing that drives basic data connectivity.

We then revisited the concept of object-relational mapping as a way to abstract the developers from some of the cumbersome tasks germane to database programming. ORM models can be ideal for keeping the developers focused on the business code, as it removes the need to write the code to support the data plumbing. Basic tasks such as reads, inserts, and updates are supported within the ORM models themselves. This pattern also helps to support uniformity in the data access layer. The benefits of this model are clear if your system is strongly data-driven, and it can help to catalyze the development process, especially when using an existing ORM framework.

Unfortunately, not all systems are ideal for Data-Driven Design. Many enterprise systems have the need to keep the business model isolated from the persistence mechanism itself. This approach is referred to as Model First development and requires a few extra conceptual layers. The domain model exists on its own. It is designed solely with the business in mind, and satisfies business requirements with little or no knowledge of other consuming or dependent technical components. A separate persistence mechanism is then introduced, commonly using the abstract repository pattern as a means to save data to any number of loosely coupled data stores. A mapping layer is then required to translate between the domain model and the repository, with the goal of keeping the domain model as persistence ignorant as possible.

The User Interface

Chapters 9, 10, and 11 discussed the enterprise patterns commonly used for the user interface (UI). User interface design has a somewhat muddled history in the Microsoft world. Much of it has fallen prey to the whims of rapid application development tools. Chapter 9 was an exploration of the history of user interface design on the Windows platform. Beginning with simple command-line interfaces and walking you through the evolution of rapid application development tools, we uncovered some of the previous shortcomings of interface design and how new patterns strive to solve those shortcomings. The chapter also discussed the evolution of the Model-View-Controller, or MVP, pattern. MVC has grown over time, spreading its tendrils into myriad platforms and frameworks, most recently (and notably) the web MVC framework model found in Ruby on Rails and ASP.NET MVC.

Chapter 10 introduced the Model-View-Presenter pattern, or MVP. MVP has become a popular pattern for providing degrees of separation in user interfaces. It is especially useful for separating existing UI code, as it allows for the modification of existing UI platforms. MVP is a natural evolution of the MVC model into a pattern specifically targeting testability. Like MVC, the Model typically contains the business code and data to be displayed and received from the end user. The View represents the physical user interface itself. This layer most often contains visible, interactive artifacts such as buttons, lists, and menus, and is usually defined in HTML or some other UI-specific construct. Views are coupled with specifically defined interfaces, exposing public methods and properties with which the Presenter can interact abstractly. The View itself implements the interface, satisfying the abstract contract with other, consuming objects. The Presenter is also coupled with a View and handles the events invoked by the user. Presenters act as coordinators of UI events and mediate data transmission between the View and the Model. Presenters hold abstract references of the View interfaces internally, setting the reference to the physical page that implements the interface when created. This allows for testing the Presenter without having to start the View engine and pass in the physical UI. MVP is popular for both its testability and its flexibility. The pattern provides for a loosely coupled model that separates out the individual UI concerns, without forcing the developer into a strict framework or runtime model. For this reason, MVP is widely used for refactoring legacy code into well-designed, testable enterprise systems.

Chapter 11 reacquainted you with the Model-View-Controller pattern for web programming. Continuing where Chapter 9 left off, you were introduced to the latest and most powerful version of the MVC model to date. This new MVC pattern takes its cue from the Ruby on Rails (RoR) community. The RoR creators defined the model for the Ruby platform, which has since been known as the Web MVC framework. Web MVC is a more rigid platform than the web frameworks with which most web programmers are familiar. Unlike MVP, Web MVC forces the developer to create various objects with different roles and responsibilities. Each of these objects has an expected interaction by the MVC engine and only functions when the objects are created and consumed correctly. Unlike many of the popular web frameworks to date, the Web MVC model is necessarily stateless. It builds on the patterns of older HTTP-based communication mechanisms, invoking controller actions as explicit actions within an HTML form. Routing in a Web MVC model is entirely different from common web routing. Rather than navigating to web pages in specific project folders, the Web MVC routing model calls for a URI that clearly contains the name of the controller and action to be invoked, along with the parameters to be passed to the action.

In the Web MVC pattern, The Model contains the business rules and data for a particular business entity. Controllers expose public methods called *actions* that coordinate between the Models and Views, as well as between Models and other Controllers. The Views are very finite user interfaces, with a brief and limited lifecycle. Views can employ the use of different engines, such as ASP.NET or nVelocity. View engines need not provide the same state-rich features of other web platforms; they need only to provide server-side scripting for dynamic HTML generation. ASP.NET MVC is a newly released, emerging Web

MVC platform. It provides the MVC engine for real-time MVC routing and processing. It also provides a series of templates for automatically generating Controllers and Views based on strongly typed models. This combination of templates, along with strict adherence to the MVC runtime routing patterns, constitutes a balance between pervasive testability and rapid application development.

The Big Picture

The power behind design patterns lies not only in their individual implementations but also in their combinations. When developing enterprise systems, it's important to understand that no one solution is right for everything. Whereas one system may benefit from the use of an MVC model calling a Domain pattern middleware server with a service locator, another may be better off with a handful of simple MVP forms that persist through an Active Record pattern. A legacy system might be due for a light refactoring into a Transaction Script pattern, while a newer system may be ideal for a strong Domain pattern with an abstract repository for persisting to many different data stores. Enterprise systems don't all have a single size, type, or flavor that lumps them all together. Like small applications, they come in different shapes and sizes and, thus, require different solutions. You should come away from Part III with a strong understanding of enterprise *thinking*, conceptually partitioning the various sections of their system according to their purpose, and applying the models or frameworks that best suit that section's need.

Being Holistic — The Big, BIG Picture

The final example posted for this book is a comprehensive mortgage processing system. Building on the concepts we've covered, it contains multiple facets comprising of all of the core patterns and methodologies discussed in this book. Each piece endeavors to extend on a chapter code sample or application. Although some of the code has been slightly altered, the spirit of each piece has remained intact. Ostensibly, the system consists of three core components: The mortgage processing service, a simple client mortgage calculator, and a separate web-based mortgage prequalification application. Figure 12.1 depicts how the different portions of the system relate to one another.

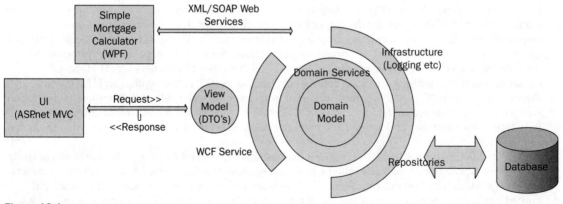

Figure 12-1

The Mortgage Service

The mortgage service is a middleware system that provides the core services needed to apply for, process, or inquire about a mortgage loan. It is comprised of multiple conceptual tiers, each contributing to an integral piece of the overall process. At its heart lies the mortgage calculations and business rules, designed using the patterns discussed in Chapters 6 and 7. The persistence layer employs the use of an abstract repository as reviewed in Chapter 8. A Service Locator pattern is used to expose its public methods to consumers, packaging the requested data into slimmed-down classes called Data Transfer Objects (DTOs). These objects are simple examples of the DTOs mentioned in Chapters 6 and 8. Readers will also note that all of the classes designed are loosely coupled and highly testable. Unit tests are available with the source code, demonstrating the benefit of a modular design pattern. Spring.Net is also leveraged here, providing an Inversion of Control (IoC) container to simplify complex object initialization.

The Simple Mortgage Calculator

The first of two systems to consume the mortgage service tier is a simple client program written with Windows Presentation Foundation (WPF). The purpose of this application is to demonstrate the flexibility of a service-based enterprise system in a multi-tiered environment. The mortgage service serves out data in a number of different fashions, some of which are fitted for generic, platform-independent calls. The calculations are served out using a web service written using the Windows Communication Foundation (WCF) pattern we reviewed in Chapter 6. Since we kept the same Http bindings defined in the configuration file, any external system provisioned for XML-based SOAP can execute mortgage calculations through this service. The design of the application is irrelevant since it uses the same WCF pattern for interpreting the XML SOAP messages into C# primitives. The Model-View-Presenter (MVP) pattern was preserved from the earlier example, with unit tests added to highlight the testability of the pattern.

The Mortgage Loan Prequalification Application

The Mortgage Application Processor is a revamping of the web sample we built in Chapter 11. Like the simple mortgage calculator, it, too, is a consumer of the mortgage service. However this application is more complicated, requiring more data from the middleware server iteratively. Using the web MVC model, the application collects data from the user and applies it to the correct object in the local mortgage model. Using a WCF service layer, data is exchanged with the mortgage service using DTOs. The DTOs are created using a mapping class that facilitates the creation of DTO instances from domain objects, and vice-versa. Business rules are applied using the same pattern implemented in Chapter 11, with extra rules added to determine the status of an application once all data has been submitted. The ASP.Net MVC framework provides the base pattern for the web model, with ASP.Net web pages used for the View engine.

The source code for all three projects can be found on the book's website at `www.wrox.com`.

Final Thoughts

Switching to enterprise development is tricky business. It requires focus, patience, and an open attitude to learning new things. The intent of this book was to provide a window into the latest enterprise trends to help ease that transition. Each topic discussed warrants deeper exploration before you can fully embrace them. We encourage interested readers to take some time to research each of the chapters' themes. An online search on any topic will yield ample blogs, forums, usenet groups, and online communities that host enterprise discussions. Perhaps the most important thing to remember during your transition is that you should always use what works for your business. The enterprise and open source communities don't always keep that in mind. Oftentimes subject matter debates sway towards the academic, focusing on the intricacies of a pattern and losing focus of broader goals. Keep in mind that the primary intent of enterprise development is to increase quality, flexibility, and ease of maintenance. If you find yourself in a position where the patterns you've implemented are causing more harm than good don't be afraid to refactor or roll it out. Too often developers marry themselves to a pattern or methodology simply because the complexity seems to justify its use. Don't fall prey to this insanity. You want your code to be modular and testable, but not overcomplicated. Like any other software project, the correct enterprise solution will be a balance between your business needs and the best tools for the job.

Summary

In this concluding chapter, we take a step back to assess all of the themes and topics explored in this book.

❑ We begin with a comprehensive review of all of the chapters in the three parts and discuss how each section affects the way you approach system design. Beginning with enterprise theory and core values, then continuing with coding and testing methodologies, you are reacquainted with the basic theory and approaches that affect the way you write your code.

❑ We then reexamine the various design patterns outlined in the second half of the book, taking the time to understand their place in the grander scheme of enterprise design.

❑ We briefly reviewed the design of the final enterprise mortgage system, discussing the three major pieces and the fundamental designs they support.

❑ The chapter concluded with some brief thoughts on enterprise design, and some important points to remember when making the transition to enterprise development.

C#.NET Primer

The term *.NET* (pronounced "dot net") has a lot of different meanings. At a high level, it is Microsoft's development platform for designing software and building applications targeting the Windows operating system. It is also a term used to define Microsoft's server platform initiatives, representing a loose collection of server-based products that run distributed applications and support large, multi-tiered systems. .NET is a term also used to define the latest system runtime environment, enabling applications written in different languages to execute and behave similarly. In this appendix, we'll be discussing how to build programs and design software using .NET languages and targeting the latest .NET runtime.

.NET is unique to all previous Microsoft development platforms and is quite different from most development platforms for non-Windows operating systems. Unlike older, more traditional programming environments, .NET programs can be written in one of many different .NET-enabled languages. Developers familiar with languages such as Visual Basic, C++, Java, or even older mainframe languages such as Cobol can leverage their skills sets by building .NET programs using their language's .NET equivalent. This helps to make the .NET learning curve a little less steep.

Of course, understanding .NET programming goes well beyond the simple syntax of disparate languages. Modern software development requires programmers to have at least a cursory understanding of object-oriented programming patterns. Object orientation, or OO, can help you separate your code into tighter, reusable components. Although not every .NET program demands a strong degree of OO design, it is important for .NET programmers to be familiar with object-oriented concepts as consumption of the .NET SDK relies on them. In this section, we will review and discuss many aspects of .NET programming, along with the basic principles behind it.

.NET Concepts

.NET represents a dramatic shift in the way we think about software. More than just a series of libraries and APIs, the .NET Framework is a collection of services that manage code development, compilation, and execution. Understanding some of the fundamental differences between .NET and previous Microsoft SDKs is the key to building well-designed, full-featured applications.

Multiple Languages

One of the facets of .NET that makes it unique is the ability to program in multiple languages. Traditional development platforms require a programmer to be familiar with a signal language targeted for a limited compiler which turned the code into platform-specific machine code. .NET works a bit differently. Rather than a single language and compiler the .NET SDK comes equipped with multiple compilers, each for a different .NET-targeted language. Each compiler creates code targeted not for a specific platform but rather for the .NET runtime environment. Because of this, programs can be created with modules and classes built in different languages. Following is a list of available .NET languages:

- ❏ C#
- ❏ VB.NET
- ❏ J#
- ❏ C++
- ❏ Cobol
- ❏ Python
- ❏ Jscript
- ❏ PHP
- ❏ JCL
- ❏ Ruby

Flexible Runtime Environment

Equally important as the language compilers is the .NET Runtime Environment. When building programs in .NET, compilers no longer turn modules of programming code into machine code. Rather, each compiler takes the .NET code and turns it into Microsoft Intermediary Language, or MSIL. MSIL is a commonly understood code base for the .NET Runtime and represents the midpoint in a program's compilation lifecycle. Once a program has been compiled into MSIL, it is the job of the runtime environment to complete the code's transformation into machine code when the program is initially executed. This is known as Just-in-Time compilation. This compilation pattern allows .NET developers to essentially ignore the target machine on which their code will run, trusting only in the runtime environment itself to effectively translate the correct code. That kind of abstraction not only simplifies development of desktop applications, it also helps developers build applications that target other devices, such as servers and portable mobile devices.

Garbage Collection

Memory management has always been a burdensome task for application developers. Previous platforms required users to null out memory blocks used to maintain code state, which meant keeping constant track of variables, pointers, references, and instance objects. Failure to effectively manage your memory often leads to memory leaks. Large amounts of leaks over extended periods of time inevitably has a negative effect on both the running application as well as the machine on which it is executing. .NET alleviates the burden of memory management by implementing garbage collection. Garbage collection is an unobtrusive service that runs within the .NET runtime. It looks for unreachable object references and variables and automatically frees up their memory space for use by other applications. You can think of garbage collection as a low-priority thread that constantly runs in the background of your runtime environment. As long as .NET applications can execute on your machine, garbage collection will sweep up after them.

The presence of garbage collection also changes the manner by which users implement their code. Since lower-level memory management is now handled by the runtime, direct access to memory blocks is not allowed. That means that coders cannot instantiate or reference objects or variables using pointers. Instead, all instances of objects are handled by way of an object reference, the .NET equivalent of the pointer. Many users of third and fourth generation languages are already quite used to coding without pointers. However, veterans of older languages such as C++ may have to adjust to a slightly more abstracted level of memory control.

No More COM

.NET replaces Microsoft's previous platform development model known as the Component Object Model, or COM. COM has its roots in much older version of Windows programming. It, too, was designed to be (somewhat) language or platform independent. However, the level of skill set needed to properly model and control interchangeable components was necessarily high. In addition, the memory management portion was unpredictable, requiring coders at almost all levels to implement object and variable cleanup to be safe. COM applications have classes that share a single interface, which it used to invoke methods on one another. Since this level of interoperability was relatively low, various aspects of state had to remain isolated. This primarily manifested itself in the COM threading model, which often made it difficult to marshal data in between objects at runtime. Thankfully, the .NET platform replaces all of this. To be fair, .NET doesn't really *replace* COM, but rather abstracts from it, providing a layer of management with which developers and users need not be concerned. COM libraries are quite prolific throughout the Windows OS. Though many COM libraries are being redesigned completely in .NET, a good deal of the .NET SDK invokes COM objects and COM servers. However what's important to understand is that the runtime environment that sits on top of COM provides the much needed level of indirection to help developers create multi-threaded, multifaceted applications without the need to understand the gross underpinnings of the core Windows framework.

> *The .NET SDK still has not completely replaced all COM libraries. For this reason, .NET applications can utilize specialty wrapper classes known loosely as interop classes. Interop is an advanced concept which falls outside of the scope of this tutorial. However, developers interested in incorporating .NET into older VB/COM/ATL applications should familiarize themselves with these classes.*

Programming in C#

C# is a relatively new language created by Microsoft for developing .NET applications. It is a C-based language, consisting of many of the same elements of syntax and flow control associated with the languages C and C++. However, unlike its pointer-laden predecessor, C# is a much cleaner language, flush with new features and simpler programmatic tenets to facilitate a shallower learning curve. Still, mastering C# takes plenty of time and experience. However web designers and developers will find that understanding some of the key concepts can help when reading Microsoft code samples, especially those pertaining to Windows Live and ASP.NET.

Types and Entities

When it comes to delivering code, web developers don't require as much design as straight C# programmers. After all, just about all web code is contained within a web page, its natural vehicle of delivery. Even though the same page-specific model is used in ASP.NET, all C# code is delivered within strongly defined templates of code called types. C# comes with a great many built-in types, some of which are basic values types, such as integers and characters, others are complex types built into external libraries in the .NET SDK. However, the power of an object-oriented language like C# is the ability to create new user-defined types. User-defined types can become a fairly in depth topic when it comes to object-oriented design, so for the purposes of simplicity let's just say that types manifest themselves most commonly in one of four C# items: classes, objects, structs, and interfaces.

System Defined Types

The following is a list of simple .NET types, their full name in the .NET SDK, their sizes, and their descriptions:

Keyword	Size (bytes)	Description
byte	1	8-bit value ranging from 0 to 255 (unsigned)
sbyte	1	8-bit value ranging from -128 to 127 (signed)
char	1	Unicode character
bool	1	true or false
short	2	16-bit value (signed)
ushort	2	16-bit value (unsigned)
int	4	32-bit value (signed)
uint	4	32-bit value(unsigned)
float	4	Single-precision floating point value
double	8	Double-precision floating point value
decimal	8	Fixed-precision number up to 28 digits past the decimal point. Does not undergo standard floating point number rounding. Requires an appended suffix of "m".
long	8	64-bit value (signed)
ulong	8	64-bit value (unsigned)
object	n/a	Base type used for references of class instances
string	n/a	An immutable sequence of Unicode characters

User-Defined Types

- ❑ **Classes:** User-defined type definitions that can contain functions, properties, variables, and other user-defined types. Classes represent a blueprint for a type; many instances can be created from a single class definition. Classes are reference types — each instance is allocated to the heap.

- ❑ **Objects:** Individual instances of a class created by using the new keyword. Each object represents a single copy of a class, maintaining its own state separate from like copies of the same class.

- ❑ **Structs:** User-defined type definitions that can contain functions, properties, and variables. Similarly to classes, structs can be instanced using the new keyword. However, structs cannot be inherited or derived from. Structs are value types — each instance is allocated on the stack.

- ❑ **Interfaces:** User-defined type containing definitions of function signatures, properties, and events without any implementation. Interfaces cannot be instantiated using the new keyword. They represent a binding contract for a type, defining a minimal set of rules for the type.

Scope and Declaration

Like all things programming, C# code requires declaration and a varied degree of scope. All C# code is compiled into classes. Classes represent a sort of blueprint for a user-defined type or entity. As classes are instanced using the new keyword, copies of the class are held in memory and are called objects. The new keyword can be used to create as many instances of a class a computer can handle, thus one class can become multiple instances or objects.

Classes generally contain functions, properties, and variables. Web developers can think of functions and variables similarly to functions and variables on a web page. Once created, they can be invoked to set values and state, or to execute various tasks from different points in your code. C# applications can have multiple levels of scope. When working with C# for web applications, one should be familiar with these basic declaration keywords (known as *modifiers*):

- ❑ **Public:** Used to declare a function, property, or variable that is accessible from any other calling or consuming object.

- ❑ **Private:** Used to declare a function, property, or variable accessible only from within the containing class or entity. Items with this declaration cannot be accessed from inheriting classes or other classes on the same assembly or library.

- ❑ **Protected:** Used to declare a function, property, or variable accessible only from within the containing entity or inheriting entities. Items with this declaration cannot be accessed or invoked from other entities on the same assembly or library.

- ❑ **Static:** Modifier that defines a method, property, or variable as class-based only. Instances of the item cannot be created, and instances of the containing entity all share access to the same state of the item.

- ❑ **Internal:** Used to declare a function, property, or variable accessible from any calling or consuming object in the same assembly or library. Items with this declaration cannot be accessed by classes or objects on different entities or libraries. Internal scope is the default accessibility for items that are declared without an explicit modifier.

- ❏ **Sealed:** Modifier used to define a class as uninheritable. Classes declared with this keyword cannot be derived from by other classes.

- ❏ **Virtual:** Modifier used to define a function or property as overridable. Classes inheriting from the declared item's container classes can reimplement the item using the `overrides` keyword.

- ❏ **Abstract:** Modifier used to define a class, method, or property as requiring derived implementation. Classes inheriting from the declared item or declared item's container must reimplement the item, using the `overrides` keyword.

- ❏ **Overrides:** Modifier used to identify a method or property as one that is reimplementing a predefined abstract or virtual entity in the parent class.

Properties, Delegates, and Events

C# has a few interesting features that can help to make your code design more efficient and compact. Properties, for example, are a C#-specific implementation that facilitates class encapsulation. As a concept, encapsulated properties are not new to object-oriented design. Languages such as C++, Java, and Visual Basic have supported propertied patterns for some time. In these languages, developers would declare private variables and then expose them through public ally accessible functions. Yet their support was more of a well-known best practice, utilizing user-written accessor functions and contrived naming conventions. In C#, properties are more compact, consisting of a single definition with either a set block, a get block, or both. In this fashion, properties can be designed much more intuitively. Likewise, developers using popular IDEs such as Visual Studio .NET 2005 will notice that properties appear as single items in an autocomplete drop-down menu, rather than as two or more disparate methods connected to one another merely through their like naming conventions. The following example shows two property definitions exposing two privately declared variables. Note that privately declared variables are often prefixed with a leading underscore, and that the keyword `value` used in the *set* blocks represents any value or state to be assigned to a property at runtime.

```
private string _firstName;
private string _lastName;


    public string FirstName
    {
        set
        {
            this._firstName = value;
        }

        get
        {
            return this._firstName;
        }
    }

    public string FirstName
    {
        set
        {
            this._lastName = value;
        }
```

```
        get
        {
            return this._lastName;
        }
    }
```

Delegates are an entirely new item for those new to C# programming and a powerful feature of the .NET SDK. Delegates are, for lack of a better description, strongly typed function pointers. They are object references that point to other methods and functions for the purpose of indirect method invocation. Programmers familiar with function pointers might remember that they are convenient vehicles for background processes and callback methods. The same holds true for delegates. As a strongly typed entity, delegates can be declared and attached/associated with a method, then passed to other portions of code without losing its initial function reference. Under the covers all delegates hail from either the System.Delegate or System.MulticastDelegate classes. However, delegate types can be declared simply by using the delegate keyword. Each instance of one defines a method signature to which all methods in its invocation list must conform. A delegate declared as accepting two string parameters and returning an integer can only invoke methods with exactly the same signature.

Designing applications for effective delegate use can be tricky. This is especially true when defining events. Events themselves receive a list of other delegates for iterative invocation. Thankfully, the .NET SDK comes with a handful of built in delegates that correspond to commonly used events. The following two examples show how to create and consume a custom delegate and how to handle a button's click event using the .NET-provided delegate, respectively.

Example 1

```
using System;
using System.Windows.Forms;

namespace Appendix _proj
{

    /// <summary>
    /// Delegate available for remotely invoking any method accepting a single
    /// string parameter and a void return
    /// </summary>
    /// <param name="name">name</param>
    public delegate string HandlerForMyDelegateClass1(string name);

    /// <summary>
    /// This class contains methods which can be remotely invoked using the
delegate
    /// declared above.
    /// </summary>
    public class MyDelegateClass
    {
        private string SpecialMethod(string myName)
        {
            //NOTE: this is another way to dynamically assemble strings in C#
without
```

Appendix A: C#.NET Primer

Example 1

```
                // using the string + string notation
                return String.Format("Hello {0}, good to hear from you!", myName);
        }

        public HandlerForMyDelegateClass1 GetSpecialMethodHandler()
        {
            HandlerForMyDelegateClass1 h = new HandlerForMyDelegateClass1(SpecialMe
thod);
            return h;
        }
    }

    /// <summary>
    /// Consuming class that uses the delegate declared above to remotely invoke
    /// methods in MyDelegateclass1
    /// </summary>
    public class MyDelegateClass2
    {
        public MyDelegateClass2()
        {
            MyDelegateClass m = new MyDelegateClass();
            HandlerForMyDelegateClass1 h1 = m.GetSpecialMethodHandler();
            MessageBox.Show(h1.Invoke("Jon Arking"));
        }
    }
}
.
```

Example 2

```
using System;
using System.ComponentModel;
using System.Drawing;
using System.Text;
using System.Windows.Forms;

namespace Appendix _proj
{
    public partial class Form1 : Form
    {

                Button myButton;
/// <summary>
        /// Simple Form class that will display a button
        /// </summary>
        public Form1()
        {
            InitializeComponent();

            //Button initialization - standard on most Windows
```

```
                //Forms applications.
                myButton = new Button();
                this.myButton.Location = new System.Drawing.Point(86, 58);
                this.myButton.Name = "myButton";
                this.myButton.Size = new System.Drawing.Size(75, 23);
                this.myButton.TabIndex = 0;
                this.myButton.Text = "MyButton";
                this.myButton.UseVisualStyleBackColor = true;

                //Single instance of a .NET EventHanlder delegate- EventHanlders
                //have a signature accepting an object, an instance of EventArgs,
                //and a void return type
                System.EventHandler buttonHandler = new EventHandler(this.myButton_
Click);

                //Attaches the EventHanlder instance pointing to myButton_Click()
                //to the button's Click event
                this.myButton.Click += buttonHandler;

            }

        /// <summary>
        /// Button click handling method with a signature matching the
        /// EventHandler delegate
        /// </summary>
        /// <param name="sender"></param>
        /// <param name="e"></param>
        private void myButton_Click(object sender, EventArgs e)
        {
            MessageBox.Show("Button has been clicked!");
        }
    }
}
```

Example 1 shows how a delegate can be created and passed indirectly to calling or consuming classes. In MyDelegateClass1, a private method labeled SpecialMethod is not accessible to objects outside of MyDelegateClass1 itself. To allow objects to call this method, another public function is declared which creates a delegate pointing to SpecialMethod() and passes the delegate to the calling class. As a result, MyDelegateClass2 can raise the private method by calling the invoke method on the delegate class received.

Example 2 consists of mostly Windows Form code with only a small example of delegate usage. All of the Windows Forms controls and ASP.NET UI controls expose events to consuming classes. All events are handled using delegates in .NET, especially in C#. Other .Net.NET languages such as VB.Net.NET use different event handling objects for events, but ultimately these types of verbose handlers evaluate to delegates at the MSIL level. As you can see, the System.EventHandler object is instantiated in a fashion similar to that of the HandlerForMyDelegateClass1 object in the first example. The delegate is then added to the Button.Click event using the += notation. Events can have multiple event handlers in its invocation list, all of which are called when the event is raised. Thus, the += notation is ideal for increasing the list one more delegate.

Namespaces

The term *namespace* defines a scope of code or collection of items under a common grouping. Items within each namespace pertain to a definition relative to the group theme and unique to all other items in the same namespace. Thus, no two items can have the same name. The .NET development libraries are separated into separate .dll files called *assemblies*, each one pertaining to one or more specific namespaces. Likewise, a single namespace can span multiple assemblies. Each namespace contains types that you can use in your program such as classes, structures, enumerations, delegates, and interfaces. Each and every type in the .NET platform can be identified using its fully qualified name with namespace:

```
System.Web.UI.WebControls.Button
System.Xml.XPath.XPathDocument
```

Likewise, every method, property, or member of a type can be referenced using the type's fully qualified name:

```
System.Text.Encoding.UTF8.WebName.ToString();
```

Type declarations can be made within namespaces declaration as well, providing an avenue of type grouping for user defined classes, structs, interfaces, delegates, and other types:

```
namespace Appendix_proj
{
    public class MyNamespaceClass1
    {
        private string _myVar;

        public string MyVariable
        {
            get
            {
                return _myVar;
            }
        }

        public void DoSomething()
        {
        }
    }

    public class MyNamespaceClass2
    {
        private int _myVar;

        public int MyVariable
        {
            get
            {
                return _myVar;
            }
        }
```

```
        public void DoSomething()
        {
        }
    }

    delegate MyNamespaceClass1 SpecialHandler(string var1, string var2);

    namespace InnerGrouping
    {
        class MyInnerNamespaceClass
        {
            public MyInnerNamespaceClass()
            { }
        }
    }
}
```

You'll notice in this sample that the classes `MyNamespaceClass1` and `MyNamespaceClass2`, along with the delegate type `SpecialHandler`, are all defined within the namespace `Appendix_proj`. Therefore, the fully qualified names of these types are `Appendix_proj.MyNamespaceClass1`, `Appendix_proj .MyNamespaceClass2`, and `Appendix_proj.SpecialHandler`.

Namespaces can also be nested within one another. At the bottom of the preceding sample, there is another namespace declaration, aptly named `InnerGrouping`. Declared inside of it is a class named `MyInnerNamespaceClass`. Since the two namespaces are coupled, the fully qualified name of this inner class is:

```
Appendix_proj.InnerGrouping.MyInnerNamespaceClass.
```

Namespaces can make type declaration names very long and unwieldy to use. If coders had to fully qualify every type instance, most C# code would be overly bloated and very difficult to read. As a convenient shortcut, C# programmers can utilize the `using` keyword to properly scope one or more namespaces within a page. The `using` keyword should be placed at the top of the code page, referencing the particular namespace containing types to be used throughout the page. As a result, programmers need only call the type by its name within the namespace. There is no need to fully qualify the type name.

```
using Appendix_proj;

public class NamespaceScope
    {
        public NamespaceScope()
        {
            MyNamespaceClass1 m = new MyNamespaceClass1();
        }
    }
```

The preceding example is based on the code in the previous code block and implements the `using` keyword to properly scope the `Appendix_proj`. So, rather than declaring the type used in the constructor using the fully qualified name as such:

```
Appendix_proj.MyNamespaceClass1 m = new Appendix_proj.MyNamespaceClass1();)
```

The namespace portion of the declaration is already scoped, allowing the much simpler:

```
MyNamespaceClass1 m = new MyNamespaceClass1();
```

As you become more proficient in C# code, you'll find the need to implement the `using` keyword quite often to slim down your syntax and make your pages simpler to follow.

> The `using` keyword can also be used for scoping type instances with controlled object lifetimes. The `using` keyword in these examples do not apply to this functionality.

C# 3.0 Language Features

With the release of Visual Studio .NET 2008 comes the latest version of the C# language specification. C# 3.0 builds on some of the topics introduced in the 2.0 version, with explicit syntax added to empower the use of newer .NET technical features. Chief among these new features is Language Integrated Query, or LINQ. LINQ itself is not covered in this book. However many of the C# language features upon which LINQ depends can be found peppered throughout the chapter code samples. The following is small list accompanied with some brief explanations on some of the C# 3.0 features we've used in this book. For a more complete list of C# 3.0 language features, visit the MSDN online documentation at http://msdn .microsoft.com/en-us/library/bb308966.aspx.

Implicitly Local Typed Variables

An implicitly typed local variable is simply a variable with a type that has been inferred by the compiler through the context in which it is being used. Implicit typing requires the use of the type named `var`. Variables of type `var` ultimately evaluate to the same strong typing they would get if declared an `int`, `float`, `obj`, or any other type. However, the use of the `var` signals to the compiler that the responsibility of setting the type belongs to the compiler.

Following are five simple examples of implicit typing, each line evaluating to a different type at compile time:

```
var i = 10;
var s = "Arking";
var d = 1.0;
var numbers = new int[] {1, 2, 3};
var purchases = new Dictionary<int,Purchase>();
```

The preceding implicitly typed local variable declarations are precisely equivalent to the following explicitly typed declarations:

```
int i = 10;
string s = "Arking";
double d = 1.0;
int[] numbers = new int[] {1, 2, 3};
Dictionary<int,Purchase> purchases = new Dictionary<int,Purchase>();
```

An anonymous type is created simply by the use of the var keyword to declare a variable with a type to be defined.

Lambda Expressions

C# 2.0 introduced the concept of anonymous delegates. These are delegates that allow for a block on inline code to be referenced as a delegate's directly invoked callback, as opposed to first declaring the delegate instance and referencing a method with like signatures as the delegate's target method. Anonymous delegates are somewhat verbose, though, and can be cumbersome to write or consume over and over again in your code. Lambda expressions provide a viable shorthand for anonymous delegate declarations. The syntax of a lambda expression consists of a parameter or set of parameters, followed by the => token to mark the point of executable code. Lambda expressions can contain explicitly typed and implicitly typed parameters. Like normal C# functions, explicit parameter declaration requires the explicit stating of type with each parameter in the list. In an implicitly typed parameter list, the parameter types are directly inferred from the context in which the lambda expression is executing. Often the compiler can refer to the delegate referenced, which provides parameter types within its own declaration. The following list depicts some of the different ways that lambda expressions can be used:

```
x => x + 1                      // Implicitly typed, expression body
x => { return x + 1; }          // Implicitly typed, statement body
(int x) => x + 1                // Explicitly typed, expression body
(int x) => { return x + 1; }    // Explicitly typed, statement body
(x, y) => x * y                 // Multiple parameters
() => Console.WriteLine()       // No parameters
```

Lambda expressions are used prolifically throughout some of the samples in this book. Many generic data collections, such as lists and dictionaries, provide lambda-friendly callback expressions for defining filters or predicate callbacks.

Extension Methods

Extension methods are static functions that can be consumed and invoked using instance method syntax. They are methods that can be tacked onto existing classes or entities, allowing developers to add functionality to existing types without using an inheritance pattern. The behavior of extension methods is more limited than that of instance methods, and overall they are more difficult for the compiler to discover. However, in limited scope they can prove to be a useful tool when adding localized features to types without modifying the type's inherent object model.

Extension methods are defined as static methods. The first parameter can have no other modifier other than this, with the type of the parameter specifying the type to receive the extension. All other parameters in the argument list are implemented as normal parameters by the consuming class. Classes consuming the extension method must explicitly declare the extension method's namespace with a using-namespace-directive notation. Lack of explicit import with a using-namespace-directive will result in the compiler's inability to see the intended method. The following is an example of an extension method used in Chapter 11:

```
namespace ProEnt.Chap8.Controllers
{
    public static class ControllerHelpers
    {
        public static void AddRuleViolations(this ModelStateDictionary modelState,
        IEnumerable<BrokenBusinessRule> brokenRules)
        {
            foreach (BrokenBusinessRule brokenRule in brokenRules)
            {
                modelState.AddModelError(brokenRule.Property, brokenRule.Rule);
            }
        }
    }
}
```

This sample code allows for consumers using the `ModelStateDictionary` class to call the method `AddRuleViolations` off of an instance of `ModelStateDictionary` as if it were defined in the parent class:

```
List<BrokenBusinessRule> brokenRules = newBorrower.GetBrokenBusinessRules();
ModelState.AddRuleViolations(brokenRules);
```

Object and Collection Initializers

Object and *collection initializers* are blocks of code that both instantiate and initialize values in object instances and collection instances. This is a form of C# shorthand that quickly and explicitly allows for a single line of code to create a new object and supply it with state. They are ideal for assigning values to class instances that do not provide for an initializing constructor. An object initialize consists of a sequence of keywords that map to property names within the object, enclosed by braces {} and separated by commas. When they are used, the compiler implicitly creates temporary variables to perform the state initialization. Each member initializer must name an accessible field or property of the object being initialized, followed by an equals sign and an expression or an object or collection initializer. An object initializer can only reference a public field once per initialization. Likewise, it is not possible for an initialize to reference the object it is attempting to create. The following is a simple class providing two public properties:

```
public class BrokenBusinessRule
    {
        private string _property;

        public string Property
        {
            get { return _property; }
            set { _property = value; }
        }
```

```
        private string _rule;

        public string Rule
        {
            get { return _rule; }
            set { _rule = value; }
        }

        public BrokenBusinessRule() { }
    }
```

Typically, instances of this class could be created by first instantiating the object and then, in separate lines of code, assigning values to the object's properties:

```
BrokenBusinessRule r1 = new BrokenBusinessRule();
r1.Property = "LastName";
r1.Rule = "You must enter a first name for this borrower.";
```

Object initialization provides for a means to execute all three lines of code in one statement:

```
var r1 = new BrokenBusinessRule { Property = "LastName",
Rule = "You must enter a first name for this borrower" };
```

This single line of code has the equivalent affect as the following, which represents the translated code by the compiler:

```
var __r1 = new BrokenBusinessRule();
__r1.Property = "LastName";
__r1.Rule = "You must enter a first name for this borrower";
Var r1 = __r1;
```

Collection initializers work similarly, allowing the developer to instantiate a collection while assigning values to elements within the collection. The collections for which a collection initialize is being applied must be of type System.Collections.IEnumerable or a compile-time error will occur. For each specified element in order, the collection initializer calls the collection's Add method on the object with the expression list of the element initialize. A List of type Employee can be created as follows:

```
var contacts = new List<Employee> {
    new Employee {
        Name = "Jon Arking",
        PhoneNumbers = { "215-555-0101", "610-882-8080" }
    },
    new Employee {
        Name = "Scott Millett",
        PhoneNumbers = { "504-555-1212" }
    }
};
```

This code is read by the compiler and evaluated to the following:

```
var employees = new List<Employee>();
var __e1 = new Employee();
__e1.Name = "Jon Arking";
__e1.PhoneNumbers.Add("215-555-0101");
__e1.PhoneNumbers.Add("610-882-8080");
employees.Add(__e1);
var __e2 = new Contact();
__e2.Name = "Scott Millett";
__e2.PhoneNumbers.Add("504-555-1212");
employees.Add(__e2);
```

Object-Oriented Concepts

C# is a strongly object-oriented (OO) language. Using it effectively means understanding the tenets of object-oriented design, and how they apply to modern software development. Object-oriented programming is in no way a new concept. Developed in the early 1990s and later embraced by third and fourth generation languages, OO programming has become the fundamental paradigm in which most modern, tiered software is designed. Some languages such as C++ have supported advanced OO for many of its own generations. Developers familiar with Microsoft Foundation Classes, or MFC, have been working with a strongly object-oriented SDK for almost 15 years. Yet later versions of OO platforms have made some important and interesting enhancements to otherwise established patterns. These enhancements have made object-oriented programming simpler to understand and design while cleaning up much of the syntax in the process. To this end, C# leverages many (if not all) object-oriented concepts and built them right into the language syntax itself.

Classes and Objects

If you're a seasoned web developer unfamiliar with object-oriented design, classes and objects represent a cultural, as well as paradigmatic shift for you. Most web applications run within the context of a web page. The page itself represents the vehicle through which your code is executed. C# runs by an entirely different model. All code in C# lives within a class. A class represents a sort of blueprint for an entity to be created at runtime. Classes can have many of the same programmatic elements you may be used to seeing in web pages, including variables, functions, and events. Different elements within a class can have different levels of scope and accessibility. Some functions might be public to outside calls, while others might be visible to other elements within the containing class. Classes should not be thought of as web page equivalents, however. Whereas web pages inevitably host executing code, the class is simply a definition of a type. With the exception of static elements, no code defined in a class executes within the class itself.

Once a class has been defined, objects can be made from them. Objects represent virtual live copies of a class at runtime called *instances*. Object instances of classes are created by declaring a variable of the class type and then using the new keyword to instantiate it. Take a look at the class definition here:

```
class MyFirstClass
    {
        private string _var1;
        private string _var2;

        public MyFirstClass()
        {

        }

        public string Variable1
        {
            set
            {
                this._var1 = value;
            }

            get
            {
                return _var1;
            }
        }

        public string Variable2
        {
            set
            {
                this._var2 = value;
            }

            get
            {
                return _var2;
            }
        }

        public DateTime GetDateAndTimeOfDay()
        {
            return DateTime.Now;
        }
    }
```

This class definition is deceptively simple. It begins with the type naming following the keyword `class` indicating to the compiler that this is a type definition. At the top of the class are two privately declared strings aptly named using the proceeding underscore (commonly used naming conventions use a leading underscore or "_" when naming private, local variables). These variables are accessible only to functions and properties defined within this class. The next two blocks of code define public string properties with *set* and *get* accessors exposing the two private variables. The coupling of public properties and private variables is an object-oriented pattern known as *encapsulation*. We'll discuss this concept in the next few sections. Finally, we see a single public method named `GetDateAndTimeOfDay`, which appropriately returns a C# `DateTime` object containing the date and time when the method is invoked.

What's needed now is a means to run the class. Unlike web pages, there is no default server that runs the page. Even if this were saved locally like an HTML file, there is no way to execute the code without an instance of the object and an application entry point.

```
class Program
    {
        static void Main(string[] args)
        {
            MyFirstClass mc = new MyFirstClass();

            mc.Variable1 = "Any value";
            mc.Variable2 = "Another value";
            DateTime d = mc.GetTimeOfDay();
        }
    }
```

The class seen here is also its own type definition with one distinct difference from `MyFirstClass`. The Program class contains a single method named Main which marks the application's entry point. Main is a *static* function, meaning that the code contained within it can be executed without an instance of the containing class. Every application, be it Windows Form app, a web app, or even a simple command-line app, must implement `static void Main()`, or an equivalent entry point, somewhere in its code to mark the beginning of execution. Most Web applications handle static void Main implicitly, abstracted from web developers. Client application requires its explicit implementation.

Inheritance

Inheritance is the act of deriving one class definition from another. A class that inherits from another class automatically receives, or has immediate access to, all properly scoped features of the class. That is, if a class A exposes three public (or accessible) functions, properties, or variables, a class B inheriting from class A automatically receives these attributes. Consider the following example:

```
class A
    {
        protected string _firstName;
        protected string _lastName;

        public DateTime GetTimeOfDay()
        {
            return DateTime.Now;
        }
```

```
    public int CalculateSomeNumbers(int x, int y)
    {
        return (x + y) * Math.Abs(x-y);
    }

    internal decimal Rate
    {
        get { }
        set { }
    }
}

class B : A
{
    private string GetTimeStamp()
    {
        this.GetTimeOfDay().ToString();
    }
}
```

In these two class declarations, class A contains a series of functions, variables, and properties all appropriately scoped for accessibility. Class B is declared with the syntax "class B : A", indicating that B inherits directly from A. B has only a single private function, GetTimeStamp(), which calls the function GetTimeOfDay off of the this keyword. The this keyword is a convention employed for reflexive class referencing. A call to an member using this indicates a reference to a member within the same containing class or entity. There is no other object reference or definition of GetTimeOfDay() within B as none is needed. Since B inherits from class A, all of the accessible definitions within the sample class can be called as if they were locally defined in B.

Advanced OO design utilizes strong inheritance models for the purposes of code reuse and abstraction. Separating code into parent classes reduces the amount of code needed to be rewritten in inheriting classes (also known and child classes). Likewise, if a particular task or function uses reusable code features but only needs to be invoked every once in a while, separating said function into an inheriting child class will keep the more heavily used classes leaner by design.

Encapsulation

Object-oriented design places a great deal of emphasis on separation of code and patterns. Proper separation of code can facilitate insulation of signatures and variables in a manner that reduces external dependencies. This process of separation and insulation is known as *encapsulation*. As a pattern, a well-encapsulated class hides its internal objects variables and functions, scoping each as private (or sometimes as protected). Another set of functions or accessors then exposes the appropriate number of these features to calling classes. This provides a level of indirection which allows for changes to the class's design with minimal impact on consuming entities. The following code sample demonstrates a poorly designed class with no encapsulation and follows up with a well-designed class utilizing proper encapsulating techniques:

Poor Encapsulation

```
class PoorEncapsulation
    {
        //local variables are public, accessible to external calling classes
        public string _firstName;
        public string _lastName;
        public bool _isFemale;
        public DateTime _dateOfBirth;

        public string GetInformation()
        {
            string gender = _isFemale==true?"she":"he";
            string retVal = string.Format("This person's name is {0}, {1}. {3} is
{4} years old.", _lastName, _firstName, gender, CalculateAge().ToString());

            return retVal;
        }

        //single method used by both the local Getinformation function
as well as external calling classes
        public TimeSpan CalculateAge()
        {
            return DateTime.Now - _dateOfBirth;
        }
    }
```

Proper Encapsulation

```
class ProperEncapsulation
    {
        //private variables are not visible/accessible to calling classes
        private string _firstName;
        private string _lastName;
        private bool _isFemale;
        private DateTime _dateOfBirth;


        //public write-only properties that set the private variables directly
        public string FirstName
        {
            set
            {
                this._firstName = value;
            }
        }

        public string LastName
```

```
        {
            set
            {
                this._lastName = value;
            }
        }

        public bool IsFemale
        {
            set
            {
                this._isFemale = value;
            }
        }

        public DateTime DateOfBirth
        {
            set
            {
                this._dateOfBirth = value;
            }
        }

        //public property returning the age separately from the Calculate age
function
        public double Age
        {
            get
            {
                return CalculateAge();
            }
        }

        //private function to calculate age internally
        private double CalculateAge()
        {
            TimeSpan ts = DateTime.Now- _dateOfBirth;
            return ts.TotalDays / 365.25;
        }

        //public function to get consumed class information
        public string GetInformation()
        {
            string gender = _isFemale == true ? "she" : "he";
            string retVal = string.Format("This person's name is {0}, {1}. {3}
is {4} years old.", _lastName, _firstName, gender, CalculateAge().ToString());
            return retVal;
        }
    }
```

Both classes in this example ostensibly do the same thing — they collect demographic information about a person and return a variable containing the information collected. In the first example, the variables and methods used by the function GetInformation() are accessible to both internal and external elements. If the design of the classes changes by, say, altering the names of the demographic variables, any class consuming those variables will throw an exception when run (more likely, they simply won't compile). The second class does the same thing as the first, with extra properties to separate the setting of the variables from the consumption of them. Since calling classes only reference the public properties mapped to internal variables, any changes to the internals will require handling only within the containing class. To this end, encapsulation plays a very important role in software consumption and component design.

Polymorphism and Abstraction

Have you ever bought a special extension for your hose to set up a lawn sprinkler? Ever bought special hub caps for your car with different designs or cool, spinning rims? Or maybe you're an iPod nut who loves to snap on different covers or cool extensions? All of these are great examples of polymorphism. Polymorphism is a big, fancy word that really translates to one simple concept: one interface, many uses. A polymorphic model defines a minimal set of functions or features that must be had in order to be considered a thing. What an object does after meeting those minimal definitions is entirely up to the designer. Consider the example of the hose and sprinkler. The hose itself is fundamentally simple. It delivers water from starting point A to endpoint B. At the end is usually a screw extension where one can snap on different types of nozzles. Once the nozzle snaps on, the hose doesn't care what happens to the water. It can be sprayed, fanned out, turned into mist, and so on. Once the nozzle meets the hose's minimal requirement of accommodating the screw-on connector, it can do just about anything. The screw-on extension is what we would call an *interface*. It defines a set of requirements that must be met in order to properly and effectively work with the hose. Nozzles are polymorphic by design. They implement the required interface for the hose and then do a great many different things.

In object-oriented design, the same polymorphic patterns can apply. Consider a class A defining a function named `AddEmployee()`. The `AddEmployee` function accepts a certain type of class, specific in design, which interacts implicitly with the internals of class A. Although any external class can call `AddEmployee()`, the item passed in needs to meet certain minimum requirements in order to work effectively with class A. To handle this minimal definition, an interface X is defined by the designer of class A containing the names and signatures of functions, properties, and objects required to work with class A's internals. Class B's designer can then define another class that implements interface X, and then add any other features he/she wishes. Note the following example code:

```
/// <summary>
/// polymorphic interface defining the Worker type
/// </summary>
public interface IWorker
{
    string WorkerName
    {
        get;
    }

    int WorkerID
    {
        get;
    }

    XmlDocument GetCredentials();


}
```

```
/// <summary>
/// class consuming instances of Worker types.
/// </summary>
class Employees
{

    IList<IWorker> _employees;
    Hashtable _workerNames = new Hashtable();

    public void AddWorker(IWorker w)
    {
        XmlDocument xdoc = w.GetCredentials();
        //...do something with the worker here

        _workerNames.Add("worker:" + w.WorkerID.ToString(), w.WorkerName);
        _employees.Add(w);
    }
}
```

The first portion defines an interface named IWorker (A commonly used convention when defining an Interface is to proceed the name with the letter 'I'). The interface is the definition of a type. That is, to be of type IWorker, an object must implement the properties WorkerName, WorkerID, and the function GetCredentials(). The second portion demonstrates a class consuming the Worker type. It defines a function named AddWorker which expects an instance of the Worker type and invokes the expected properties and methods accordingly. Like the hose example, once the Worker instance fulfills its obligations (i.e., provides the properties and functions expected) the calling class is unaware of whatever else the instance may or may not be capable of doing. Now observe the next example showing a class of type IWorker:

```
class SpecialWorker : IWorker
    {

        protected string _workerName;
        protected int _workerID;


        /// <summary>
        /// this function is a constructor - it is called as soon as the class
        /// is instantiated with the "new" keyword
        /// </summary>
        public SpecialWorker()
        {
            //initialize class here
        }

        public string WorkerName
        {
            get
            {
                return this._workerName;
            }
        }
```

```
public int WorkerID
{
    get
    {
        return this._workerID;
    }
}

public XmlDocument GetCredentials()
{
    XmlDocument creds = new XmlDocument();
    ///Create XML containing worker info and credentials
    SendWorkerDataToWebService();

    return creds;
}

private void SendWorkerDataToWebService()
{
    //Do something else here...like call a web service and post the
worker's data
}
}
```

The class is declared using the colon-type notation (class SpecialWorker : IWorker) indicating inheritance or implantation of a type. In this case, the class SpecialWorker is indicating to the compiler that it is of type IWorker, and should thus be checked for IWorker-required items. The class implements the properties WorkerName and WorkerID, satisfying the first two requirements of the IWorker interface. The function GetCredentials() is also implemented. Yet notice that another function, SendWorkerDataToWebService(), is also defined in the same class. Moreover, when the GetCredentials() method is invoked, the SendWorkerDataToWebService() function is also called implicitly. This is our first example of polymorphism. The SpecialWorker class meets all of the minimal requirements to be considered an instance of type IWorker. Yet when consumed, this instance of IWorker not only returns the requested XMLDocument, it also sends worker data to a proverbial web service located completely outside of the scope of either calling or consuming class. The class Employees doesn't care (or better put, doesn't know) exactly what happens when the GetCredentials() function is called. As long as the IWorker definition is met, each instance of IWorker can operate completely differently from one another while still being able to be consumed similarly by the Employees class.

C# and the Web SDK

Developers using C# for web development should familiarize themselves with types in the .NET web-related namespaces. The .NET SDK provides a vast multitude of classes, structs, and namespaces, which can be used to enhance web-enabled programs for more advanced features. The documentation for the following .NET namespaces is from the MSDN online reference guide.

System.Web

The `System.Web` namespace supplies classes and interfaces that enable browser-server communication. This namespace includes the `HttpRequest` class, which provides extensive information about the current HTTP request; the `HttpResponse` class, which manages HTTP output to the client; and the `HttpServerUtility` class, which provides access to server-side utilities and processes. `System.Web` also includes classes for cookie manipulation, file transfer, exception information, and output cache control.

System.Web.UI

The `System.Web.UI` namespace provides classes and interfaces that allow you to create ASP.NET server controls and pages that will appear in your Web applications as user interface elements.

This namespace includes the `Control` class, which provides all server controls, whether HTML server controls, web server controls, or user controls, with a common set of functionalities. It also includes the `Page` class, which is generated automatically whenever a request is made for an `.aspx` file contained in your web application. You can inherit from both of these classes. Also provided are classes that provide the server controls with data-binding functionality, the ability to save the view state of a given control or page, and parsing functionality for both programmable and literal controls.

System.Web.UI.WebControls

The `System.Web.UI.WebControls` namespace contains classes that allow you to create web server controls on a Web page. Web server controls run on the server and include form controls such as buttons and textboxes. They also include special-purpose controls such as a calendar. Because web server controls run on the server, you can programmatically control these elements. Although web server controls are rendered as HTML, their object model does not necessarily reflect HTML syntax.

The `System.Web.UI.WebControls` namespace contains classes that are rendered as HTML tags, such as the `TextBox` control and the `ListBox` control. The namespace also contains classes that are not rendered on the web page, but support data operations, such as the `SqlDataSource` and `ObjectDataSource` classes. Other controls, such as the `GridView` and `DetailsView` controls, support data display and editing. The `WebControl` class serves as the base class for many of the classes in the `System.Web.UI.WebControls` namespace.

System.Web.UI.HtmlControls

The `System.Web.UI.HtmlControls` namespace contains classes that allow you to create HTML server controls on a Web Forms page. HTML server controls run on the server and map directly to standard HTML tags supported by most browsers. This allows you to programmatically control the HTML elements on a Web Forms page.

System.Web.Services

The `System.Web.Services` namespace consists of the classes that enable you to create XML Web services using ASP.NET and XML web service clients. XML web services are applications that provide the ability to exchange messages in a loosely coupled environment using standard protocols such as

HTTP, XML, XSD, SOAP, and WSDL. XML web services enable the building of modular applications within and across companies in heterogeneous environments, making them interoperable with a broad variety of implementations, platforms, and devices. The SOAP-based XML messages of these applications can have well-defined (structured and typed) or loosely defined parts (using arbitrary XML). The ability of the messages to evolve over time without breaking the protocol is fundamental to the flexibility and robustness of XML web services as a building block for the future of the web.

To get started creating XML web services using ASP.NET, look at the `WebService` class, which XML web services can derive from to get access to the ASP.NET intrinsics and the `WebMethodAttribute` class, which must be placed on any method that you want to programmatically expose over the web.

System.Web.Security

The `System.Web.Security` namespace contains classes that are used to implement ASP.NET security in web server applications.

The `Membership` class is used by ASP.NET applications to validate user credentials and manage user settings such as passwords and e-mail addresses. The `Roles` class enables you to manage authorization for your application based on groups of users assigned to roles in the web application.

Both the `Membership` class and the `Roles` class work with providers, classes that access your application's data store to retrieve membership and role information. Membership and role information can be stored in a Microsoft SQL Server database using the `SqlMembershipProvider` and `SqlRoleProvider` classes, in an Active Directory using the `ActiveDirectoryMembershipProvider` and `AuthorizationStoreRoleProvider` classes, or in a custom data source using implementations of the `MembershipProvider` and `RoleProvider` classes.

You configure ASP.NET membership using the membership `Element` (ASP.NET Settings Schema). When an application using membership is accessed, ASP.NET creates an instance of the `Membership` class that you can use to query membership information. Provider-specific implementations of the `MembershipUser` class contain information about the user accessing the page. You can create custom implementations of the `MembershipUser` class for your application.

You configure ASP.NET roles using the `roleManager Element` (ASP.NET Settings Schema). ASP.NET creates an instance of the `Roles` class that contains information about the role membership of the current user.

ASP.NET provides server controls that interact with the `Membership` class and the `Roles` class. The `Login`, `CreateUserWizard`, and `ChangePassword` controls work with the `Membership` class to simplify creating an authenticated web application, and the `LoginView` control uses role-specific templates to customize web pages for specific groups of users.

System.Web.Mobile

Microsoft ASP.NET provides three namespaces that are used to implement the runtime and design-time behavior of mobile components and controls. These namespaces include the fundamental interfaces and base classes for implementing attributes, classes, controls, and elements. The list contains the namespaces in ASP.NET for mobile controls and the classes that constitute them:

- ❑ **System.Web.Mobile:** Core capabilities, authentication, and error-handling classes. See the MobileCapabilities and MobileFormsAuthentication classes.

- ❑ **System.Web.UI.MobileControls:** Core ASP.NET mobile control classes. See the IObjectListFieldCollection interface, ITemplateable interface, AdRotator class, and DeviceSpecific class for some examples of interfaces and classes.

- ❑ **System.Web.UI.MobileControls.Adapters:** Core adapter classes that you can implement to create adapters for targeted devices.

System.NET.Mail Namespace

The System.NET.Mail namespace contains classes used to send electronic mail to a Simple Mail Transfer Protocol (SMTP) server for delivery. The MailMessage class represents the content of a mail message. The SmtpClient class transmits email to the SMTP host that you designate for mail delivery. You can create mail attachments using the Attachment class.

System.Web.Mvc Namespace

The System.Web.Mvc namespace contains classes and interfaces that support the ASP.NET Model-View-Controller (MVC) framework for creating web applications. This namespace includes classes that represent controllers, controller factories, action results, views, partial views, model binders, and much more.

System.Web.Mvc.Ajax Namespace

The System.Web.Mvc.Ajax namespace contains classes that support AJAX scripts in an ASP.NET MVC application. The namespace includes support for AJAX scripts and AJAX option settings.

System.Web.Mvc.Html Namespace

The System.Web.Mvc.Html namespace contains classes that help render HTML controls in an MVC application. The namespace includes classes that support forms, input controls, links, partial views, validation, and more.

System.Data

The System.Data namespace provides access to classes that represent the ADO.NET architecture. ADO. NET lets you build components that efficiently manage data from multiple data sources.

In a disconnected scenario such as the Internet, ADO.NET provides the tools to request, update, and reconcile data in multiple tier systems. The ADO.NET architecture is also implemented in client applications, such as Windows Forms, or HTML pages created by ASP.NET.

The centerpiece of the ADO.NET architecture is the DataSet class. Each DataSet can contain multiple DataTable objects, with each DataTable containing data from a single data source, such as SQL Server.

Each DataTable contains a DataColumnCollection — a collection of DataColumn objects — that determines the schema of each DataTable. The DataType property determines the type of data held by the DataColumn. The ReadOnly and AllowDBNull properties let you further guarantee data integrity. The Expression property lets you construct calculated columns.

If a DataTable participates in a parent/child relationship with another DataTable, the relationship is constructed by adding a DataRelation to the DataRelationCollection of a DataSet object. When such a relation is added, a UniqueConstraint and a ForeignKeyConstraint are both created automatically, according to the parameter settings for the constructor. UniqueConstraint guarantees that values that are contained in a column are unique. The ForeignKeyConstraint determines what action will happen to the child row or column when a primary key value is changed or deleted.

Using the System.Data.SqlClient namespace (the.NET Framework Data Provider for SQL Server), the System.Data.Odbc namespace (the.NET Framework data provider for ODBC), the System.Data .OleDb namespace (the.NET Framework data provider for OLE DB), or the System.Data .OracleClient namespace (the .NET Framework Data Provider for Oracle), you can access a data source to use together with a DataSet. Each.NET Framework data provider has a corresponding DataAdapter that you use as a bridge between a data source and a DataSet.

System.IO

The System.IO namespace contains types that allow reading and writing to and from files and data streams, and types that provide basic file and directory support.

System.NET

The System.NET namespace provides a simple programming interface for many of the protocols used on networks today. The WebRequest and WebResponse classes form the basis of what are called pluggable protocols, an implementation of network services that enables you to develop applications that use Internet resources without worrying about the specific details of the individual protocols.

System.Xml

The System.Xml namespace provides standards-based support for processing XML.

The supported standards include:

- ❑ **XML 1.0:** http://www.w3.org/TR/1998/REC-xml-19980210 - including DTD support.
- ❑ **XML Namespaces:** http://www.w3.org/TR/REC-xml-names/ — both stream level and DOM.
- ❑ **XSD Schemas:** http://www.w3.org/2001/XMLSchema
- ❑ **XPath expressions:** http://www.w3.org/TR/xpath
- ❑ **XSLT transformations:** http://www.w3.org/TR/xslt
- ❑ **DOM Level 1 Core:** http://www.w3.org/TR/REC-DOM-Level-1/
- ❑ **DOM Level 2 Core:** http://www.w3.org/TR/DOM-Level-2/

Summary

The Microsoft .NET platform is a powerful, flexible environment for building Windows-based and distributed software applications. The .NET SDK supports many different languages and language compilers, all of which can be used to build applications that run in the .NET Runtime Environment (also known as the Common Language Runtime, or CLR).

Programming in .NET is markedly different than previous Windows SDKs. Memory management is built into the runtime environment via the use of a process known as garbage collection. Garbage collection allows developers to effectively ignore memory management and cleanup within their code, putting the responsibility of cleanup on the runtime environment itself.

The .NET SDK replaces, both conceptually and in many cases physically, older programming models and libraries. Where once there were multiple development models available for software development, such as COM, MFC, ActiveX, ATL, and Win32, there is now one unified development kit for all things Windows.

C# is a powerful .NET programming language with a rich set of code-based features and tools that help programmers develop advanced applications. C# is object-oriented; with it, developers can create classes, structs, enums, and types conforming to all manner of object-oriented design patterns. Features such as properties, delegates, and events facilitate advanced object-oriented design, while also helping to keep one's code clean and readable.

.NET uses namespaces to separate types into logical groupings. Namespaces can be contained within a single .NET library called an *assembly* or can span multiple assemblies for effective splitting of the group. Likewise, an assembly can contain a single namespace or many namespaces at the same level or nested within one another. Namespaces are used as a naming convention for otherwise like-named types, wherein the fully qualified name with a leading namespace name properly identifies the entity. The `using` keyword can be used to scope a namespace to a page of C# code.

Object-oriented patterns play an important role in .NET development. Many built-in .NET types require an inherent understanding of object orientation to make use of their features. Principles such as inheritance, encapsulation, and polymorphism can be powerful allies when designing software using C#.

Although there are a great many namespaces available in the .NET SDK, some of them lend themselves particularly well to web development. Namespaces such as `System.Web`, `System.Web.UI`, `System.Web.Security`, and `System.Data` are worth understanding before endeavoring to build large .NET web applications.

Index